1866 - 1991

125th

ANNIVERSARY

COMANDOS

COMANDOS

The CIA and Nicaragua's Contra Rebels

SAM DILLON

Henry Holt and Company/New York

Published by Henry Holt and Company, Inc.
115 West 18th Street, New York, New York 10011.
Published in Canada by Fitzhenry and Whiteside Limited,
195 Allstate Parkway, Markham, Ontario L3R 4T8.

Library of Congress Cataloging-in-Publication Data
Dillon, Sam.
Comandos : the CIA and Nicaragua's Contra Rebels / Sam Dillon.
p.   cm.
Narrative based largely on the personal experiences of Luis Fley.
Includes bibliographical references and index.
1. Nicaragua—Politics and government—1979– 2. Military
assistance, American—Nicaragua. 3. Fley, Luis. 4. United States
Central Intelligence Agency. 5. Fuerza Democrática Nicaragüense.
6. Counterrevolutionaries—Nicaragua. 7. Nicaragua—Military relations
—United States. 8. United States—Military relations —Nicaragua. I. Title.
F1528.D56   1991
972.8505'3—dc20   91-20172
                                                              CIP
ISBN 0-8050-1475-6

Henry Holt books are available at special discounts
for bulk purchases for sales promotions, premiums,
fund raising, or educational use. Special editions
or book excerpts can also be created to specification.

For details contact:
Special Sales Director,
Henry Holt and Company, Inc.,
115 West 18th Street,
New York, New York 10011.

First Edition—1991

Designed by Katy Riegel
Photographs by Jason Bleibtreu
Map designed by Jackie Aher

Printed in the United States of America
Recognizing the importance of preserving
the written word, Henry Holt and Company, Inc.,
by policy, prints all of its first editions
on acid-free paper. ∞

1   3   5   7   9   10   8   6   4   2

Contents

Acknowledgments

Many people helped me write this book. I thank them heartily.

The Alicia Patterson Foundation financed my research, and the Foundation's Margaret Engel helped me with many administrative details.

In Miami, Ed Wasserman, with extraordinary generosity, read and edited my first draft. John Rothchild edited an early proposal and offered other helpful advice. Bill Prochnau and Laura Parker offered hospitality during a reporting trip.

At the *Miami Herald*, colleagues who criticized proposals, helped with research, or contributed in other ways included Don Bohning, Alfonso Chardy, Elisabeth Donovan, Tiffany Grantham, Guy Gugliotta, Gene Miller, Gay Nemeti, Andres Oppenheimer, Nora Paul, Mark Seibel, and Juan Tamayo. Pete Weitzel and Janet Chusmir, the *Herald*'s late executive editor, extended me a sixteen-month leave.

In Managua, Carmen María Baez transcribed more than two hundred hours of tape, Aracely Acosta arranged interviews, and Lino Hernández helped me find Isaac Blake. Richard Boudreaux generously loaned me several interview transcripts.

In Tegucigalpa, Jason Bleibtreu, the photographer who spent more time with the contras than any other mainstream journalist, offered me many insights to the movement. He and Rebecca Ramos also opened their home to me on several visits to Honduras. Rafael Tercero let me view old footage from the CBS News video collection, while Wilson Ring shared with me his extensive knowledge of the contra army.

Others, elsewhere, who aided me with advice or other help included Enrique Baloyra, David Burnham, James Chace, John Dinges, Jorge Dominguez, Alma Guillermoprieto and Aryeh Neier.

Thanks to William Strachan, editor-in-chief at Henry Holt and Company, for his skillful editing, encouragement, and good judgment, and to Joseph Spieler, my agent, for his patience as I toyed with different approaches at the beginning of this project.

Many of the people I interviewed were so generous with their time and information that they became more than just sources. Included were several U.S. officials who I've agreed not to name; they know who they are.

My mother, brothers, sisters, and in-laws in the Dillon, Berliner, Smith, Preston, and Barnes families cheered me up and on when I grew discouraged. Julia Preston, my wife, urged me to write the book, read and edited early drafts, and put up with me through it all.

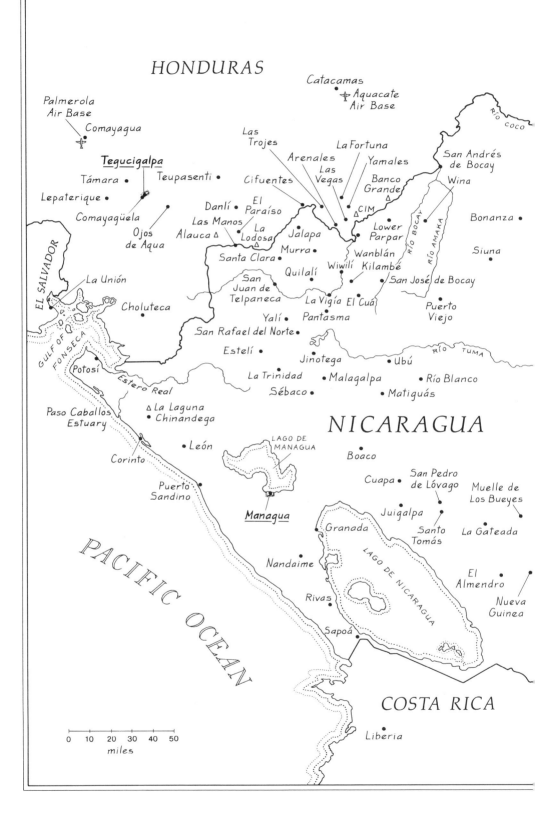

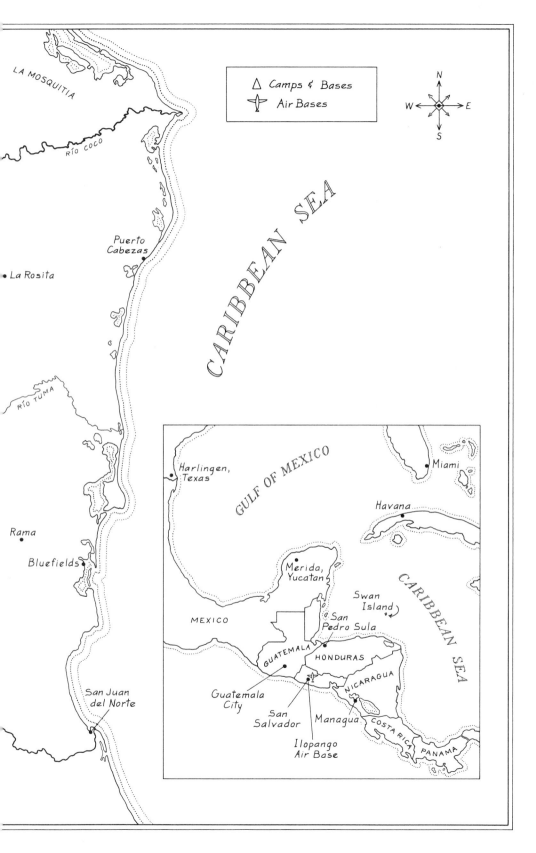

Preface

At the peak of Nicaragua's contra war, Luis Fley had led a rebel battalion, commanding hundreds of fighters in combat ranging over three provinces, but by the time I met him in 1988, he'd taken a U.S.-financed rearguard post that put him in charge of investigating crimes committed by contra fighters.

A contra detective? That idea fascinated me from our first meeting, a long conversation about the war over *churrasco* and beer in a smoky barbecue joint in Tegucigalpa, Honduras.

I'd written my first story about Nicaragua for the *Miami Herald* in 1983, when the contra war was beginning to explode. I had covered the conflict ever since, watching as it burgeoned into the most controversial U.S. foreign policy involvement since Vietnam. But like most reporters who followed the covert war, I'd been able to learn very little about the contras themselves or about their uneasy alliance with American officials.

Was the rebel force just the latest in a long string of CIA proxy armies, recruited this time to punish the leftist Sandinista government of Nicaragua, one of the poorest countries in the hemisphere, for rebelling against Washington? Or was this an indigenous insurgency, rebels fighting for a just cause against a ruthless regime?

Throughout what became the Nicaragua Decade, the contradictory images vied in the minds of most Americans who cared enough to try to understand the conflict.

When the fighting stopped after a 1988 cease-fire, Nicaragua was in ruins, and few Americans wanted to hear anything more about the country. One side of me was sick of the whole wretched mess and wanted to move on to another story. But I still had more questions than certainties, and my curiosities won out. As Ronald Reagan left office, I took a leave from my newspaper job and began puzzling over the war's continuing riddles.

For answers, I turned to scores of contra fighters at their bases along the Honduran border and in the bleak apartment blocks ringing Miami, where they were settling as illegal immigrants. I drove my jeep through the Nicaraguan outback, visiting old battlegrounds and talking to the war's victims, tracking the conflict's eight-year path. I looked up several of the CIA men who had managed the covert action on the ground.

And I met repeatedly with Luis Fley. In the contra army, he'd taken the nom de guerre "Jhonson." He said the peculiar spelling was "just a whim," but it reflected his own and other Nicaraguans' mixed-up relations with the succession of Americans who have left their imprint on Nicaragua. Over time, I pieced together his rebel career—and realized that he was as close to the "freedom fighter" of U.S. government rhetoric as you could find.

Fley, now forty years old, had been a disillusioned rural functionary of the revolutionary government when he joined the contra rebellion a decade earlier. An impetuous man, he was an idealist hoping to "rescue" the revolution for which he himself had once fought. When he took up arms, the CIA was not yet involved in the rebellion, but in Honduras, he began learning the realities of covert war. Fley watched as the CIA installed former soldiers from ousted Nicaraguan dictator Anastasio Somoza's National Guard in the command of the rebel movement. He learned demolition techniques from CIA agents who put him in charge of an elite sabotage team. At U.S. behest, he infiltrated Nicaragua repeatedly to blow up bridges, construction equipment, and other targets. Later, commanding a U.S.-equipped, 1,200-man rebel battalion, Fley returned to the hills around his own village, directing combat by field radio over a 2,500-square-mile battle zone. Then, after the U.S. Congress cut off military funding for the contras in February 1988, Fley watched as the contra force—Latin America's largest peasant army since the Mexican revolution—crumbled into a horde of hungry refugees.

That's when I met him, after the government and the rebels signed a cease-fire in March 1988, not long after he'd become the rebel army's chief investigator. As he went about his duties, Fley, like me, was trying to make sense of the war.

I was used to dissembling rebel politicians and spokesmen paid by the CIA to deal with reporters, but Fley was different: candid, sincere, and now angry. And this wasn't just the smoldering resentment the contras had always felt for the Sandinista government. Fley was fed up with the leaders of his own army and with the American agents behind them as well.

From our first meeting, I began to learn from him about the underbelly of the covert project. At one of our first meetings, he complained that rebel officials were raffling off the army's airplanes, boats, and other assets for personal gain. At another, Fley reviewed a string of cruelties that top contra commanders had committed against their own peasant troops.

"A lot of abuses have never been punished," Fley said.

We looked back together across a war in which Washington had worked systematically to destroy the Nicaraguan economy. Over the years, the U.S.-financed war levied heavy costs—more than 30,000 died in a country of 3 million, and 35,000 others were left widowed, orphaned, or disabled. And Fley hadn't slipped through untouched. He lost several relatives, including his younger brother, a Sandinista army lieutenant slain in a fiery ambush mounted by Fley's own rebel colleagues. Fley was embittered by Washington's refusal to take more than token responsibility for the war's heavy costs.

He wanted me to see the abandoned sugar plantation outside Tegucigalpa where the contra army's hundreds of wounded veterans were hidden from public view; U.S. funds were converting the farm into a refuge. Fley introduced me to dozens of hurting, used-up rebels loitering around an open-air courtyard, most missing arms or limping on prosthetic legs. Several bore devastating facial wounds.

"Our wounded and our widows are an enormous burden for us," Fley said.

As I got to know Fley better, I began to see that he embodied characteristics of the rebel movement that few Americans had recognized. He wasn't a thug or a thief; he was neither a mercenary nor a murderer. Like the vast majority of the rural men who'd joined the contras, he was fighting for a simple vision of good government. He was a decent man, often brave, among the best that the rebel army had to offer.

The climax of Fley's rebel career came at war's end, when he put the contras' CIA-backed intelligence chief—one of the most powerful former National Guardsmen in the force—before a tribunal of young commanders on charges of torture and murder. During his investigation, Fley acted with courage in pursuit of justice. I saw that he was a man who would take risks for his own convictions.

As I learned more about the case, however, I became aware of Fley's ambiguities. One was his relationship with Enrique Bermúdez, the former colonel whom the CIA had installed and controlled as the head of the contra force. Fley knew Bermúdez had tolerated and occasionally ordered many vile crimes, yet Fley always retained a certain loyalty to his longtime military commander. On another level, Fley recognized and despised Bermúdez's servile relations with his American handlers.

"It was difficult for Bermúdez to be a legitimate commander, because we were footing the bills," a former CIA agent who had overseen Bermúdez's work for a time in Honduras told me. "If he didn't want to play ball, then we had the resources to throw him out of the camps and get somebody that would."

Gradually I became aware of Fley's own subordination to American officials—and realized that that was the problem with the entire U.S.-financed proxy force.

"Behind every contra there's an American," one rebel told me, and I realized that it was true for Fley, too. As an investigator, technically Fley was "an outside contractor" for the U.S. State Department, and U.S. officials monitored nearly every move he made. Were his end-of-the-war investigations really aimed at setting things right in the rebel army? Or were they just more U.S. public-relations gimmickry designed to persuade congressmen and reporters like me that the contra army was cleaning its own house? I found it difficult to distinguish what Fley did for his own reasons from what he did after prodding from Bermúdez or the Americans.

For a time, as the contra's top investigator, Fley moved—with State Department backing—against the contra army's most brutal men, but the CIA, protecting a longtime asset, eventually undercut Fley's tribunal. That's when I saw Fley most bitter.

"I'm not taking any more risks for the Americans," Fley told me.

Before the elections scheduled for February 1990, Fley reexamined the contra war's roots. He'd joined the rebel force because the Sandinistas had shut down the political space for Nicaraguans like himself. The Sandinistas reopened it nine years later, partly as a result of the rebels' own sacrifices, and Fley saw that the time for war had passed. He left the contra army and became the only top contra fighter to return to Nicaragua from exile to campaign for the Sandinistas' electoral opponents.

The CIA-backed contra leaders reacted with fury to Fley's decision, expelling him from the rebel force, branding him a traitor, ransacking his Tegucigalpa office, and broadcasting threats against him over their propaganda radio. Fley shrugged it off.

"They have made war a way of life," he said of his former comrades.

The night the opposition overwhelmed the Sandinista Front in free elections, the contra army's top leaders were still in Honduras, sulking and scheming, dreaming of new military campaigns. Fley was in Managua, his choices vindicated.

The elections were a victory for Nicaragua's people, a step toward reconciliation in which both the Sandinistas and their victorious opponents displayed considerable dignity. The entire country repudiated war.

Back in Washington, the war's end brought curious reactions. At first, the election results set off more unseemly squabbling, as swaggering American politicians of every stripe rushed to ascribe the opposition victory to their own policies. Then, in the months of economic hardship that followed in Nicaragua, the U.S. abruptly forgot about the country whose plight had been a decade-long obsession. That illustrated the truth of what rebel official Ernesto Palazio told me:

"Nicaragua was too small a country to serve as psychotherapy for an America trying to get over its Vietnam syndrome."

COMANDOS

1

The Pit

November 22, 1988

Commander Jhonson had barely arrived at the general staff headquarters of Nicaragua's contra rebel army when he first heard about the murder.

Jhonson, the contra army's chief legal prosecutor, had only minutes earlier wheeled his four-wheel-drive pickup truck along the mountain track leading into the headquarters camp, pulling to a stop in front of the cast-off U.S. Army field tent that served as his office.

Upon setting his parking brake, Jhonson climbed out and dusted himself off after the morning's five-hour race out from Tegucigalpa, the Honduran capital, over two mountain cordilleras to the contra base camps in the valley surrounding the hamlet of Yamales, along the Nicaraguan border.

It was a majestic day. Morning sun streamed through the eucalyptus trees, and the air was crisp. But from the moment Jhonson caught a glimpse of his friend and main assistant, Frank Mercado Matús, he sensed trouble. Mercado, a twenty-five-year-old rebel with the nom de guerre "Joshua," had greeted him with a handshake and a tight smile, but he seemed agitated. He was glad—too glad—to see Jhonson.

Jhonson liked Joshua; he was such an easy fellow to work with. Though Joshua was thirteen years Jhonson's junior, the two men had a common past. Both had been born and schooled in Matagalpa, a northern provincial capital in Nicaragua. After the 1979 defeat by Sandinista guerrillas of Nicaragua's longtime dictator, Anastasio Somoza Debayle, both Jhonson and Joshua had served for a time in the revolutionary Sandinista army before fleeing into exile and joining the contra guerrilla force. Since then, both men had dedicated their energies to building the rebel army, financed by Washington in what was now an eight-year war with the Sandinistas.

Jhonson had risen through the rebel ranks to become one of the army's top field commanders. Then, after a cease-fire took effect earlier in 1988, though he had no training as a lawyer, he was put in charge of the rebel army's legal office, with Joshua as his assistant. They were the rebel army's top legal investigators. Together they organized military tribunals to discipline contra soldiers for everything from drunkenness to murder. Their work, bringing legal order to a force of guerrillas, was an often contradictory mission, and it earned them many enemies within the insurgent army. It also sealed their friendship.

Jhonson worked out of a crumbling safe house in the Honduran capital where he kept the contra army's legal files and could meet with the Honduran and U.S. authorities. Joshua was based in the border camps. During trips to Yamales once or twice a week to monitor Joshua's work, Jhonson had become increasingly sensitive to his deputy's moods. And this morning, though Joshua was grinning as they discussed Jhonson's drive and exchanged the latest camp gossip, Jhonson sensed unease. He cut through the chitchat. "What's up?" he asked.

Joshua said nothing, but turned and beckoned Jhonson into the legal affairs tent. Inside, he pulled two sheets of paper from a ledger and tossed them onto a rough wooden table in front of Jhonson.

"Two notes that a couple of commandos left for us here. I found one on Saturday, the second one Sunday," Joshua said.

Each had been torn from a cheap spiral binder. Both had been folded many times into a small wad. They were written in the scrawling handwriting common to most of the barely literate soldiers in the rebel army, who referred to themselves as "commandos."

Jhonson examined the first note. Dated 19 November 1988, it bore no signature:

I want to inform you that the commando Israelita is trying to force all the girl prisoners to screw him. He's done it with Sandra and Rosita. And for the rest of the personnel detained in the counterintelligence section, there's nothing but drastic treatment.

The second scribbled page was longer, dated 20 November 1988. Its author had penciled across the top: "From the Quilalí Regional Command."[1]

The Quilalí Regional Command was one of the two dozen units that were the twelve-thousand-man contra army's equivalent of combat battalions, each numbering about five hundred men. Each regional command was, in turn, divided into several task forces, the rough equivalent of companies, numbering about one hundred or so fighters. When the contras were inside Nicaragua, these were fighting units. After U.S. military aid ended in March 1988 and the contra army retreated into its Honduran base camps, each regional command had bivouacked in separate campsites, most of them within a few miles of the rebel general staff's Yamales headquarters. So "the Quilalí Regional Command" meant the Quilalí's campsite about five miles east of the general staff headquarters.

The note went on:

> Tuesday 14 Nov. at midnight in the counterintelligence section where Israelita is in command, a prisoner w/ the pseudonym "Managua" was killed by severe blows. I was ordered to bury him under a ceiba tree near the prison where the detainees are beaten with severe kicks in the stomach. . . . With the women, he tells them to confess everything, that they are infiltrators. But if they go to bed with him, he'll let them out. I want to tell you: I'm a cadre with seven years in the struggle. What Israelita is doing isn't just.

"Killed by severe blows?" Jhonson muttered to himself. This was going to be very complicated. Jhonson had never heard of any commando called Israelita, but the references to the rebels' counterintelligence section made him nervous.

The section was a mysterious team of anonymous rebel agents, most of them ex-members of Nicaragua's brutal prerevolutionary National Guard. In principle, the section was dedicated to preventing infiltration of the contra force by Sandinista spies, but it was widely feared in the rebel army because in the early years of the contra war it had been little more than a death squad, seizing commandos denounced as spies and "disappearing" them into the Honduran night. More recently, the section had seemed to become a bit more professional. Through his legal work, Jhonson had learned that American CIA agents were working in direct liaison with Luis Moreno Payán, whose pseudonym was "Mike Lima," the ex-Guard lieutenant who now headed rebel counterintelligence. But all in all, the counterintelligence section still had a grim reputation. Men with knives. Dark rumors.[2]

Neither of the notes were signed. Jhonson looked up at Joshua. He was about Jhonson's height, five six, and of medium build. Not fat, but pudgy. He was wearing a U.S. Army–issue camouflage cap. His dark eyes were set widely apart, over cheeks scarred slightly with acne. His mustache was well trimmed. Joshua wasn't really handsome, but he had a meticulous look about him: nicely cared-for uniform, a crucifix around his neck.

Joshua's bemused smile seemed to ask, What are we going to do about *this* situation?

"Did you have a chance to talk with the guys who wrote these?" Jhonson asked.

"Nope. Just lying here in the tent when I came in after breakfast," Joshua said. "But 'Galaxias' thinks he knows who left the second note. He's a guy they call 'Chino.' He's from the Quilalí."

Galaxias was the pseudonym of one of the ten junior investigators on Joshua's staff, the young commandos, most of them in their late teens, who ran errands for Joshua and Jhonson, carrying messages on foot to the regional command camps and calling witnesses to testify.

"What do you think? These sound credible?" Jhonson asked Joshua.

Joshua nodded. "Two notes, a day apart? Something fucked up is happening," he said.

Still, these were just anonymous notes, unsigned, Jhonson thought. He knew he could move with confidence to investigate abuses only after somebody signed a complaint. Furthermore, counterintelligence appeared to be involved. Those guys could be very ugly. Jhonson had to admit he felt a little nervous about running up to them accusing them of abuses without more information, or more backing.

His first thought was to call Enrique Bermúdez, the former National Guard colonel who commanded the rebel army, but Bermúdez was in Miami, and the telephone closest to the camps was a four-hour drive away. In Bermúdez's absence, power in the border camps was held by the army's chief of staff, Juan Ramón Rivas, whose nom de guerre was "Quiché" (pronounced kee-CHAY), or whichever member of Rivas's general staff was on duty.[3] Jhonson's official title was "legal adviser" to the general staff, a post that gave him the power to collect evidence and to recommend tribunals, but it wasn't his job to make routine arrests. Jhonson decided to walk up the hill to staff headquarters to see who was around who might help.

As Jhonson walked past his pickup, two sweaty young commandos were splitting logs with axes next to a small mountain of firewood heaped for burning in the camp cooking fires. A few yards beyond, a half dozen peasant men and boys wearing camouflage fatigues were standing over the bloody carcass of a newly slaughtered steer, knives in hand. They had slit the hide of the dead animal and pulled it back from the carcass on all sides, so that it lay like a blanket around the exposed meat. Covered with blood up to their elbows, the men were butchering the carcass into long strips of beef.

Jhonson strolled on. To his left, he saw the cooking hall for the general staff camp, a long barracks-like structure of rough plank siding, roofed with black plastic. It had no chimney for the four big earthen stoves inside, and wood-smoke poured out through cracks in the planking. Piled at the far end of the cooking shed under a canopy of plastic roofing were several dozen hundred-pound sacks of sugar, rice, beans, and onions. A dozen peasant women, also in camouflage fatigues, were bustling about the mess hall, scrubbing the breakfast skillets, patting tortillas, stirring cauldrons of beans.

The staff camp straddled a rib of hills running from southwest to northeast, overlooking the clear waters of the Yamales River and the dirt road that ran parallel to it. Turning to look back to the southwest, Jhonson could see several miles down the wooded valley, where he knew thousands of commandos were bivouacked in a string of regional command camps. The whine of a chainsaw echoed from somewhere in the valley. Looking three hundred yards or so farther up the hill, Jhonson could see the edge of a small clearing that served as a landing strip for the Americans who helicoptered from Tegucigalpa to visit the rebel camps.

Jhonson continued into the muddy parking area. Beyond a barbed-wire perimeter were the five army field tents, pitched in a half-moon cluster, that constituted rebel headquarters.[4]

There Jhonson caught sight of an American official, and he immediately decided he'd found just the man he needed. It was William Meara, a political officer in the U.S. embassy in Tegucigalpa. Meara was twenty-nine, a former U.S. Army captain, with cocky good looks he liked to show off by wearing his shirt open three buttons down. Jhonson knew Meara worked as a special assistant to Washington's ambassador to Tegucigalpa, Everett "Ted" Briggs. For about five months, Meara had been Jhonson's main liaison with the embassy. The two men had met many times—over coffee, in the embassy, at Jhonson's office—to discuss Jhonson's work.

Meara was the perfect person to help in a situation like this. The Americans paid for virtually every aspect of contra army operations and wielded the tremendous control that comes with complete financial backing. Maybe he could even get Meara to go with him to ask a few questions at counterintelligence.

Meara was making the rounds of the staff tents, collecting information—what they called in the military "the situation"—to report back to Ambassador Briggs. When Jhonson saw him, Meara had just emerged from the G-1 tent, where they kept the army personnel lists on U.S.-supplied Radio Shack computers, and was heading for the G-2 section to talk with the intelligence group.

Jhonson caught Meara's eye, the two men exchanged pleasantries, and then Jhonson motioned for Meara to follow him several paces away from the staff tents where they could talk quietly.

"Look, I've got some bad news," Jhonson told Meara. "We've had some reports of abuses in the counterintelligence section. It looks kind of bad. One prisoner has died from torture, it appears. There are others detained who are being mistreated. And it looks like there've been some rapes."

He was studying Meara's face for reaction, hoping he could enlist the official's support. With an American at his side, Jhonson was sure he could find out quickly what was going on and get it stopped.

Meara was impassive.

"Yeah, well, you know, those kind of things can happen in any army in the world," Meara said, Jhonson recalled later. Meara had grown up in El Salvador and spoke excellent Spanish.

"Even in the U.S. Army there are abuses. I wouldn't make too big a thing of it." The tone was cold. Meara seemed uncomfortable that Jhonson had shared this secret with him.

"Okay, but they have to be investigated, corrected," Jhonson said.

Meara shrugged, then repeated himself: "I wouldn't make too big a deal out of it." He was in a hurry, had a lot of errands to run. He walked on toward the intelligence tent and resumed his rounds.[5]

Jhonson stood for a time, stunned, thinking. He'd really expected to find Meara willing to throw his influence behind him to look into the troubling reports. Instead Meara hadn't even asked Jhonson to explain the reports twice. He hadn't asked for a written report, hadn't even bothered to scribble notes.

Now what? Jhonson wondered. Should I go on to the general staff, ask for their help? But now he'd muddied the waters. With Meara in the camp, the first thing anybody on the staff was sure to ask would be: What does Meara think?

And the one gringo adviser in the camp had just dismissed the abuse reports.

What was the problem here? Jhonson wondered. Was it that anonymous notes had too little credibility to raise concern? Maybe he was reacting too strongly. He and Joshua needed to get a stronger description of what had happened—and get it signed—before starting a scandal. And before doing anything further, Jhonson decided he'd better call Bermúdez in Miami.

He went back to his staff tent to talk to Joshua. He didn't mention his encounter with Meara. "This could be sensitive, so we better put ourselves on firm footing," Jhonson told Joshua. "We need to get signed statements from the commandos who left these notes. Can Galaxias put you in touch with them?"

Joshua thought that with some legwork, his guys could identify those who wrote the notes. Then he could call them in for detailed questioning.

"Okay," Jhonson agreed. "But first I'm going back to Tegucigalpa to call Bermúdez. Don't do anything until I send you a message."

Jhonson took the road back to Tegucigalpa the same afternoon. It was another grueling drive, four hours along a twisting, dusty gravel road to the border town of Danlí, then another hour and a half across a mountainous shoulder to the Honduran capital. Along the way, he had a lot of time to think.

He was depressed. He'd been fighting in Nicaragua's civil war for eight years. It had torn his life apart, yet as far as he could see, the conflict was as far from resolution as ever, even though the Americans had cut off military aid to the rebels and a cease-fire had stopped most of the fighting eight months earlier. Jhonson had watched thousands of rebel fighters straggle back into Honduras, waiting to see what the Americans would do next. Two weeks earlier, a new U.S. President had been elected, George Bush. That set off enthusiastic celebration in the rebel camps, with hundreds of fighters firing their automatic rifles into the air, because Bush had said several times in his campaign that he wouldn't let Nicaragua's freedom fighters down. Jhonson wasn't so sure, and neither were a lot of other fighters. Some were drifting away, deserting from the rebel force to journey north from Honduras through Guatemala and Mexico into the United States, where they were settling illegally. The contra army wasn't really disintegrating, but Jhonson knew the commandos in the camps were frustrated and bored. They were guerrillas, yet all they'd had to do recently was play volleyball. Ahead, there were too many questions: What were the Sandinistas planning? What were the Americans up to? What should the rebel army do next?

Jhonson's office was in a stucco safe house two blocks down a deteriorating street from the entrance to Toncontín Airport in Comayagüela, the southern sector of the Honduran capital. He arrived there late, and the next morning prepared to call Bermúdez.

Several months earlier, Bermúdez had moved from Honduras to Miami, to take a seat on the directorate, a junta of seven exiled Nicaraguan politicians that was supposed to be the rebels' political arm. But Jhonson knew Bermúdez was still the de facto leader of the contra army—the Americans still dealt with the rebel force through him. Jhonson didn't expect Bermúdez to offer much help, but if he and Joshua were going to get anywhere with an investigation, they'd have to be able to say they had Bermúdez's backing. He dialed the twelve digits to Bermúdez's suburban Miami home.

Bermúdez answered. *"Comandante,"* Jhonson said, "I think the boys from counterintelligence got a little out of hand this time. I think they put somebody to sleep. What should we do?"

"Really? Shit!" Bermúdez said. He seemed surprised. He asked for a few details, and Jhonson told him what little he knew. "Okay, better look into it. Start investigating," Bermúdez said.

After his call to Miami, Jhonson typed out a message to Joshua and drove across Tegucigalpa to a contra safe house along a tree-lined street within earshot of Tegucigalpa's noisy outdoor vegetable market. It was the rebels' communications office, where the CIA had installed a powerful radio transmitter and printer linking all the contras' main Honduran installations by radio-teletype.

Jhonson handed the message to the commando working the keyboard that transmitted the radio messages. Within minutes it was clicking across a computer printer, powered by a U.S.-supplied gas generator at the Yamales general staff camp. A young commando strolled down the hill to the legal affairs tent to deliver Jhonson's message directly to Joshua.

"On instructions of Cmdte. Bermúdez, begin investigating the Quilalí case."

November 30–December 1, 1988

Bert Charneco was worried. He was picking up reports of screams echoing through the Honduran valley where twelve thousand Nicaraguan contra rebels were bivouacked.

For over a year Charneco, forty-six, had been the State Department official overseeing the U.S.-financed training program aimed at improving the contras' human-rights record. Six feet tall and stocky, Charneco had salt-and-pepper hair and eyes with dark rings that revealed the long hours he put into his job. As an active-duty U.S. Air Force colonel,

Charneco had plenty of experience with military bases. In his most recent posting, he'd been base commander at Torrejon Air Base, the U.S.'s main airfield in Spain, in charge of four thousand airmen and dozens of F-16s. Now Charneco, a native of Puerto Rico, was on loan to the State Department.

That morning, Charneco had jetted from Miami to Tegucigalpa and helicoptered east to the base camps. From the Yamales helicopter landing strip, he hiked forty-five minutes downhill past the contras' general staff tents, to the valley bottom. The previous night's rain had turned the camps into a vast bog. Charneco had no boots, only his brown low-topped docksiders, one of which was immediately sucked off his foot by the mud. But he was in a hurry. He just picked it up and plodded on.

Charneco headed for the wooden shack housing the Yamales offices of the Nicaraguan Association for Human Rights, the organization to which Congress in 1986 voted $3 million to finance work aimed at ending contra rights abuses. His plan had been to review the rights training, but soon after Charneco's arrival, one of the Association's instructors pulled him aside to pass on a chilling report: People were hearing horrifying shrieks echoing down the valley during the night.

Later, during a campfire chat over a dinner of sticky brown rice, laced with a dollop of dark beans and with a hand-patted tortilla, another Association worker told Charneco he'd talked with a contra fighter who, during a recent shift as a night sentry, had seen a young woman running naked through the woods near one of the regional command camps. The woman's arms had been tied, and several commandos had been trotting along behind her laughing. Charneco looked the teenager telling the story straight in the eyes. He wasn't kidding.

The next morning, Charneco heard still another disturbing story. An Association official introduced him to a peasant woman in her late thirties who said she had something to report. Charneco wanted her to talk freely, so the two sat down on a log about fifty yards from the Association campsite. The woman said she was the mother of a teenage girl who, for much of a year, had been living in the contra camps with her boyfriend. A week or so earlier, contra authorities had seized the girl, without explanation. But her mother said she was sure the girl had been seized because there were commandos who wanted to . . . well, to abuse her.

Charneco told the woman he'd do what he could for her daughter. He thought the best way to learn more was to visit the contras' Yamales prison, located atop a hill across the valley from the general staff camp. But just as Charneco and a contra officer were about to begin the hour-long climb up the hill to the prison, a Huey helicopter clattered into view and landed on the summit. It was a delegation of officials from the General Accounting Office, the congressional office overseeing the U.S.-financed humanitarian aid program that had been feeding and clothing the contras in their base camps for eight months.

Charneco, seeing that the GAO officials were visiting the prisons, decided to abandon plans for his own visit, as he was already late for his helicopter flight to Tegucigalpa, where he was scheduled to catch an Eastern flight back to Miami. Instead of investigating the reports himself, he would pass them on to Commander Jhonson, who, as the head of the contra army's legal adviser's office, was in charge of investigating abuses and was Charneco's main contact in the rebel army.

Charneco thought highly of Jhonson. He'd been one of the contras' top battalion commanders during the rebels' largest offensive, in 1987, financed by $100 million in U.S. funds. Jhonson's men had shot down two Sandinista helicopters and fought their way into control of a big chunk of Nicaraguan territory. Now Jhonson had made the transition from field commander to military investigator, and was showing the same leadership in human-rights work that Charneco had admired in his combat record.

Back in Tegucigalpa at Toncontín Airport, Charneco headed with his bags to the Eastern check-in counter and put himself at the end of a line of passengers. Moments later, he felt a tug on his arm. It was Jhonson; knowing that Charneco would be passing through, he'd driven over from his office just blocks away to say hello.

"Hey, great, nice to see you," Charneco said, clasping Jhonson's hand and looking him over. Jhonson was wearing Levi's and a blue polo shirt. A pair of aviator sunglasses were clipped in a case to his belt. He had the light copper complexion common across rural Nicaragua, but what distinguished him were the gray-green eyes he'd inherited from his grandfather, an Englishman who had settled in Nicaragua to grow coffee in the 1920s. Charneco began immediately with the rumors.

"You need to take a look at the situation of the prisoners in the camps. There's something screwy going on out there, some rumors I don't like," Charneco said. He'd barely begun talking when they were joined by another American, carrying a walkie-talkie. Jhonson introduced the man to Charneco as William Meara.

Charneco knew Meara as a political officer at the Tegucigalpa embassy who served as a special aide to Ambassador Briggs. The three of them chatted briefly in Spanish, and then Charneco turned again to Jhonson.

"Like I was saying, you've really got to take a look at the prisoners," Charneco said.

Suddenly Meara interrupted. Facing Charneco, he switched to English.

"Don't discuss this with anybody else," Meara told Charneco. "We don't want to hear any more from you about prisoners, we just don't want to hear any more about it." There was a silence. Charneco wasn't sure he'd understood.

"You know what I mean," Meara went on. "Don't mention that to anybody else. Just don't talk about it."

Charneco was stunned. This sounded like a threat. He'd never heard any other U.S. official, anywhere, talk like this.

"This is not coming from me, this is coming from above. This comes from the guy I work for," Meara said. And at that he walked away.

Charneco was taken aback. He glanced at Jhonson, who—suddenly excluded from the conversation by Meara's switch into English— appeared bewildered. Charneco wasn't sure how much of the incident Jhonson had picked up.

"Did you get what he said?" Charneco asked Jhonson. "That kid just threatened me, told me not to meddle with the prisoners."

Charneco tried to calm down. His flight was already boarding, and in the few moments remaining, he hurried to finish his briefing for Jhonson about the reports of abuses. He gave Jhonson the name of the teenage commando said to have been detained by the contras and the name of her mother. Jhonson said he'd look into it. Charneco boarded his plane back to Miami.[6]

December 8–9, 1988

Jhonson was broke. The legal office he ran for the contra army, known officially since 1987 as the Nicaraguan Resistance, was completely funded by Washington, and since early October, he had faced a financial crisis.[7] Squabbling between the State Department, the Congress, the White House, the CIA, and, he assumed, other agencies he wasn't even aware of had delayed approval of new funding for his legal operation.

When he'd taken over the legal adviser's post seven months before, he'd inherited as his office a dilapidated, single-story house surrounded by a steel-grate fence. Inside, faded curtains were falling off the windows. Jhonson and an old man who served as his bodyguard and had been his camp cook when they were fighting together inside Nicaragua were sleeping on cots in one of the ruined back bedrooms. The living room was crammed with three desks, where Jhonson was managing more than a dozen cases at any one moment, involving scores of documents.[8] And now, not only had he not paid the rent since September, but worse, he could pay neither the two Nicaraguan exile lawyers who advised him nor the two Honduran secretaries who typed up legal statements for him. He'd had to plead with his staff to work for half pay in November. Jhonson was cajoling friends at the phone, water, and electric companies not to cut off the utilities. He didn't even have gas money.

He finally beat back the crisis by begging a personal loan, which allowed him to fund his office through January and to fuel up his pickup for a trip to the camps. So when he finally met Joshua at the Yamales legal affairs tent at eleven o'clock on December 8—two weeks after he'd left his aide to investigate the anonymous notes—there was a lot to catch up on.[9]

Jhonson sat down backward on a wooden chair and grabbed the back of the seat. Joshua looked harried. Jhonson asked for an update.

"Well, those notes we got were certainly accurate, as far as I can tell," Joshua said. "I got hold of the guys who wrote them, and I've gone over their stories."

"How'd you find 'em?" Jhonson asked.

"Galaxias followed his hunch back to his friend out at the Quilalí camp," Joshua told him. "Turns out he was right. The guy who left the notes is a character named 'Chino.' I finally persuaded Chino and a couple of other commandos from the Quilalí to come in and make statements. I went out to the Quilalí once, too. Informally," he added.

Jhonson could see that Joshua was spooked. Jhonson knew Joshua as a gutsy investigator who would take risks. Jhonson also knew that some months earlier, a rebel commander they'd been investigating had threatened Joshua. Jhonson had never heard all the details, but he knew Joshua hadn't forgotten.

"Look, here's what I've collected so far," Joshua told Jhonson, handing him three typewritten statements.

Jhonson knew how Joshua had produced them. He'd seen him do it dozens of times: He'd bring witnesses into the legal affairs tent, one at a time, sit them down at the table across from his typewriter, and ask them to tell their story. He'd type it up—hunting-and-pecking with two index fingers—as they talked, interrupting occasionally until he'd catch up. At the end, Joshua would follow up with a Q-and-A, typing his own questions along with their answers.

"Why don't you read these now?" Joshua said. "Then I've got a couple of other things to tell you."

The first statement had been taken from Eugene "Chino" González, a foot soldier in one of the task forces of the Quilalí Regional Command. On several occasions Jhonson had driven from the general staff camp east along the dirt road through the Yamales Valley to visit the Quilalí camp. He remembered it as a smoky bivouac of wood-and-plastic huts next to the road on the valley's western slope. Across the road from the main camp, the commandos had set up volleyball courts in a large clearing.

Chino, now twenty, had joined the contras as a twelve-year-old and had been fighting since the very dawn of the war. Jhonson assumed his pseudonym came from the slightly oriental cast of his eyes.

This was the story he told Joshua:

Several months earlier, a burly fighter in his late twenties from Nicaragua's Atlantic coast (his dark complexion looked to be part black and part mestizo) had shown up at the Quilalí camp. He had a strange pseudonym—"Israelita"—but Chino had met him years earlier in another regional command where he'd called himself "The Black Commando." Chino knew his real name: Isaac Blake.[10]

Blake was a mystery from the start, Chino said. He'd built his own hut, across the road from the main body of the camp, beyond the volleyball courts and a stand of pines.

He didn't participate in the life of the unit. In the morning, he didn't grunt through the calisthenics with the other commandos, nor did he line up for the twice-daily ration of beans and tortillas. Yet his strange presence seemed to have the acquiescence of the Quilalí battalion's commander, Roberto "Nolan" Martínez.

In fact, it seemed to Chino that Nolan was afraid of Blake. Nolan was only twenty-two, and inexperienced. He was a former student from Managua, while most of the fighters he commanded were tough country boys. Nolan had assumed command of the Quilalí about the time of Blake's arrival.

Starting on November 13, Chino had been assigned to work with Blake. The first day Chino reported to Blake's hut, a rough shed near a swampy stream, he'd learned Blake's real mission: counterintelligence. Chino discovered he was joining a gang of nearly a dozen young commandos, mostly the bullies of the Quilalí camp, whom Blake had recruited as his aides. They were helping Blake seize and interrogate prisoners. Blake was accusing the detainees of being Sandinista infiltrators, but Chino's account made it sound as though the accusations were arbitrary. Chino sounded to Jhonson like a fighter whose sensibilities would be plenty tough after eight years of war. But what Chino saw in the Quilalí made him sick.

On the very first day of his work with counterintelligence, Chino had seen Blake's men drag in Isaac González, a fighter in his mid-teens whom other commandos had dubbed "Managua" because he'd grown up in the Nicaraguan capital. Managua's wrists were tied with rope, his eyes were blindfolded, and an old rag had been stuffed into his mouth. The guards guided him with punches and kicks, dragging him inside Blake's hut. Immediately, Chino began to hear the sounds of a savage beating. Chino stood listening, horrified by Managua's cries. The torture appeared to continue, without much respite even for questioning, for a couple of hours. At about midnight, Chino saw Managua dragged out, bruised and groaning, and up a hill dotted with coffee bushes overlooking Blake's hut, out of sight.

Chino didn't discover Managua's destination until the next afternoon, November 14, when he accompanied another commando carrying a message to Blake up the hill. A couple of hundred yards up the coffee slope, Chino came upon an earthen pit, about ten feet square and some seven feet deep, used as a makeshift detention center. A few branches and an old tarpaulin used to cover the pit had been pulled off to one side. Two contra prisoners, who seemed to have been pulled out of the pit, were bound and lying facedown in the earth nearby.

In the pit was Blake, standing next to Managua. Managua's hands were lashed together over a timber pole laid across the top of the hole. Managua was dangling from his bonds, clad only in his undershorts. His upper torso glistened crimson. Blake was kicking Managua in the stomach. Managua was spitting blood.

Chino was stunned at the sight. Blake did not appear to be questioning his captive, just dishing out punishment. Chino handed the note to one of Blake's guards watching from the edge of the pit and withdrew, his head reeling.

Back at Blake's hut, several of his aides were talking about his methods. One said he'd told Blake that the other prisoners being held in the pit hadn't had food or water in three days. "I don't give a shit if they die of hunger," the commando said Blake had told him. Later the same day, after Blake had returned to his hut, leaving Managua in the pit, one of his aides warned Blake that Managua was heaving with convulsions.

"Let him die. I don't give a fuck. He's a Sandinista spy!" Chino heard Blake shoot back.

The same evening, just twenty-four hours after Managua's initial detention, Blake sent two aides to fetch Managua from the pit again. They had to drag him back down the hill, supported from the shoulders. He could barely stand, let alone walk. Once Managua was inside Blake's hut, Chino heard Blake shout: "Are you gonna tell the truth this time, you son of a bitch?" Chino couldn't hear any response—only shrieks as the kicking and beating began.

At about 10 P.M., two commandos dragged Managua out of the hut and down a slope to a marshy swamp, where, Chino learned later, it had become routine to torture prisoners by holding their heads under the surface of the muddy slime until they were drowning—and then revive them. The two brought Managua back forty-five minutes later and dumped him on the ground outside Blake's hut.

"Leave me, brother, leave me. I can't take any more," Chino heard Managua groan.

Later that evening, Blake emerged from his hut. Managua was crawling along the ground, moaning, still spitting blood. Blake screamed for aides to drag him back down to the swamp. A half hour passed, then one of Blake's men came running up the slope to announce that Managua was dying. Chino and several others ran down the slope. They found Managua, stretched out alongside the swamp, covered in slime and blood. His eyes were fluttering.

Somebody called for Roberto "Robespierre" Aguilar, one of the Quilalí's staff officers, who had undergone U.S. training as a paramedic. Robespierre arrived and checked Managua's pulse. It was just after midnight. Managua was dead.

Blake ordered Chino, along with two prisoners, to drag Managua's corpse back up the coffee slope, past the interrogation pit, for burial. Chino said he and the prisoners had chosen a spot under a gigantic ceiba tree to excavate the crude grave. They finished their spadework just before dawn. One of the prisoners helping to dig was a sixteen-year-old peasant with the nom de guerre "Cerrano." The boy was himself badly bruised and torn from beatings, and he collapsed to his knees at graveside as Chino lowered Managua's corpse. Cerrano began to sob over the body. He stammered out an Ave Maria in the chill air.

Chino said he'd seen a total of thirteen prisoners dragged out of the Quilalí camp to the pit for interrogations. Four of them were teenage girls, two of them sisters, Rosa and Sandra. Chino said Blake appeared to have seized them as concubines.

One day Chino had seen Blake bring a tape player to the side of the pit, to listen to the heavy-metal music of Led Zeppelin while he tortured a prisoner. Halfway through a rhythmic session of kicks and blows, he grabbed Sandra. He danced with her, in front of the other prisoners, down in the pit.

Chino said he'd worked under Blake for just one week before Blake had grown suspicious of him. Then Blake had dispatched him back to the main Quilalí camp, warning him not to return to the interrogation area. The next day, Chino had written an anonymous note and sent it with a friend to Joshua's legal affairs tent.

Jhonson felt queasy. "This isn't even war!" he said to Joshua. "Our army is camped in Honduras. There's a cease-fire. If this is what our army does, why are we fighting the Sandinistas?"

Joshua stood up. "*Comandante,* let me tell you something else. It gets worse. I think there are big men involved in all this—from the general staff," he said. "Chino and the others told me they'd seen two members of the staff meet with this Blake character out at the Quilalí. They were too scared to tell me that officially—it's not in their statements. But they wanted me to know."

Jhonson stared at Joshua. Of course! There had to be higher officers involved. A single commando in the Resistance couldn't just one day set up a detention center and start seizing prisoners. In the contra army, only three sections were empowered to hold or interrogate prisoners: the intelligence and counterintelligence sections and the military police. And they were all dependencies of the Resistance's general staff.[11]

From Chino's account it appeared that Blake was carrying out some kind of perverted counterintelligence mission. If that was true, he'd be working for Mike Lima, the Resistance's twenty-nine-year-old counterintelligence chief.

Jhonson had known Lima throughout the war. Mike had been a second lieutenant in Somoza's National Guard during the last war. After joining the contras, Mike had become a favorite not only of Bermúdez but of the American CIA agents working with the contras. Mike had been a prominent field commander in 1982 and 1983, until a mortar accident had blown off his right arm. Then Bermúdez had put him in charge of intelligence, and he'd quickly racked up a bloody reputation. In the years since, he'd held several other staff posts; mainly, he hung around Bermúdez as a personal aide. Jhonson got along with him personally, but he knew Lima could be a vicious bully. As a result, Jhonson had questioned the wisdom of Bermúdez's decision in February 1988 to put Mike Lima in charge of the rebel army's powerful counterintelligence section.

That gave Mike Lima command over the contras' central, computerized counterintelligence safe house in Comayagüela, base for a dozen secret agents, as well as control over secret staffs in the Yamales base camps and in Danlí, Choluteca, and several other Honduran towns. It was too much secret power for an officer as unpredictable as Mike Lima, Jhonson thought.[12]

Now, with the brutality he'd just discovered, Jhonson suddenly felt angry, and a bit panicked. He glanced at a calendar. "Managua" had been murdered on November 15; it was now December 8 and no one had yet intervened. Blake was probably still out there at the Quilalí, still holding other prisoners. He had to be stopped.

"Joshua, we can't help who's involved," Jhonson said. "We've got to get this thing stopped."

Jhonson stalked out of the legal affairs tent. He didn't have the power to make routine arrests, but the time had come to do something. He walked up the hill to the general staff camp to find out who was on duty. Quiché, the chief of staff, was gone. The only members of the general staff in camp were Pastor "Denis" Meza, the personnel officer, and Oscar Sobalvarro, another rebel staff officer who used the nom de guerre "Rubén." He'd known them both for a long time.

Jhonson knew the way word spreads in the contra camps. By now both officers had to know all about what was happening in the Quilalí. If they hadn't heard about it before, they would have found out two weeks ago from his own radio message to Joshua that an investigation was beginning. In fact, Jhonson was irritated that none of the rumors floating around about the Quilalí had provoked any reaction from the general staff. He'd started to consider this thing a real emergency.

"You've heard about what's happening out in the Quilalí?" Jhonson asked Rubén. "They killed a guy."

"That's what people are saying," Rubén answered.

"Look, Rubén, this is serious," Jhonson said. "There are going to be other deaths. We've got to stop this. Let's go out there, you and I. Or let's go to counterintelligence."

Rubén shook his head. "You do it. I've got a lot of things going on."

"Rubén, what the hell do you mean by that?" Jhonson said. "This is our responsibility! You as a staff commander. Me as legal adviser. We can't act like nothing has happened."

"No thanks," Rubén said.

Jhonson glared at him for a moment, steaming. Then he turned and stalked out. He went straight on through the eucalyptus trees to Denis's tent.

Pastor "Denis" Meza, the thirty-four-year-old son of a prosperous Nicaraguan landowner, was the contras' quartermaster, and in charge of the army's computerized personnel lists.[13]

"You heard about the guy they killed out in the Quilalí?" Jhonson asked Denis.

"Uh-huh," Denis said, nodding.

"All right, let's go," Jhonson said. "You and I are going to go stop this thing."

"What do you propose doing about it?" Denis asked.

"Your choice," said Jhonson. "We can go straight to the Quilalí and detain this fellow Israelita ourselves. Or we can go to counterintelligence and let them bring the guy in."

"I'll go with you to counterintelligence," Denis said.[14]

As he and Denis drove in Jhonson's pickup east along the dirt road toward the counterintelligence camp, Jhonson recalled what he'd learned about the section from the couple of visits he'd made as part of his legal work. Its headquarters was a cluster of about a dozen wood-and-plastic huts dispersed through a stand of banana trees set three hundred meters back from the dirt road. Each hut was surrounded by barbed wire and was designed to hold three or four suspects undergoing interrogation. The section had been set well away from all other contra bivouacs and was at least a mile from the nearest Honduran house. Just about everybody in the Resistance—including Jhonson—feared the place. The section's commander at Yamales, Mike Lima's representative in the border camps, was José Zepeda, a former National Guard sergeant known in contra ranks by the nom de guerre "Joel."[15]

Commandos who were suspected of being infiltrators were normally dragged off for questioning and held completely incommunicado until Joel's counterintelligence guys had finished with them. Jhonson knew Joel and Mike Lima to be extremely strict about this rule: Nobody—not even Bermúdez—got into the section to visit a commando "under investigation." If the suspect came through unscathed, he was released. If he was declared to be an infiltrator, he was passed on to the Yamales prison, a cluster of log barracks set in a barbed-wire corral and guarded by the eighty-man military police detachment.

Jhonson and Denis pulled up at the rough wooden sentry post marking the entrance. Several commandos standing guard with automatic rifles eyed them suspiciously. Jhonson told the guy wielding a U.S. Army field radio that they'd come to talk to Joel. The guy transmitted a message in to Joel, who crackled back word for the two commanders to wait. About twenty minutes passed. Then a young commando came ambling down over a low slope, led them past the guard post, about a hundred meters up a low rise, and into a dirt-floored, plastic-sided hut, surrounded by barbed wire. Inside were three stout tree logs used as stools. Jhonson assumed it was an interrogation cell.

Presently, José "Joel" Zepeda arrived, accompanied by two heavily armed commandos whom he posted outside as sentries. Joel was a man who wouldn't look you in the eyes. Jhonson had heard rumors about Joel's methods, but had never found anybody willing to sign a denunciation. Mike Lima, Joel's boss, was based five hours away in Tegucigalpa. That meant Joel wielded a lot of power by himself.

Joel was a rotund man, maybe five six and 180 pounds, in his mid-thirties but looking older. Today he was carrying his AK-47 rifle and had a Browning pistol strapped to his hip. He had longish dark hair, a sloppy mustache, and, for a Nicaraguan, a heavy beard, giving him a slightly menacing appearance.[16]

He entered and sat down opposite the two commanders. Both men were technically of higher rank, but he still seemed to be playing the heavy.

"So to what do I owe the pleasure of your visit?" Joel asked.

"You know they killed a commando out in the Quilalí?" Jhonson asked him.

"Yep, we heard about it. Not our operation. I checked with Mike Lima about this guy Israelita," Joel said, referring to Blake by his pseudonym. "His work isn't authorized."

Jhonson wasn't surprised that while an atrocity was still unfolding, the counterintelligence section's main worry seemed to be covering its own ass. But for the moment, Jhonson didn't want an argument about chains of command and areas of responsibility.

"Look, Joel. The important thing is to get this thing stopped," Jhonson told him. "If we don't act, somebody else is going to get killed. This thing could mushroom into a huge problem."

"Okay, okay," Joel answered. "I'll shut Israelita down, no problem. But on whose responsibility? Are you ordering me to detain Israelita?"

"Yes, this is an order from Commander Denis and me," Jhonson said.

"Put it in writing?" Joel asked.

Jhonson glared at Joel. "Okay, fine. Got any paper?" he said. Jhonson scribbled out a note ordering Blake's detention, using the rhetorical flourishes customary in contra documents: "To Joel, Chief of Section 6, Zone 2. Resistance Army of the North. . . . In accordance with this affair, detain the commando Isaac Blake, pseudonym Israelita, and hold him for questioning. On orders of Commander Denis, G-1, General Staff and Commander Jhonson, Legal Officer." Jhonson signed it. Denis did too.[17]

Jhonson and Denis drove back to the general staff camp. There, Jhonson told Joshua that he'd arranged for Joel to detain Blake.

"We should be able to question him in a couple of days," Jhonson said. "What we need now is for you to go back out to the Quilalí, inspect the area, find this detention pit they dug, locate this kid's grave. Sketch a little map of the area. And make a list of the prisoners and the staff out there. We'll need to get statements from everybody."

Jhonson left the same morning for Tegucigalpa. He knew he'd gone out on a limb—it wasn't really within his authority to order arrests. That power rested with the chief of staff or with the contras' commanding general. He was eager to talk with Bermúdez and with the Americans.

Jhonson knew Bermúdez was in Tegucigalpa, but when Jhonson

arrived back at his office and called Bermúdez's safe house, the commander didn't answer. Jhonson dialed Charneco, his State Department liaison, at his office in Washington. Charneco greeted Jhonson in his rapid-fire Puerto Rican Spanish.

"Colonel, I have some bad news," Jhonson said. "The guys from counterintelligence put a guy to sleep."

"What do you mean?" Charneco asked. Jhonson had to be more direct.

"One of the prisoners was tortured and beaten to death," Jhonson said.

There was a long pause. "Oh, God," Charneco said. "I can't believe it. Who was it?" he asked.

"A commando named Isaac González, pseudonym Managua," Jhonson said.

"Have you told Bermúdez?" Charneco asked.

"I haven't been able to reach him today. But he already knows. I'll keep calling."

"What have you done so far?" Charneco asked.

"We're investigating," Jhonson said.

"Have you detained anybody?"

"We're working on it."

"Look, Luis," Charneco said, "I'm sure you know, this is really serious. This could be a huge scandal. It can damage your organization a great deal. The Congress will cut off the aid for sure if you guys don't handle this right. You've got to investigate this thing and punish whoever's guilty."

"I know, Colonel, we're working on it," Jhonson said. "I wanted to let you know."

Minutes later, Bermúdez answered the phone at the Tegucigalpa safe house that was the rebel army's communications headquarters.

Jhonson said he wanted to talk. He'd drive right over.

Jhonson figured that since his first call two weeks earlier, Bermúdez had probably learned all about the crime from his ex-Guard friends in the contra army. But Jhonson wanted Bermúdez to know just how serious it was, and to tell him of his own decision to order Blake detained. Furthermore, Jhonson wanted Bermúdez to know he'd reported the murder to the Americans. That way, Jhonson knew, Bermúdez would have no real choice but to back his investigation—however reluctantly. When he was face to face with Bermúdez, Jhonson laid out the bad news.

"*Comandante*," he said, "the counterintelligence guys really screwed up out in the Quilalí. You know that, right?"

Bermúdez was noncommittal. "How's your investigation going?"

"I called Charneco this morning and gave him details," Jhonson said. "This is serious. Some of the officers on the general staff were involved out there."

Now Bermúdez reacted. "What a bunch of idiots," he said. "Something like this would never have happened if I'd been in charge. Have you gone out to the camp?"

"Yeah, Joshua was out there. But he hasn't taken any statements from the Quilalí staff yet."

"Okay," Bermúdez said, "you've got to do that. And you've got to do an inspection, maybe make a map of the site."

Jhonson sent a radio message to Yamales.

To: Joshua
Continue with investigation Quilalí case. On instructions Commander Three-Eighty. Try to do an inspection of the site.

Signed, Jhonson.[18]

December 12–13, 1988

Who was Blake, anyway? Jhonson had never run into him, either inside Nicaragua fighting or around the Honduras base camps. Working at his Comayagüela office, Jhonson checked with his staff to see if anybody recalled the name. Nobody else had been able to put together any solid information on him either.

Then Jhonson recalled that Chino had said that earlier in the war Blake had used a different pseudonym: "El Comando Negro"—The Black Commando. That rang a bell for Jhonson.

Jhonson had a list in his office of all the commandos who'd been investigated and tried by the Resistance. It was an index of the contra army's investigations files, packed into three battered metal cabinets. He grabbed the list. Sure enough, there had been a "Comando Negro" investigated and tried in July 1987. Jhonson asked one of the Honduran secretaries to pull the file.

It was a curious case. Three Hondurans, two men and a woman, rural merchants who had established a rustic beer joint at the side of the road leading in to the contras' Yamales general staff headquarters, had complained to the Resistance military police. They claimed that the Black Commando, Isaac Samuel Blake, had "caused scandals while inebriated, firing his regulation AK-47 rifle and exploding hand grenades at all hours of the night, without taking into consideration the families living close by." The record showed that Blake had been called before a tribunal of three Resistance commanders for questioning.

The panel was one of the tribunals established at U.S. State Department bidding, starting in late 1986, to investigate and punish rebel fighters accused as human-rights abusers. Defendants were called before three rebel field commanders, questioned, and sanctioned under the terms of a code of conduct modeled on the old military justice code of the former Nicaraguan National Guard. The tribunals generally heard cases in a field tent at the rebels' Yamales border base or, in 1987, at the CIA-run Aguacate Air Base outside Catacamas, Honduras. Although the State Department had demanded the tribunals in hopes of improving the rebels' human-rights record, during the first years they functioned, until 1988, they mainly heard internal discipline cases like Blake's.

Blake had denied all the charges. He'd never fired his rifle like the complaints said, nor exploded any grenades. Faced with contradictory accounts, the tribunal had called in the three Honduran complainants to explain their charges. At that, the two Honduran men had a striking change of heart. Overnight, they withdrew their complaints. For her part, the Honduran woman who had signed the original complaint against Blake came before the tribunal. Once seated across the wooden table from the three commanders in their U.S. Army camouflage, she, too, claimed there had been a terrible misunderstanding. She'd never raised an accusation against Blake, or anyone else in the contra army. She knew nothing about any shooting incident. She had never seen Blake drunk. Her signed complaint? That wasn't her signature. Blake? As far as she was concerned, he was innocent. Innocent of whatever anybody might accuse him, she said.

The tribunal cleared Blake.

What had caused the three Hondurans to change their minds so dramatically since they'd filed their original complaints? Jhonson, familiar with the thuggish ways of the Resistance's military police units, figured Blake had gone to the Hondurans and threatened them.

On Tuesday, December 13, Jhonson drove back to Yamales. He'd given Joel three days to bring Blake in. Now was the time to take a complete statement and to determine who Blake was working for.

When Jhonson's pickup ground its way up the slope to his legal affairs tent, he saw a small group of young commandos loitering out front. As Jhonson climbed out, a skinny, slightly emaciated commando, who looked to be about twenty, approached him and saluted.

"*Comandante*, I'm 'Alí,' the S-2 from the Quilalí. I just finished giving a statement to Joshua," he said. The term "S-2" meant that Alí was the head of intelligence for his unit, the Quilalí Regional Command.

"Okay, good," Jhonson said. Joshua must have been out to the

Quilalí and called some of the staff officers in for questioning, he thought.

Alí was about five feet five inches tall and slight, about 130 pounds, Jhonson thought, sizing him up. His hair was black, longish, and wavy. His skin was pale, the ivory color common among many Nicaraguans from the north. A scar ran up from the bridge of his nose between his eyebrows. He looked to Jhonson like an intelligent character, but at the moment apprehensive. Alí's mannerisms told Jhonson he knew he was in trouble. He was contrite, saluting, hat in hand. Jhonson suddenly realized that commandos scattered across the entire general staff camp- site were watching his conversation with Alí. It looked as though the investigation had become big news.

"Another commando is inside with Joshua now, guy named 'Rambo,' " Alí said.

"Nice to meet you," Jhonson said. He turned and walked over to the legal affairs tent. Inside, Joshua was seated at his typewriter, across from a powerfully built commando, around twenty-four years old.

Joshua nodded in greeting. Jhonson didn't like to interrupt Joshua when he was taking statements, nor did he ever listen to the question- ing. It made witnesses nervous to have an audience.

"Just briefly," Jhonson said to Joshua. "You've been to the Quilalí?"

Joshua nodded again.

"Is Israelita detained?" Jhonson asked.

"Yep. Joel's got him."

"Okay," Jhonson said, "I'll go see if I can get him and bring him over here for a statement—or arrange for you to question him over at the mil- itary police."[19]

Five miles east, at Joel's counterintelligence section, Jhonson encountered the same routine as the week before: the wait at the road- side sentry post for Joel's radioed permission to enter, the hike in to one of the plastic interrogation huts, and finally, Joel's appearance.

"Have you got Israelita?" Jhonson asked.

"Yeah, he's here," Joel said.

"I need for you to loan him to me. I want to take him to make a statement," Jhonson said.

"Well, today I'm pretty busy," Joel told him. "I've got a lot of interro- gations under way. Better another day. But I'll tell you what. I'll bring Israelita out and you can talk to him briefly right now."

Joel disappeared, leaving Jhonson to think. What's he up to? Is he really too busy?

Presently Joel was back, ushering in a black man, maybe five eleven and heavily built for a Nicaraguan, probably 190 pounds, well-muscled. He had a goatee and short Afro hair. He was unarmed, but without bonds. He was smoking.

"This is Israelita," Joel said.

Blake and Joel sat down facing Jhonson.

"As you know, we're investigating what happened in the Quilalí," Jhonson said to Blake. "I want you to make a formal statement to the legal office."

"Look, *chambelán*, I'll give you a statement," Blake said.

He'd used the slang word "chambelán," meaning "buddy," roughly. Jhonson knew the word was used only by former National Guardsmen, as kind of a password. Blake was talking in measured statements, broken by pauses.

"But I want you to know," Blake went on, "that I did what I did on orders of Mike Lima."

Blake glanced at Joel. Joel sat stone-faced, silent.

"That's fine," Jhonson said. "But don't tell me now. I need you to say all this in a formal declaration. And I want you to tell me the truth."

"Well, like I say," Blake said, "that's the truth, *chambelán*. I did my work there on instructions of Mike Lima."

"Well, you're going to have to give a statement and then sign it," Jhonson said.

Joel interrupted. "That'll be okay, but not today. I'm just too backed up here with interrogations. Come back tomorrow or Thursday."

Jhonson felt he couldn't really argue. He'd have to come back himself or send Joshua. "All right, I'll be back," he said. He excused himself, walked out to the road, and drove back to the general staff camp.

It was mid-afternoon, and Joshua's interviews had ended for the day. Alí, Rambo, and the other commandos who'd been outside the legal office were gone. Joshua wasn't around either.

Inside the tent, on Joshua's worktable, Jhonson found the stack of statements Joshua had produced in two days of questioning. Jhonson sat down to look over the latest documents.

The statement from Alí, the Quilalí's intelligence officer, was the longest: eight pages, single-spaced. He started by telling Joshua about himself.

Antonio "Alí" Herrera Hernández had, like many of the commandos in his unit, grown up in the town of Quilalí, a coffee marketing town of a few hundred residents, 140 miles north of Managua and 31 miles south from Yamales across the Honduran border. In July 1980 Quilalí had been the scene of the very first serious anti-Sandinista uprising. In the years since, scores, perhaps hundreds, of Quilalí teenagers like Alí, male and female, had streamed into contra ranks. The Quilalí Regional Command was named after the town.

Alí's parents were comfortable landowners, with more than five hundred acres of coffee and pasture land. Alí joined the contras in 1982 when he was thirteen, cutting short his schooling after just six years. In seven years as a rebel, he received basic infantry, radio, and office maintenance courses. In 1987, at the beginning of the U.S.-financed $100 million offensive, he'd taken a course in intelligence methods.

Jhonson knew that the intelligence-methods course was for elite rebel cadre, taught at the Honduran Army's pine-shaded Sixth Battalion base along the highway from Tegucigalpa to the border camps. The instructors were Honduran and CIA.[20]

In contrast to Chino's earlier account, which was limited to one week in November, Alí's testimony seemed to lay out an overview of the Blake affair. There were many horrifying details to Alí's statement, depressing to Jhonson because the brutality, turned on the Resistance's own cadre, seemed to degrade the contras' struggle into a mindless vendetta. Alí couldn't hide his shame as his own participation came to light under Joshua's questioning. He'd gotten his hands dirty once Blake's work had begun, but Alí kept returning to a central argument: Blake had authorization from above.

Alí said Blake had just shown up, as a kind of menacing onlooker, at the Quilalí in late summer or early fall 1988. Rumor had it that he'd been hanging around another regional command earlier in the summer. Jhonson thought this detail itself was further evidence that Blake was working for someone else, probably Mike Lima, just as Blake had claimed.

Commandos in the Resistance couldn't move freely from one camp to another without orders or direction. They were detailed to a unit, as in any army, and if they were ordered to a new unit, they were to report to their new commander. They didn't just show up and start hanging around—unless they were working for counterintelligence.

Alí found that Blake immediately came into conflict with what he saw as his own intelligence duties. In late October, Alí had received reports that two teenage commandos in the Quilalí were planning to desert from the Resistance. But when Alí informed Nolan, the Quilalí's twenty-two-year-old commander, Nolan told him that Blake already had gathered information on the potential deserters. That surprised Alí. Why had Blake been gathering information on commandos? Was Blake an intelligence or counterintelligence agent? Nolan didn't seem to want to give a clear answer, but he told Alí to coordinate his work with Blake. Alí went to Blake directly and asked him if he had information on the

suspected deserters. Blake said yes, he did, and that he'd already reported it to Nolan. Nolan knew about Blake's work. To Alí, it all added up
to one thing: Blake was working undercover, with the consent of higher
authorities in the Resistance—probably for counterintelligence.

Alí questioned Nolan and Blake on October 29. He began to work
together with Blake for the first time that same night. Jhonson checked
the date. October 29 was about two weeks before Managua's murder.

Blake had already recruited Roger Medal Rodríguez, a burly twenty-
four-year-old commando using the nom de guerre of "Rambo," and several other fighters as aides. Blake told the group that any commandos
considering desertion were probably Sandinista spies who'd been sent to
infiltrate contra ranks. He ordered them to seize the two suspect fighters from their sleeping hut.

One was a seventeen-year-old fighter who had taken the nom de
guerre "Gangman." He was a dark, clean-shaven boy with a large nose
and straight black hair, from impoverished peasant parents. The other
boy, his friend, was just sixteen. His pseudonym was "Cerrano." On
Blake's orders the two youths were tied and blindfolded and old socks
were stuffed into their mouths. Blake and Rambo dragged Gangman up
the hill near the pit, beating and kicking him. "Tell the truth!" Blake
screamed. Gangman, terrified and confused, didn't know what to say.
The beating continued.

Down the hill, Alí and several others were slugging and kicking Cerrano. He had been conscripted into the Sandinista army in May, but had
deserted weeks later, joining a contra column retreating to Honduras.
He'd been with the contras just three months. When the beating began,
he burst into tears. "You came to Honduras with Gangman to carry out
missions for the Sandinistas, didn't you?" Alí shouted at the boy. The
boy—blindfolded, surrounded by older fighters kicking and punching
him—began making up the answers his tormentors seemed to want.

"Yes, I'm an infiltrator, I came to commit sabotage, to eliminate
commanders!" Cerrano screamed. Alí and the others, perhaps surprised,
stopped the beating. They dragged him to Blake's hut, and Alí took out a
tape recorder to begin taping a statement.

About that point, Blake and Rambo showed up dragging Gangman,
bleeding and bruised from the beating. Alí told Blake that Cerrano had
"confessed." Blake grabbed him and tore off his blindfold. "What the
fuck are you crying about?" he shouted, seizing Cerrano by the feet.
"Let's take them to Acapulco!" The name Acapulco appeared to be
Blake's little joke, because he dragged the boy down a slope and into a
bog of fetid water. The others dragged Gangman down. Blake held Cerrano's head under the water for a while, then raised it to let him revive.

Finally Blake shoved the boy aside and waded out of the muck. It was well past midnight and he appeared to have tired of his sport.

Blake shouted at the youths lying in the swamp not to move or things would go badly for them. Then he and his commandos walked back up to their huts and went to bed.

Gangman and Cerrano lay in the swamp until morning, when Blake ordered Cerrano brought to his hut. This time, Blake was holding his heavy-bladed knife with the head of an eagle carved into its steel handle. He let the youth see the knife, then ordered him blindfolded. He began to prick the boy in the neck, face, and scalp. Cerrano screamed and broke into sobs.

"Who are the other infiltrators?" Blake asked.

"I don't know," the boy answered, gasping. Blake stabbed him again in the scalp. Blood was trickling down the boy's head.

"Who are your spy friends, you little shit?" Blake asked.

The boy decided to use the tactic he'd tried the night before. He said he was part of a group of twenty-five infiltrators. He began to list names of acquaintances, other commandos he'd met, anybody. Blake was pleased. Alí taped his sobbing statement.

When his aides brought Gangman into his hut, Blake jumped on top of the blindfolded youth, forcing him to all fours. Blake began pretending he was riding a bucking horse. He turned the youth over and began kicking him. Then he got out his eagle-handled knife to let Gangman feel the terror of the little stabs.

"You're a captain in the Sandinista army, aren't you?" Blake yelled at him.

"Yes, yes, I am," Gangman whimpered.

Jhonson could see that on the face of it, Gangman's was an absurd confession. Jhonson knew that the rank of captain in the Sandinista army was a relatively senior position. A typical Sandinista captain would be in his late twenties, would have studied a year or two in the East bloc, and would probably have led an entire combat battalion for a couple of years. Blake was questioning a weeping seventeen-year-old.

Blake accused Gangman of stealing a U.S.-supplied field radio from the Quilalí staff tent. Gangman "confessed" to that, too. He said he had given it to a commando named Sandra, a teenage girl. He began naming other commandos he said were Sandinista spies. Alí wrote down all the names carefully in his notebook.

Alí and Blake were pleased with themselves. They'd uncovered an entire infiltration ring in the Quilalí! They swaggered off to Nolan, the Quilalí's commander, to report their finding. Their reports confused Nolan. What should he do? He decided to check with top Resistance commanders, and hiked five miles west down the Yamales Valley to the general staff camp.

Alí didn't see Nolan again until the next day, November 1, when he walked over to Blake's hut. Inside the hut, Alí, to his shock, found two visitors meeting with Nolan and Blake. They were two officers from the Resistance general staff, Commanders Israel "Franklyn" Galeano, twenty-eight, the contra army's operations chief, and José Benito "Mack" Bravo Centeno, forty-four, the rebels' top intelligence officer. Alí, an ambitious young officer, liked to consider Mack, even more than Nolan, his real commander.

The group was gathered around two blindfolded, bloody prisoners. Blake had brought in Gangman and Cerrano with their hands lashed behind their backs. They were covered in mud from the interrogation session in the swamp.

At first, Alí was afraid that Mack and Franklyn had heard about the torture under way in the Quilalí and had shown up to punish him and Blake. Then he saw that there was no problem. Mack and Franklyn were engaged in an earnest discussion about how the investigation should continue. Alí, watching, saw no sign of disapproval by the commanders about the condition of the prisoners.

They had apparently just about finished their visit when Alí arrived; the two commanders began making moves to depart. Pleased, Alí ran to his hut and got the tape recordings he had made during the interrogations of the two prisoners, as well as a list he'd typed of the names of commandos the prisoners had accused of being members of the infiltration ring. He brought the materials back and personally delivered them to Commander Mack. Mack thanked him.

After their visit, everything began to fit into place for Alí. Of course the general staff would have known about the sensitive work Blake was doing. The commanders had given Blake the green light, so Alí said he felt a lot more confident about working with Blake after that.

Jhonson, reading this passage in Alí's statement, thought back. This was the visit Chino had mentioned to Joshua. No wonder Joshua had been worried.

Jhonson knew Mack and Franklyn well. Mack was a former National Guard sergeant whom Colonel Bermúdez had put in command of the contra army's main training base in 1982, at the dawn of the war. Along with Mike Lima, Mack was a key figure in the clique of Bermúdez's ex-Guardsmen. He had rarely entered Nicaragua to fight. Instead Mack had preferred to hang back in the camps, pursuing black-market businesses, selling rebel food for private gain, and running after his many girlfriends. Mack had accumulated a long record of camp brutality.

Ten months earlier, in February 1988, Bermúdez had arranged for Mack's appointment as intelligence chief. That meant he had at least two American CIA officers working with him directly.

Mack's involvement in torture and murder didn't surprise Jhonson, any more than he'd been surprised to hear Mike Lima's name connected with the savagery. But Franklyn was a different story. Like Jhonson, Franklyn had been a farmer in Nicaragua and spent much of the war fighting the Sandinistas in Nicaragua's central provinces, far from the easy life in the Honduran camps. Franklyn's problem, in Jhonson's view, was that he was still young, impressionable, and had gotten too friendly with Mack in recent months. Now it looked to Jhonson as though that had gotten Franklyn into trouble.

If there had been any doubts at the outset among Alí and Blake's other helpers about whether Blake had the authority to carry out his tortures, they all disappeared after the visit by Franklyn and Mack.

Alí said Blake laid down a new rule after the commanders left: Blake said he suspected that some members of Nolan's staff on the Quilalí might themselves be double agents, so from now on, none of the Quilalí staff would be allowed to visit his hut or the area behind it, where he had dug the detention pit. These would be "restricted areas."

Alí considered that absurd. Technically, the rule would apply to him, too, since he was on Nolan's staff. He went to Nolan. Nolan defended Blake's right to restrict the area.

At that point, Alí said he felt he had little power left to question Blake's behavior, but he said he'd asked Blake directly: Who authorizes you to do this kind of work?

"Mike Lima," Blake had said. "I take my orders directly from Mike Lima, without any intermediaries."

That same night, Blake's men seized Sandra, the dark-haired sixteen-year-old girl to whom Gangman claimed to have given the field radio he said he'd stolen. They seized Sandra's two sisters, Rosa, who was just twelve, and Otilia, seventeen, shortly thereafter. They, too, were tied, blindfolded, insulted, punched, kicked, and shoved. Not even Otilia, who was four months' pregnant, was spared.

"Take her to Acapulco!" Blake shouted after Sandra was detained. So Rambo took Sandra, bound, to the swamp. Pressured, she "confessed" to having accepted the field radio from Gangman. Weeping, she promised to lead Rambo and Blake to the place it was hidden, but of course there was nothing there. Fearing more torment, Sandra suddenly said she'd given the radio to a fifteen-year-old girl named Mirna. So Blake's men dragged Mirna in and interrogated her. She named another female commando living at another regional command camp miles down the Yamales Valley.

Blake contacted Joel, the counterintelligence chief at the Yamales base. Joel, who had the use of a U.S.-supplied four-wheel drive, seized the woman in the other camp and brought her to the Quilalí to face her accuser. Under more torture, the women had meanwhile produced other names. The number of prisoners grew.

A few days into Blake's widening dragnet, half a dozen prisoners were crammed into the pit, waiting for interrogation. Blake had noticed that once Gangman had begun to accuse other commandos of being infiltrators, he'd grown increasingly willing to cooperate. Blake named Gangman "chief prisoner," to watch over the others. Sometime later Blake allowed Gangman out of the pit and ordered the seventeen-year-old boy to mete out the same kind of torture he'd been enduring.

Alí came to the pit one day and found Gangman, though still a prisoner, beating another bound commando savagely with his fists, then kicking him when he fell. There was no apparent motive. Gangman told Alí that Blake had "authorized" him to punish the other prisoners.

So it was that when Managua was detained and Blake had worked him over for two days in the pit, well after the first signs of internal hemorrhage had appeared, Blake had turned the injured prisoner over to Gangman and another commando with the order "Take him for a bath in Acapulco."

Gangman knew what to do with Managua. It was Gangman, Alí said, who was mounted on top of Managua in the swamp, meting out the pain, at the end, when Managua's life finally faded.

Alí said he was concerned about the consequences of Managua's death. He considered it of the highest importance to type out a detailed report for Nolan, and also for Mack, the intelligence chief, about the suspect's death during interrogation. He hiked to the general staff camp to deliver his report personally to the intelligence section. He sought advice.

Instead Alí got silence. The general staff did not respond to his report. Nolan had left the camp. Alí had no idea where he was.

Blake, for his part, at first appeared nervous that one of his torture victims had died. In the hours after Managua's death, he called his men together to "explain" the prisoner's death. He said the youth had succumbed to cholera, even though his men had all watched the fatal beatings. But soon Blake regained his confidence. Even while Chino and Gangman were still digging Managua's grave, Blake was pacing around the edge of his interrogation pit, screaming at the other prisoners. "All right, this son of a bitch is dead," he said. "He's the first one. This should be an example to the rest of you."

In the days that followed Managua's death, the torture sessions became public knowledge around the Quilalí camp. Several Hondurans living nearby complained at the camp about the nighttime screaming. The rest of the commandos in the Quilalí, who had seen their comrades dragged away, were terrified.

On November 17, two days after Managua's death, Alí saw Commander Mike Lima, the Resistance's counterintelligence chief, stop his four-wheel-drive pickup at the Quilalí base. He had apparently visited his assistant, Joel, at the Yamales detention center. Blake ran out to the road, and Alí watched as they talked. After Mike Lima left, Alí went over to Blake's hut, and Blake said he'd discussed with Mike Lima the work he was doing. "He told me to keep giving the Sandinista spies hell," Blake told Alí.

After that, it seemed as though Blake and his interrogators went mad. Blake began stripping the teenage girls naked before "questioning" them. He tortured the girl Sandra, then offered to end the pain if she would have sex with him. Blake slept with her a few times, then went after her younger sister, Rosa. He coerced her into having sex with him, too.

To Jhonson, the whole affair spoke of rank degradation. Blake detained so many commandos that his pit became crowded; he had close to a dozen bound prisoners crammed into it at once. They were given food and water only occasionally. Then Blake's helpers would throw a few tortillas onto the earthen floor of the pit. The ravenous prisoners, their hands bound, fell to their stomachs to eat the tortillas off the ground.

Blake invented other tortures. One day he called for one of his men to bring him several pounds of cool ashes from a cooking fire. He took one of the U.S. Army rain ponchos that the Americans had supplied and cut it with his knife, fashioning a hood. Blake grabbed his cassette player and Led Zeppelin tape, and he and two of his aides went up to the pit. He switched on the music, jumped down in with the prisoners, took off his shirt, and grabbed a young kid, José "Gorrión" Siles. Blake used his T-shirt to blindfold the boy. Then he turned him over on his stomach, put his knee on the boy's back, and put the hood filled with ashes over the boy's head. He let the choking boy inhale the ashes to the point of suffocation, removed the hood, then replaced it. Eventually he got the kid to mumble a few names of other commandos who were supposed infiltrators.

Blake wielded his eagle-handled knife with abandon. One night in his hut he was interrogating a sixteen-year-old named Luis "Vidal" Maldonado, when suddenly he just slashed the boy in the knee, clean to the bone. Alí could see that it was a potentially crippling wound.

On November 8, the night George Bush won the U.S. presidency, the entire Yamales Valley erupted in gunfire as commandos throughout the rebel camps, hearing the news by radio, began firing their AK-47 rifles into the air. But while others celebrated, the firing drove Blake into a frenzied anger. He ran to a U.S. Army field radio he had in his hut and began to transmit, howling over the radio that those who were shooting were spies, and that his men should seize them and bring them to him so he could teach them a lesson.

On another occasion perhaps a week after the murder of Managua, Blake took a guitar, along with his field radio, to the detention pit. He ordered the prisoners' hands untied, gave one of the boys the guitar, and ordered everyone in the pit to begin singing evangelical hymns. Once the bewildered prisoners began to sing, Blake began to transmit with his field radio, holding the microphone toward the singing prisoners.

Alí got angry about this use of the field radio. He shouted at Blake to turn it off.

"The enemy has scanning equipment!" Alí shouted. "Discipline yourself! It's not a good idea to let the enemy hear this."[21]

Jhonson was just finishing reading Alí's statement when the flaps to the legal affairs tent swung open. In walked Joshua. Jhonson hadn't had a chance to talk with his aide all day.

"What happened with Israelita?" Joshua asked, referring to Blake by his pseudonym.

"Joel said he couldn't release him today. Too busy. Said maybe tomorrow," Jhonson answered. "You'll have to try over there, 'cause I've got to return to Tegucigalpa tonight. I've got a meeting with the Honduran Army and the Americans tomorrow."

"This guy Alí had a lot to say," Jhonson said, shoving Alí's testimony across the table toward Joshua. "Tell me about your visit to the Quilalí."

"I got to the camp yesterday morning," Joshua said. Nolan, the unit's young commander, wasn't around. In Nolan's absence, it appeared that Alí was in charge, and Alí was nervous but helpful.

Joshua had asked immediately about the whereabouts of Blake and his prisoners. Alí said he had "detained" Blake on Saturday, two days earlier. He said a messenger from Joel had arrived at the Quilalí camp, ordering Alí to bring Blake to the counterintelligence section. There, Joel had informed Blake he was no longer authorized to carry out counterintelligence work, and while Blake was to stay in the counterintelligence section, Joshua got the impression from Alí that Blake had not really been detained, but rather placed under loose house arrest.

Joel had ordered Alí to bring Blake's prisoners to his own counterintelligence section. Joshua learned that they had been removed from the pit and taken away at night. Nobody said why, but Joshua thought it was because Alí was worried that if they were moved by day, people would see them battered and cut.

Together with Alí, Joshua had compiled a preliminary list of the victims. So far he had fifteen names. Joshua had also met the gang of young interrogators Blake had recruited, including Rambo and at least nine others. He'd found them loitering in a sullen clot around one of the cooking fires. Joshua had taken names and scheduled separate appointments with each of them in the legal affairs tent this week.

Later, Alí had led Joshua on a tour of Blake's "restricted area," to view the detention pit, the swamp called Acapulco, and the unmarked grave under the ceiba. "I sketched the site," Joshua said to Jhonson, shoving a crude map across the table.

Joshua continued uneasily: "Yesterday I interviewed a kid named Enrique Aguilar—'Panchito,' they call him. He's the human-rights delegate in the Quilalí. I wanted to know why he didn't report this thing earlier. He said he'd gone to Nolan a month ago to inform him that some of the Honduran residents were complaining about the screams from Blake's hut. Panchito claimed he told Nolan that Blake was making the camp look bad."

"What did Nolan do?" Jhonson asked.

"He said he was trying to quiet the screaming. And then he threatened Panchito. He told him he would disappear if he opened his mouth to the human-rights association. That brings me to my second point. Franklyn, Mack, and the others on the general staff are angry about our investigation."

"Why? What have they done?" Jhonson asked.

"They haven't really *done* anything. But they're looking at me around the camp like they're going to . . . well, I don't know. They don't say anything. It's just ice, everywhere I go. When I tried to requisition some fuel for the electric generator this morning, they told me there wasn't any. They claimed there weren't any lantern batteries, either."

"Well, brother, do the best you can," Jhonson said. "We're mounted on this horse now. We'll just have to ride on."[22]

Jhonson left for Tegucigalpa that night. Tearing in his pickup along the washboard gravel road through wooded foothills between the Yamales camps and Danlí, he thought back over the accumulating evidence in the Quilalí case.

What depressed him as much as anything was that he felt that the commandos of the counterintelligence section had shown themselves to be incompetent amateurs. Jhonson knew the Resistance needed a professional counterintelligence effort, because the rebels faced a real threat of Sandinista infiltration in the camps. Tomás Borge, the Sandinista government Interior Minister and spy chief, had sent agents into the camps successfully many times before.

But if there were spies in the Quilalí with real information to disclose, Blake hadn't found them. Instead, he wrung pathetic lies from his victims. All the "confessions" didn't add up to anything. There was no pattern. But the incoherence of the confessions didn't seem to bother Blake and his gang of interrogators in the slightest.

Most frustrating of all, those holding responsible command positions in the rebel army hadn't done anything to end the madness.

Mack and Franklyn had visited Blake and seen two prisoners hours after they'd been tortured, and they'd left behind the general staff's implicit stamp of approval. Blake had announced loudly to many people that he was working directly for Mike Lima, the counterintelligence chief. He'd even sustained his claim in front of Joel, Mike Lima's second. Then Mike Lima had shown up at the Quilalí to chat with Blake just days after Blake had tortured Managua to death.

It seemed that the Resistance army's most powerful commanders were in trouble.

November 30–December 2, 1988

Patrick McCracken, an auditor from the U.S. Congress's General Accounting Office (GAO), knew that the contra army was holding prisoners, but he'd never visited their jails. On November 30, 1988, McCracken and two other American auditors carried out a surprise inspection.

McCracken, forty-five, was a curly-haired former Marine and Vietnam veteran who had been monitoring Reagan Administration policies in Central America since the beginning of the decade. With him on a U.S. Agency for International Development (AID) helicopter that clattered out of Tegucigalpa's Toncontín Airport was a second GAO auditor and a third from the New York auditing firm Price Waterhouse. Their helicopter headed over the heavily timbered countryside, bound for the remote border hamlet of San Andrés de Bocay, 137 miles to the east.

The three were part of a troupe of U.S. auditors who had been poking about in the contras' Honduran operations throughout much of 1988. On February 3, 1988, Congress had refused to vote further U.S. military aid to the rebel army, instead voting only to continue feeding and clothing the insurgents while peace talks with the Sandinista government continued. As a result of that vote, U.S. administration of the contra army had passed from the Central Intelligence Agency, which had been in direct control since October 1986, to the Agency for International Development. AID was to spend U.S. funds on the contras exclusively for "humanitarian purposes." The Democratic-controlled Congress, angry about how Reagan Administration officials had in 1986 secretly allowed the contras to take funds from a $27 million appropriation specified for nonlethal purchases and use the money to buy grenades and other items, had ordered the GAO to keep watch over AID's shoulder.

After hearing that the contras were holding prisoners, McCracken had asked for details and learned from Resistance officials the locations of two prison camps, one at San Andrés, along the remote Coco River forming the border with Nicaragua, and the other at the Yamales camps. McCracken and the other auditors wanted to know how many prisoners there were, how long they'd been held, and how they'd been treated.

Near San Andrés, the helicopter circled above a steep mountain peak covered in dense jungle canopy. Looking to the horizon in all directions, McCracken could see nothing but a sea of timber. Then, through the treetops below, a cluster of huts surrounded by barbed wire came into view: the contras' San Andrés military police detention center.

The helicopter set down and McCracken and the other auditors clambered out the side bays. The two dozen or so Military Police guards at the center, taken aback by the sudden appearance of McCracken and the other American auditors, cooperated meekly.

McCracken and the others toured two crude jails. They found three teenage girls imprisoned in an eight-by-ten-foot canvas-roofed log hut, encircled by five strands of barbed wire. In a second log cell block, fifteen by forty with an adjacent barbed-wire enclosed prison yard, the auditors found forty-nine miserable men. All fifty-two detainees at San Andrés had been labeled by the contras "politicals," meaning they were either Sandinista prisoners of war or contras accused of being infiltrators.

Once the interviews started, McCracken realized his team had uncovered a shocking underworld of cruelty. All three of the girls complained that they'd been raped at the time of their detentions by contra counterintelligence officers. Every single one of the males accused of being infiltrators said they'd been tortured during interrogations that followed their detention. Some of the forty-nine male prisoners reported that they'd been held in contra jails for four years.

After several hours of interviews, McCracken and his team helicoptered fifty miles to the southwest, following the course of the Coco River, then circled over the Yamales Military Police detention center, located at the summit of a hill overlooking the counterintelligence interrogation camp run by Joel.

At Yamales, McCracken's team found ninety-two detainees. Nineteen were being held for marijuana possession and other common crimes. The remaining seventy-three were "politicals," accused of being spies. The picture in Yamales proved just as appalling as at San Andrés.

The sixteen female "politicals" were held in a ten-by-twenty-foot log hut with a canvas roof, surrounded by barbed wire. Fifty-seven males were jammed into a second log barracks the same size.

The Yamales camps straddled a border cordillera where days are hot but nights can be frigid. Half the women said they were given no bedding or hammocks and were forced to sleep on the ground in the mountain cold. Four out of five of the males lacked bedding. Furthermore, all seventy-three prisoners accused of being infiltrators—sixteen young women aged fifteen to twenty-five, and fifty-seven men—reported that they'd endured extended torture during questioning.

In the late afternoon, McCracken's team flew back to Tegucigalpa. The next day, McCracken typed up the findings, and they added up to an explosive portrait of brutality. He'd found rude jungle concentration camps, jury-rigged together with logs and barbed wire inside a perimeter of armed guards. He'd found that everyone seized by the contras as an infiltrator faced torture. He'd also found systematic rape of the teenage girls.[23]

McCracken went to the walled U.S. embassy compound built into a hill overlooking downtown Tegucigalpa to report on the inspection. He briefed Tim Brown, the fifty-year-old American diplomat working as Ambassador Everett Briggs's main liaison officer with the contra army. Days later, McCracken flew back to Washington and briefed key congressional leaders about the Resistance prisons.

McCracken's inspection raised a disturbing question. How could so many people have been tormented for so long by a U.S.-financed army without this outrage coming to the attention of the U.S. military and intelligence officers working closely with the force? Or had Americans known all along about the abuses and looked the other way?

The GAO inspection raised these concerns within days of Jhonson's own initial investigation into the Quilalí torture-murder case. So the two developments echoed off each other. Jhonson's probe drew attention to the auditors' report. And the GAO's findings made clear that Blake and his abuses in the Quilalí Regional Command were just one theater in a much broader war on accused spies, a witchhunt throughout the Resistance involving the systematic use of torture, rape, and other degradation.[24] It was a vendetta that had intensified in the second half of 1988—but which hard men in the Resistance had been pursuing for years, with virtual impunity.

For the first time in the war, the contra army's most powerful and brutal men were called to account. That provoked extraordinary tension between the rebel leadership and the rival American bureaucracies administering the force. It brought months of handwringing in the Tegucigalpa embassy, forced an angry visit to the camps by a deputy assistant secretary of state, and dominated several White House interagency discussions.

Coming at the close of the war when Washington was preparing to dispose of the rebel army, the case was little more than an asterisk in the Nicaraguan saga, and it passed largely unnoticed in the press.

For the contra army, however, the Quilalí case was a watershed. Jhonson became the central protagonist in a symbolic drama of crime and punishment. The case pitted him against the rebel army's most powerful clique: the former National Guardsmen installed with CIA blessing in the rebel army's top commands early in the war. As a result, Jhonson's fortunes depended almost entirely on how firmly he was supported by one wing of U.S. officialdom, and how relentlessly he was undercut by another.

Throughout his contra career, Jhonson had dealt with many U.S. officials, men and women from the Tegucigalpa embassy, from the CIA and the State Department, from the Pentagon and the National Security Council, from the Agency for International Development and the General Accounting Office. For him and other contras, it was always a confusing panorama. Every American, it seemed, had a different agenda, but in the Quilalí case, otherwise chaotic squabbling boiled down to a clear confrontation. Some American officials—those likely to have known for some time about these and other crimes—fought to cover up the reports of contra brutality. Others, pursuing a reform agenda in their dealings with the rebels, pushed for investigation and punishment of the guilty. They worked through Jhonson.

The Quilalí case became a climactic showdown between the idealism for which the conflict was said to be fought and the cynicism and deceit that were in fact its driving forces. And so, played out in the moral twilight at the end of Washington's covert action, Jhonson's investigation revealed as much of the character and meaning of the larger conflict as any earlier episode.

It forced Jhonson to do a lot of thinking about the war—and he wasn't the only one. Several of the army's younger commanders, men who'd joined the rebel cause in mid-war as teenagers, began asking Jhonson some suddenly very introspective questions: What were the origins of our army? Who's really in charge? What have we become? Where are we going?[25]

2

Insurgent Roots

1951 through 1978

Before he became contra Commander Jhonson, Luis Fley had been a Sandinista. In July 1979, he tramped victoriously through the northern
Nicaraguan town of Jinotega with hundreds of other bearded Sandinista
guerrillas, his *compañeros*, celebrating their defeat of the forty-three-
year Somoza family dictatorship. Just two years later, Fley helped a band
of desperadoes set an ambush that left four local Sandinista officials
dead in a burning jeep along a back road. Then, with his coconspirators,
he fled north on foot for two weeks through forests, farms, and mountains into neighboring Honduras. He escaped into exile six months into
the Reagan Administration, just as CIA agents were beginning to put
together Washington's contra army. Fley became one of the first contras.

Over the next years, thousands of other Nicaraguan youths—perhaps
as many as thirty thousand—made a similar trek into Honduras. They
made the U.S.-sponsored army the largest guerrilla force in Latin America since the Mexican revolution.[1]

Like Fley, most were farm boys who grew up in Nicaragua during the
final decadent years of the Somoza dynasty. Like Fley, they soured quickly on revolution, especially on Sandinista attempts to press-gang thousands of wilderness pioneer peasants into radical mass organizations. But
Fley's upbringing made him different from many contras in ways that
eventually set him apart, and often above, his comrades-in-arms.

Fley's grandfather was an Englishman who in the early years of the century had taken a fancy to coffee cultivation, settling in the heavily wooded mountains of the north-central province of Matagalpa. In the 1940s, Fley's blue-eyed and fair-skinned Nicaraguan-born father inherited the family farm, rambling across six hundred hilly acres of what was then still Nicaragua's eastern agricultural frontier. Fley's father carried on the cultivation of coffee, cacao, fruit orchards, even some sugar cane, and built up a dairy herd of sixty cows.

Fley's father married a witty, cinnamon-skinned Nicaraguan woman who adopted his Seventh Day Adventist religion and patiently bore him fourteen children. Luis Adán Fley, born on March 5, 1951, was the sixth. He grew into a sturdy child with a Roman nose, greenish gray eyes beneath a high forehead, and lighter skin than average in rural Nicaragua. The family farm thrived, but Fley's father had a second woman, by whom he sired some ten additional children. That stretched the father's earnings.

As a result, Luis grew up, not poor, but in humble surroundings, accustomed to hard work in a countryside populated by siblings, half-siblings, and cousins. Fley absorbed many of the pleasing traits common to the Nicaraguan peasantry: a quiet, friendly manner, humble courtesy, patience. Yet because of his grandfather's onetime prosperity, Fley never experienced the extreme privation and precarious existence of the common peasantry.

When Fley was school-age, his father sent him to live with his grandmother in Matagalpa, the provincial capital thirty miles west from the Fley farmstead. Matagalpa was a charming town of stucco-and-timber homes set around a belled cathedral. Straddling a highland valley, the settlement was surrounded by fragrant pine forests; backyard gardens blossomed in its cool air.

Fley grew to adolescence in this invigorating climate, attending school for six years. He was intelligent, a quick learner, and picked up reading, writing, and some minimal mathematics, but there were other, younger children to educate, and his father couldn't keep more than a couple in school at any one time. When Fley reached his early teens, he had to quit school and go to work. He got his first job in a local sawmill, loading trucks and stacking lumber. Later, at fifteen, he took a post with the National Health Ministry, where he became a rural fumigator. This was a job, the first of several, that gave Fley an intimate knowledge of Nicaragua's northern farm country—the terrain in which he eventually fought. His boss would drive Fley from Matagalpa to the end of one of the several roads extending into the provincial backlands. From there, either on mule-back or foot, carrying a backpack, a tank of DDT, and a hand pump, Fley would travel the valleys, spraying farmhouses and out-buildings against malarial mosquitos. It was a job where he met farmers, and they met him.

Three years later, Fley earned a better job, this time with the Nicaraguan Agrarian Institute, the Somoza-era agency which in several frontier sections of Nicaragua rented idle government lands at low prices to landless peasants. Fley was the *cobrador*, the official who drove and walked through the back country, visiting farm sites, collect-ing rent, and sharing conversation. He visited hundreds of farm sites each harvest season, crisscrossing Nicaragua's rural byways from the south of Matagalpa province north through Jinotega to the Honduran border. The only paved road through the region in Fley's youth wound northwest from Matagalpa twenty-one miles over a mountain rib, then descended again to Jinotega, a smaller market center with cobbled streets and as many mules as cars, which was perched in a narrow pass through mountain slopes thick with black pines. Past Jinotega, the roads became mere earthen ruts, extending north and east through a vast, sparsely populated region the size of Connecticut of coffee farms and cattle ranches. Over the next decade, Fley trekked through virtually every mountain hollow in this wilderness.

Fley was a friendly young man with a gentle gift of gab. People knew his family, and he had an easy way with everyone, from the poorest hardscrabble hillbillies to the wealthiest ranchers. He made friends everywhere.

He also saved some money. By the early 1970s, he had accumulated enough savings to establish a little farmstead of his own. He kept his government job, but bought about fifty acres of land near the town of El Cuá, forty-five miles northeast of Jinotega. He planted garden crops—radishes, onions, carrots—and bought a dozen milk cows, good ones for Nicaragua, Brown Swiss, their milk rich with butterfat.

Around this time, Fley met and married a young woman named Magda, whose father's farm he had passed many times on his fumiga-tion route. Soon she gave birth to their first son.

The town of El Cuá stood on the edge of Nicaragua's agricultural frontier. It was a place where a man willing to clear and plow could acquire fertile land cheaply, and hundreds of humble pioneer families were moving northeast from the crowded countryside around Jinotega and Matagalpa to settle on pristine land. Fley's El Cuá was a string of one- or two-room houses, rough wooden planks spiked together over dirt floors, facing a muddy track. No electricity, no municipal water or sewage. Fley and his wife turned the front of their house into a general store, stocked with salt, soap, rice, beans, cooking oil, and crates of warm Coca-Cola.

Fley had never picked up damaging vices, no smoking or drinking; he wasn't a carouser. Instead, he concentrated on his family and his work. Traveling back and forth to the Agrarian Institute in Matagalpa in his pickup truck, he began supplementing his business by hauling sacks of coffee and corn to the capital. For a reasonable commission, he'd ferry back rolls of barbed wire, milking pails, and other farm supplies for El Cuá farmers. The farm blossomed, the store grew, Fley prospered.[2]

1978 through June 1981

In those years, Nicaragua was ruled by Anastasio Somoza Debayle, the last in a series of dictators from the family dynasty founded by Somoza's father, Anastasio Somoza García, in 1936. U.S. administrations in Washington had consistently backed Somoza family rule, channeling money and weapons to the dynasty's security force, the Nicaraguan National Guard.

During the nineteenth and early twentieth centuries, Nicaragua had been torn by civil feuds between peasant armies raised by the wealthy leaders of two warring parties: the Liberals and the Conservatives. Generally their differences had more to do with family ties and territorial prerogatives than with political ideology. (Like other Latin American "Liberal" parties, Nicaragua's Liberals were in fact extremely conservative.) American businessmen found the turmoil inconvenient and engineered repeated U.S. interventions. U.S. Marines occupied Nicaragua for a dozen years after 1912, then withdrew, only to intervene anew in 1926 to quell a Liberal revolt that broke out in the wake of presidential elections two years earlier.

A U.S. Marine expeditionary force helped found Nicaragua's National Guard in 1927, ironically hoping to build an apolitical constabulary that could end decades of civil conflict. The force, known in Nicaragua simply as "the Guard," became a monument to U.S. naïveté, however, when Somoza García—the officer handpicked by the Americans to be its original commander—deployed the force to overthrow President Juan Bautista Sacasa and to install himself in the presidency in 1934.

Over four decades, the Guard became Nicaragua's most powerful institution, as well as the Somoza family's private army. Somoza García's son, Anastasio Somoza Debayle, who assumed the presidency in 1967, turned command of one of the Guard's best units over to his half brother, Somoza García's illegitimate son, José Somoza Rodríguez.

Later, Somoza Debayle created another, even more elite unit, and passed it to his own son, Anastasio Somoza Portocarrero.[3] Platoons of Guardsmen attended to every family need, swarming over the Somozas' several estates as uniformed gardeners, watchmen, mechanics, valets, drivers, even baby-sitters.

In the countryside the Guard evolved into a typical Latin garrison army, with all the vices, high-handedness, and corruption that implies. Deployed in each of Nicaragua's fourteen provincial capitals, often occupying a walled fortress with medieval parapets, the Guard was less an army than a police force with machine guns and tanks, deployed to enforce order and put down dissent and labor unrest. The local Guard commander was the de facto provincial governor. Together with the *jefe político*, the provincial political representative from Somoza's Liberal Party, the Guard commander ran the network of pistol-packing rural sheriffs called *jueces de mesta*. These were local bosses and informers who enforced Somoza rule at the hamlet level.

For Nicaragua's country people, this would have been a familiar and perhaps not unbearable system when crops were good, had it not been for the proliferation of corruption. But by the 1970s, the corruption that commonly accompanies unbroken rule was out of control. Somoza set the example for his followers, systematically embezzling the international aid sent to Nicaragua after a 1972 earthquake. In Managua, the plunderers were members of the Somoza clan themselves, along with the gang of businessmen who surrounded the dictator, but in the northern countryside, the greed of the era marched in a Guard uniform. No doubt imitating the example of their commander-in-chief, Somoza's rural Guardsmen were running wild. Quasi-official thievery became the dismal routine; every minor flunky was on the take.

That's how Fley developed his first distaste for the Guard: He was flagged down and fleeced for a bribe at a roadside checkpoint by an overbearing and overweight sergeant, smelling of rum. Driving his pickup truck throughout the Nicaraguan north, Fley was routinely forced to grease Guard hands.

And yet if peacetime rule by the Guard was bad, it became savage when the Sandinista guerrillas finally began to threaten the Somozas' stability. In 1977 and 1978, as the guerrilla movement made its alarming if not powerful presence felt throughout Nicaragua, the Guard developed a paranoid suspicion: Everyone was a potential subversive. And, in line with the rest of the Guard's procedures, their intelligence methods were not sophisticated. Once the 1978–1979 Sandinista war got under way, the Guard began to seize, torture, and execute. Visiting rural farmsteads, Fley witnessed their methods up close. Talking with peasant friends, he learned how Guardsmen had occupied a mountain chapel to rape a farmer's teenage daughter. He would hear how Guardsmen had lashed a country youth to a tree, torturing him with knives under the guise of questioning.

The Guard, fearing for its survival, developed a brooding hatred for everyone who was not part of its extended family circle. Guard soldiers began to see virtually every Nicaraguan who had no Guard relative as a potential Sandinista. And Fley, on his fumigation rounds through the back country, was no exception.

In the fall of 1978, Fley was visiting farms for the Agrarian Institute on the slopes of a northern volcanic peak called Kilambe, where several dozen guerrillas were camped under the command of a Sandinista named Omar Cabezas.[4] Fley encountered the rebels by chance in the course of his work. He chatted with them, looked over their munitions, heard their sermons, considered their chances. He was friendly, but he made no commitments.

Nonetheless, Guardsmen tipped off by an informant seized Fley a day later as he returned through Jinotega, accusing him of being a Sandinista collaborator. They pulled him out of his car, roughed him up, and dragged him into their cement fortress overlooking the town park. Within a few hours, though, he was allowed to send a message to a defense attorney, who secured his release with a bribe. Fley was lucky the payoff worked, but it deepened his contempt for the Guard.

Back in El Cuá, Fley received a surprise visit from his brother Francisco, then twenty-one, six years his junior. For a year Francisco had studied law at the University of León, then a hotbed of clandestine Sandinista organizing on the sweltering cotton coast to the west. Francisco arrived home in Matagalpa in time for the Sandinista uprising that rocked the provincial capital in September 1978. Francisco and two more of Fley's younger brothers took to the streets to hurl Molotov cocktails. Somebody in the government got a glimpse of Francisco's face behind his red-and-black kerchief, which identified him as a Sandinista, forcing him to flee underground. To hide out, Francisco traveled incognito to his brother's home in El Cuá, more than fifty miles northeast of Matagalpa. Luis Fley was glad to see his brother and to catch up. The two of them talked into the night about the teetering dictatorship and the glories of insurrection. Not long thereafter, Fley and his brother made contact through a messenger with one of the Sandinista units operating in the Jinotega hills.

To Fley, the Sandinistas' war was nothing exotic. Over a century and a half, Nicaragua had become a country not of elections but of civil wars. Periodic revolts against unpopular rulers had become routine, a traditional form of political expression, almost a civic duty.

Gradually, though, the fever of revolution consumed Fley. When the Guard began to bomb Nicaragua's cities and towns, he saw the beginning of the end. He sent Magda and his infant son to stay on her father's farm, and slipped off to join the guerrillas.

Fley joined the Bernardino Ochoa column, named after a rural labor organizer. Like other Sandinista units proliferating through the northern hills, it was an ill-trained militia, a mixture of revolutionary students and working-class kids from the cities and recruits like Fley from the countryside. They were armed with shotguns, pistols, and a few rifles.

It was ragtag, but in that theater of the war in early 1979, that didn't matter. The Guard's final surrender, in Managua, came on July 18 and 19, 1979, but in rural areas, it had begun weeks earlier. As the regime tottered in Managua, León, and the other Pacific coast cities, the Guard's central commanders called in the smaller garrisons from the provinces as reinforcements.

In El Cuá, the lieutenant, two sergeants, and a handful of troops who had been Somoza's Guard presence abandoned their posts and retreated to the provincial capital in early June. Dozens of their counterparts in other settlements across the north also retreated from the countryside at the same time, so Fley's Bernardino Ochoa column never saw heavy fighting. Instead it just followed the Guard's retreat, occupying the posts it abandoned. The Bernardino Ochoa column finally reached Jinotega amid the final Somoza collapse, just in time to see scores of frightened Guard officers and enlisted men from the Matagalpa and Jinotega garrisons surrendering to the Red Cross.

At the moment of triumph, virtually every Sandinista left the hinterlands for Managua to celebrate. Fley, a foot soldier, stayed behind in Jinotega, hanging around with his revolutionary comrades, watching the celebration play itself out. There were several lynchings of particularly odious Somoza-era functionaries, but the takeover was by no means the bloodbath that might have been expected. No one, however, seemed to know who was in charge.

Fley and other troops from the Sandinistas' northern columns were camped out on the hillsides. In the post-triumph anarchy, no normal military logistical system had been established. Food rations were intermittent. There was no system for providing—much less cleaning—uniforms, and in Jinotega's cool and drizzly northern climate, many troops didn't even have ponchos. There was little discipline. Troops were drinking, and there were abuses. What made it worse was that the guerrilla chiefs who inherited command moved themselves into a mansion on the town's outskirts, confiscated from a wealthy coffee farmer who had fled to Miami. They celebrated their victory with a series of wild debauches.

Within weeks of the triumph, Fley saw new Sandinista Front officials arrive, deployed to the provincial capital to begin building the local Sandinista revolutionary apparatus. Transforming the guerrilla columns into regular army units was a top priority. The new military authorities began dividing men into squads, platoons, and companies, selecting unit leaders, and organizing a primitive logistical system. Cuban military advisers appeared to help.

Fley faced a choice. Like most of those who fought with the Sandinistas, Fley was a fighter, a sympathizer, but not one of the full-time revolutionary organizers who were the elite party members. Now he could choose to plunge in further by committing himself to a career with the revolutionary army, or he could return to his pastoral life in El Cuá. Three of his younger brothers—Francisco, twenty-two, Enrique, twenty-one, and Jorge, nineteen—chose the former path. But Fley, twenty-eight, was older. He had joined the Sandinistas to throw out Somoza and the Guard. He had a wife and child, a farm and shop. By late summer 1979, he informed his superiors that he wanted to resign from the army. They, however, had seen his abilities, and knew his sympathy for the revolution. They found Fley a third way.

One of the revolutionary government's first measures had been to confiscate the businesses of Nicaragua's private coffee buyers and exporters. The state was to control the country's most precious export through a monopoly on coffee marketing, and they needed government agents to purchase coffee from farmers at the local level. Fley's Sandinista superiors considered him a potential party cadre, especially since his three brothers were moving on the path to militancy. What better person than Fley to return to El Cuá as the agent of the government coffee-buying monopoly (to be known by its Spanish acronym Encafe)? A party functionary traveled to Jinotega to lure Fley with the offer, which he accepted. In September, he retrieved his wife and child from his father-in-law's farm and returned to El Cuá as a representative of the revolutionary state.

When Somoza fled Nicaragua, the Sandinista Front was a party that enjoyed vast popular sympathy across Nicaragua, but had barely a few thousand charter members. If it was to carry out the social revolution that its leaders considered their mission, the Front not only had to consolidate its grip on state power, it had to grow, to transform itself from a tiny group of conspirators into a political organization capable of controlling an army, police force, and dozens of mass organizations with hundreds of thousands of members. It had to organize.

The Front's leaders dispatched young agitators to the countryside to build the party. In 1980 they sponsored a literacy campaign, in which thousands of university and high-school students who'd joined the Front during the insurrection took to the backwoods to teach peasants how to read and write. Hundreds of other organizers fanned out across the country to assume other tasks.

In El Cuá, Fley was proud of the revolution, supportive of its program, and eager to help out. He joined the Sandinista militia and attended innumerable meetings of the fledgling Sandinista Defense Committee, the CDS, formed to organize neighborhood watches against counterrevolutionaries. Here, too, he began to meet the new kids with smooth hands who were to make revolution. He listened to their agenda for northern Nicaragua.

The newcomers formed study groups in which the newcomers tried to bone up on local history, concentrating on the periodic conflicts between peasant workers and large landowners. Their aim was to fit local residents into Marxist categories, to figure out who among the area's backwoods people belonged to the rural "working class," who were the "semi-proletarians," who were "classic peasants," and so on. After a little study, the Sandinista newcomers began to mark up the provincial maps, penciling in the peasant communities and large farms targeted for special organizing efforts. They began making lists: Which farmers were potential revolutionary leaders? Who in El Cuá would likely sit on the fence when class warfare broke out? Who were the workers' class enemies?

This entire approach began to make Fley uneasy. He was irritated by the young zealots' conviction that after a few weeks of brainstorming, they'd know what was best for an entire region, and he was annoyed by their clinical approach, their cool analysis of people he knew intimately, by name, family by family.[5]

Because the revolutionary government had taken over the businesses of all Nicaragua's former private coffee buyers, Fley's Encafe office became the only coffee market in El Cuá during that first harvest of the new regime. As a result, virtually every coffee farmer in the El Cuá zone came to visit Fley. He knew them all anyway from his years of traveling the back country, and he loved the opportunity to chat as he graded, bagged, and weighed their coffee and recorded the transaction in his Encafe ledger.

He soon realized that he wasn't the only one getting irritated. By the spring of 1980, many peasant farmers were so fed up with government policies, they were already looking back with nostalgia to a romanticized time before the revolution. As they saw it, even if the National Guard had been repressive and corrupt, Somoza's Nicaragua had rewarded hard work with the freedom to pursue independent lives. Poor peasants who, before the revolution, had made decent livings cropping land rented from large farmers now, overnight, learned that they were "semiproletarians." Sandinista functionaries like his boss were confiscating the properties of the largest ranchers. In many cases, this meant that the former tenants were physically removed to state-run cooperative farms. There they were expected to work collectively, under the direction of Sandinista administrators. In the same way, those who had been wage laborers on the Somoza-era haciendas found themselves working for new revolutionary administrators, young people telling the workers that the lands were now "theirs." This was, at first, a popular idea, because the peasants—accustomed to seeing their *patrónes* wintering in Miami—assumed they'd get a slice of the farm profits they knew could make the good life possible. But they soon found that the new *patrón*, the Agrarian Reform Ministry, was only marginally more generous than the last. And under the inexperienced new managers, despite revolutionary rhetoric about better wages and conditions, workers began to see "their" haciendas crumble into disrepair.

The complaints mounted as the seasons turned from harvest to planting. The Front, determined to extend political control over Nicaragua's hitherto unorganized small farmers, decreed that the state-run banks would extend crop loans only to those who presented membership credentials in a Sandinista cooperative. Dozens of Fley's farmer friends stomped into his office, infuriated, to complain. A similar Sandinista measure prohibited gas station owners from selling fuel to farmers without co-op cards.

In May 1980, a delegation of ranking Sandinista officials touring backwoods villages came to El Cuá. Fley watched the meeting in a packed schoolhouse, where an official from the Agrarian Reform Ministry was explaining the government's agricultural goals. The farmers' resentments began to surface; they didn't like being lectured on what to plant, they didn't like meetings, and they didn't like land confiscations. They began to shout insults. The Sandinista officials and their security contingent shouted back, calling the farmers "bourgeois counterrevolutionaries." Later several of the most vocal peasants were arrested. Others saw their farms confiscated, then given to Sandinista party people. Fley had applauded the seizure of Somoza's vast properties as well as the takeover of lands that had been sitting idle while other, landless farmers lacked the rent money to plant crops. But now the government began taking farms from mere peasants—just because they had been labeled anti-Sandinista.

Many mornings over coffee, Fley liked to listen to a portable radio, and the news he was hearing told him that the same process of alienation he was watching in El Cuá was occurring elsewhere in the north. He began to hear of bloodshed. In late May 1980, the government news programs broadcast reports about the knife murder of a Sandinista literacy worker in the northern province of Chinandega by "counterrevolutionaries."[6] In late July, Fley heard a newscast reporting an even more dramatic development. A group of armed men had attacked the headquarters of the Sandinista police in the town of Quilalí, twenty miles northwest of El Cuá, killing three Sandinistas and wounding five. Later the same day the attackers ambushed a government car along a road outside the town, killing several more Sandinista officials.[7] The attack on Quilalí, coming amid a visit to Nicaragua by Cuban President Fidel Castro to commemorate the revolution's first anniversary, triggered a vast dragnet through the countryside surrounding Quilalí by Sandinista army and Interior Ministry troops, supported by helicopters. Fley listened closely to the news. The first Sandinista accounts Fley heard said the assailants were former National Guardsmen who had invaded Nicaragua from Honduras.

Fley, however, had a friend, a tractor driver on a Sandinista Construction Ministry crew working to widen the road through El Cuá, who had relatives in Quilalí, and the friend told Fley that there was a lot more to the Quilalí attack than the government was saying. The friends said the attack had been planned and led by a man named Pedro Joaquín González, who, far from being an ex-Guardsman, had actually been the Sandinista guerrilla who had liberated Quilalí from the Guard in 1979 and had served as the town's revolutionary commander. Seven months before the Quilalí attack, González had resigned his Sandinista command post in disgust over the way other Sandinista officials were treating the townspeople. He'd recruited men who'd fought with him against Somoza, as well as farmers unhappy with the revolution's path—a total of some eighty men—to carry out the Quilalí attack.

In September, the government confirmed much of what Fley's friend had told him. The Sandinista newspaper *Barricada* identified González as the author of the attack, and trumpeted the news that Interior Ministry police had killed him in a combat outside Quilalí. The government accounts referred to González as "the principal chief of the counterrevolutionary gangs in the north." These Sandinista accounts conceded that González had served as Quilalí's revolutionary commander, but claimed that he had turned on the revolution after he was refused a post in the

Sandinista army, supposedly because of his own abuses against the population. The government accounts also admitted that González had a number of followers who had eluded capture. They were still armed and in the hills.

The attack on Quilalí was the first time Fley had ever heard of any organized, armed opposition to Sandinista authority inside Nicaragua. He knew that hundreds of defeated National Guardsmen had fled into exile in Honduras, the country bordering Nicaragua to the north, and that Sandinista authorities still considered them an armed threat. As a matter of fact, Fley still considered them a threat as well. He remembered the Guard's corrupt, brutal ways, and didn't want them returning. But armed resistance to the Sandinistas by rebels who weren't ex-Guards? That was a new development. Also, González sounded a lot like himself. Fley, too, had fought against Somoza's Guards because he'd seen them repress country people. And now, like González, Fley was getting angry watching citified students shove around farmers in the name of revolution.

Fley wasn't ready to shed blood against the revolution, but he began to examine his own anti-Sandinista anger. How serious was he?

Soon after the government announced that it had killed González, Fley learned from local farmers that another group of armed peasant rebels had begun operating, this time in the hills right around El Cuá. Its leader was said to be Encarnación "Tigrillo" Baldivia. Fley knew a number of Baldivias working the land around El Cuá, and he located several of the rebel's relatives. They described Tigrillo as an illiterate former sharecropper who, like Fley, had fought with the Sandinistas against Somoza. Tigrillo had trained with the Sandinista army for a year after the triumph, then deserted, carrying off a few Kalashnikov rifles into the hills. Now he'd persuaded nearly three dozen men, many of them his cousins, to join his tiny insurgency.

Once word spread about Tigrillo's presence near El Cuá, Fley began to see State Security agents, young toughs carrying Uzi automatic rifles, visiting the town's Sandinista Front offices. Townspeople heard that they were compiling lists of suspected counterrevolutionaries. Meanwhile, Fley's relations with many of his Sandinista comrades had grown ugly. There were no more friendly arguments over revolutionary policies—you were with them or against them. As Fley's mounting irritation festered, he found it harder and harder to mouth revolutionary rhetoric with the fervor necessary to convince his *compañeros* that he was still a true believer. Finally, he quit pulling his duty in the Sandinista militia. That's when Fley first began to feel the sting of the murmured insult from former comrades: "counterrevolutionary."

Things were going badly at Encafe, too, as the 1980–1981 coffee harvest got under way. Sandinista authorities in Managua decreed the prices that would be paid to the nation's farmers for the coffee crop, and this year they were well below world levels, far less than what the private buyers had been paying to farmers two years before. However, disgruntled farmers no longer had any other place to go. Fley had no power to pay more, and worse, he began to quarrel with his boss, who would drive out to El Cuá from Jinotega to supervise his work.

Encafe's regional chief, Adrian Molina, was a longtime Sandinista militant who'd been imprisoned by Somoza, then liberated in a mass release of political prisoners negotiated during a widely publicized 1974 Sandinista hostage taking in Managua, and flown to Cuba.[8] Molina returned to revolutionary Nicaragua after the Sandinistas' triumph. Fley thought his boss was fast becoming a petty tyrant in his dealings with coffee farmers. Fley saw no need to wear a military uniform to weigh coffee, and he knew it bothered the locals, but his boss swaggered through every minute of the day in olive drabs, side arm strapped to his hip. More outrageous still were his business practices. To boost Encafe's earnings, he ordered Fley to grade coffee beans strictly, knocking down the price paid to farmers even for minor blemishes on the berries, or dirt in the bags. Fley saw that as cheating, pure and simple.

In March 1981, Fley made his first move toward protest. Alfonso Robelo, a member of the junta that had taken the reins of the original revolutionary government in July 1979, had resigned in protest ten months later and was now leading the anti-Sandinista opposition. He announced a rally for the town of Matiguás, near Fley's birthplace in eastern Matagalpa. Fley, curious, decided to drive to the rally, filling the rear bed of his truck with peasants he picked up along the way. The rally itself was uneventful—a few hundred people, a few hours of speeches—but days later Sandinista State Security police seized Fley, yanking him out of his pickup truck when he drove into Jinotega and shoving him into jail. It was the same provincial lockup in which Somoza's Guardia had thrown him three years earlier.

Fley was held for six days. He wasn't tortured, but the State Security officers who did the questioning humiliated him, insulting him and pummeling him with false accusations, certain in their arrogance that he was a dangerous counterrevolutionary. Meanwhile, in other areas of Nicaragua, the period brought a watershed crackdown. Sandinista mobs reacted violently to another Robelo rally in the town of Nandaime, thirty miles from Managua, beating demonstrators and sacking opposition leaders' homes while revolutionary police arrested dozens of other government opponents. It was a watershed for Fley as well. When the

Guard had seized him three years earlier, Fley had not been a Sandinista—but he became one soon thereafter. Jailed by the Sandinistas, he wasn't what his accusers labeled him this time, either, but the indignity permanently outraged and embittered him.

Fley's three brothers in the Sandinista army were scandalized by his arrest, but prevailing upon authorities in Matagalpa, they soon obtained his release. Upon returning to El Cuá, Fley found his life had turned a corner. He was fired from Encafe, and soon discovered that the entire Sandinista apparatus now considered him a counterrevolutionary. His life quickly became unbearable. The Sandinista militia and CDS unit he'd only recently left now turned their watchful eyes on him. Revolutionary punks began strolling past his store and shouting insults at him and his wife. Local Agrarian Reform officials began moving to take over his farm.

Talking with some of his closest friends in El Cuá, men who'd been in the militias and had shared other experiences with him, Fley realized things were going badly for them, too. Several had been detained; all were desperate.

Finally, Fley decided to go into exile with his family, to build a new life in Costa Rica, but when he applied in Matagalpa for the Nicaraguan passport he'd need in order to travel, Sandinista migration authorities refused his request. He was forced to wait—and worry. His life was closing in around him.

One day he learned that his friend, the tractor driver for the Construction Ministry, had left his job and family and was in the hills with Tigrillo. Fley was curious, and through an intermediary, arranged a meeting at a farm a few miles outside El Cuá. The two men hiked to a clearing along the bank of a river to guard their secrecy, and Fley heard his friend's own story of mounting desperation and final decision to join the rebels. To Fley, the rebels' plans for a new guerrilla war seemed quixotic, even foolhardy, but he felt a tugging admiration for his friend's defiance of the self-righteous revolutionaries.

Fley listened, making no commitments, but agreed to meet again for another chat a few days later and to bring cigarettes and other supplies back with him. Without sensing the change, he'd already become a rebel messenger. He began meeting, one-on-one, with a handful of his closest friends, feeling them out. They were showing interest in breaking out of the closing Sandinista circle, but they were looking to him. What was he going to do?

One day, a distant cousin of his wife's made a mysterious visit to Fley's home, bearing disturbing news. He said that he'd been working for some time, secretly, for the Sandinistas' State Security Directorate.

In the course of his work, he'd learned that secret police agents had labeled Fley an enemy of the revolution and were plotting to attack him. The cousin said he had come to Fley because he felt unable to stand by silently while his own family was in danger. He was warning Fley to be careful. Fley believed him, but what good was the warning? There were few ways he could protect himself, and without a passport, he couldn't leave the country.

Fley's desperation fed his anger. He began to scheme, wild plans racing through his head. The rifle-toting Sandinista CDS vigilantes continued to hound him, calling him "Corporal Fley." They'd invented an entire, fictitious former Guard career and were laying it on Fley. Fley was fed up.

The next time he met his rebel friend, Fley said he wanted to help out more actively. Why didn't Tigrillo's insurgents work out a plan and just take over El Cuá? Fley had friends inside the town, and he knew every Sandinista official there as well. Fley could help the rebels pick an opportune moment, when the authorities' guard would be down. They could overrun the small militia post, seize rifles, rob the bank, and be out in the hills long before army reinforcements could arrive.

His friend was interested. Fley's knowledge of the local militias' patterns and willingness to collaborate made the plan seem eminently feasible.

At their next encounter on a nearby farm, Fley's friend brought Tigrillo. He was a short, dark man with long shaggy hair hanging down from beneath a baseball cap that bore the brand name of a fertilizer. He had small, yellow eyes set close together above a broad nose—hence, Tigrillo, the "Little Tiger." He talked big to Fley about making war on the Sandinistas, just as the Sandinistas had made war on Somoza. Tigrillo spoke a rapid-fire Spanish so crammed with mountain expressions and peasant syntax that it was practically a separate dialect.

Fley wasn't impressed, but he plunged ahead, renewing his suggestion for an attack on El Cuá. Tigrillo liked the idea. The attack would start with a road ambush by Tigrillo's people on the town's Sandinista leaders when they drove out of town. Then the rebels would rush into El Cuá to link up with Fley and his men, who could lead them through an assault on the militia post and the hit on the bank. It looked good. They shook hands in parting, and in early June, Tigrillo moved all his men—now nearly thirty—into the zone.

Finally, Fley saw his moment. Juan Ramón Correa, one of El Cuá's most prominent Sandinista militants, just back in town after training in Cuba, announced a rally to enroll farmers in a new Sandinista cooperative. It was set for the following Sunday morning in the hamlet of Pedernales, near El Cuá. Fley knew Correa, knew his vehicle, and quickly envisioned his ambush.

Fley rushed to prepare. He met with a rebel contact and told the ambushers to be ready to move into place Saturday night. He contacted a half dozen friends inside the town. It's now or never, he told them. They signed on, too.

Fley took a drive toward Pedernales. About three miles out of town, he picked a stretch where the road took a sharp left curve along a wooded bank. That was the spot to drop a tree across the road, Fley figured. Ambushers could shoot down on the vehicle from the overlooking hillock.

By late Saturday night everything seemed ready. Fley threw two spare pistols, ammunition, and a rifle he'd saved from the war against Somoza into his pickup and drove to a meeting point on the road. Several of Tigrillo's men, rough-looking farmers with unkempt beards, walked out of the bush. Fley led them to the ambush site and reviewed final details for a postambush rendezvous with his own group of new contra volunteers in El Cuá. He turned over the three firearms and his ammunition to Tigrillo, to bolster the band's firepower. Then he went home to wait.

On Sunday, June 13, 1981, just as the first rays of sun were streaking over the verdant hills, Fley saw Correa's jeep creaking along El Cuá's main road, heading toward Pedernales. With Correa were five others: two Sandinista militia members carrying M-16 rifles, a couple of small farmers who'd been helping Correa organize Sandinista co-ops, and a stranger carrying an Uzi. It turned out that the man was Jorge Escoto Paguaga, a friend of Correa's and a plainclothes officer in the State Security Directorate.

At an intersection outside El Cuá, Correa stopped his jeep to pick up a peasant family of four. They jammed inside with the rest. Some twenty minutes later, Correa's jeep rounded a curve and, seeing a tree across the road, pulled to a stop. Immediately, Tigrillo's men opened fire from the embankment above. The rebels were armed only with shotguns, pistols, and one M-3 carbine, but they rained down considerable gunfire. One of the militiamen leaped out of the jeep, trying to fire a clip from his M-16. Tigrillo's younger brother, firing from close range, blew the man's face away with a shotgun blast. Paguaga sprayed bullets from his Uzi frantically, then fell. Correa was hit. When the firing stopped and Tigrillo's men crept forward, they found six dead. One was Jesús Lumbi, an old woman who'd hitched a ride. One of the farmers was groaning on the pavement, wet with his own blood. He would survive to tell his story for the Sandinista papers.

Tigrillo's men were ecstatic. After starving in the hills for a year, hungry for weaponry, they'd finally captured two M-16s and an Uzi! They were so jubilant, in fact, that they abandoned their plan to seize El Cuá. Instead, they hijacked a farm truck and drove west fifteen miles to celebrate at a collaborator's remote farm. They forgot all about Fley.[9]

The ambush was just far enough out of El Cuá so that the gunfire was inaudible to Fley. He waited an hour. Had Tigrillo ambushed the jeep? What was keeping them? Fley paced the floor of his shop, looking at his watch. Two hours. What had gone wrong? The sun was getting high in the sky, the town bustling. The delay was ruining all chances for any surprise attack inside El Cuá. What had happened with the ambush? Did it fail? Was Tigrillo captured? Or had they pulled it off? Either way, Fley was in trouble. Finally, he decided, it was now or never. He walked down the dirt road and told one of his coconspirators that it was time to leave. Back in his shop, he grabbed fifty dollars in savings and a photo of his two boys from a drawer, and kissed the baby and his wife. Then, in a voice loud enough that the CDS vigilante could hear from the street outside, he told Magda he was going to the farm to look over the crops. Joined by his friend, he walked out the door and into the hills.

In less than an hour, three military troop trucks crammed with infantry rolled into El Cuá to occupy the town; they were the first of numerous reinforcements that over the next years turned the village into a virtual garrison. A month later, State Security agents came to Fley's shop to inform his wife that Fley had been identified with a band of armed counterrevolutionaries. The Sandinistas seized the house and shop and, the same day, a platoon of soldiers moved in to establish a barracks. Fley's sobbing wife fled to her sister's in Jinotega.

In his first panicked flight from El Cuá, Fley's biggest mishap came when he tried to ford a river swollen by the June rains, and raging waters swept away his savings along with the photo of his kids. After making contact with rebel messengers, it took him a week to locate, on a nearby hacienda, the contras who'd stood him up. Fley stalked forward to confront Tigrillo; a screaming match ensued. But Tigrillo was in charge. He wasn't sorry for his decision to abandon the El Cuá attack, and he was still elated about the success of the Pedernales ambush. Overnight, the Sandinista papers had made Correa, Paguaga, and his other victims into martyrs—and Tigrillo into a dangerous warrior! Among local farmers his stature had surged.

At the same time, however, a Sandinista dragnet through the area was building momentum. Tigrillo ordered the group to keep on the move.

Fley began to take stock of the rebel band he'd joined. Tigrillo's men had survived a furtive, illegal existence in Nicaragua's hills for a year, talking insurgency to disgruntled farmers, plotting small conspiracies, stealing chickens from government farms. They'd carried out two small attacks before the Pedernales ambush. But since they had absolutely no outside help and only mediocre hunting weapons, their military impact had been inconsequential. Yet the Sandinista response was mounting fast: increased infantry patrols, more State Security visits to local farms.

By June 1981, despite Tigrillo's rhetorical bravado, his followers were acutely aware of their own limitations as a rebel threat, yet listening to radio stations broadcasting from Tegucigalpa, 110 miles to the northwest, they knew that neighboring Honduras was boiling with anti-Sandinista activity. It was the new refuge not only for hundreds of ex-Guards camped there, but also for the remnants of Pedro Joaquín González's rebels from Quilalí and thousands of other Nicaraguan exiles. Tigrillo decided that now was the time to go to Honduras. He had captured two M-16s and an Uzi, trophies that could prove he was fighting a real war. Maybe he could get donations for more weaponry from the Nicaraguan exiles; maybe some kind of international backing. Fley, too, was curious about Honduras. How much international support was there for a revolt against the Sandinistas? And Fley had a sister living in exile in Honduras who could probably help him out.

Tigrillo's band marched north toward Honduras, and Fley trudged with them. His war had begun.

3

The Rise of the Ex-Guards

Mid-1981

When Fley waded across the Coco River into Honduras, he was filthy, sunburned, and ravenous. During the three-week trek northward through thick forests, he'd been separated from Tigrillo's band and his boots had given out, leaving his feet bloody and swollen. He was, moreover, illegal, without documents. He looked more like a refugee than a guerrilla. The distinction blurred further over the next months. Fley fought as much to survive in Honduras as to reclaim Nicaragua.

Fley still had two pistols thrust under his belt. One, he wrapped in an old corn sack and buried just over the border inside Honduras. Furtively avoiding Honduran Army border patrols until he found the right peasant buyer, he sold the other for enough cash to buy a few days' food.

Then, in the border hamlet of Arenales, a Honduran Army lieutenant at the head of a fifteen-man patrol detained Fley. Who was he? What was he doing in Honduras without papers? The lieutenant held Fley for two days, eyeing his ragged clothing and desperate gaze, considering Fley's extravagant claims to be a Nicaraguan rebel, fighting the Sandinistas.

The young officer might have been still more skeptical, but he'd already encountered other, similar desperadoes, hungry men fording the river, claiming to be Nicaraguan insurgents. The lieutenant's orders were to keep the Nicaraguans together so they wouldn't make trouble.

There was a camp of Nicaraguan exiles in a valley called Maquengales not far to the northeast, and he dispatched a private to guide Fley to the site.

Fley was hopeful. There was already a rebel camp? There'd be food, drink, shelter, and, perhaps, decent rifles. He'd be able to get his bearings, sound out the others about the prospects for further help. But when he trudged into the rebel "camp" at Maquengales, Fley's heart sank.

Several dozen men were living in rough brush lean-tos, virtually destitute. There was no steady food besides wild bananas, no extra clothing, no money. About half of the men were former members of Anastasio Somoza's National Guard and were loyal to the leader of the camp, a thirty-five-year-old former Guard captain. Another two dozen or so were farmers and ex-Sandinista militiamen who'd participated in the July 1980 takeover of the town of Quilalí led by Pedro Joaquín González. Tigrillo and his men had straggled into Maquengales just days before Fley.

Fley was aghast. He'd walked all the way to Honduras for this? In Nicaragua, when they had to beg, at least they'd gone to their own countrymen. When they shot wild game, at least they'd been able to eat it without sharing. Now, to the Honduran authorities, Fley, Tigrillo, and the other civilians were no different than the ex-Guards—just Nicaraguan illegals. The Hondurans shoved them all together in the same camp. Tigrillo's group had to break scarce bread with a clique of drunken Guardsmen.

Fley and the others in Tigrillo's band were among a few of the hundreds of civilians who fled Nicaragua for Honduras during this period and who eventually ended up fighting in the contra army. Many were small-business owners like Fley, or poor dirt farmers like Tigrillo, who had fought with the Sandinistas against the National Guard. Some were cattle traders or other rural merchants whose independent commerce the Sandinistas suppressed. Some were Protestant preachers who saw their frontier congregations harassed by zealous local revolutionary officials. The sons of wealthy ranchers whose lands had been confiscated were few: Men fleeing Nicaragua with access to real wealth didn't hike to Honduras, they jetted to Miami.

They were all, like Fley, furious at a revolution turned harsh. Many, like Fley, had dreamed of a new insurrection to set things straight. Virtually none, however, entertained any sophisticated vision of Nicaraguan geopolitics. If some had begun to consider the Somoza years as a time of peace, when hard-working people ate beef, few considered themselves to be "counterrevolutionaries."

Most, like Fley, still harbored extreme antipathies toward the

National Guard. Yet over the next months, Fley, Tigrillo, and hundreds more of these men would join a fledgling army, financed by the CIA and commanded, in its entirety, by Somoza's former Guardsmen. American officials would portray the civilians as the heart and soul of the U.S.-financed force. For the American public, they would become the very symbol of the Nicaraguan war: the "freedom fighters." But within the rebel army, they would wield little influence. Power would be held by the ex-Guards.

Fall 1981

The men of Maquengales were a despairing lot of gaunt refugees when, a couple of months after Fley's flight into exile, a jeep bumped its way down an earthen track and stopped at the edge of the campsite.

A Nicaraguan man, forty-eight, with slightly Asiatic eyes crowned by dramatically dark, bushy eyebrows, climbed out and greeted the curious men of the camp. He was wearing blue jeans and a nylon windbreaker. Fley had never seen him before. He introduced himself as Enrique Bermúdez, a former National Guard colonel.[1] With him were two middle-aged Argentines. Bermúdez introduced one as Santiago Villegas.[2]

Bermúdez gave an informal speech. He said he was visiting Maquengales because he was interested in building an armed struggle against the Communists in Nicaragua. His Argentine companions, he said, wanted to help. He said he'd never doubted that the Sandinista revolution would result in a totalitarian, Marxist-Leninist regime. Nor had he ever doubted that the Nicaraguan people would reject such a regime. Bermúdez said he had been exploring all along the Honduran border with Nicaragua, stretching nearly two hundred miles from the southern, cotton-growing province of Choluteca northeast through the coffee country of El Paraíso province. He said he'd met a lot of ex-Guards, men with professional military backgrounds like his own, who wanted to continue the fight against the Sandino-Communists. And he was finding a lot of civilians—even former Sandinistas—who wanted to take up the fight, too. What was needed now was for all the groups camped in different areas of Honduras to join forces.

Bermúdez said he knew that some of the men at Maquengales had already begun fighting the Sandinistas, but without connections in Honduras and international backing, they would never get anywhere. Bermúdez said that he had international friends, lovers of freedom who were committed to helping this anticommunist fight, if the Nicaraguans would only unite into a single guerrilla army. He was willing to be its commander.

When Bermúdez finished his introductory speech, he turned to the scruffy men of Maquengales. Where were they from? What were their intentions? Did they want to fight the Sandino-Communists? Were they willing to fight in a real army? How many men could they recruit?

Bermúdez and his Argentine friends seemed particularly interested in Tigrillo's band. Tigrillo brought out the Uzi and the two M-16s they'd recovered in the Pedernales ambush. Tigrillo was swaggering.

"Here's what we have to show!" Tigrillo said. "We're already waging war! These are our trophies. This is the evidence of what we can do."

Bermúdez looked the weapons over. He seemed partly impressed, partly bemused. How many men did Tigrillo have inside Nicaragua? he asked. How many men could he recruit? Tigrillo claimed hundreds of followers.

The banter went back and forth. Finally, Bermúdez said he would press on with his efforts to unite all the Nicaraguan exile groups into one army and to organize more backing from his international friends. Looking at the gaunt faces and the ragged clothing, Bermúdez said he knew what the men of Maquengales were going through. He wanted them to be patient; help was coming.

Now, Bermúdez said, I want you to have a token of our commitment. He gestured to Villegas, the Argentine, who opened the back of their jeep and began pulling out bags of new combat boots. There were sixty pairs, enough for every refugee at Maquengales. Villegas opened a briefcase, removed fifteen hundred dollars, and gave it to the ex-Guard captain in charge of the camp. That's to buy food for these men, he said. Then Bermúdez and the Argentines left.

Bermúdez's visit disoriented Fley. He had turned on the Sandinistas because he'd come to loathe their arrogance and self-righteousness. But if he'd dreamed of waging peasant rebellion against the Sandinistas on his own terms, he was uneasy now at Maquengales, sharing a refugee camp with a ragtag assemblage of former National Guardsmen, listening to a middle-aged colonel rant against the revolution. Nevertheless, Fley's abhorrence of the National Guard was fading before his loathing of the Sandinistas. The humiliation he'd suffered at the hands of State Security police in the Jinotega jail just months before was still stinging. Furthermore, he now had Sandinista blood on his hands; he had burned his bridges.

Bermúdez had left enough money to buy a steer to slaughter, perhaps enough to keep the dozens of men at Maquengales in rice and beans for a week or two. But Bermúdez had given the money to the ex-Guard commander, who had already accumulated some food debts, and would likely spend at least some of the money on liquor. If Fley was to survive, and to get his wife and family out of Nicaragua, he would have to rely only on himself.

A day or two later, Fley hitched a ride on the back of a farm truck, hiding under a tarpaulin from the Honduran migration authorities. He rode six hours over mountains to the west into the capital, Tegucigalpa. There, he linked up with other Nicaraguan exiles who helped him get started. He worked construction around Tegucigalpa for a few months, then sent word to his wife and sons through a messenger. They joined him in Honduras, where he set them up in a shabby, windowless cubicle he rented for the equivalent of twenty dollars a month. There, Magda could live with the boys and take in sewing piecework. When Fley had saved a few lempiras, the Honduran currency, he hopped a bus northwest to Honduras's commercial capital of San Pedro Sula to visit a sister who found him more construction work. And so it went for Fley, hand-to-mouth, fighting to pull his family back together after his life had fallen apart.

He was a refugee, not a rebel. But he learned from friends the location of the safe house where Bermúdez and other military men were organizing their anti-Sandinista force. For more than a year, Fley kept in touch with Bermúdez's army—while keeping his distance.

1932 through August 1981

Former Guard Col. Enrique Bermúdez hardly fit the profile of a rebel chieftain.

Born December 11, 1932, the third of eight children of a free-lance mechanic who repaired electric motors, Bermúdez lived as an infant in Nicaragua's sweltering city of León near the Pacific coast. Later his father moved them to Managua, where Bermúdez grew up.

By 1948, when Bermúdez was sixteen, the National Guard had become one of the most generous avenues of advancement for working-class boys. Watching Somoza's soldiers parade through Managua's streets in their uniforms, reading advertisements offering foreign scholarships for Guard cadets, seeing the tidy houses Somoza provided his Guard officers, Bermúdez decided on a military career. He entered the Military Academy as the school's 380th cadet (Bermúdez later took "Three-Eighty" as his contra nom de guerre) and graduated as an infantry lieutenant four years later, in 1952.

Over the next twenty-seven years, Bermúdez built a career by steady, undistinguished competence. "In the Guard, I was always a deputy, never the commander," Bermúdez recalled later.

From 1954 through 1956, he studied military engineering in Rezende,

Brazil, but back in Nicaragua, he remained a lieutenant for nearly fifteen years, spending most of the period teaching chemistry and math to cadets in the Military Academy. In 1965, Bermúdez traveled to the Dominican Republic as the deputy commander of the two-hundred-man infantry company Somoza contributed to the U.S. intervention in that country. There, he married his wife, Elsa, a Dominican beautician, the daughter of the administrator of Santo Domingo's Bridgestone tire dealership. Back in Nicaragua, Bermúdez rose in ten years from lieutenant to lieutenant colonel, passing through a series of minor headquarters jobs in Managua. His two most notable posts were as purchasing officer for Somoza's general staff, and later as deputy to Managua's traffic police chief. "Hubcaps and fines," other Guard officers would recall derisively.

Bermúdez also attended a series of regional security exchanges at the U.S. Southern Command in Panama and in other Central American countries, which were opportunities for him to get acquainted with U.S. officers and to improve his minimal English. In August 1975, he went to Washington, D.C., for a term at the Inter-American Defense College, where he wrote a thesis on the "Psycho-Social Causes of Subversion." At the end of the term, Bermúdez was named by Somoza Debayle—Somoza García's son, the last ruler of the dynasty—to remain in Washington as the military attaché at the Nicaraguan embassy. A year later, in 1977, while still in Washington, Bermúdez made full colonel.

When Bermúdez left Managua, Somoza had been facing a bothersome little guerrilla problem, the obscure Sandinista National Liberation Front. While Bermúdez was in Washington, the problem escalated into a full-scale civil war that left tens of thousands of casualties, ravaged the National Guard, and brought down Somoza's regime. Bermúdez never fought in any of it: Somoza's flight to Miami on July 17, 1979, simply put Bermúdez out of work. He took a truck-driving job, delivering *Newsweek* magazines.[3]

Then, in the fall of 1979, Bermúdez got a call from Maj. Gen. Charles E. "Chuck" Boyd, the U.S. Air Force's western hemisphere chief. Boyd, a former POW in Southeast Asia, was alarmed by the Sandinistas' takeover. He'd seen the Sandinistas from the start as Communists with dangerous ties to Cuba's Fidel Castro, bent on destabilizing the entire Caribbean. Boyd had met Bermúdez at several get-togethers of military officers from the hemisphere at the Washington headquarters of the Inter-American Defense Board. One suggested that Boyd give Bermúdez a call, invite him to the Pentagon, sound him out about his plans.

Bermúdez was glad to come. In a long afternoon discussion over coffee with Boyd and a handful of other U.S. officers in one of the Pentagon meeting rooms, Bermúdez said he shared Boyd's view about the Sandinistas' totalitarian intentions, as well as the hope that something could still be done to turn back the revolutionary catastrophe. Boyd told Bermúdez that he knew somebody at the CIA, an informal acquaintance, who he was confident would be interested in talking to Bermúdez. General Boyd would put Bermúdez in contact.

Within a few months, by the mid-1980s, Bermúdez was on the CIA payroll.[4] He began to travel frequently, but kept his new status as a CIA employee quiet; his meetings with case agents were secret. As he reached out to Nicaraguan exiles, he struck a patriotic pose. He presented himself as a concerned Nicaraguan nationalist, working pro bono for the good of the *patria*, the homeland. How was he financing his new activism? He told many people he was living off the proceeds of the sale of his house in Washington.[5]

At first Bermúdez just collected information. He flew to Miami and Guatemala to look up old friends from the Guard. He checked out the dozens of Nicaraguan politicians who had already formed an alphabet soup of political parties in exile communities throughout the region, each a new acronym, each a handful of exiles. In the mid-1980s, Bermúdez moved his wife, Elsa, and their three children from Washington to a suburban Miami ranch house. Then he traveled to Guatemala and joined the leadership of the September 15 Legion, a self-proclaimed "army" of ex-Guardsmen hiding in a Guatemala City safe house and plotting to continue the war against the Sandinistas. Several dozen angry ex-Guards had already rallied to the cause. One contingent, the detachment of hapless bodyguards who had watched over Somoza's Paraguayan exile, flew up from Asunción in the fall of 1980 after Argentine guerrillas assassinated the fallen dictator, blowing apart his Mercedes-Benz with a rocket-propelled grenade on September 17, 1980.

One of the ex-Guard officers Bermúdez found working with the Legion was former Col. Ricardo Lau, known as "El Chino" because of his oriental look. In the Guard, Lau had been a top "investigator" in Somoza's secret police agency, the Office of National Security, a corps of plainclothesmen whom the Sandinistas accused of seizing, torturing, even executing suspected subversives.

After Somoza's fall, Lau had fled to Guatemala, which was then under the military dictatorship of Gen. Romeo Lucas García. In Guatemala nearly three decades of conflict between the army, Marxist guerrillas, and rightist landowners were culminating in an especially bloody period of insurgent sabotage and rightist murder. For someone with Chino Lau's training, that meant opportunity, and Lau enlisted a gang of former Guardsmen to carry out contract killings. One of the crimes in which Lau was later implicated was the March 1980 assassination of Monsignor Oscar Romero, the Catholic archbishop in neighboring El Salvador.[6]

Bermúdez was several years older than Lau, and their careers in the Guard had not brought them together, but in the weeks after Bermúdez joined Lau in the September 15 Legion in Guatemala, the two became inseparable collaborators and friends.[7]

The Legion needed financial support to grow. In its crucial first year, the money was provided by the Argentine Army. A military junta in Buenos Aires had been fighting left-wing guerrillas since taking over the government in 1976. In this dirty war, the Argentine Armed Forces had practiced, and they believed perfected, techniques of kidnapping and murder. An estimated twelve thousand Argentines disappeared during a relentless state-directed campaign aimed at eliminating "subversion." After the Sandinista triumph, an Argentine Army intelligence battalion dispatched numerous military officers on clandestine missions to Central America, following the trail of Argentine guerrillas who had fled to Managua as a safe haven.

Starting in 1980, Argentine officers helped teach counterinsurgency to government forces in Guatemala, El Salvador, and Honduras. That year an Argentine Army intelligence battalion also began financing the September 15 Legion—along with several other anti-Sandinista gangs—in the hopes that the ex-Guardsmen could help them hunt down the Argentine rebels in Nicaragua. In the spring of 1981, Bermúdez flew to Buenos Aires to meet with the head of Argentine intelligence and came away with a pledge of continued support and an attaché case stuffed with cash to fund the Legion's anti-Sandinista work. The exact amount Bermúdez received became the focus of an immediate dispute within the Legion. Bermúdez's rivals, claiming he had absconded with fifty thousand dollars, resigned from the group weeks after Bermúdez's trip.[8]

By this time, Ronald Reagan had been elected President. Bellicose men were taking over U.S. Central American policy, and plenty of American money—more than Bermúdez had ever dreamed possible—began to flow through his hands. In March 1981, Reagan signed a presidential document that authorized the CIA to begin covert activities against the Sandinistas, and later in the year the CIA fleshed out the covert-action concept, proposing to build a five-hundred-man "action team" to engage in paramilitary activities inside Nicaragua. The Administration allocated $19.9 million for the task.[9] Dozens of CIA agents were converging on Tegucigalpa, a sleepy cobblestoned capital that would be the nerve center for Washington's new paramilitary project. In

Honduras, the Americans encouraged the Argentines, who were working not only with the contras but with the Honduran Army's intelligence section. The CIA negotiated a deal: To take advantage of the experience the Argentines already had with the Nicaraguan rebels, a group of Argentine officers led by Col. Osvaldo Riveiro would stay on as case agents. Washington would pick up the financing.

The CIA designated Bermúdez as their front man to put together the paramilitary force. Bermúdez and Lau moved the September 15 Legion's headquarters out of Guatemala to Tegucigalpa, into a rambling stucco safe house behind an eight-foot brick wall with an iron gate in the upper-middle-class neighborhood known as Florencia South.[10]

In August 1981, the Argentines and the Americans decided it was time to end the petty rivalry between the September 15 Legion and two other Nicaraguan exile paramilitary groups. Working with Bermúdez, they arranged a Guatemala City meeting where the Legion merged formally with two other tiny sects. Some of the exiled Somocistas involved argued that the new army should be called the Nicaraguan National Guard—"to preserve the name"—but the Americans were in charge, and they wanted a name that would appeal to American ears. They settled on the Nicaraguan Democratic Force—in Spanish, FDN. CIA agents drafted documents for a signing ceremony. Bermúdez, Lau, and the rest of the general staff from the Legion became, with the stroke of a pen, the military leadership of the new FDN.[11]

Fall 1981 through March 1982

A little over a year after Bermúdez began his travels, reporting to the CIA on the Nicaraguan diaspora, he'd emerged as the point man for the Agency's most ambitious project in Latin America since the Bay of Pigs. To those who knew him, including many Guardsmen, Bermúdez seemed a curious choice, given his lackluster background—no guts, no charisma, no accomplishments—but to the CIA, Bermúdez was the ideal asset for the covert operation they had in mind. They were seeking a recruiting officer, a paymaster, a supply sergeant, and a training camp administrator. They didn't want a warrior or a man with particular political vision or battlefield valor. They needed a man who could accomplish logistical tasks—the kinds of things Bermúdez, as a desk man and procurement officer, had learned how to do. He spoke English, needed money, and didn't mind following orders. Obedience was his strong suit.

"He fit the profile," said a U.S. official who worked with Bermúdez closely. "He was malleable, controllable, docile."

And he proved an efficient recruiter. With his "general staff" installed in the safe house in Florencia South, Bermúdez set to work in earnest pulling together what remained of the National Guard. At its peak, the Guard had been seven thousand soldiers, including six hundred officers and three hundred policemen.[12] And while hundreds were now in jail inside Nicaragua, Bermúdez needed only a few dozen able men in order to get started. He worked the phones and dispatched emissaries to search them out in the exile communities in Miami and Central America, cajoling former comrades to take up the cause.[13] Once the CIA financing began to flow, Bermúdez's aides had the wherewithal to offer plane fare, lodgings, and small salaries for the services of ex-Guard officers. Bermúdez called the payments "family aid."[14] The senior officers, the majors and colonels, had been beaten once; most of them didn't want any part of it. But lieutenants and captains signed on, along with a number of sergeants. Guardsmen were converging from San Salvador and San José, from Miami and Panama.

Once Bermúdez had the nucleus of an officer corps, he needed fighters, lots of them. Bermúdez was hearing rumors about angry peasants straggling into Honduras, claiming to have staged little uprisings against the Sandinistas, so he toured Honduras's nearly two-hundred-mile border with Nicaragua, visiting the refugee settlements, compiling a human inventory. By the fall of 1981, he had put former Guard officers in charge of three border camps in Honduras: one in southern Choluteca province, another called Pino Uno in eastern El Paraíso province, and a third at Maquengales.[15] The recruitment prospects appeared most promising at Maquengales, mainly because of the peasant named Tigrillo. Bermúdez was skeptical about Tigrillo's pretensions as a warrior, but impressed with his recruiting possibilities. Whenever Bermúdez thought about his need for more troops, Tigrillo came to mind. Months later in late 1981, Bermúdez and Tigrillo ran into each other at Xally's, a Danlí bar. Over beers, Bermúdez grilled Tigrillo again about how many followers he really had inside Nicaragua. Hundreds, Tigrillo insisted.

Prove it! Bermúdez said. March them up to Honduras. We'll train them. We'll arm them to the teeth, if they join the FDN.

But Tigrillo resisted. He'd been a Sandinista. He didn't like National Guardsmen, and he didn't want to join the FDN. He was running his own army.[16]

Villegas and the other Argentines argued with Bermúdez. They were excited about Tigrillo's description of the angry breach developing between the Sandinistas and Nicaragua's northern peasants. Tigrillo was a real peasant rebel! Why force him to join the FDN? Why not just give him weapons and let him arrange to get them into Nicaragua to arm his people inside?

Bermúdez, however, thought it was ridiculous to give arms to people with uncertain loyalties. When he caught up with Tigrillo again in Danlí in early spring 1982, Tigrillo had begun to see the need to train his peasant followers. He wanted the weapons Bermúdez was offering.

Bermúdez, sensing that the pursuer had suddenly become the pursued, raised his price. He laid out the same glorious promises: uniforms, weapons, full infantry training. But now Bermúdez said Tigrillo would have to "pay" for the training and weapons already given to Tigrillo's first batch of recruits, with a promise to return to Nicaragua and recruit more peasants for the FDN. Each time Tigrillo brought back recruits, Bermúdez would train and arm them, in exchange for Tigrillo's promise to recruit still more peasants. Tigrillo accepted and Bermúdez drew up a written agreement they both signed. Tigrillo went to get his men.

Bermúdez began to arrange the training. The site would be a mountain clearing, just miles from the Nicaraguan border, at the end of a dirt road leading south from the Honduran town of El Paraíso. Bermúdez named two ex-Guardsmen to lead the training: former M. Sgt. José Benito Bravo Centeno and former 2nd Lt. Luis Moreno.

1959 to March 1982

Bravo and Moreno were good examples of the men Bermúdez was pulling together for his officer corps. In the Guard, one had been an enlisted man, the other a cadet. In the FDN, they would both become top officers.

Moreno was born on March 21, 1959, in Managua, the son of the chauffeur for the administrator of Somoza's empire of sugar plantations. From his earliest days, Moreno wanted a military career, and he worked throughout his early teens to get into the Guard. At seventeen, he triumphed, obtaining a commission to the Military Academy.

By entering the Guard, Moreno moved into a secretive subculture of codified machismo, of pain and privilege, a brotherhood with its own vocabulary, vision, and worldview. He learned how it functioned as Somoza's personal army and was able to meet the dictator, who, along with all the other attributes he'd accumulated, was the Academy's director. Moreno was smart, and though he wasn't a big man, he was pugnacious. In the Guard, those qualities made him the top cadet in his class.

In 1978, Moreno traveled to West Point on an annual exchange. There was a side trip to Washington, where he toured the FBI building and did some other sightseeing. He was dazzled by the United States.

Back in Nicaragua the next year, Moreno saw his first combat while he was still a cadet, in May 1979, fighting on the Pacific coast highway to León. The Sandinistas had taken the military initiative, and they weren't giving any quarter. They were attacking Guard officers' families, at home, and luring Somoza's men into deadly traps. Sensing its control ebbing, the Guard was giving vent to its own fury as never before, even smashing poor neighborhoods with aerial bombing. The jails and hospitals were filled; many Guards just executed the rebels they wounded or captured in battle.

During the Sandinistas' final offensive in June, Somoza himself called in Moreno and the rest of the Academy's third-year cadets and summarily graduated them a year early. There was a shortage of officers, Somoza said. Senior cadets would become second lieutenants, and they were going into battle. That same afternoon, Moreno was thrust into command of a platoon of thirty raw, untrained, terrified teenage recruits and ordered into one of the Guard's ugly "mop-up" operations through Managua's hostile neighborhoods.

Within weeks, Somoza and all his top officers had flown to Miami. Moreno learned the news on July 18 when he reported for duty to the EEBI, the elite unit commanded by Somoza Debayle's son, Lt. Col. Anastasio Somoza Portocarrero, known as "Tachito." Moreno's commander had already fled to Miami with his father.

"What are my orders?" Moreno asked a Guard captain who had taken over command.

"Do whatever the hell you please," the captain replied. "The Guard is just negotiating now to see if the Sandinistas will spare our lives."

Moreno couldn't believe that the Guard had lost the war, that it was, in those moments, ceasing to exist. He took command of ninety Guardsmen holed up in a Managua movie theater and organized them for a new patrol; he volunteered to walk point. But by that time Sandinista snipers had taken up positions all through the capital. Within an hour, one shot Moreno in the back with a .22 rifle. It was just a flesh wound, and doctors extracted the slug minutes later at what had been Somoza's Military Hospital, but it set up the bitter end to Moreno's first war: On July 19, 1979, the day Nicaragua celebrated the Sandinistas' victory, Moreno awoke in a hospital ward, sobbing.

The hospital was surrounded by Sandinistas. Moreno stifled his tears, sneaked out past a Sandinista barricade, and hitched a ride north out of Managua toward Honduras. There were numerous Sandinista checkpoints along the highway, but when adolescent Sandinista militiamen detained him, Moreno was glib. He denied his own Guard past and began parading as a jubilant, though wounded, Sandinista combatant.

He talked his way free and took asylum in Managua's Spanish embassy. Weeks later, he slipped across Nicaragua's southern border.

Three years of ignominious exile followed: table-waiting in a sleazy Costa Rican nightclub, slopping hogs on a Costa Rican pig farm, sanding cupboards in a Panamanian cabinet factory. When the FDN got in touch with him in February 1982, Moreno was in Guatemala, working as a bodyguard. He showed up a month later at the Tegucigalpa safe house of the FDN's general staff.

Bermúdez gave Moreno his first mission. Covered trucks bearing an FDN commando team, back from a sabotage raid into Nicaragua, had rumbled into Tegucigalpa at night, stopping at a safe house to deposit their secret human cargo. But the ex-Guard captain whom Bermúdez had assigned to care for the safe house was drunk and out with some Honduran whore. The commandos had been unable to get in. The trucks had been forced to circle for hours until somebody found a spare key. Moreno's first assignment was to administer the safe house.

He was twenty-four, with a baby face: soft eyes, a peach fuzz mustache, plump lips. But he was dying to get back to war. He took the nom de guerre "Mike Lima."[17]

1946 to March 1982

José Benito Bravo Centeno, a muscular, mustachioed, thick-necked man, was fifteen years older than Moreno. He was the kind of person who, in Somoza's Nicaragua, amounted to nothing at all—he was a peon, the oldest of six children born to a peasant who grew bananas for the United Fruit Company in Nicaragua's central ranch country—but he'd joined the Guard at twelve and had clawed his way up until he was somebody. At first he was one of the little boys who hung around the Guard barracks, running errands, picking fights with bigger kids, begging for free food. As a teenager, when Nicaraguan kids from a higher station were beginning to date or think about college, Bravo was toiling in Somoza's personal household as a kind of a nursemaid for the dictator's kids, shining their shoes, cleaning up their messes. When he was twenty-one, Bravo flew to the Dominican Republic with the Nicaraguan delegation, headed by Bermúdez, that was Somoza's contribution to the American intervention.

Bravo's years in the dictator's household had won him a special place in the Somozas' hearts, and he in turn had been able to study the intrigues, the corruption, and the behind-the-scenes violence of the dictatorship. He grew especially close to Somoza's second son, Julio, and became Julio's driver and, some said, his pimp. Bravo was poor and servile, but he wasn't dumb. He was learning.

Somoza Debayle eventually approved Bravo's appointment to sergeant major, assigned to the EEBI. If the Guard was Somoza's army, then the EEBI—with Tachito, Somoza's Harvard-educated son at its head—was a Guard within the Guard, the battalion that received the best equipment, the best food, the most press attention. Many believed that Tachito would one day be Nicaragua's new ruler, and generals and full colonels stood aside for the young lieutenant colonel.

In 1979, there were no funds to send a class of officer cadets to Panama, where they would normally have received command training. Instead, Somoza organized a class in the EEBI for them. Bravo was their instructor. Normally, drill sergeants threw their weight around with the students, but Bravo, knowing that one day the cadets would be officers, took a different tack. Arriving at the EEBI barracks each day, Bravo made it his practice to salute the teenage cadets idling around a table. "Good morning, gentlemen cadets," he'd say in a saccharine voice, tipping his hat. Years later, Bravo's ingratiating manner with superiors still set some of his former students' teeth on edge.

During the 1979 war, Bravo was sent to the Southern Front, where EEBI troops were hunkered down in a war of positions, blocking heavily armed Sandinista forces trying to advance north toward Managua. But Bravo didn't see combat; his connections with the Somozas landed him a soft job overseeing supplies for the field kitchen.

More so even than for most of Somoza's men, Bravo's whole life was the Guard. When the EEBI disintegrated on the Southern Front in July 1979, so did Bravo's world, and it filled him with fury. He followed the Somozas to Miami, with his wife, Lesbia, and his four children. They rented a dilapidated house in Little Havana, and Bravo tried to adjust, but it didn't work out. At the first rumor that there would be another chance against the Sandinistas, Bravo showed up in Guatemala to join the September 15 Legion and took the nom de guerre "Mack."

In early 1981, Mack was one of sixty Legionnaires who traveled to Buenos Aires to receive intelligence and other training from the Argentine Army.[18] Bermúdez went too. He knew Mack only vaguely from the Guard, but, sizing up his credentials, Bermúdez saw that he was as experienced a trainer as he could find—perfect for making real soldiers out of Tigrillo's peasant rebels.

March through December 1982

At the new FDN training site in the border hills south of the Honduran village of El Paraíso, Mack, Mike Lima, and a handful of other ex-Guardsmen cleared away the underbrush and erected a few rough huts in which to sleep. By that time, the spring rains had started and the new training base was slick with mud. Its name quickly became "La Lodosa"—The Mudhole.

Tigrillo marched sixty of his peasant followers north from their homes around El Cuá to the end of Honduras's primitive network of border roads, just past the village of Las Trojes, where they climbed aboard Honduran Army trucks for the drive to La Lodosa. From the moment they jumped out from beneath the tarpaulins to begin their training, there was trouble between Tigrillo's peasants and Bermúdez's Guards.

The peasants had learned, under Somoza, to detest the National Guard's arrogance and cruelty; hating the Sandinistas didn't sweeten their memory of the Guard. Mack's people, meanwhile, considered Tigrillo's people little better than Sandinistas. Some might even be infiltrators, they thought, preparing to murder them.

The first showdown came immediately. Tigrillo's brother Dimas had a long beard; he vowed to let it grow until Nicaragua was "liberated." One of the precious few things left of the National Guard was its training doctrine, and one of the norms was the clean shaving of recruits, both heads and beards. Dimas was told he was going to cut that fucking shag off his fucking chin now, or he wasn't setting a foot on their base.

There was a standoff. Tigrillo and Dimas conferred. Finally, Dimas backed down. Two Guards dragged him down and shaved off his beard with a knife.

"Soldiers understand a kick in the ass," said Mike Lima.

That set the tone for the training. There were the normal rigors of any boot camp: pre-dawn calisthenics, scores of punishing knee-squats, endless shouted insults. The food was bad and scarce, and the rain incessant. But at La Lodosa, all these evils of boot camp were magnified, because Mack's Guard trainers were settling a score with the Sandinistas. There were plenty of kicks and slugs, and peasants with bloody noses and teeth knocked out.

Mack watched approvingly. "Teach them how to be soldiers," he said.

Tigrillo's peasants had grown up hardened by ill-treatment, but this was too much even for them. The training went on for six weeks, and Tigrillo had all he could do to keep his men from revolting. But he kept soothing and cajoling: Hold out, endure—then we'll get the rifles, he said.[19]

Visits from a few well-placed outsiders aggravated the tensions. Once a week, a Honduran Army helicopter would set down at the edge of La

Lodosa, and Bermúdez, Villegas, and an American CIA agent would jump out. The American introduced himself as "Captain Alex." He was a muscular character, about thirty, with pale skin and black hair cut short on the temples, military-style. He spoke a Caribbean Spanish that some Nicaraguans took for Cuban, others for Puerto Rican.[20]

The Argentines loved Tigrillo. The image Tigrillo presented as a peasant guerrilla tickled them: the illiterate farmer who had taken up arms against the revolution. Villegas brought Tigrillo a sleek AR-15 automatic rifle as a gift on one trip, along with several new Browning 9-mm. pistols, still packed in oil, for him to take to his lieutenants inside Nicaragua. Tigrillo, no fool, saw the enthusiasm he could generate when he strutted his stuff as a peasant commander.

Alex, the CIA man, also encouraged Tigrillo's peasant-fighter image. Bermúdez went along. Whenever he'd take photos of the troops in training, Bermúdez would put Tigrillo up front: the peasant leader with his troops. He would grab Mike Lima and Mack and the other Guards, pulling them out of the frame. He'd wink.

"This is the image that they're selling to the Americans," he'd tell Lima.

Mike Lima understood the game, but it irritated him. Was there only room in this war for illiterate peasants? What about real soldiers like himself and Mack?

The training ended in mid-June. Honduran Army choppers ferried Tigrillo's long-awaited arms out from Tegucigalpa. The Argentines handed them out from crates to Tigrillo's sixty men, who were divided into three detachments. Each unit got sixteen FAL rifles, a 60-mm. mortar, a machine gun, an M-79 grenade launcher, one sniper's rifle with telescopic sight, forty hand grenades, and a sleek little disposable rocket called a LAW, or Light Anti-Tank Weapon.[21]

Tigrillo was elated. So were his detachment leaders—they each got to strap a 9-mm. officer's pistol to their hips. The troops were overwhelmed, especially the machine gunners. They loved to sling those long cartridge belts across their chests.

Bermúdez had complied with his half of the bargain. Now it was Tigrillo's turn. He wanted Tigrillo's men to get back into Nicaragua and bring out more recruits. Tigrillo promised to do so. With the recruits already waiting inside Nicaragua, and those he figured he could convert quickly, he'd bring back a hundred farmers in two months. But Bermúdez wondered.

Alex wondered, too, about a lot of claims Tigrillo made so glibly about conditions in Nicaragua. He wanted a man with military experience to accompany Tigrillo, someone who could keep an eye on him and gather a bit of intelligence.

Mack wouldn't do—Bermúdez wanted him to remain in charge at La Lodosa—but Mike Lima volunteered. Alex assigned him to Tigrillo, formally, as a radio operator, but he asked Mike, in a discreet aside, to "coordinate" Tigrillo's efforts.

So it was an odd couple—Mike Lima, the ex-Guard lieutenant once trained at West Point, and Tigrillo, the onetime Sandinista soldier turned peasant chieftain—that infiltrated into Nicaragua from Honduras at the head of a sixty-man FDN column in June 1982. It was one of the first major CIA-sponsored contra infiltrations of the war.

The column crossed the gurgling Coco River in the dead of night, four men at a time, in a dugout canoe, eluding Sandinista patrols on the southern bank and moving on south. Immediately they began to learn what it was like to fight in the FDN. Bermúdez's logistics men had packed only twenty pounds of cheese for each man, and in no time the men were trading their new ponchos for hens and tortillas. Mike Lima snorted in contempt.

Then Tigrillo got lost, walking his men in a vast circle around the same mountain for two days. Infuriated, Mike seized a compass to plot a course straight south. Mike's regard for the importance of his own military background began to swell, but when a Sandinista army scout picked up their scent and several patrols moved in, Lima had to admit that Tigrillo had some assets. The FDN column made its way to a peasant farm, and the farmer rushed out and embraced Tigrillo. The farmer was awed, even stunned, to see the array of arms Tigrillo's men had brought back. The two men established an immediate rapport, communicating with each other in a direct flow of Nicaraguan peasant vernacular almost unintelligible to outsiders like Lima.

Soon there were peasants converging on the farm from several directions, bearing reports on the Sandinistas' movements. It was an impressive display of the country people's informal intelligence network. Tigrillo's friend soon figured out an evasion route through a valley; the FDN column slipped out of striking range of the government patrols. Mike Lima was humbled.

Now in home territory, Tigrillo was eager to begin his recruiting. He began to give little talks before gatherings of country people, denouncing the revolution that, he said, had turned godless, and pitching his own band's growing strength. He pointed to the new U.S.-supplied weaponry wielded by his men, dazzling symbols of new power and mounting strength. If he had enjoyed great respect among peasants before, now he had dozens of farmers offering up their sons to his band.

Demonstrations of force speeded the recruiting process. Less than a month after the incursion began, peasants in a hamlet called Parpar Abajo denounced a farmer named Tomás Barreda as a Sandinista informer and suggested a way to entrap him. Lima organized the seizure, and soon Tigrillo's men had the man, tied up and shaking. "He belongs to State Security," Lima announced before a gathering of farmers— though Barreda was really just a peasant collaborating with the government. One of Tigrillo's men pulled out his long-bladed commando knife and gashed the prisoner's throat, leaving him to bleed to death.[22]

The bloodletting created a certain tenuous bond between Tigrillo and Mike Lima. Six days later, other peasants denounced a man named Gerardo Rivas, another "State Security" agent. He, too, was seized, tied, and knifed before a peasant gathering.

The temporary camps that Tigrillo's men cleared in the jungle to hold his conscripts filled quickly. Some of Tigrillo's "volunteers" really were; others were seized by commandos and marched away at gunpoint. Within weeks, Tigrillo had 160 "recruits." Lima urged Tigrillo to leave his brother Dimas inside Nicaragua with their original, sixty-man column. The odd couple would march the new fighters back to Honduras.

Tigrillo was smug. Mike Lima was triumphant. And Bermúdez, Alex, and the Argentines waiting in Honduras were flabbergasted. One hundred sixty recruits in two months! The possibilities for making the force grow were extraordinary.

Alex and the Argentines sat Mike Lima down in a Tegucigalpa safe house, took out legal pads, and began firing questions about everything he'd seen, heard, and smelled in Nicaragua. What were the Sandinista troops like? What bridges could be blown? How were the weapons holding up in the rainy season? And, especially, how many recruits could he and Tigrillo bring out?[23] Bermúdez ordered Tigrillo's 160 peasant recruits trucked to a new training base, then sent Tigrillo and Mike Lima back into Nicaragua for more. Within two months, they had marched back with hundreds of new FDN commandos.

Meanwhile, Tigrillo's brother Dimas, left behind in Nicaragua with his sixty heavily armed men, was building a rebel army his own way. He was twenty-eight years old, and a stocky five feet two inches tall, but recent developments had greatly inflated his sense of self. His men were calling him "Dimas Tigrillo," adding on his brother's nom de guerre to distinguish him from others called Dimas. Together, he and his brother were known as "The Tigrillos." The way he saw it, they were the only real guerrillas, the ones with genuine peasant following. In fact, the sixty automatic rifles and all the other weapons were now his and Tigrillo's. Why not? They'd traded 160 recruits for them!

This was the War of the Tigrillos! They had started it, Dimas thought, not Bermúdez. It was time to be clear about one thing: The Tigrillos were at war to drive the Sandinistas out of peasant Nicaragua, not to march a bunch of Guardsmen back into power in Managua.[24]

Dimas felt that he needed a stronghold, so he built one at a heavily jungled place in upper Jinotega called Wina. To make it comfortable, he had his men construct a series of elaborate bamboo tree houses for himself and his staff. To relax, he seized two fifteen-year-old peasant girls as his ladies-in-waiting. He set up a network of messengers, dirt farmers who would bring him not only intelligence, but daily offerings of roasted hen and corn on the cob.

Dimas became a *cacique,* a peasant warlord. He set his men—wielding European rifles, they were now little *caciques,* too—to rounding up more peasant recruits, and using machetes, they cleared a training field and obstacle course for infantry instruction and close-order drill out of the jungle. Dimas began thinking about where to plant crops, and even began to plot out a primitive taxation scheme.

With those who opposed his ambitions, Dimas proved harsh. When twelve of his "recruits" attempted to escape from his Wina camp, he declared them military deserters and ordered several shot. The others he confined to a crude bamboo cage. His newfound powers, in fact, quickly overwhelmed him. He fell in love with two tall and fair sisters, the daughters of a local farmer named Chilo Osorio. When they resisted Dimas's advances, he ordered Osorio murdered, along with three of his sons. Then Dimas added the sisters to his harem, and Osorio's two youngest sons to his army.

Dimas carved out his sultanate with astonishing speed during some twelve weeks in the fall of 1982, but his enemies moved quickly, too. Sandinista military authorities infiltrated spies in with Dimas's recruits, and soon they knew the exact coordinates of Dimas's "stronghold." The Sandinistas brought in heavy mortars, long-range artillery, helicopters, "push-and-pull" bombers, and hundreds of troops. They surrounded the Wina base, pummeled it with bombs and shells, and overran it with waves of infantry. Dimas's sixty-man army and more than two hundred unarmed recruits fled. Dozens died.[25]

By this time, Tigrillo and Mike Lima, heading separate forces, were returning from Honduras for their third recruiting mission. Mike Lima heard about Dimas's "stronghold" just as it was being obliterated. Furious, he began to stalk Dimas through the Nicaraguan outback, determined to administer a little National Guard discipline to the hillbilly who'd provoked such a setback.

Eventually, Dimas's force was able to regroup, and Mike Lima closed in on them in mid-December. He caught up with one of Dimas's platoons first. Interrogating its leader, Lima discovered that during Dimas's fleeting halcyon days at Wina, a commando named "Coyote" had guzzled too much green mountain rum and had hurled a grenade into a farmhouse. Three men and a woman had died amid the tearing shards. Mike Lima called for discipline: Coyote was executed.

Mike Lima finally caught up with Dimas's disheveled force at a place called Gacho Mountain. They had words. How could Dimas have been so stupid? Guerrillas don't have bases, Mike said. What the fuck took you so long? Dimas said. They argued over what to do next. Mike Lima wanted to camp. Dimas wanted to move out. Mike Lima thought it was time to feed the men a barbecued steer. Dimas said they were soldiers, they could march hungry for now.

"These are my soldiers, I give the orders here," Dimas said.

"Bullshit!" Mike Lima shouted back. "This is the FDN, those are FDN rifles you're packing. And here, *I'm* the FDN."

They ended up drawing on each other, in front of the gawking troops. Neither fired. Amid the confrontation, Dimas's brother Tigrillo showed up, marching down a valley with a sixty-man detachment. Soon he'd taken his brother's side. More curses, more threats, more tension.[26]

Finally, Mike Lima broke contact. He marched back to Honduras and reported to Bermúdez and the FDN general staff in Tegucigalpa, laying out what had happened. He talked with Alex and the Argentines. There were meetings and discussion. It was obvious to the Americans and Argentines that Tigrillo's peasant recruits could make good fighters, but only if they were well-trained—and well-led. The CIA's military men felt more comfortable with military professionals at the head of rebel units, an attitude they would maintain, despite mounting criticism, to the end of the conflict.

Out of the deliberations came a decision. Tigrillo and Dimas were worthy recruiters, but unreliable commanders. Better to systematically strip them of any conscripts they marched out of Nicaragua. Best for the recruits, best for the FDN.

In late December, the Tigrillo brothers appeared in Honduras with their latest harvest, several hundred peasant farmers. During the last six months of 1982, the Tigrillos had conscripted nearly a thousand rural men into the CIA's army. All were transferred from the Tigrillos' command to create new FDN units—headed, of course, by ex-Guardsmen. Tigrillo and Dimas were left with a sixty-man force. They headed back into Nicaragua for more recruiting.[27]

Mid-1982 through October 1983

Fley watched the guerrilla army Bermúdez had promised become a reality. If the squalor he'd found at the Maquengales camp had disheartened him about the possibilities for fighting a real war against the Sandinistas, now he was reconsidering.

Fley began to meet the ex-Guards Bermúdez was bringing to Honduras to command the force, and his tolerance for them expanded amid the privations of exile. They were no longer just drunken policemen hitting him up for bribes. Now he saw most of them as penniless exiles, on the skids, like himself.

He met ex-Guard Lt. Roger Sandino during one of his visits to the Florencia safe house. They had long chats, and Sandino kept inviting Fley to join the FDN force. This was going to be an army that would force the Sandinistas to take its opponents seriously, Sandino said. Fley had heard a lot of big talk from other exiles, but in March 1982, he read newspaper reports that made him take notice. Counterrevolutionary rebels had carried out two daring sapper attacks in northern Nicaragua that had simultaneously crumpled two key bridges. The sudden, devastating sabotage shocked the Sandinistas, who declared a state of emergency and announced that they were at war and were the victims of foreign aggression.

Then Fley heard through the grapevine that his friend Lieutenant Sandino had led one of the sapper teams! Good for him, Fley thought, smiling to himself.

Fley was no scholar. He had no idea that the FDN was, to the CIA men putting it together, just another in a long string of native insurgencies they had organized around the world. What Fley saw was that war on the Sandinistas was becoming a reality. It appeared that Washington was putting its enormous weight behind the struggle. Fley's difficult months in exile had kicked all the bravado out of him. All his dreams about "rescuing" the revolution, all his patriotic pronouncements to his wife, were just *mierda,* so much crap. He'd never have the wherewithal to confront the Sandinistas again on his own. He had become just a refugee. If he and all the other anti-Sandinista rebel sects gathered in Honduras—Tigrillo's men, Pedro Joaquín González's people—wanted to settle accounts in Nicaragua, they needed weapons, food, cash. They needed a leader who'd speak for them internationally. When all was said and done, Fley felt he had little choice. Having shed blood against the

Sandinista revolution, he couldn't turn back. Midway through 1982, Fley decided to join the FDN army.

Fley showed up one evening at the FDN's Florencia safe house in Tegucigalpa, where he found Lieutenant Sandino out front, lashing a tarpaulin over crates of cargo piled on the bed of a one-ton truck with dual tires parked near the walled entryway. Fley saw other guys with guns standing guard. "What's inside?" he asked.

"Rifles," Sandino said, pulling up the tarp to let Fley see.[28]

Bermúdez had put Sandino in charge of one of the training bases the FDN was establishing by the border, and Sandino was leaving that night to deliver the rifles to the men at his base. He was selecting men for a special project. Why didn't Fley come along?

Fley shook his hand. "I'm in," he said.

Fley took the nom de guerre Jhonson.

He and two dozen other Nicaraguan men from Sandino's base arrived a week later at La Quinta, a rambling forty-acre farm, about seven miles west of Toncontin Airport, that the Argentines had rented from its absentee French owner to use as a training base for FDN commandos. A crumbling stone wall ringed the property. Inside, a farmhouse and a couple of outbuildings faced on a central yard, shaded by malinche trees. Everything was in disrepair. A few tattered army field tents had been set up near a stand of mango trees to house the commandos. It was hardly a satisfactory training site for an army; the only available water had to be drawn and carried from a distant well.[29]

At La Quinta, Jhonson experienced his first real military training in the contra army. The sixty men who eventually amassed there were divided into two commando units of thirty each. Their teachers were Argentine, all apparently military officers in their mid-thirties with pseudonyms like Raul, Chingolo, and Melena. Their leader was Villegas, the silver-haired gentleman with a taste for aviator sunglasses and gold chains whom Jhonson had first met with Bermúdez at the Maquengales camp months earlier.

The Argentines were autocratic and aloof. The Nicaraguans were here to learn how to make war, secret war, the Argentines said. The Nicaraguans were to ask no questions about who their teachers were. They were to shun all contacts with anybody outside their commando units. They could not leave the base.

The curriculum was ambitious: an hour of racking pre-dawn calisthenics and jogging, then a day crammed with infantry patrolling exercises, blackboard theory on explosives, sabotage and special operations, direct practice in map reading and compass orientation. After dark the training intensified. The commandos, their faces painted black, would slip out of La Quinta to steal their way across Tegucigalpa's suburban farmland in simulated nighttime patrols. There were a couple of day trips as well, to a Honduran Army shooting range about fifteen miles west of La Quinta for some hands-on target shooting with automatic rifles and some demonstrations and practice with plastic explosives, blowing up old wrecked cars.

After two weeks of crash training, nineteen hours a day, the Argentines began equipping the two commando teams for their operation. Each fighter was given boots, a uniform (not military fatigues, but blue Dickey's workingman's togs), a heavy Belgian FAL automatic rifle and ammunition, a long knife, U.S.-made freeze-dried rations, and as much C-4 explosive and detonators as they could carry. Under cover of night, Jhonson and the other heavily laden men were loaded onto the beds of two Honduran Army trucks. Hidden beneath tarpaulins, they were driven through Tegucigalpa streets and on east, through Danlí, to the end of the dirt road by the border just past the village of Las Trojes.

A month of heavy marching began. The commander of Jhonson's unit was Pastor "Denis" Meza, the son of a wealthy landowner near Jinotega. Jhonson had first met Denis at Maquengales, after Denis had participated in Pedro Joaquín González's 1980 attack on Quilalí. After a couple of days' march south from Las Trojes, when the unit was barely into Nicaragua, Denis confided to Jhonson their target. The Sandinistas were cutting a dirt road east from Matagalpa to gold mines in the north-central savannahs, and on to the Atlantic coast. The Argentines had targeted a construction site along the route, near a hamlet called Puerto Viejo, where dozens of costly building machines were parked.

Laden like pack animals under the burden of heavy weaponry, the commandos sweated their way south. At first they trudged along in daytime, talking to peasants along the way, buying food. Despite his exhaustion, Jhonson felt the exhilaration of coming home. The column tracked through terrain he knew well, valleys and hollows he'd visited years before. He met farmers who recognized him. He just smiled, saying nothing, and they smiled back. But when Jhonson's team was within a week's march of the target, they began to move only at night, off the roads, keeping out of sight, eating only sweet candy.

The unit was more than a week behind schedule when they arrived. There had been days of marching in circles, trying to locate Puerto Viejo and link up with the second group, but finally they made contact and got a look at their target: a remote construction yard, surrounded by a cheap cyclone fence, crowded with rows of heavy new Fiat dump trucks, more than two dozen of them, all gleaming chrome. There were two jeeps, four heavy backhoes, even a nicely stocked tool shop with several welding plants. There was no military guard, only a couple of dozen Construction Ministry machine operators camped out in huts adjacent to the site. It was going to be easy.

Jhonson's team rested a day, then marched into staging areas as the Argentines had taught them. Just past midnight, the two teams rushed to surround the Puerto Viejo yard and the settlement of construction workers. When they burst the gate, a car horn in an old Chevrolet station wagon, rigged as a makeshift siren, began to shriek. A lone watchman, hearing the racket, ran out of the machine shed to the car. One of the contras' FALs belched out a line of heavy slugs, and the man spun around, hit and screaming; other commandos had already taken the machine operators prisoner. The rest was simple: rigging the C-4 explosive on each of the truck motors, on the hydraulic systems of the backhoes, underneath the jeeps, in the machine area, then stringing the detonator cables neatly as the Argentines had insisted. Everybody moved back. The concussion echoed across the valleys. The yard blazed brilliant orange. When the smoke cleared, the line of once-gleaming trucks was all disembowelled. The commandos scattered a few blue-and-white paper Nicaraguan flags, released their hostages, and left.[30]

Jhonson found the march out of Nicaragua considerably more pleasant than the infiltration. He was rid of his burden of explosives. The commandos chatted with peasants along the way, bought steers to barbecue, and set a slower pace. Jhonson felt good. He'd struck his first heavy blow against the Sandinistas.

It had been more than a year since Jhonson's first collaboration with Tigrillo in their deadly ambush at Pedernales del Cuá. Ever since, attacks like the sabotage at Puerto Viejo had been happening weekly, almost daily, and in late 1982, the international media discovered the mounting U.S. involvement in the secret war. In October and November, reports of the contras' fast-mounting war and of the U.S. and Argentine backing for it appeared in the *Miami Herald, Newsweek,* and other U.S. publications.[31]

Jhonson was confident that he'd made the right choice. With the FDN carrying out strikes like this, and with the enormous power of Washington behind the rebels, what he had heard Bermúdez and others say had to be true: The Sandinistas wouldn't last long.

Jhonson had shown himself a capable soldier and a valuable cadre during his first FDN operation. Once he was back in Lieutenant Sandino's Honduran base camp with the rest of the sabotage unit, word got around. A few days later, Sandino called Jhonson aside. There was good news. The FDN's international "friends" were increasing their backing. The fledgling rebel force was now in a position to pay Jhonson two hundred Honduran lempiras monthly, the equivalent of about a hundred dollars. It wasn't a lot, but it would keep his family in food while Jhonson fought a war. He could quit scratching for construction work. An FDN officer would drop off the cash at Magda's Tegucigalpa flat the first of every month.

Furthermore, the Argentines were so pleased with the FDN's recent sabotage work that they had decided to assemble a permanent, elite sapper squad that would receive more advanced training in the destructive arts and carry out new high-stakes raids. They had selected Lieutenant Sandino to be its commander, and they wanted him to handpick a couple of dozen of his best men to join the new contra special forces unit, which was to be called the Commandos for Special Operations. Jhonson was one of Sandino's first choices, and he quickly agreed.

Jhonson's ego swelled when he joined the special forces unit. The mystique surrounding the unit was macho, the hopes were high, and the expectations exalted. Villegas, the chief Argentine trainer, laid on the superlatives in a chalk-talk about goals and procedures a day or two after the force assembled at La Quinta.

"You all have been selected as the Commandos for Special Operations!" Villegas said, pacing in front of a blackboard, slapping his palm with a pointer. "You must make yourselves the best! You have to harden yourselves, become capable of anything, any operation, capable of taking out any target! You have to become the quickest, the strongest, the most tenacious, the meanest, the deadliest. You must become commandos who never say no!"

That set the tone for the training. There were more visits to the Honduran military base at Lepaterique, eighteen miles west of Tegucigalpa, for explosives and sharpshooting practice. A secluded lake offered the opportunity for Jhonson and his fellows to learn the silent use of rubber rafts and ropes in water infiltration.

Although Jhonson's unit was, supposedly, to be capable of hitting any target anywhere in Nicaragua, he gradually deduced that the unit's managers were hoping to deploy it mainly for attacks along Nicaragua's northwestern Pacific coast, a region adjacent to Honduras and the Gulf of Fonesca that had been left largely untouched despite the FDN's constant attacks all over the country's mountainous north-central highlands. The fifty-mile-wide strip of land adjoining the Pacific coast was Nicaragua's most strategic chunk of real estate, including the capital, the vast majority of its industry, scores of huge farms producing most of its cotton, banana, and other agricultural exports, as well as two-thirds of the country's population.[32]

The FDN's problem was that conditions were poor for waging guerrilla war on the Pacific coast. The terrain in Chinandega and León, the Pacific coast provinces closest to Honduras, was hot and flat, much of it dedicated to vast, unshaded cotton plantations, without much cover. There were few of the frontier-style farmers who had provided so much intelligence and food to the contras in the highlands. There wasn't even much water. Because of all this, Jhonson's commandos were being prepared for another kind of war, one of stealthy incursions, devastating strikes, and silent withdrawals. They would infiltrate into Chinandega or León by land or by sea, carrying everything they needed, staying only as long as necessary to carry out one mission.

Jhonson's first operation with the elite unit underscored the Argentines' elevated ambitions. The target was "La Laguna," The Lagoon, a new military base seven miles north of the capital of Chinandega province where the Sandinistas had deployed a dozen newly acquired Soviet T-55 tanks. Some one hundred Sandinista soldiers, about a company, were guarding the tanks behind a barbed-wire perimeter. Thousands of other soldiers were bivouacked in bases nearby. The Argentines sent the contras to destroy the tanks—not with mortar fire from a respectful distance or by aerial bombing, but by penetrating the base itself. The contras were to knife the guards, disable the tanks with meticulously located charges of C-4, and steal away. Jhonson was the second-in-command of the forty-man sapper team, equipped with CIA-supplied infra-red night-vision goggles (worth $25,000 each) that allowed Jhonson to make out clear images at 150 yards in pitch dark.

Despite the CIA gadgetry, on the first try Jhonson's unit never even came close. Trucked secretly to the Nicaraguan border, Jhonson's men bogged down after an all-night moonlit march in hip-deep mud as they crossed the Estero Real, a broad estuary cutting twenty miles across Chinandega province from the Gulf of Fonseca. Twenty-four hours later, several men got lost on a hacienda. Out of drinking water and luck, Jhonson's unit retreated back to Honduras and radioed Tegucigalpa. The Argentines sent trucks to ferry them back to La Quinta. There were no recriminations. After all, it was a new unit.

Months later, in October 1983, Jhonson's Special Operations commandos had a second shot at La Laguna tank base. This time the Argentines had equipped the commandos with U.S.-supplied rubber boats, inflatable with cans of pressurized gas. The crossing of the Estero Real was a breeze. The hike south was easy, too, because the commandos had studied aerial photographs taken by U.S. spy planes of the topography between the Honduran border and La Laguna. The same photos, passed from the CIA to the FDN by the Argentines, also clearly highlighted the location of the tanks within the base.

The commandos arrived near La Laguna's barbed-wire perimeter at 11 P.M. and regrouped. They had diagramed their mission extensively and practiced their movements to exhaustion. Eighteen men would remain at the base perimeter as security. Twenty-four would enter: three four-man explosives teams and three four-man elimination squads. This time, each of the three explosives teams had one pair of the infra-red goggles.

The Sandinistas had hidden the dozen tanks in twelve separate earthen pits, each covered by a small, hangar-like shed with a zinc roof. Two soldiers, serving as guards, lived and slept beside each tank. The commandos' plan was to cut through the barbed-wire perimeter, slip inside, silently eliminate the guards with knives, attach the explosive charges and a time detonator to the tanks, and slip back out. They counted off, set their watches, and moved in. The barbed-wire fence was no problem. Furthermore, some of the Sandinista sentries had wandered away from their posts to visit with other guards. Jhonson could hear their voices through the chatter of the cicadas in the Chinandega night. With the guards absent, the commandos succeeded in locating and placing their charges on three tanks. Jhonson was crouched alongside one tank, placing a charge. Other commandos were moving across the dark turf toward an adjacent bunker.

A shout rang out. "*Compañeros!* Who goes there! Identify yourselves! Now! Or I'll shoot!" It was a Sandinista sentry no one had noticed, crouched in a kind of a duck blind atop a tree shading the base.

One of the commandos had a clear line of fire. The rhythmic crash of automatic rifle fire cut the night, and the Sandinista soldier pitched off his perch. But his call had alerted the entire base, and the gunfire had awakened the countryside. The night erupted with shouts, shots, cries, flashlights.

Jhonson raced for the perimeter. The Sandinistas were firing their AK-47s wildly. Jhonson reached the fence, slipped through, and sprinted back along the approach trail. The escape plan called for the unit's men to regroup at several preestablished rendezvous points. Jhonson heard the sudden roar of the Sandinista tanks, revving into action. They were clinking their way across the cotton fields, firing in delirium from their machine-gun turrets amid the shouts of infantry.

The commandos didn't return the fire, because in the nighttime confusion, it wasn't clear who was who. Furthermore, the Sandinistas would be executing a preestablished defensive maneuver within their own terrain. The commandos had no hope of prevailing in combat. The idea was to retreat, fast. Along the way, to Jhonson's satisfaction, they heard the explosions of the charges they'd left on three tanks with time-delay detonators.

About 150 yards out of the base, while crossing a clean field, one of Jhonson's commandos took a burst of machine-gun fire. He was the only casualty until frantic hours later, when another commando drowned during the return crossing of the Estero Real, halfway through the sixteen-hour dash to the border. A third commando, "Ulysses," separated from the column and was given up. The column beat its final retreat into Honduras.

The Special Operations commandos had destroyed three tanks, but had lost three men. Militarily, it had been neither the unit's greatest success nor its worst debacle, but politically the operation, like most of the other sabotage operations, became a dismal failure.

"Ulysses" was later captured and gave extensive statements about the secret history, training, and procedures of Jhonson's unit to Sandinista interrogators. The Nicaraguan authorities turned the attack into a propaganda victory, portraying it as a tremendous fiasco by hapless contra mercenaries.

Fall and Winter 1983

In the fall of 1983 there were many changes for the Special Operations commandos. Lieutenant Sandino requested permission from Bermúdez to travel on leave to Miami, and never came back. Carlos "Gustavo" Guillén, a medical student whose father had been a National Guard physician, took Sandino's place as commander of the unit, and Jhonson became Gustavo's second, leading a thirty-man sapper squad. A few weeks later, Villegas and the other Argentine trainers disappeared. One of Bermúdez's general staff officers came out to La Quinta to explain. The political situation had changed in Buenos Aires, civilians were taking over the Argentine government, and they didn't want to help the FDN anymore. Now, Bermúdez's staff officer said, "American friends" would be taking over the training of the special forces.

At this point, Jhonson's unit was transferred away from La Quinta. Too many journalists had been asking questions about the mysterious goings-on at the ramshackle farm outside Tegucigalpa surrounded by Nicaraguans with guns. Jhonson's unit boarded trucks—as always, at night, and covered by tarpaulins—for the drive eighteen miles west to Lepaterique, the shooting range where he had earlier received some basic sabotage training.

Lepaterique was a Honduran military installation, with the Honduran flag overhead, uniformed Honduran military guards at the front gate, and Honduran soldiers patrolling the perimeter, but the CIA had arranged with the Hondurans to use it for training various rebel units. For the next months, Jhonson and the Special Operations commandos would be based there.

At Lepaterique, Jhonson for the first time came into direct contact with some of the CIA men who, though he just knew them as "the American friends," had taken control of the Nicaraguan war. In command was "Col. Bill Clark," a gigantic man, well over six feet tall, with short, straight brown hair, a chunky body like a boxer's, and weight lifter's muscles. He appeared to be in his early forties. He liked to do all the calisthenics and jog with Jhonson and the other commandos in the morning. When he ran, it would take Jhonson about five steps to match every one of Colonel Bill's.[33]

"I'm a big mule," he told Jhonson.

Over time, Jhonson began to piece together Bill's background. He didn't have a wedding ring, but seemed to be married; he mentioned a son studying at an American university. He talked a lot about Vietnam, and it was obvious that he'd seen a lot of combat. He had scars from operations he'd undergone to extract bullets and shrapnel. During calisthenics, Bill would pull up his sweatshirt to show the scars across his stomach and back.

"Be careful with mines," he said at one point.

Colonel Bill headed a staff of five or six American CIA officers at Lepaterique. They all dressed in civilian clothes, but they were all military men. His second was "Major Thomas," a fellow with Hispanic, or perhaps American Indian, features, about thirty-five.[34] He had a wiry, tightly muscled frame that contrasted humorously with Colonel Bill's beef. Speaking slightly more flowing Spanish than "Bill," Thomas taught Jhonson and the other commandos the techniques of close-up war, such as ways to stab with a commando knife.

A handful of other CIA trainers also worked with Jhonson's men. There was a "Major Sean," who had been a Green Beret. "Tom Ecker" taught a course in cryptography, but he couldn't make himself understood in Spanish, so the CIA provided an interpreter, "Roberto," who also spoke Spanish with a thick American twang.

For Jhonson and his men, conditions were better at Lepaterique than they'd been at La Quinta under the Argentines. There the men had camped in field tents and washed out of a barrel; the food had been rice, beans, rice, beans. Now, under the gringos, although they still weren't allowed to leave the base, there were wooden barracks; there were eggs and bacon, cornflakes, a red apple, and coffee for breakfast after the morning jog—even a glass of cow's milk! Furthermore, most of the gringo instructors were friendlier than the Argentines had been, though they maintained a certain distance. On weekends most of the gringos would leave Lepaterique, driving to Tegucigalpa to get drunk and get laid, Jhonson figured. One American, however, always stayed behind with the Nicaraguans as a sort of baby-sitter. The gringos never left them entirely alone.

The American instructors built their own barracks apart from the Nicaraguans, and Jhonson's Special Operations commandos were also kept isolated from other Nicaraguans training at Lepaterique. Each Nicaraguan unit was separate, and everyone was urged to mind his own business. "Compartmentalized" was the word. As a result, Jhonson remained ignorant of many things. He didn't know that besides his own special forces unit, other Nicaraguans at Lepaterique were also learning about "psychological operations." Some were training as paramedics, others as radio operators. He didn't know that the sabotage he carried out was just one aspect of an enormous CIA counteroffensive aimed at beating back revolution all across Central America.

He didn't know, at first, about the dozens of other programs the CIA was undertaking to enlarge and remake the FDN, nor was he aware that the FDN was just one of four separate Nicaraguan exile armies the CIA was now managing: There was a force of Indians that the CIA was arming and training in the Honduran Mosquitia, the eastern savannah region bordering on Nicaragua; another, separate CIA-armed Indian force based in Costa Rica; and Edén Pastora's "southern front," yet another army financed and armed by the CIA.

There was a fifth secret CIA force, too, smaller but perhaps more deadly than the others, an elite sabotage unit operating frequently out of neighboring El Salvador's eastern port of La Unión. Composed of mercenaries from Colombia, Ecuador, Honduras, and other Latin countries, and under direct CIA control and command, they were the Agency's "Unilaterally Controlled Latin Assets."

Jhonson still thought that this was a Nicaraguan war. Seeing only a tiny part of the CIA's total involvement, he viewed Colonel Bill and the other CIA men simply as allies, eager to help. They seemed to be just what they said they were: "American friends."

4

The Project

1981 through 1983

By the time the Reagan Administration was installed, had considered how best to punish Managua's upstart revolutionaries, and had written secret proposals for clandestine contra armies and approved them, the Nicaraguan rebel force had already taken primitive shape. Enrique Bermúdez, working with the Argentines and reporting to the CIA, had recruited many officers, established a number of base camps, and begun to field some troops. Now Washington had a vision of much bigger things.

Building on this rudimentary foundation, the CIA utterly transformed every aspect of the rebel force, creating an army that rivaled the regular armed forces of Honduras in size and was equipped with sophisticated weaponry none of the government armies in Central America possessed. If, when Jhonson first took up arms, the Nicaraguan rebellion had been an independent, if sputtering, peasant revolt, it now became a U.S.-sponsored covert action. For the rest of the war, the CIA—or, during a period, Oliver North's National Security Council—maintained strategic control over the rebel army, directing the course and pace of contra initiatives through domination of supplies, logistics, and intelligence. At key periods, the CIA took tactical control as well, issuing direct battle orders that were radioed to troops fighting on the ground inside Nicaragua. Yet the CIA sought to maintain the image that the war continued as an indepen-

dent peasant insurgency, seeking always to mask its master-client relationship with the FDN. The Agency encouraged FDN leaders to pose as
independent patriots charting their own course.[1]

1981 and 1982

While the Nicaraguan paramilitary force became the Reagan Administration's pet project, Reagan and his advisers were angry not only about
Nicaragua's Sandinistas, but also about the insurgency flaring next door
in El Salvador and about a fledgling guerrilla movement in Honduras.
They were determined to stop arms moving from Nicaragua across
southwestern Honduras to the Salvadoran rebels. Honduran cooperation
in confronting all these leftist adversaries was essential, so American
officials cultivated a key ally. They threw their influence behind Honduran Army Col. Gustavo Alvarez, a hard-line anticommunist trained in
Argentina who shared Washington's hankering for an all-out brawl with
communism. With Washington's backing, Alvarez soon rose to general,
took command of the Honduran Army, and signed off on a sweeping list
of U.S.-financed programs designed to hit the region's Communists
hard. The Americans transformed a Honduran military airport at
Palmerola in central Honduras into a sprawling U.S. base, the headquarters over the next years for dozens of maneuvers and training exercises.
U.S. military advisers began to remake General Alvarez's armed forces,
greatly expanding U.S. military aid, training, and routine contacts. And
the CIA and General Alvarez cooperated enthusiastically in the creation
of the FDN.

Mindful of the magnitude of the task it was undertaking in Honduras—CIA agents referred to it as "The Project"—the CIA began by
beefing up its own local organization. The contra war was going to
transform the CIA station at the Tegucigalpa embassy from a backwoods intelligence-gathering post with minor operational capabilities
into a major paramilitary command center. With President Reagan and
CIA Director William Casey both personally dedicated to the FDN more
than to any other CIA project, Tegucigalpa would become virtually the
most important Agency station in the world. It would need extra hands.

In 1981 and 1982, about fifty full-time American CIA agents moved
quietly to Honduras: old paramilitary warriors, pilots, mechanics, and
logisticians. Some took up diplomatic cover at the walled limestone-
block U.S. embassy on Calle La Paz overlooking downtown Tegucigalpa,
or at the Americans' burgeoning military complex at Palmerola Air
Base, forty miles northwest of Tegucigalpa. Scores of other CIA contract
agents moved to Honduras in the same period, mostly retired CIA and

Pentagon people—nearly a hundred including the secretaries, code clerks, and communications specialists.[2]

Many of those who signed on had earned their credentials during service in other, not-too-glorious American projects: the Bay of Pigs, Vietnam, Laos. Others had been diplomats in Somoza's Managua. Washington's relations with the Somoza government had been long and complicated, and after his fall, there were many U.S. officials whose warm ties to the Nicaraguan government and to the Guard weren't much use anymore—until the Project.

"They were hired like you would hire somebody to paint your house," a U.S. official who was involved at the time said later.

The CIA agents streaming into Honduras formed a secret network of substantial size even for a large country. In Honduras, a sleepy backwater of just four million, they became a large—if largely unseen—presence.

At first, the tall, fair-haired, athletic CIA station chief at the U.S. embassy, Donald Winters, was riding herd on the entire project. Winters was what CIA agents call a "standard foreign intelligence case officer," meaning he had no experience in paramilitary war. He and his agents were plotting the contra buildup in furtive meetings with their Nicaraguan assets in parking lots and restaurants around Tegucigalpa. And the Argentine advisers working for the CIA were even more disorganized.[3]

"The Argentines were basically drawing attack plans on the dust of a car hood, telling the contras, 'You're going to go over here and attack this town.' It was chaos," one CIA officer who worked in Honduras during this period recalled later.

To impose order, the Agency divided its labors between the embassy station, which would coordinate all U.S. intelligence activities in Honduras, and a second CIA outpost—a "base," in intelligence jargon—that would take primary operational responsibility for the war. It was an administrative practice that had become standard wherever the CIA intended to develop a major paramilitary project.

The base was not only an administrative entity, but also a physical workplace. CIA agents rented a rambling house near Toncontín Airport in Comayagüela, Tegucigalpa's twin city, and converted it into a high-security CIA safe house. The base became the true strategic command of the rebel army, the nerve center for the war, the top-secret headquarters for dozens of CIA agents and U.S. military officers operating under the Agency's control. Bedrooms became logistical and administrative offices. The living room became an operations center, crammed with radios and maps, where CIA agents tracked rebel combat units and

Agency aircraft. They set up powerful radios and computerized encoders that could bounce secure radio communications off a satellite to CIA headquarters at Langley.[4] The CIA's successive base chiefs were the FDN's shadow commanders, the American agents who made virtually all the important decisions for the force.

1982 and 1983

The first base chief was Ray Doty, a grizzled, fifty-seven-year-old former U.S. Army master sergeant who arrived in Honduras in 1982. He had little formal education, spoke only broken Spanish, and knew next to nothing about Central American history. But he was an expert in arms acquisition and paramilitary war. Doty, who introduced himself around Honduras as "Colonel Raymond," became the contra army's behind-the-scenes architect.[5]

Doty had learned most of what he knew about paramilitary operations during a three-year stint in Laos, halfway through the CIA's thirteen-year war in that Southeast Asian country. That project began in about 1962, when CIA agents began to secretly recruit and train what grew to be a forty-thousand-man force of illiterate Meo and other peasants. The Agency recruited a Laotian general of Meo origin to command the force, built a major air base north of Vientiane, the Laotian capital, as its secret headquarters, and supplied its units in the field with air drops from a fleet of planes belonging to a CIA-run airline, Air America. The CIA station in Vientiane farmed out direct management of the war to a subsidiary CIA base hidden at the sprawling Udorn Air Base across the border to the south in Thailand. The CIA used the Laotian peasant force to fight the homegrown Communist Pathet Lao guerrillas as well as to harass North Vietnamese regulars moving weapons along the Ho Chi Minh trail down through eastern Laos to South Vietnam. Trained to fight with light arms as guerrillas, thousands of the CIA's hapless peasant fighters were eventually ordered, as the conflict built in intensity and scope, to defend hilltop positions like regular soldiers, pounding the Communist enemy with mortars and other artillery in coordination with American B-52 strikes. What journalists called "The Twilight War"—it never received the attention focused on Vietnam—ended with the proxy force's 1975 collapse and the flight of its CIA-recruited leader into U.S. exile. It left 30,000 Meo peasants dead and another 400,000 displaced from their tribal homelands.[6]

Ray Doty lived and fought with the CIA's client Laotians from 1967 to 1970, directing guerrilla operations around the Bolovens Plateau in the south and later around the Plain of Jars in the Laotian north. Like many other Americans who served in Laos, Doty went off to a new post-ing before the final debacle, and he left with his confidence in the problem-solving capacities of paramilitary technology and technique unshaken. A dozen years later, Doty brought this same certitude with him to Tegucigalpa.

So, too, did a striking number of other CIA officers who worked with the contra army during the 1980s. All three of the CIA base chiefs who directed the Nicaraguan rebels during the Reagan Administration had learned their paramilitary craft in Laos. Two of the four Tegucigalpa sta-tion chiefs and dozens of other CIA agents who served in Honduras dur-ing the contra war began their Agency careers in Laos. Most, like Doty, had a view of war that tilted strongly toward materials-handling. There were munitions to buy, guns to deliver, cargoes to drop, explosives to place. Though Doty worked hard, sometimes he seemed a little over-whelmed.

"The Project could only be as good as Doty was, because he didn't delegate anything," one former CIA officer who worked with Doty in Honduras recalled. "He made every decision, so it was all kind of small-scale, and all very conventional. To us, Doty was a lovable, gruff old bear that you couldn't help but respect and love. But to the contras, he was very authoritarian and gruff. He counted every bean and bullet. He yelled and screamed a lot. I don't think they really understood him. I don't think he understood them very well either."

Despite his limitations, Doty left an extraordinary imprint on the contra army and on the way the contras fought. During Doty's tenure, he and his men oversaw the construction of the contras' main base camp, and they cut a thirty-mile road through virgin hills to supply it. They rented a string of secret warehouses to store rebel supplies, and a fleet of trucks to move them. They acquired an airport for the contras and assembled an air force to use it. They established a string of contra medical clinics and hired doctors to tend them. They set up a field radio network for the contras to communicate with one another and a clan-destine radio transmitter for the contras to beam propaganda at Nicaragua. They hired logistics technicians to move supplies and hired accountants to bankroll them. In Miami, CIA agents even recruited Nicaraguan exile politicians to speak for the contras in Washington. How CIA agents made all these things happen is the story of Washing-ton's rebel army in its early years.[7]

When Jhonson first fled to Honduras in July 1981, the war had already taken shape in two forms. The ambush he had plotted at Peder-nales del Cuá was an example of one: spontaneous internal anti-Sandinista uprisings. The war took a second form when ex-Guardsmen, squatting in a handful of Honduran border camps, mostly in southern Choluteca province, began carrying out short incursions to murder Sandinista officials and rustle cattle. But there was no formal rebel military organization at that time—the war was chaos.

The network of border camps reflected the anarchy. Maquengales, the first exile camp Jhonson saw, was then one of just three such FDN centers, and yet more than a dozen other rough settlements of counter-revolutionary Nicaraguan exiles had sprung up along Honduras's long border with Nicaragua. Some were populated entirely by former Guardsmen, others held scores of angry exile civilians. The geography of the border camps owed more to the exigencies of exile life than to the needs of counterrevolutionary war.

One of Bermúdez's first tasks was to consolidate this chaotic sprawl of mini-settlements into a coherent border military network. He designated two new camps, bringing to five the number of rough FDN installations dispersed along the nearly two-hundred-mile-long border winding through the hills in southern Choluteca province northeast to El Paraíso province.[8] The locations were selected for their convenience as staging areas for attacks on the most important northern Nicaraguan towns. For example, Mack's training camp at La Lodosa was established in the hills south of El Paraíso because that was the most convenient border site from which to mount attacks on Ocotal, Nicaragua, a farming center barely ten miles across the border.[9]

The rebels in the five main FDN camps were deployed in armed battalions called "task forces," which numbered anywhere from a few dozen to a few hundred men, and each task force was commanded by an ex–National Guardsman. In addition to staging areas for border combat, the rebel camps were to function as headquarters, training, and supply areas for their respective task forces.

Supplying the task forces in these camps with food, uniforms, guns, ammunition, and all the other needs of a primitive army was tough. The first lots of weapons, ammunition, and supplies were small, purchased in the U.S. or Honduras. The Argentines, spending U.S. money, originally bought the FDN three hundred Ruger Mini-14 automatic rifles, and about fifteen four-wheel-drive vehicles, assigning one to each task force commander. Those jeeps, sagging under loads of rice, beans, and bullets, carried a lot of the army's early supplies to the border camps. Cattle trucks and troop transports rented from the Honduran Army joined the supply fleet later. But some camps were miles past the last Honduran road, and rivers of mud made passage to several other camps impossible during the rainy season.[10]

When American money began to flow and the rebel army began to swell, this original, jury-rigged supply system proved too primitive. CIA agents soon modernized the flow of weaponry and other supplies into Honduras. Container ships docked on Honduras's Atlantic coast with secret cargo, cargo planes landed at Palmerola Air Base, and fleets of semi-trailer trucks shuttled between the ports and CIA warehouses in Tegucigalpa. But these tonnages just couldn't be moved out to the border camps in jeeps over washed-out roads.[11]

In one early solution, the CIA rented Huey helicopters from the Honduran Army—at $750 per hour—to airlift the mounting supplies out to the camps. This worked for a time, but as FDN ranks grew, the tonnages mounted and the helicopter rental costs grew exorbitant.[12]

Originally, the FDN's task forces had specialized in border incursions, darting twenty miles south into Nicaragua to mortar a town or murder a Sandinista. But by early 1983, the war was changing as well. Now commanders like Mike Lima were marching sixty, eighty, even one hundred miles into Nicaragua. The potential theaters of war expanded from a string of northern border towns to embrace Nicaragua's entire peasant backlands. Reflecting the new conception of the war, the FDN's old task forces were reorganized and renamed. They became "regional commands," each assigned an operational region inside Nicaragua. As the concept evolved away from the border raid, the function of the camps as combat staging areas diminished even as the supply problems grew more acute.

Finally the CIA decided to consolidate the unwieldy string of FDN border bases into one main camp that could serve as a resupply center and headquarters for the entire rebel army. The site the CIA chose was a pine-forested valley surrounding the Honduran hamlet of Las Vegas in eastern El Paraíso province, not far from the Maquengales camp. It was located in a parrot's beak of hilly, wooded terrain formed by the confluence of two rivers, the Poteca and the Coco, a region only sparsely settled by a few coffee farmers and known in Honduras as the "recovered zone," because, after years of diplomatic wrangling with Nicaragua, Honduras had won its sovereignty in a 1960 decision in the World Court at the Hague. CIA agents gave the region around Las Vegas their own name. They called it "the salient," because it was a slice of Honduras that thrust out into Nicaragua.

The only problem with the Las Vegas site was that it was accessible by no improved road. Heading from Tegucigalpa toward Las Vegas, the paved roads turned to gravel just past Danlí, and the gravel petered out to nothing at Las Trojes, at the northwestern corner of the salient. Most coffee farmers working the zone could penetrate to their slopes only by mule-back, following narrow and treacherous earthen tracks. The CIA needed a new camp and a new road, and an agent known to the contras as "The Engineer" built both.

The Engineer, about fifty, was lanky and, six feet tall, towered over the contras, especially in his cowboy boots. He had a weatherbeaten face and short, curly hair, and often wore a camouflage baseball cap. He showed up riding on a road grader, and he liked to jam a big dab of Skoal tobacco chaw under his bottom lip to keep the juices flowing while he cut a road through the hills to Las Vegas.

The Engineer worked on the construction project with another American agent who introduced himself to the contras as "Mr. Ted," a man about sixty years old but in good shape. Mr. Ted had long paramilitary experience, having served in Korea, Indonesia, Thailand, and Laos. In the last station, he'd been a CIA unit chief, outranking Doty in the intelligence hierarchy. Fifteen years later, Doty had become Mr. Ted's superior—and didn't trust him—so Doty put him to building roads with the Engineer.[13] Besides a contingent of gunmen in charge of security, the Engineer and Mr. Ted had three Honduran machine operators, a couple of bulldozers, and a grader, all rented. Neither man spoke much Spanish, but everybody communicated somehow. The Engineer would climb up on the grader himself when he wanted the excavating work done just right. They cut a wide swath through the broad valley east from Las Trojes to Las Vegas, then called in the dump trucks to lay down a gravel topping that was good enough for eighteen-wheelers, at least part of the year.

The Engineer built the main core of the Las Vegas rebel base camp, too. Las Vegas was designed as the rebel army's major resupply point, to which contra units would return for rest, relaxation, and rearming between operations inside Nicaragua. Rather than a single dirt clearing with a few huts, it had to be a cluster of bivouacs, spread across several hills and valleys, connected by secondary roads, and it had to have a resupply infrastructure. The CIA cut the roads and built the camp.

Las Vegas also needed an arms warehouse. The Engineer brought his dozers into the camp and graded a hill, slicing a series of parallel gouges into the side of the slope, then trucked in a half dozen cargo containers, backed them into the gouges he'd cut in the hillside so that their open ends faced out, and covered them with backfill. They made a series of weatherproofed mini-warehouses, undetectable from the air. A driveway along the front of the slope allowed supply trucks to keep them stocked with C-4 explosive, mines, automatic-rifle ammunition, mortar shells, and other weaponry. The Engineer graded off another area for the rebels' "logistical supply center," a string of field tents that would serve as a food and dry-goods warehouse.

The headquarters the Engineer and his Las Vegas construction crew built for Colonel Bermúdez reminded many who saw it of a U.S. Army Vietnam-era troop settlement, a series of prefab wooden "hooches," set on concrete decks and roofed with zinc panels. They weren't huge, maybe sixteen feet deep and twelve feet wide, but they were off the ground, and they had windows with screens. Bermúdez's five main aides—his personnel, intelligence, operations, logistics, and psychological operations officers—each got one. Bermúdez's was the best. His men hung up Nicaraguan maps, and there was a desk with the latest radio printouts from the field—just as though this were the war's real command center. Among other things, Bermúdez's was the only hooch with a kerosene-driven refrigerator, stocked with beer.

The Engineer also built two hooches to house the CIA men who would be working with the FDN at Las Vegas. Journalists would be visiting the camp, and the FDN was supposed to be an independent insurgency, so the CIA's hooches needed to be out of sight. The Engineer picked a spot about seven hundred yards beyond the Strategic Command, behind a stand of trees. He excavated a lot out of a hill, and the carpenters put up two prefab houses. One house, which soon bristled with antennas, was for the three or four CIA men who'd be living in the camp; the second was for transient agents who would come out for special meetings. Even from the parade ground the Engineer graded nearby, where Bermúdez would review the troops at graduations, you could just barely see the top of the CIA's hooch.[14]

The FDN "air force" also grew. The Argentines had bought a couple of light planes, a Beechcraft Baron and an Aztec, so they and Bermúdez wouldn't have to fly commercial as they traversed the region preparing for war.[15] But the CIA had bigger plans. The FDN was turning out to be a lot like Washington's client paramilitary army that Doty had worked with in Laos in the late 1960s—heavily armed for an irregular force, insurgents with mortars, "guerrilla-conventional." Doty was urging FDN units to fight for extended periods inside Nicaragua—for four, five even six months. They'd need supplies, and there were only two ways to get them. They could create Nicaragua's version of the Ho Chi Minh trail, or they could be supplied by air.

So the CIA needed a secret airport. Honduran aviation maps showed a little-known facility 129 miles northeast of Tegucigalpa: the Honduran Air Force's Aguacate Air Base. CIA agents flew out to take a look. What they found wasn't much, really just a shed next to a 4,300-foot dirt strip on Honduras's remote savannahs, outside the cowboy town of Catacamas, but it had potential. The CIA rented the entire base from the Hondurans.

CIA men put up a new control tower and several industrial warehouses and hangars. Then the U.S. Army's 46th Engineering battalion went to work on Aguacate during a military exercise, called Big Pine II, in 1983. Why was the Army lengthening the Aguacate strip? reporters asked. Just good practice, the military flacks said. Among other thoughtful improvements, the Army engineers extended Aguacate's runway to eight thousand feet, built barracks and a dining hall, and installed a new water system. Then they turned it back over to the CIA.[16]

In the first stage of the war, Nicaraguans piloted the FDN's air force. Bermúdez appointed Col. Juan Gómez—Somoza's personal flyer, and Bermúdez's old chum—as the FDN's "Air Force Commander." Gómez called airports and crop-dusting companies throughout Central America looking for pilots, mechanics, and other air personnel from the old Nicaraguan Air Force, offering flyers $1,000 a month, and mechanics, $750. In early 1983, he called ex-Guard Maj. Roberto Amador in Miami. Amador had flown as a fumigator in the Honduran banana fields after Somoza's defeat, then moved to Miami, but he was a little old to break into commercial aviation in the gringos' world. Gómez's offer sounded good. Amador signed on, and Gómez threw in the plane ticket to Tegucigalpa.

In Tegucigalpa, old comrades from the last war met Major Amador at Toncontín Airport and took him to a CIA-paid safe house already hopping with a dozen other pilots and mechanics. It was old home week for a while, then the CIA conducted a course in aerial photography, taught by an agent named "John," a young American about twenty-eight years old. In August, Colonel Gómez, Amador, and the rest of the FDN air force flew to Aguacate. They found an air-conditioned barracks and American-style mess hall that turned out hamburgers and hot dogs.

There they met more CIA agents. "Major West," a short, wiry man of fifty, was Aguacate's commander. He spoke no Spanish, but over time Amador figured out that he'd been an Army Special Forces paratrooper in Southeast Asia. "Mark," a twenty-five-year-old aide, was in charge of packing the airdrop bundles. A few days later, the FDN air cargo wing arrived: two aging C-47s. Two Americans nosed the planes to a halt in front of the Aguacate tower, then climbed out blinking into the Honduran heat, dressed in civilian clothes. Amador wasn't impressed by the C-47s. They were old and battered, with poor avionics.

There'd been a lot of other pesky details that CIA agents had been forced to tend to, among them the acquisition of a series of radios for FDN field commanders to use to transmit their map coordinates back to Aguacate. CIA agents also had to train the radio operators, the "kickers" who would be shoving the five thousand pounds of cargo out the rear bays of the C-47s, and so on.

Finally, in September 1983, the first cargo bundles began to float down over Nicaragua to FDN troops. Amador flew five missions. On the sixth, October 3, a Sandinista rocket slammed into motor number one on Amador's C-47. Amador crashed, and Sandinista authorities seized, tried, and sentenced him to thirty years in jail.[17]

Despite that setback, the CIA's air-resupply program continued. Doty and the other Americans, locked in their vision of guerrilla-conventional warfare, were dreaming of an air combat wing. They sent Nicaraguan pilots to El Salvador for aerial rocket training, and in early 1984, the CIA delivered three Cessna O-2 observation planes, equipped with rocket pods, to the "FDN air force." They hoped to use them for close air support for combat in northern Nicaragua.[18]

Another of the CIA's additions to the rebel army was a modernized medical system. This was a war; there would be wounded. Bermúdez and the Argentines had made a start, establishing rustic little clinics in the early FDN border camps and appointing a colonel from the old National Guard medical corps, Ernesto "Dr. Tomás" Matamoros, to head the FDN's fledgling system. Now Bermúdez's people recruited half a dozen more doctors, mainly financially strapped Nicaraguans unable to practice medicine in exile.

An American agent using the pseudonym "Doc"—though he was only a paramedic, not a physician—supervised the FDN medical corps. Doc was a bespectacled, mustachioed fellow of about twenty-eight, with fine brown hair, a light complexion, and, to hear the Nicaraguan doctors tell it, an arrogant spirit. He drove around Honduras in a white Honda Civic, tending his little piece of the Project. The CIA had rented a crumbling mansion in the Honduran village of Támara, twelve miles west of Tegucigalpa, and converted it into the FDN's first relatively civilized, though makeshift, clinic. By early 1983, the Támara clinic had become the heart of the FDN system, with a fifty-bed ward, two permanent doctors, and a dentist. Doc's job was to supply it, support it, supervise it.

The doctors said they worked for the FDN, but really they worked for Doc; he could transfer them or, if he wanted, fire them. He told one of the Támara doctors he was to be transferred to another FDN facility where his particular skills could be better used. How do you know about my skills? the Nicaraguan doctor asked. Doc began to recite biographical details, culled from the Nicaraguan's youth, as well as data from his educational and professional career. Doc played it all back to the doctor in a clinical tone, like a personnel officer who'd just reviewed an employee's file.

The Támara clinic was ample, at first. When FDN task forces invaded northern Nicaragua to attack towns, however, it was too far from the action. The CIA equipped the FDN medical corps with a forty-bed field hospital, and after a bit of practice, the Nicaraguan doctors became so proficient, they could be ready on twenty minutes' notice to race out to the closest border site, throw up the olive-drab field tents, and begin to do first aid, bullet extractions, and triage as contra units dragged their wounded back to Honduras. During a September 1983 attack on Ocotal, Nicaragua, the CIA was so bold as to order the FDN's medical tents pitched in an open field along the road leading south from the Honduran town of El Paraíso.

As the war mounted, though, the Támara clinic just wasn't big enough. The ward that was set up for fifty beds soon had one hundred rebel wounded crammed into the hallways and corners, and when the Sandinista army began to bring its Soviet-made Katyuschka multiple rocket launchers to bear on contra units, the flood of shrapnel cases overwhelmed Támara. Furthermore, the Honduran military was starting to complain. Támara's public profile—not to mention that of the CIA's field hospitals—was just too brazen.

So the CIA modernized the medical system. After the Engineer's crew built the Las Vegas base, Doc supervised the transfer of the Támara clinic to a new site fifteen minutes' walk from the FDN's new headquarters. Once the CIA opened its new base at Aguacate, other new possibilities opened up. Instead of the old field hospitals along the border, the CIA acquired a medivac helicopter and began to air transport FDN wounded to Aguacate. There, the CIA had thrown up two wooden warehouses and five hospital tents, housing thirty beds each, as medical wards, along with an operating chamber. The Aguacate hospital complex was handling up to 250 wounded during heavy combat. A contingent of volunteer Cuban exile doctors from Miami was visiting regularly to help out, and press attention focused on them, but the CIA's medical service was largely based on the full-time services of salaried physicians, more than a dozen by 1984.[19]

1981 through 1983

During the first years of the war, intelligence gathering by the contra army was primitive at best.

For tactical combat, rebel units operating inside Nicaragua learned about Sandinista army movements from friendly peasants or from Sandinistas they seized and interrogated. But the information that field commanders collected this way stayed within their units because the army had no system for communicating intelligence back to headquarters for analysis and redistribution to other units.

In advance of contra sabotage operations, the CIA provided the contras the intelligence they needed, arranging overflights of Nicaragua by U.S. spy planes to shoot aerial photos used to target objectives for FDN sapper squads. But during the first three years of the war, the Agency placed little emphasis on developing the contra army's own intelligence-gathering capacity.[20]

Nor did the FDN's own section, headed by the former National Guard Col. Ricardo "El Chino" Lau and operating out of general staff headquarters in Tegucigalpa, gather intelligence on the Sandinista enemy in Nicaragua. Instead, Lau focused on counterintelligence work: He ran a death squad.[21]

Lau's killers were ex-Guardsmen he recruited into the FDN as paid agents, and during his first months in Honduras, Lau sent them to eliminate Nicaraguan exiles he suspected might be Sandinista spies plotting an attack on Bermúdez or on other contra leaders. Some of Lau's victims were FDN commandos. One contra fighter executed on Lau's orders was Iván Bendaña, a twenty-year-old Nicaraguan student exile who had joined the September 15 Legion in Guatemala and then moved to an FDN camp in Honduras. In early 1982, Bendaña wrote several letters from Honduras to his brothers in Miami complaining that he feared for his safety because he had run afoul of Bermúdez and Lau. Accounts differ about the reason for the rift. Some contras believed that Bendaña's infraction had been only to complain too insistently about the food served during a leadership course run by Argentine advisers at La Quinta. But Lau's personal secretary later told Bendaña's brothers that Iván had threatened to reveal crimes committed by Lau in Guatemala. On April 23, 1982, contra gunmen shot Bendaña thirty-seven times at close range in an ambush near the Honduran border hamlet of Los Bajas. Two days later, his Miami relatives received a terse telegram from Bermúdez: "We announce that Mr. Iván Bendaña has died. Signed, Enrique Bermúdez."[22]

Lau's death squad also worked for the Honduran military, which was engaged in its own assassination program aimed at exterminating a tiny guerrilla movement operating in the country, as well as student and labor leaders considered to pose a subversive threat. In 1980, Colonel Alvarez established a secret Honduran Army intelligence unit, later known as the 316 battalion. The participation of Honduran soldiers in state-sponsored murder posed an obvious security problem for Alvarez, so to maintain secrecy, he recruited most of his triggermen from Tegucigalpa's Central Penitentiary and later ordered the execution of many of his own executioners.

In late 1981, however, the FDN's Argentine advisers proposed to

Alvarez another solution for this problem: Lau's FDN gunmen could cooperate by executing subversives previously kidnapped and interrogated by the Honduran military.[23]

During the period from 1981 to 1984, when Alvarez operated his death squads, nearly 250 political killings and "disappearances" were reported in Honduras. Lau's recruits played an important role in the extermination campaign. They seized and killed Salvadorans targeted as arms traffickers, Honduran labor or student leaders, and Nicaraguans denounced as Sandinista spies.[24]

One contra who worked for Lau later described the murders of two Honduran men to a U.S. reporter. The contra, who identified himself as "Miguel," said a Honduran military officer called him to arrange the pickup of two "packages." The contra said he took delivery of two detainees from a Honduran military jeep on a highway near Tegucigalpa and drove them south to Choluteca. There, one was forced to dig his own grave and lie in it, where he was stabbed and shot. The other was driven on toward the Nicaraguan border, stabbed and shot, and left on the highway as a warning to other leftists.[25]

"Miguel's" identity has never been discovered, but the decision to murder the Hondurans in Choluteca is significant. That steamy southern province, straddling the Panamerican Highway just north of the Nicaraguan border, became a major focus of FDN murder. It was the first stop for many Nicaraguan refugees streaming into Honduras, so it was perfectly situated for the work Lau considered his main counterintelligence task: identifying and eliminating Sandinista spies. Choluteca was also the crossroads of the arms traffic from Nicaragua, across southern Honduras to the Salvadoran guerrillas.

Several of Lau's most notorious killers—one used the nom de guerre "La Bestia," or The Beast—took up residence in Choluteca, where they worked closely with the intelligence section at the Honduran Army's 101st Brigade, a unit advised by U.S. military officers. Eighty-two Salvadorans disappeared in Honduras between 1980 and early 1984, many in Choluteca. Honduran authorities later blamed Lau's death squad for killing most of them.[26] The bodies of some of the victims were burned in the ovens of a gold mine in Choluteca province operated by two of Lau's Nicaraguan exile friends.[27]

Whether or not the CIA was involved remains unclear. During the period Lau's agents were carrying out their murders, Lau's section was funded by the CIA, according to several former FDN officers.[28] Whether the CIA helped Lau's men carry out their murders by targeting victims remains an open question. At a time that CIA Director William Casey and other Agency officials were justifying the contra program to Congress as an effort to interdict arms shipments from Nicaragua to Marxist guerrillas in El Salvador, CIA-funded FDN gunmen working for Lau routinely murdered suspected Salvadoran arms traffickers in Honduras.

Perhaps this was a coincidence. One CIA officer who worked in Honduras during the period insisted later that Lau kept the work of his assassination squads secret from the Agency officials who occasionally visited his office in FDN general staff headquarters, but it seems unlikely that the CIA remained completely unaware of Lau's activities. One reason is that the CIA was closely monitoring the activities of the Honduran Army intelligence units involved in the assassination campaign of which Lau's squads were one part. Some of the Honduran agents who served on the 316 battalion received interrogation training in Texas by CIA officers in 1980, and in Honduras American agents maintained extensive contacts with the secret unit, often visiting detention centers during interrogations and routinely receiving written statements taken from the torture victims.[29]

Furthermore, the Agency established numerous mechanisms to monitor the activities of the FDN; one of the CIA's own agents reported full time on the rebel army. Known to the rebels as "Major Ricardo," a heavyset, Colombian-born agent in his early forties, he visited every base camp, every safe house, making his way from rebel officer to rebel officer, asking questions about everything, especially anything that might be irregular, and scribbling notes on a legal pad.[30] In addition, the Agency recruited paid informants from within rebel ranks, from every base and every unit, from virtually every staff section, to spy on the FDN. One of the rebels the CIA routinely paid for information was Bermúdez's own longtime personal secretary, Ernesto Ortega, a former Guard lieutenant.

In late 1982, the CIA's base chief Ray Doty boasted to a visiting U.S. senator on the effectiveness of his program to spy on the FDN. Nothing happens in the contra army we don't find out about, Doty said.[31]

Late 1982

The CIA built its Project, piece by piece, in a remarkably short time, but almost immediately there were people who began to wonder about the quality. As the pieces of the CIA's jigsaw fell into place, the face that began to stare up from the puzzle began to look disconcertingly like Somoza's old National Guard.

The comparisons were inevitable, what with the commanders of the FDN army, air force, "navy," medical corps, intelligence service, and a string of other major posts drawn straight from corresponding posts in the Guard.[32] But as the FDN took shape, the Guard legacy emerged in countless other unexpected ways as well. When the FDN got around to writing up a code of conduct, a set of internal laws, the lawyer to whom Bermúdez delegated the task just grabbed the Guard's old *Código de Enjuiciamiento*, or Trial Code, jiggered a few things around, and called it the FDN's. When the FDN set up a basic training school, Mack and a dozen other former Guard instructors closely modeled it on Somoza's Escuela de Entrenamiento Basico de Infantería, the EEBI. And when the FDN established an "internal front" within Nicaragua, Bermúdez assigned the task to one of Somoza's former Liberal Party political bosses, who recruited the FDN's underground of collaborators from his list of old Liberal Party *jueces de mesta*, Somoza's network of village sheriffs.[33]

The Somoza era also lived on in the person of an exiled businessman whom CIA agents recruited early to work closely with Bermúdez. Aristides Sánchez was born in León, the traditional power center of Somoza's Liberal Party, and Sánchez's family was one of the preeminent Liberal families, with a web of family ties to the Somoza clan itself. Aristides was the grandson of Fernando Sánchez, a cacao planter who had accumulated more than a hundred thousand acres of plantation land tilled by thousands of illiterate peons. When Aristides was growing up, he could walk from León southwest more than ten miles to the Pacific and never leave his father's land. And there were other vast parcels in Nicaragua's northern wilds, concessions from Liberal governments, that the family had never had time to visit.

Aristides's father, Enrique F. Sánchez, was at different times Somoza's ambassador to Mexico, Somoza's agriculture minister, and Somoza's public works minister, as well as a Liberal Party congressional deputy from León. Aristides got an aristocrat's education, studying law at Managua's Jesuit University and later in Italy. He married Cecilia Rodríguez, herself the daughter of one of Central America's wealthiest families, with interests in liquor, agriculture, and shipping.

Aristides Sánchez distinguished himself as a quiet plotter who liked to control events from behind the scenes rather than work in the limelight. Instead of practicing law or following in the family tradition of Liberal Party politics, Sánchez carried out a family coup d'etat, taking control from his siblings of much of his father's lands, then went to work managing his properties, commuting between Managua and León. He got to know the National Guard well, cultivating relations with each successive local Guard commander in León to secure their help in watching over the family properties and guarding against labor unrest. But through the 1970s, the Guard's grip on Nicaragua's peons slipped, and to salvage his fortune Sánchez had to shift from accumulation to liquidation. In 1979, as the revolution closed in, he worked frantically to sell off as much as possible of the family's estate, and trucked between fifteen thousand and twenty thousand head of cattle from the family's vast herds to slaughter in Honduras. Then he fled with his family into Miami exile.[34]

As the Argentines and Americans began to finance the Guard's rebirth, Aristides was the first of three Sánchez brothers to sign on to the Project. In 1981, he moved to Honduras, where from the start he worked closely with Bermúdez, adopting the role he'd favored in business: the behind-the-scenes manipulator. He reported to the CIA daily and, like Bermúdez, generally followed their dictates. But his wealth gave Sánchez what one U.S. official later called "fuck-you money"—the wherewithal Bermúdez lacked to defy his American handlers.

The very atmosphere around the FDN leadership smelled of the Somoza era. Ensconced in a series of CIA-paid, Spanish colonial Tegucigalpa safe houses, Bermúdez, Sánchez, and the rest of the FDN clique were whiling away evenings in candle-lit elegance, murmuring over wine and beef about the way things were—and still might be. And yet the FDN's identity as a group of has-been Somocistas was becoming increasingly obvious, to the dismay of the CIA, especially since by late 1982 the "secret war" had become big news. The U.S. Congress began to consider cutting off funds.

From the moment they created the FDN, CIA agents conceived of a division of labor: The contra army would carry out military strikes inside Nicaragua—but stay out of politics—while a junta or "directorate" of exiled Nicaraguan businessmen would do the rebels' political work.[35] Mainly, that meant lobbying the U.S. Congress to vote money the CIA could spend on the contras. The CIA had chosen three members for the original FDN directorate, created in the fall of 1981: Aristides Sánchez and two others.[36] By mid-1982, the other two had quarreled with Bermúdez, and now the FDN needed a new public face. In November 1982, a team of CIA agents moved into Miami, rented a suite at the Four Ambassadors Hotel, and began to recruit. Tony Feldman was their leader.

Feldman thought the way to counter the doleful image Bermúdez and his Guards were developing in Tegucigalpa was obvious: Put together a junta of exiles with ties to Nicaragua's Conservative Party, Somoza's traditional opposition. Naturally, Feldman also wanted bright, educated people who could speak English and who knew how to work under American direction. So he recruited exiles with experience working in U.S. corporations.

One was Edgar Chamorro, then fifty-one, a member of one of Nicaragua's most prominent Conservative families and a former Jesuit with a master's degree from Harvard University who had traveled into exile to Miami after the Sandinista takeover. Living on Key Biscayne, Chamorro was working for Cargill, Inc. when the first call came.[37]

A stranger, "Steve Davis," said he was speaking in the name of the U.S. government. Washington was interested in increasing the size of the contras' political leadership. Was Chamorro interested?

A week or so later, Davis took Chamorro to dinner and introduced Feldman. "He was about forty years old, alert and good-looking. He had thinning hair, a long face, an easy smile, and a gentleman's manner. He would have made a superb car salesman," Chamorro later said of Feldman.

Feldman said that the contras enjoyed Washington's full backing. He was sure they'd be in power in Managua within a year. For now, he wanted to put together a seven-member directorate of Nicaraguans with no ties to Somoza, a group that could persuade Congress that the rebels were worth supporting. Chamorro agreed to cooperate.

At a subsequent meeting, Chamorro met another CIA agent, a man who called himself "Tomás Castillo" but whose real name was Joseph Fernández. Born in New York, Fernández had moved to Miami at age thirteen and had attended St. Peter and Paul Catholic High School. He was a police officer in Dade County for eight years before his recruitment by the CIA in 1969. During the 1970s, Fernández had done stints under diplomatic cover in Uruguay and Peru and had also served at Langley.

By late 1982, he was forty-five, an olive-skinned, heavyset man, maybe five ten, with black hair graying at the temples and buckish teeth that occasionally rested on his lower lip. He wore dark, quality suits and took a special care with clothes that impressed Chamorro.[38]

Fernández coordinated preparations for a press conference, designed to introduce the new FDN directorate publicly. Chamorro, with a handful of other Nicaraguan exiles, wrote a political manifesto typical of dozens of others the exile community was churning out at the time: anticommunist, all about the right to private property. It was submitted to Fernández for review.

"Shit, who wrote this?" Fernández burst out. "It sounds like all you want is to get back what you lost. You have to write something more progressive, more political. We'll get somebody to help you."

So John Mallett flew down from Washington and introduced himself to the contras as "George."

Then thirty-five, Mallett was a huge bear of a man, six five maybe, with a brown mustache and bushy hair, graying at the temples, parted on the left. He had poor eyes, so that he peered down at Chamorro and the other Nicaraguans through thick glasses. One of Mallett's first tasks was to write a completely new political manifesto for the FDN. Then, before the December 8, 1982, press conference in the Fort Lauderdale Hilton at which the CIA unveiled its directorate, Mallett coached the Nicaraguans carefully about the questions journalists were likely to ask. One thing was very important, he said: The Nicaraguans were to say they had no contact with U.S. government officials. The press conference went smoothly. Chamorro and the others denied indignantly that they were receiving CIA backing.

The men portrayed themselves as a group of concerned Nicaraguan patriots who'd been meeting spontaneously in one another's homes in exile, struggling to forge an independent democratic leadership that could oppose Marxism in their land. In reality, they hardly knew one another. Alfonso Callejas, a former Nicaraguan vice-president whom the CIA had recruited as another director, had flown in at the last moment from Texas, where he was living in exile. Chamorro had never met him, nor had he met Bermúdez, who flew up from Honduras. None of the directors, except Bermúdez, had the slightest idea how the army was shaping up.

Weeks later, the CIA added another recruit to the new directorate. Adolfo Calero, then fifty-two, a 1953 Notre Dame graduate, was the manager of Managua's Coca-Cola bottling plant. Although he was married into the Somoza clan, Calero had been a prominent Conservative Party activist, and Somoza had even jailed him briefly during a business strike. But Chamorro believed Calero had worked for the CIA in Nicaragua for a long time, serving as a conduit of funds from the U.S. embassy to various student and labor organizations. Now Tony Feldman persuaded Calero to go into exile to join the FDN. Feldman saw Calero as the perfect FDN leader. He was tall, maybe six three, with receding silver hair, and despite an acne-pocked face, he cut a commanding figure. He spoke English with a Southern accent, and he wore his Notre Dame class ring everywhere. Within a few weeks, Calero had become "President of the National Directorate and Commander-in-Chief of the FDN Armed Force."[39]

The CIA set up its new FDN directorate with offices in an elegant suite at the David Williams Hotel in Coral Gables, and Fernández worked out some administrative details. At first, Fernández paid Chamorro and the others lavishly for expenses, handing them stacks of hundred-dollar bills from a briefcase. He was adamant about receipts.

"They have a little old lady in Washington who'll be very upset if we don't get receipts," Fernández liked to tell Chamorro.

Later Fernández negotiated a system of monthly base salaries, with a sliding scale to account for directors' dependents and other factors. Chamorro received two thousand dollars a month; others got more. Calero, for instance, argued forcefully that he'd given up a good job and left behind a sumptuous Managua home that the Sandinistas had seized when his FDN involvement became public. He wanted more. Calero also negotiated for life insurance. The question of taxes came up. Should the directors declare? Langley said no.[40]

The process of recruiting the FDN directorate seemed so mechanical to Chamorro and others that it suggested the Agency had done it before. It had, two decades earlier. In 1961, the CIA had carried out a remarkably similar exercise, building its Bay of Pigs invasion force, the 2506 Brigade.

There were striking similarities between the two. As with the National Guardsmen of the FDN, an important minority of the members of the 2506 Brigade had been officers in the defeated army of Cuban dictator Fulgencio Batista. As with the FDN, the CIA made "family aid" payments to 2506 Brigade officers, a small salary that allowed fighters to train for war full time, but also created dependence. The parallels were, however, nowhere more striking than in the political sphere. In advance of the Bay of Pigs, CIA agents recruited Cuban exile politicians to serve on a puppet front, known as the "Frente," whose members posed as independent patriots. Later, when the CIA grew annoyed at the Cuban Frente's rightist image, the Agency dissolved it to form a new, more liberal group, known as the Cuban Revolutionary Council. The CIA would repeat the pattern several times with the FDN.[41]

1983

Edgar Chamorro moved to Tegucigalpa in early 1983 to take over the FDN's public-relations effort, where he found that the CIA was thinking big: The CIA gave Chamorro a thirty-thousand-dollar monthly budget that paid for a staff of nearly twenty. They managed the Radio 15th of September, which broadcast FDN propaganda to Nicaragua from a shortwave transmitter perched atop a volcanic slope behind the U.S. embassy, and also began publishing a slick FDN monthly, *Comandos*, with feature articles on the mounting size and sophistication of the rebel force and praise for the dedication and vision of its leaders. Chamorro oversaw another CIA fund used each month to bribe Honduran journalists—"to smooth things over, exaggerate the good things, diminish the bad things, be soft on us, tell half-lies," as he put it later. And there was also a CIA program to bribe officials in the main headquarters of the Honduran telephone utility, Hondutel, paying them to monitor all the news—papers, radio, and television—flowing across telephone lines.

The CIA's John Mallett had made a parallel move to Tegucigalpa at about the same time as Chamorro, taking up diplomatic cover as a Second Secretary in the U.S. embassy. Actually, he became Donald Winters's deputy chief of station, Chamorro's handler, and they worked together. Meeting daily over coffee at an FDN safe house, Mallett and Chamorro would exchange impressions about the Radio 15 broadcasts, discuss the latest news out of the U.S. Congress, plan for impending visits to Tegucigalpa by U.S. leaders, and so on. Chamorro came to like Mallett. He was well-spoken, a bit of an intellectual, and he argued his positions clearly and with authority. He seemed as if he'd been around.

He had. Mallett had grown up in Central America, the son of an executive of the United Fruit Company, the firm that symbolized American regional domination. After Mallett graduated from Johns Hopkins University in 1966, he joined the army and became an intelligence officer. The Vietnam War was under way, but because Mallett's Spanish was native and his familiarity with Latin America intimate, his superiors decided to station him at the army's Southern Command in Panama rather than send him to Asia. Then the CIA recruited him, and Mallett joined the U.S. embassy in Santiago in the aftermath of Gen. Augusto Pinochet's 1973 coup in Chile. In May 1980, he took up a posting under diplomatic cover at the U.S. embassy in Managua. That was a tough period: poking about with the fledgling anti-Sandinista opposition, listening to the daily government diatribes against the United States, watching the revolution flex its muscles. Eventually, Sandinista intelligence quietly identified him as CIA, but he was out of Managua before his name was ever publicized—on to his new assignment managing the FDN. Now he was "George," or, to most contras, "Jorgón"—Big George.[42]

Mallett didn't work only with Chamorro. Perhaps his closest FDN contact came to be Aristides Sánchez, then working as Bermúdez's civilian partner, who had become the FDN's major behind-the-scenes fixer and manipulator. Sánchez would rarely do anything important without calling the CIA agent. Some FDN officers around the elegant general staff headquarters, located in the exclusive Tegucigalpa suburb of Ciudad Nueva, began to kid Sánchez about his dependency. "The gringos are the ones putting up the money," Sánchez would respond.[43]

For his part, much of what Mallett knew about the FDN army itself came from Sánchez, so the towering CIA agent and the Machiavellian former landowner worked together to unplug the counterrevolutionary army's bottlenecks. The FDN had carved out an entire subterranean world—the rebel army's rear guard—and it was growing fast. There were hundreds of problems associated with running the string of CIA warehouses scattered around Tegucigalpa's industrial parks, with stocking the prodigious tonnages of food, clothing, and other supplies moving to the army, and with storing and moving weaponry and munitions to the troops. The armaments were a particularly touchy business, so the CIA recruited professional logistics people and brought them from Miami to keep inventories and make sure there was no leakage. A human services staff channeled food out to the combatants' families that were squatting in warrens of refugee huts ringing all the major rebel camps. These and all the other FDN people on the CIA payroll—the pilots, mechanics, kickers, warehousemen, doctors, dentists, optometrists, nurses, messengers, office boys, typists, secretaries, translators, broadcasters, drivers, electricians—were living and working in a growing network of Tegucigalpa safe houses. There were scores of others, guards and cooks and cleaning people, just to keep up the FDN real estate. The CIA had set up a bogus lumber company to rent the dozens of safe houses, which over time had become another administrative challenge. Joe Fernández visited Tegucigalpa, and he took that one on himself, renting a car, visiting the embassy, and then making the rounds of the FDN's rental properties. He tried to visit them all, making sure they were all in order and worth the price.[44]

Another complexity was the payroll. Just about everybody except the foot soldiers doing the fighting was getting paid, so there had to be bankers and accountants, paymasters and bagmen.

With the FDN directors, the system was tidy—neat monthly deposits to their Miami bank accounts. But the FDN rear guard in Tegucigalpa and the officer corps had to be paid in cash. The CIA brought in hardened steel safes to store the money it was turning over each month to the FDN in suitcases.

The money, not surprisingly, was soon stoking the passions of a rivalry. Neither Bermúdez nor Sánchez had welcomed the CIA's sudden, unilateral decision to install Calero as the master of the FDN domain. The way they saw it, Calero hadn't paid any dues during the lean years of the September 15 Legion. He hadn't helped bring the Project together. How could he pretend now to be "Commander in Chief"? The tensions took further substance as Calero began to flex his muscles, using his CIA backing to put his own people in the FDN's most lucrative positions.

From the beginning, the CIA had provided Bermúdez with cash to administer the army (his $2,750 monthly salary was deposited in his Miami bank account), but in addition, he had enjoyed the power to fix his officers' salaries, and at times he'd been high-handed. This caused frictions, leading the CIA to urge a standardization of officers' salaries: Staff officers would receive from one thousand to two thousand dollars monthly; regional commanders would get eight hundred; task force and group leaders four hundred or less. But even so, Bermúdez retained the power to put cronies on the payroll. There was no FDN "navy," for instance, but Bermúdez nonetheless installed an old buddy from the Guard, Col. Isidro Sandino, as the navy commander and listed him for monthly CIA payments.

Bermúdez could also purge. "Strike him from the list," he could say if somebody annoyed him, and the CIA funds would stop. That was power. But in addition to paying their salaries, the CIA had also budgeted Bermúdez, and Aristides Sánchez, with extra petty cash to resolve the army's minor problems. By counting out fifty lempiras to this sick commander, or arriving at a Tegucigalpa flat with a hundred lempiras for the pregnant wife of that fighter, both Bermúdez and Sánchez curried favor with the corps. "Grease," U.S. officials called the cash: the lubricant that kept the FDN rolling smoothly, quieting occasional squeaks of discontent. It was a pattern the Nicaraguans recognized from the Somoza years, when "El Jefe" handed out boxes of liquor-filled candy during visits to poor neighborhoods.

Now, however, Calero was in town, he had CIA backing, and he had his own people to keep happy. If Bermúdez paid the army, Calero took charge of the CIA's payments to the FDN rear guard, and soon Calero, too, had his patronage list. He appointed a relative, Orlando Montealegre, as the paymaster, and installed him in a new CIA-paid safe house. Montealegre, in turn, built an entire staff of men to work Tegucigalpa's streets, searching for the best black-market rate on lempiras before each rebel payday.

5

Dirty War

Mike Lima had an appetite for war, and 1983 was a feast. Throughout the year, he led four hundred heavily armed contras through northern Nicaragua, attacking state-owned farms, blowing up power lines, and executing government officials. He fought with singular intensity and flair. Mike Lima's brand of warfare was exactly what the CIA had in mind for Nicaragua.

Colonel Doty had marked the Nicaraguan map into several war zones, and the FDN general staff, following the CIA strategy, had assigned Mike Lima the vast farming region of lower Jinotega. It was an area of coffee *fincas* straddling mountain highlands and cattle ranches nestled in river valleys. Like other contra task force commanders under the CIA's 1983 campaign plan, Mike Lima was instructed to maneuver through his zone, bloodying the enemy and destroying economic targets, especially farm machinery and road equipment. And he was to try to seize a town, even briefly, to publicize the mounting contra challenge to Sandinista rule.

Mike Lima carried out his marching orders in exuberant style. He named his task force the Diriangén, after an indigenous Nicaraguan warrior, and deployed his four hundred men through valleys and ridges in a single, serpentine infantry column more than three miles long from point man to rear guard. Mike Lima himself, astride a white steed he'd rustled from a state farm, cantered alongside with a thirty-man staff escort.

He came to love the burning of government trucks after a deadly ambush: the shattered glass, the blood on the pavement, the rush of flame.

By mid-year, Mike Lima had racked up the most successful combat record of any rebel field commander. His campaigns were the most aggressive, his sabotage the most destructive, his ambushes the deadliest. His men, in jest, began calling him "Napoleon."

Despite his rising prominence, the Sandinistas had still not figured out that Mike Lima's real name was Luis Moreno. Both his parents were still living quietly in Managua's San Judas barrio, raising the five of their ten children younger than Luis. Their continuing anonymity even allowed them to drive north 140 miles during the Sandinistas' Fourth Anniversary of the Revolution festivities on July 19 for a secret reunion with their son at an uncle's home in the village of San Juan Telpaneca. Mike Lima marched to meet his family at the head of a detachment of heavily armed contras. His parents beamed with pride, their eyes wide at the sight of all the U.S. weaponry.[1]

Still, Lima was just twenty-four, and over the year there occurred what his men would later call "anomalies." Perhaps they were a result of his intoxicating success and sudden, life-and-death powers.

"He's a man with compulsions to kill and to rape," one of the officers who served under him would recall later.

Rumors lingered later about how he forced his way with peasant girls, ordering his men to carry them off to secluded farm sites to await his arrival for a cat-and-mouse game of coercive lust. Other stories circulated about his murder of a commando named Antonio Villagra. Mike Lima had been drinking at a Honduran farm near one of the base camps with Villagra and a handful of other commandos. Nobody recalled the substance of the dispute, but a woman, apparently Villagra's girlfriend, was involved. Villagra drew a pistol, but several commandos wrestled it away. Then Lima pulled out his own side arm and pumped most of a clip of bullets into Villagra's chest at close range. One version circulated that Lima ordered Villagra buried on the spot, then several days later ordered him dug up and moved.[2]

The murder of Antonio Villagra was one of several Lima committed in 1983. Most occurred inside Nicaragua, in the moral twilight of a war that was mounting in intensity and bitterness. He would speak candidly of these killings later, at the war's end, not with remorse, but with the introspection of hindsight.

"I killed a lot of people," Lima would recall. "But I considered it just part of my profession."[3]

If his CIA handlers disapproved of any of the "anomalies," they never let on. Though Mike Lima's image as one of Somoza's discredited ex-Guards wasn't the best—he wasn't a romantic peasant insurgent like Tigrillo—he was nevertheless bloodying the Sandinistas inside Nicaragua. That's what counted to the CIA. Mike Lima was a champion, and they praised him generously whenever he marched back to the border bases in Honduras to resupply his troops. The applause was loudest after his October 18, 1983, attack on the town of Pantasma, eighty miles north of Managua.

Militarily, Lima's attack on Pantasma was a brilliant surprise strike, a classic town takeover—one of the few that the rebel forces ever achieved. It was also one of the most destructive contra rampages in the entire war. The Sandinista government called the attack a "massacre" and an "atrocity." Busing hundreds of international visitors up from Managua to tour the town over the following years, government guides sought to turn Pantasma into a premiere example of contra plunder and havoc that endured for the rest of the war.

But Lima's commanders saw things differently. They saw Pantasma as a virtuoso performance. FDN propagandists crowed about the rebel victory on Radio 15th of September for months. Mike Lima's CIA handlers were jubilant.

October 1983

For more than a month before his attack on Pantasma, Mike Lima and the Diriangén had been wandering across northern Nicaragua, skirmishing with government forces, ambushing an occasional convoy, looking for a target of opportunity. By late September, he was short of supplies. For weeks, he had been radioing Honduras, calling for one of the new supply airdrops that the general staff had promised. Finally, the drop had come: crates and crates of the wrong ammunition. They contained shells for FAL rifles, while Lima's men were carrying AK-47s. Nor were there any boots, nor cash to buy food.

So Mike Lima decided to seize a town with a bank. In his operating zone, there were banks in only four towns: San Juan, Yalí, San Rafael del Norte, and Pantasma. He marched his men in a vast arc, preparing to attack each of the first three, but chance combat alerted each town to the contra presence. Finally, Lima feinted with a few contra platoons as though preparing to attack Yalí, then forced his men to march at double time through the night to the east, regrouping his entire task force at a hacienda he'd chosen as a staging area just ten miles west of Pantasma. On the eve of the attack, Lima called together his twenty-five top officers. He didn't have to introduce his men to the geography of the town; most were from nearby villages.

Pantasma, a settlement of timber shacks and stores where cowboys and minor coffee farmers rode mule-back to buy supplies, sat on the fertile floor of a broad valley fifteen miles north of Jinotega's provincial capital. Spruce-covered ridges loomed to the south and north. The town's internal geography was linear; homes, stores, offices, warehouses, and garrisons lined a straight gravel road for nearly four miles through the valley.

Mike Lima assigned targets, ordering his men to assault militia posts guarding the bank and other government offices, the fifteen-man Sandinista police outpost, and—the town's principal defense—an army battalion headquartered in a roadside garrison. Munitions stockpiled at the battalion could supply the Diriangén for months, he told his men. He arranged an ambush along the road leading from Jinotega, to hit arriving army reinforcements. He sent other rebels to attack two Sandinista cooperatives near Pantasma defended by some 125 militiamen. Finally, he ordered another unit to hit the Ministry of Construction yard on the town's far northern edge, where a dozen dump trucks and other construction machines were parked. The government was punching a new gravel road north to the Honduran border, hailing it as a major contribution to economic development, but the road had another military purpose, enabling military convoys to move, fast, all the way to the border for anti-rebel operations.

Pacing before his men under a harvest moon, Mike Lima outlined the stakes. The risks were high, very high, he said. If the Diriangén attacked but failed to overrun an exposed town like Pantasma, it could be pounded by a terrible Sandinista counterattack. Retreat would be bloody. He knew everybody was exhausted, but he wanted this attack to leave an impression on the Sandinistas, to say something about what kind of men were fighting in the FDN.

"I'm tired of fighting for hilltops. Let's seize a real prize," Lima said. "We have to sacrifice. Take this town at all costs!"

He ordered his men into a second night of double-time march, east across the mud of the valley floor toward Pantasma. To ensure that the Diriangén's lightning move would raise no alarm, Lima and a squad of his best men, wearing captured Sandinista army uniforms, led the way and detained every peasant who chanced across their path. The contra units slipped into positions in and around the town under cover of darkness. Mike Lima himself, along with a staff detachment of sixty, quietly penetrated to the center of Pantasma, setting up a radio command post in the town school. Then, just before dawn on October 18, Mike Lima's men opened fire.

Much of the town fell within an hour. Armed activists at the Sandinista Front's party headquarters put up the least resistance; taken completely by surprise, they fled the town. Eight militiamen on guard at the state-run Agrarian Development Bank offices gave up without a shot. Within minutes, the contras were carrying off bags stuffed with 830,000 cordobas—then worth about $30,000. The rebels sent the prisoners from the bank to Lima's command post, then set the bank afire. Across the road at Encafe, the government coffee agency, and at the warehouse of the Agrarian Reform Ministry, the rebels encountered only minimal gunfire. Inside, they put to the torch more than a dozen tractors and jeeps. At the government medical clinic, a doctor and three nurses emerged pleading for their lives. Mike Lima's men ordered them to load all their medicines onto mules.

Other offices weren't so easily taken. The Sandinista Police fought fiercely from inside their sandbagged command post, and after a half hour of combat made a strategic retreat, crossing the road through a culvert and taking up positions in a privately owned sawmill. From there, they drew the first contra blood with sniper fire. Several dozen Sandinista militiamen at a farming collective a half-mile away took up good defensive positions; only slowly, over several hours, were the contras` able to overwhelm them. The attack on the army battalion headquarters, the town's principal defense, came late, and from the start it was tough going because of fire from a government machine-gun nest. The most surprising resistance came from ten Education Ministry employees who holed up inside their offices, a warehouse made of wooden planks, piled inside with bags of food. Seven employees were teachers, three were women. Armed only with Czech automatic rifles but with plenty of revolutionary zeal, they refused to yield to the contra calls for surrender.

"Eat shit, Guardia swine!" the teachers yelled from inside the building. "We're not chocolate-assed militias. We're Sandinistas!" Some thirty-five contras had surrounded the offices with automatic rifles, a machine gun, and grenade launchers, and the teachers' insults threw the contra company leader into a rage.

"Blast the fuckers!" he shouted to his men. Moments later, a grenade slammed into the building, showering the teachers in burning phosphorus and setting the walls ablaze. Hundreds of Pantasma residents heard the teachers' screams as the building collapsed in flames around them.

The explosions aroused emotions on all sides. One of Lima's squad leaders took fire from the offices of the government's grain distribution agency. Enraged, the contra charged the office, killing two defenders and seizing two prisoners, one of them wounded. These he dragged into the road, where before dozens of residents he executed them both with a burst of automatic-rifle fire.

Mike Lima, a mile to the northeast at his command post in the Pantasma school, ordered a shack-by-shack search of the town for arms, Sandinista documents, or government officials. Contra fighters ordered residents to the plaza in front of the school, separating those who were wearing combat boots or who for some other reason looked like Sandinistas. By 7 A.M., more than five hundred terrified residents jammed the plaza, standing in silent rows facing the school. Lima's men were guarding twenty Sandinista suspects at one side.

Mike Lima was, intermittently, shouting through a field radio to his company commanders, then stalking back and forth in front of the building crowd. His men, still attacking the battalion and the Police garrisons, were facing tough resistance. He didn't know how strong the Sandinista defenders were at either stronghold. He wanted his prisoners to tell him—right away. He ordered aides to pull out two men they believed were Sandinista military leaders, one an army lieutenant, the other a local officer for State Security, the Sandinista political police.

"If you don't cooperate, you're going to die!" Lima shouted at the two men. "Now, how many Sandinistas are at the battalion?" The prisoners stood mute. Mike Lima signaled to one of his soldiers, who dragged the lieutenant off and stood him against a wall, a few yards away. Then the contra blasted him in the face with several shots from an AK-47 rifle. Lima turned back to the other prisoner.

"How many Sandinistas are at the Police?" Lima screamed at the State Security officer. Silence. A contra shot him, too, next to his comrade-in-arms.

At that, first one, then several other prisoners, agreed to cooperate. There were only a handful of police in the sawmill, they said.

Mike Lima also used his encounter with the people of Pantasma to propagate his version of the political message of the contras' cause. To Lima, that message was starkly simple. In his speech, he didn't talk about Sandinista meddling in farming and commerce; he didn't mention the Sandinistas' intolerance for those peasants who were less than full-bore revolutionaries. He just wanted the people to know that the contras were determined, and implacable.

He and some of his men "gave long speeches in which we made it clear that we were willing to take this fight to the final consequences," Mike Lima remembered later. "We wanted to show those peasants, and the people of Nicaragua, that we were ready to do anything."

Some of the townspeople seemed pleased by the executions of two Sandinistas they said they hated, but many others remained mute with fear.

Armed with the information he'd extracted from the prisoners, Mike Lima ordered a new assault. His commandos rushed the mill with knives drawn, stabbing to death the final handful of Sandinistas. The wooden structure, already blazing, burned to the ground.

Most of Pantasma was in the hands of contras who were exhausted, ravenous, and lost in the delirium of certain victory. They slaughtered a pig; soon it was roasting over an open fire. Some townspeople began to bring out tortillas, beans, and beer. Many contras were soon feeling the drink. Some fanned out for mischief, stealing combat boots off residents' feet, dragging teenage girls into the weeds. For a while, Mike Lima lost control of his men, but he thought they deserved a break. He was throwing back beers himself. Buying boots, clothing, and food from local merchants with the booty from the bank, he spent 430,000 cordobas that afternoon, the equivalent of about $14,000.

Meanwhile, two miles to the north, the battle still raged at the battalion. By early afternoon, however, Mike Lima's men knocked out the machine gun, allowing them to storm close enough to fire a rocket-propelled grenade. The projectile crashed into the battalion's main munitions stockpile, setting off a blast that hurled men and metal hundreds of feet and sent a mushroom cloud of inky soot billowing skyward. Those Sandinista soldiers who survived fled. It was a lucky shot; it ended the army's resistance. On the other hand, it utterly destroyed the arms stockpile that had been Mike Lima's major objective.

The only prize remaining was the construction yard, where militiamen forced the attackers to fight for every truck. But eventually the yard fell, and the Diriangén's demolitions men went to work. They burned ten government dump trucks and crippled six heavy road graders.

Finally, Mike Lima rallied his drunken troops and ordered a retreat to a nearby hacienda. He left behind the bodies of nearly fifty dead soldiers, police, militiamen, and residents—including the charred remains of seven teachers—strewn amid the ruins of every government installation in town. The government estimated the damage at $2 million to the road equipment alone.

Mike Lima had utterly vanquished his Sandinista foe, but, ironically, he was still short of munitions and other supplies. He marched his men north, radioing for another CIA airdrop. A Sandinista battalion caught up with him just days later, forcing him to retreat, on the run for two weeks, all the way north to the Honduran border.

In mid-November, he and his men, exhausted and starving, staggered into the FDN recruiting base at Banco Grande, a clearing on the banks of the Coco River several days' march northeast of the Las Vegas salient. Mike Lima got a hero's welcome. The CIA dispatched a helicopter to Banco Grande to fly him to Tegucigalpa, where Alex clapped him on the back, and carried him to a laudatory tête-à-tête with Colonel Doty in a CIA safe house.

"I was the CIA's golden boy," Lima recalled later.[4]

1983

If Mike Lima's attack on Pantasma was remembered as a classic contra strike, it was only one of a type. Like the Diriangén, many other CIA-supplied FDN units were carrying out sabotage and executions inside Nicaragua during 1983. The war was escalating. World attention was riveted on Nicaragua as the destruction mounted.

During the same period, however, what amounted to a second front in the war opened in Honduras, a largely silent, secret campaign of torture and murder. Hundreds died in and around the rebels' border camps, along Honduran roadsides, and in the back streets of Tegucigalpa. It was a dirty war waged largely by the ex–National Guardsmen commanding the contra army.

Some of the victims were leftist labor and student leaders. The Honduran Army, with American support, was targeting and systematically eliminating "subversives," suspected arms traffickers, as well as a small Honduran guerrilla movement. Colonel Lau's FDN counterintelligence squads made hits on contract to the Hondurans. These murders were centrally planned and coordinated.

Scores, perhaps hundreds of other murders, however, resulted from the caprice of the ex-Guardsmen installed in command of each of the half dozen FDN base camps, where they wielded life-and-death power over thousands of rebel recruits. The killing flourished against the bloody backdrop of the no-holds-barred counterinsurgency warfare the Reagan Administration was financing throughout Central America. In and around the base camps, there were murders of prisoners and recruits, murders of suspected spies and confirmed rivals, murders of rejected lovers and personal enemies.

In the southern province of Choluteca, there were killings in and around the FDN camp called Zebra, where ex-Lieutenant Armando "The Policeman" López and former EEBI Private Marcos "Black Dimas" Navarro were in command. To the east near the border hamlet of Arenales, the bloody reports focused on the FDN camp called Pino Uno.[5] In 1983, in fact, virtually every FDN base camp had its team of assassins, its clandestine graveyard, its dark stories.[6]

Some of the worst surrounded La Lodosa, "The Mudhole," where former Sgt. Benito Bravo, pseudonym "Mack," was in command.

Mack had prospered since he and Mike Lima had trained Tigrillo's men at La Lodosa. In fact, compared to his days as a sergeant in Somoza's EEBI, Mack had really risen in the world. By mid-1983, he had money, women, and plenty of raw power.

Mack had formed his own Nicarao Task Force of several hundred commandos, and following Colonel Doty's 1983 campaign plan, Mack's men were attacking towns and villages in the Nicaraguan border province of Nueva Segovia, just south of La Lodosa. But they never distinguished themselves. Mack botched the Nicarao's biggest operation of the year, an attempt to seize the town of Ocotal, by arriving late for the attack and showing little stomach for combat. But despite his scant military success, things had rarely been better for him personally.

As a military commander, Mack was demonstrating how much he'd learned from the Somozas. While his men were fighting in Nicaragua, he hung back in Honduras. He'd expanded his border domain from La Lodosa, establishing a couple of smaller bases nearby, in the same border mountains just south of the Honduran town of El Paraíso. He was earning a thousand dollars a month from the CIA as one of the FDN's top commanders, and he'd forged ties with Bermúdez, the Argentines, and some of the CIA men. Bermúdez had assigned him a U.S.-supplied yellow Toyota Land Cruiser. He even had a driver!

Sexually, Mack's life was a dream. He'd appointed one of his longtime lovers, a silent, twenty-three-year-old Miskito woman named "Clarita," as his radio operator at La Lodosa. His men were bringing plenty of other light-skinned northern Nicaraguan girls back to La Lodosa from incursions as "recruits," and Mack was having his way with them, too. But most of the time, Mack wasn't even staying overnight in the bases. His driver, a Honduran, owned a house in El Paraíso, the lovely palm-shaded village a few miles down the slope from La Lodosa. The driver fixed the house up for Mack's use, and Mack raised a military antenna there and installed one of his U.S.-supplied field radios. That way he could communicate with his men while leading a vigorous social life in town—dining, drinking, and pursuing his romantic liaisons. Soon he had a child by his driver's sister, but there were other women, too, and he couldn't very well bring them to his driver's house. So Mack spent many nights in the Hotel Eva, a Spanish-style rooming house with green tile floors facing the park. Eventually, he sired several children in El Paraíso.

A routine developed. Evenings, Mack would spend in El Paraíso or Danlí. Mornings, he'd drive back up into the mountains to La Lodosa or out to his other base at Alauca—almost like a farmer visiting his fields—to see how the war was going.

At the camps, Mack had surrounded himself with old colleagues from the National Guard. His best friend and executive officer was José Espinales, known as "Zero-Three," a muscular, mustachioed twenty-nine-year-old former National Guard police sergeant. His intelligence officer was Ramón Peña Rodríguez, "Z-Two," a hunched, forty-five-year-old former National Guard police corporal. Another close aide was Britolde Cruz, "X-Seven," a former Guard enlisted man with sinewy muscles and hard eyes who'd been with Mack and Bermúdez in the 1965 Dominican Republic intervention. They were truculent men, embittered by their defeat in the first war and now paranoid about Sandinista infiltration, men who killed as though they enjoyed it. Their weapons of choice were wire for strangling and heavy knives for slashing.

One man who found this out firsthand was Dr. Francisco Rugama. The son of a respected Nicaraguan National Guard physician, Rugama had graduated from a Mexican medical school in 1979. He returned to Sandinista Nicaragua to practice medicine for two years, then traveled into exile in New Orleans. Recruited into the contra medical corps in February 1983 at age twenty-seven, Rugama worked at the FDN's main Támara clinic for a couple of months, then, in May 1983, was sent to La Lodosa as the task force doctor for Mack's Nicarao.

Rugama supervised the building of a little clinic, just a bamboo hut on a hill with a couple of cots, but suitable for bullet extractions and other simple treatments. In his first days at La Lodosa, Rugama saw that many of the commandos of the Nicarao were terrified of Zero-Three, and of Mack. The reason, he soon discovered, was that they were killing people.

Soon after Rugama's arrival, Mack's men dragged in three Nicaraguan prisoners, peasants they had seized during an incursion: a father in his forties, his son, and a nephew, both about twenty. Mack's men suspected that they were Sandinista informers, so they lashed them to a tree—that's how all prisoners were held—pending an "investigation." In the meantime, one of Mack's men beat them bloody. It wasn't an interrogation, Rugama recalled later. Mack's men just took advantage of the opportunity to torment the prisoners. Soon Mack learned from FDN collaborators that they were not informers; they were just peasants. But, in Mack's mind, they were still a problem: Now they knew the location of his main base camp.

The next morning, the prisoners were gone. What happened to them? Rugama asked. Mack said they'd gone back to Nicaragua. Three days later, Rugama noticed a dog clawing the ground a few yards from his clinic. Rugama watched more closely. The dog unearthed a human foot. Upon investigating, Rugama discovered the three men's bodies. He went to Mack.

"The bodies of those peasants are buried up there by the clinic. A dog is digging them up," Rugama told Mack.

"Mack told me to be quiet about it—for my own safety," Rugama recalled. Mack ordered rebel fighters to rebury the men. Rugama asked several of his patients what had happened to the peasants. He learned that Mack had ordered them hung.

Not long thereafter, Rugama was treating a commando known by the pseudonym "El Tío" (The Uncle). One day El Tío failed to show up at the clinic. When Rugama began to ask around for him, other fighters told Rugama that Mack had fallen in love with the commando's girlfriend and had ordered El Tío murdered. Rugama was stunned, unbelieving. Then he saw Mack with El Tío's girl.

Rugama learned details of more than a dozen murders in Mack's camp in a period of weeks in mid-1983. Several of the victims were commandos whom Mack or Zero-Three murdered in punishment for minor camp infractions. After Rugama connected Zero-Three to several of the murders, Mack's deputy turned on the young doctor himself. Rugama fled the camp, returning to the Támara clinic. Shaken, he reported the La Lodosa assassinations to Colonel Bermúdez, to the FDN general staff, and to the head of the FDN medical corps, Dr. Ernesto Matamoros, but nothing was done to Mack. Eventually Rugama left the FDN in disgust.

Another contra who bore witness to Mack's killings was Marlon Blandón, a former Guard lieutenant recruited into the FDN officers corps from exile in Costa Rica and installed as Mack's operations officer at La Lodosa. Later, Mack transferred Blandón to his second border base, which he had established outside the nearby Honduran hamlet of Alauca. On a rainy day shortly after Blandón's arrival at Alauca, a Honduran farmer who lived adjacent to Mack's base approached Blandón and pointed up a slope.

"Look, there are some poor bastards up there whose bodies are sticking out of the ground," the peasant told Blandón. "It looks bad. Why don't you send some men to bury them?"

After hiking up the hill, Blandón found some twenty shallow graves on the side of a grade. Torrents of rain had eroded the topsoil, uncovering several bodies. Some wore commandos' uniforms, others were in peasant garb. Several fighters told Blandón that Z-Two—Peña Rodríguez, Mack's intelligence officer—had executed most of the dead. Blandón approached Mack to report the cemetery.

"Yeah, sometimes I just don't know what to do with Z-Two," Mack told Blandón. "He'll have a prisoner, he'll tie him up and fuck him over. He'll kill him—and he doesn't really get any information."[7]

Few of those who bore witness to the murders at Mack's bases survived. But in August 1983, Blandón and dozens of other commandos watched three rebel officers killed in a chilling display of brutality that appears to have been designed to teach a lesson to potentially insubordinate contras. These—unlike other murders that were simply Mack's whims—were executions ordered by higher officers.

The victims were all ex-Guardsmen. One was Julio César Herrera, twenty-eight, whose pseudonym was "Krill"; the other two are remembered only by their war names, "Cara de Malo" ("Scarface" in English) and "Habakuk." The three had all been staff officers to Pedro Ortiz Centeno, an ex-Guard sergeant turned contra commander known as "Suicide."[8]

Ironically, the joint command of Honduran, Argentine, Nicaraguan, and CIA officers then administering the war accused the men of committing their *own* camp murders, with Krill alone said to have killed more than thirty contra recruits over a period of months. But the joint command was more upset about accusations that Suicide had embezzled contra funds by padding task force payrolls and even, perhaps, selling weapons to El Salvador's Marxist guerrillas.[9] Most serious to the contra leadership was the mounting challenge that Suicide and his men represented to their own authority. The last straw came when Suicide, clutching an M-60 machine gun, led his men in a brief seizure of the Ciudad Nueva safe house where Bermúdez and his general staff were living. That frightened everyone.

The war's managers decided to set an example to other contra units. Suicide and his men were seized and held under extremely tight security, bound and confined for about a week in separate closets in an old farmhouse at La Quinta, where they were interrogated by Argentine and Honduran military officers.

FDN and CIA officers later said that Suicide and his men were "court-martialed" by a panel of ex-Guardsmen before their executions, but some contra officers later expressed doubts that there was any such formality.[10] Several accounts have circulated describing how Suicide was killed, but no eyewitness has ever stepped forward to confirm details. There were, however, plenty of eyewitnesses to the executions of Habakuk, Cara de Malo, and Krill. Mack and his men did the dirty work.

The FDN general staff radioed Mack at La Lodosa, calling him in for a meeting at La Quinta, Blandón recalled. With Blandón, his bodyguard, and driver, Mack drove eighty miles west to the Honduran capital, finally pulling his Land Cruiser up the lane into La Quinta. Mack entered the crumbling farmhouse serving as FDN offices to meet with the general staff while Blandón waited in an outer room. About an hour later, Mack emerged with his orders.

From La Quinta, Mack radioed to Zero-Three at La Lodosa, telling him to march with about forty soldiers to an agreed-upon meeting place in the border mountains. Bring picks and shovels, Mack said.

Another Toyota Land Cruiser was brought to the farmhouse at La Quinta, and the three blindfolded prisoners were dragged out. Their wrists were handcuffed and their feet bound with rope. Blandón said he believed they'd already been tortured, but that wasn't clear, because of another problem: Their mouths and noses had been bound tightly with adhesive tape, so breathing was nearly impossible.[11]

The prisoners were shoved into the back of the Land Cruiser and forced to lie down. Since this was a special, joint operation between the Honduran Army and the FDN, a Honduran Army captain participated.

It was past dark by the time the rebel vehicles headed for the border, driving in a virtual convoy: Mack and Blandón in the lead Toyota, the Honduran Army captain in the second, the prisoners in the third, and other jeeps filled with contras following. At Danlí, twenty-five miles from the Nicaraguan border, one of the contras bought gasoline in a portable container, then the convoy drove southwest for half an hour, finally pulling off the dirt road onto a mule trail an hour's march from Mack's Alauca camp. It was about 1 A.M.

Mack's ex-Guardsmen were waiting: Zero-Three, X-Seven, Z-Two. As the rebels climbed out of their jeeps into the chill of the mountain air, the Honduran Army captain asked Mack if they were close to the Nicaraguan border. His orders, the Honduran said, were to bury the prisoners inside Nicaragua—there wasn't to be any trace left of these men. Mack argued—the border was a full day's march away—and the Honduran relented.

There were no farms nearby, and the mule trail was little used, but Mack ordered his men to set up a security perimeter anyway, to order off any peasant who might chance by.

The Honduran captain gave the order for three graves to be dug, and Mack's men set to it with picks and shovels about ten yards off the trail. It was rocky soil, and the digging was tough. After an hour, the graves were only four feet deep, but the Honduran was impatient.

"It's time," he said. "It's late."

Several dozen of Mack's contra fighters stood ringing the jeeps, silent in the night air. The prisoners were lying motionless in the Land Cruiser. Two of Mack's contras opened the rear door, grabbing Habakuk first. They pulled him out like a sack of potatoes, and it wasn't clear to Blandón how much life was left in him after the hours of gagging from the tape. He fell to the ground. When he was pulled to his feet, still bound, one of the contras came up behind him, tossed a length of rope around his neck, and yanked it tight. It took less than a minute.

Habakuk fell limp to the ground. Two contras dragged him by his boots to the edge of one of the graves. Cara de Malo was next. This time, X-Seven was the executioner, and when he pulled the rope tight around Cara de Malo's neck, it was over quickly.

That left Krill, but he was still very conscious. Probably the tape over his nose and mouth was looser, because when the Toyota door opened, he heaved out a muffled, haunting plea that stunned Blandón. His words were just comprehensible.

"Shoot me, please, don't stab me. Don't make me suffer!" Krill pled.

Nobody responded. Instead, Krill was yanked from the jeep. Zero-Three caught hold of Krill's neck from the rear with the cord. Krill's body slumped after about a minute. Two contras began dragging him through the underbrush toward the grave.

Then one of the rebel officers burst out: "Hey! Wait! He's still alive!" It was true. Krill was gasping for air through the crumpled tape. "Please don't kill me in this way!" Krill mumbled.

X-Seven shoved Zero-Three aside in order to climb on top of Krill, planting his knee on the prisoner's chest and curling the cord tight again. After a longer time, Krill was completely limp. X-Seven climbed back to his feet.

But as the gravediggers began dragging Krill toward the pit again, the gasping sobs came back. Krill's rib cage was heaving.

"You son of a bitch!" grunted X-Seven. "We'll see if you survive this one!" He hurled himself back on top of Krill's prostrate body, by now facedown in the dirt. This time the former Guard seized Krill's head with his bare hands, twisting it violently upward and back, until Krill was practically looking straight backward, his spine apparently shattered. Finally, Krill was dead. The struggle had lasted at least twenty minutes.

At the Honduran captain's direction, the gravediggers stripped the three rebel bodies of their handcuffs and boots, then slashed the bottoms of their feet with knives. The Honduran claimed this would permit the bodies to burn more completely. Then the bodies were pitched into the graves. Somebody fetched a can of gas from one of the jeeps. Ignited, the bodies burned like three torches for more than an hour in the Honduran night. Then the smoking ashes were covered. It was nearly 5 A.M. by the time Mack and his aides pulled out.

On the drive to La Lodosa, higher in the mountains, Mack told Blandón that the general staff had ordered him to carry out the executions in front of his men so that they would see the consequences of defying the central command.[12]

Late 1982 and early 1983

Jhonson was a platoon leader in the Special Forces commandos, hidden with his men in isolation at La Quinta and at the CIA's Lepaterique training base. Though he emerged only for sabotage strikes inside Nicaragua, throughout late 1982 and early 1983 Jhonson was hearing dark rumors from commandos visiting La Quinta.

He received his first detailed account of the clandestine violence during one boring weekend when a group of commandos, lying around in hammocks, began trading stories. A new fighter with the pseudonym "Jonathan" told of his own experiences leaving Nicaragua months earlier. He was a twenty-nine-year-old dirt farmer from the northern province of Nueva Segovia, just south of La Lodosa, who, along with other peasants, had fled Nicaragua and joined the contras at La Lodosa. He'd been at the camp for a few months, during which time he saw several of his friends "disappear." Eventually, he, too, had been accused of being an infiltrator and lashed to a tree.

Jonathan's "investigation" by Mack's men—he mentioned Zero-Three, X-Seven, Z-Two, and others—had lasted several harrowing days. He'd given himself up for dead, but in a moment when his interrogators were distracted, he slipped free of his bonds and fled the base. Later he'd made contact with relatives who were also in the FDN, and they persuaded him that he would be safe with the FDN Special Forces. Jonathan claimed that during his ordeal at La Lodosa he'd learned of more than one hundred murders in the camp. Jhonson thought he must be exaggerating, but Jonathan insisted there were unmarked cemeteries all around La Lodosa.

Not long thereafter, Jhonson heard a similar story from another young commando, Antonio González, "The Giant." Jhonson was González's detachment commander, and the boy, trusting Jhonson, called him "Papa."

González was also from Nueva Segovia province, and like many

Nicaraguan border residents, he had many Honduran relatives. González left Lepaterique with a signed FDN leave to visit his Honduran family in El Paraíso, and there he'd learned distressing news: Mack had seized his cousin, accusing him of being an infiltrator. His people were frantic, believing that the cousin would probably be killed.

"They've murdered a lot of commandos out there, Papa," González told Jhonson back at Lepaterique. He wanted help.

Jhonson thought a moment. What could he do? The answer was obvious—go to the Americans. He and his men were under the gringos' responsibility and instruction at Lepaterique. If anybody had the authority to stop the killing, it was the Americans.

"I'll do what I can," Jhonson told González.

It was a Sunday, about 10 A.M., when Jhonson left the wooden barracks where he and the other FDN Special Forces were quartered, and walked the two hundred yards along a stand of pines to the "House of the Gringos," the smaller building divided into little apartments where the CIA instructors lived. There he found Colonel Bill, the hulking, friendly Vietnam veteran who was the chief CIA instructor, sitting in his shorts, cleaning his boots. Jhonson told him he wanted to talk; he had a favor to ask.

Jhonson laid out the problem; one of the Special Forces commandos in training at Lepaterique had a cousin whom Mack was holding prisoner at La Lodosa. He thought they might be torturing him. His family feared for his life. Could Colonel Bill help get him released? Or could he at least make some emergency calls so that they'd treat him fairly?

Colonel Bill seemed shocked. He grabbed a pad and pencil and asked Jhonson to repeat the commando's name, all the details.

"These things shouldn't be happening," he said; he'd investigate. Jhonson thanked him and left.

Jhonson never found out whether the American agent did anything about his plea for help. He was sent away from Lepaterique on a sabotage mission a couple of weeks later, and when he got back, Colonel Bill had been transferred. So had González. Jhonson didn't catch up with the young commando until some months later, in Danlí. González had left the FDN and was working as a stoop laborer on a Honduran farm.

"What happened to your cousin?" Jhonson asked.

"They killed him, Papa," González said.[13]

Late 1983 through mid-1984

Jhonson's report to Colonel Bill was certainly not the first time the Americans running the contra army heard about murders by the FDN's ex-Guardsmen. The reports were flowing into the CIA stations in Nicaragua and Honduras not only from commandos like Jhonson, pleading for help on behalf of friends, but from the network of salaried spies whom Colonel Doty's men had recruited throughout rebel ranks, as well as through their extensive contacts with the Honduran Army's intelligence apparatus.

At the same time, news reports were pouring out of Nicaragua about FDN murders of civilians, and in Honduras, the routine killings in and around the FDN camps had become common knowledge. Members of the U.S. Congress, in fact, were beginning to ask questions. Colonel Doty's boss, Dewey Clarridge, the chief of the Latin American section of the CIA's operations directorate, tried to set the lawmakers straight during a classified briefing in late 1983: Of course there were murders, Clarridge told the congressmen. Yes, FDN fighters had killed civilians. Yes, FDN fighters had murdered Sandinista officials. Yes, FDN fighters had killed leaders of cooperatives, judges, nurses, doctors, Clarridge told them.

"This is a war, a paramilitary operation," Clarridge said.[14]

But Clarridge wasn't only hearing criticism of Bermúdez and his ex-Guardsmen from the liberals in the U.S. Congress. Clarridge had begun channeling funds to another rebel leader, Edén Pastora, a former Sandinista commander building an army in Costa Rica, and now Pastora was refusing to work with Bermúdez.

For a time, the CIA treated the problem as an image question. It started with agents criticizing the fiendish pseudonyms adopted by the FDN fighters. The entire army had taken on animal names: The Serpent, The Wolf, The Shrimp, The Stag, The Deer, The Jaguar, The Ram, The Ostrich.

"What is this, a goddamn zoo?" one CIA agent snapped.

But the zoological pseudonyms were much better than some of the others: The Executioner, Suicide, The Devil, Atila, Vengeance, Ironfoot, Lost Man, Primitive, Trickster. The CIA passed the word along to Bermúdez: Clean up the names. The word went out, and dozens of commandos changed their noms de guerre. The Serpent became "Rubén"; the Executioner became "Iván"; and so on.

The CIA, however, had other, more substantive concerns: thievery, inefficiency. Although commanders like Mike Lima were making a lot of fireworks inside Nicaragua, Clarridge and other CIA men weren't satisfied with the FDN's military progress.

The CIA irritation began with the annoying realization that nearly three years into the war, Bermúdez's military "headquarters"—the safe houses serving as offices and residences for Bermúdez and his general staff—were still in Tegucigalpa. In 1982, Bermúdez had given up the old September 15 Legion safe house in the middle-class neighborhood of Florencia South for a rambling stone-walled affair underneath a stand of eucalyptus trees in the upper-class, suburban barrio of Llanos de Potrero. In 1983, Bermúdez moved up in the world again, this time to an elegant two-story place, all dark wood and balconies, overlooking the Tegucigalpa basin from a lovely hillside lot in the exclusive neighborhood of Ciudad Nueva.

Bermúdez, Sánchez, the general staff, and a whole string of other hangers-on were enjoying themselves amid this old Spanish elegance. Nights were for drinking, for playing the roulette tables at the Hotel Maya casino, for companionship. Colonel Lau and some of the other men on the staff liked chasing Tegucigalpa's whores. For his part, Bermúdez had developed a taste for the teenage girls his men were recruiting in Nicaragua. Bermúdez was inviting them from the base camps back to Ciudad Nueva, one at a time, to try out as his "secretary." The CIA might not have minded Bermúdez's little passions, but living a hundred miles from the FDN base camps—not to mention the battlefield—Bermúdez and his men were paying less and less attention to the war.

The dissipation, moreover, was descending into outright greed. The CIA was channeling tens of thousands of dollars a month to Bermúdez's general staff to pay the "family aid" salaries of his field commanders, and other prodigious sums to buy food for the thousands of FDN fighters. By mid-1983, however, the CIA was picking up lots of complaints about hunger, both in the camps and on the march inside Nicaragua. Alex and Colonel Doty's other CIA men did some checking. They found that many FDN field commanders weren't being paid their salaries. Bermúdez's staff officers were pocketing the money. They were also stealing half the CIA's food budget. Though they routinely shipped only half the necessary beans, rice, and other foodstuffs to the base camps, they were billing the CIA for full rations.[15]

What this meant was that the troops were hungry at a time of mounting CIA ambitions for spectacular military offensives against the Sandinistas. These were the heady weeks following the Reagan Administration's October 1983 invasion of Grenada, and perhaps CIA planners hoped to pave the way for a similar direct intervention in Nicaragua. Colonel Doty urged the FDN to seize a chunk of territory in Nicaragua and establish a field command post—the Americans dubbed it "The Tactical Operations Command"—from which to call in air-supply drops and direct further FDN military campaigns inside Nicaragua. Then the

FDN directorate could declare a "liberated zone" and seek international recognition for a provisional FDN government.

The notion of beating the Sandinistas in a conventional engagement was completely unrealistic. Even a year earlier, when government forces had overrun "Dimas Tigrillo" Baldivia's ill-conceived base at Wina, the Sandinista army had demonstrated that it could deliver crushing blows to any position the FDN tried to seize and hold. Now, by late 1983, Sandinista forces were growing fast. Thousands of tons of new Soviet weapons were pouring into Nicaraguan ports, and Sandinista units were bearing down on FDN units with hundreds of new Soviet howitzers and rocket launchers.[16]

However foolhardy, Doty's plan to seize territory offered the CIA a way to clean up FDN corruption. Once the new Commander of Tactical Operations had been named, the CIA thought, he'd be a kind of theater commander—essentially the FDN's top field officer. Doty could begin channeling all food and other supplies through him, neatly bypassing the FDN general staff in Tegucigalpa. Doty figured he could just cut Bermúdez and his general staff hacks out of the loop.

The man Doty appointed as theater commander was ex-Guard Capt. Hugo Villagra, a former officer in Somoza's EEBI. Villagra had joined the September 15 Legion in 1980, and after serving prison time in Costa Rica for a December 1980 Legion terrorist attack on a radio station in that country, he had rejoined the FDN in 1983. Colonel Doty launched a campaign to build support for Villagra's leadership among other FDN commanders, and throughout November 1983, Doty's CIA agents met with FDN field officers, one-on-one and in groups, discussing the embezzlement of salaries and supplies by the general staff and encouraging the officers to accept Villagra as the FDN's top field officer.

Mike Lima was helicoptered to Tegucigalpa to meet with Colonel Doty and Villagra directly. Doty promised Lima that if he would accept Villagra's leadership, the CIA could guarantee the end of his logistical problems—like the air-supply drops he had received of ammunition that was the wrong calibre for his weapons.

Alex, the young CIA trainer with Caribbean Spanish, did other agitating himself. With Villagra, he helicoptered to Banco Grande, the FDN recruiting base on the banks of the Coco River, for one November meeting with Tigrillo, Lima, Mack, and several other top commanders. Huddling with the FDN officers in the Banco Grande house of a Honduran farmer, Alex warned the commanders that the general staff had been embezzling their salaries. To make his point, he pulled a hundred-dollar bill from an attaché case.

"Have you ever seen one of these?" Alex asked Tigrillo. Tigrillo looked confused.

"We've been paying you five hundred dollars—five of these—every month since last year," Alex told Tigrillo. "The general staff has been stealing them!"

This kind of CIA agitation tapped an angry vein of resentment among FDN officers. Although the CIA had originally planned simply to bypass Bermúdez and his staff with money and supplies, the FDN's rank and file moved quickly to call for their expulsion from the rebel army. Many commanders had long since figured out that Bermúdez and his staff were stealing, and Tigrillo and the other commanders at Banco Grande signed a call for the mass resignation of the FDN's military high command.

Other sectors of the FDN were angry, too. The doctors of the FDN medical corps were upset over corruption in the purchase of medical supplies; almost unanimously, they welcomed Villagra's rise. Furthermore, the fear created by Lau's ruthless counterintelligence dragnets now backfired against the general staff. Lau's men had abducted and killed many commandos suspected as infiltrators, frightening fighters throughout the FDN. Another, larger meeting of dozens of FDN officers at a Tegucigalpa safe house produced a new written petition demanding the resignations of Bermúdez, Lau, and the rest of the staff. The document complained that the staff had for two years lived "300 kilometers from the theater of operations" and that corruption had caused "hunger and lack of attention for our troops." The document also warned that in case of any "violation of the physical integrity of any of the signers," the FDN officers would hold Bermúdez and his staff responsible.

Despite the widespread resentment, the CIA's plot didn't turn out as planned. First, FDN attempts to seize a Tactical Operations Command post inside Nicaragua met with defeat. Colonel Doty had rented a safe house in Danlí for Villagra in late 1983 and equipped it with powerful field radios, topographical maps, and other equipment so that it could serve as his theater command post until the FDN could seize territory inside Nicaragua. In mid-December, Villagra led an FDN force in an attack on a Sandinista outpost near the village of Wanblán, at the southern tip of the Las Vegas salient, while hundreds of other FDN troops attacked the villages of San José de Bocay, El Cuá, La Vigía, and Quilalí. The goal was to tie the Sandinistas down while Villagra established control over an easy-to-supply outpost. But none of the FDN units succeeded in overwhelming Sandinista defenses—Villagra's own forces took a pounding at Wanblán—and the offensive was an utter failure.[17]

And while Doty's military offensive was collapsing in northern Nicaragua, his CIA superiors were changing their minds about

Bermúdez. Within days of the time Doty's men had begun their agitation, the FDN commander, working with his closest associates, Aristides Sánchez and Colonel Lau, had learned of the CIA's effort to displace him. Meeting with a series of FDN officers, bribing several with cash payments to loosen their tongues about the plotting, Bermúdez and Sánchez had soon put together the mosaic of CIA intrigue.

Bermúdez complained to CIA higher-ups. Seeing the dangers in dumping the obedient asset who'd helped construct their entire project, they cut a deal. The CIA would fire the rest of the FDN staff. Bermúdez would stay on and appoint new aides, this time more firmly under his own centralized control. The staff officers would be called "strategic command assistants." Bermúdez would get a new, more glorious title: General Commander of the FDN Strategic Command. In exchange, Bermúdez promised to move his headquarters from Tegucigalpa to the base camps.

Villagra began to sense that the CIA had encouraged him to challenge the FDN leadership, then betrayed him. He drove to Tegucigalpa to see Colonel Doty.

"What happened?" Villagra asked. "I thought I was getting CIA support."

"I'm sorry. I'm just part of a larger hierarchy," Doty told Villagra. "I've got to follow my orders."

Villagra realized that his new title as Tactical Operations Commander wasn't worth much, nor, he figured, was his life. Colonel Lau had targeted him for retribution. He demanded a U.S. visa and fled to Miami.

Villagra was angry, eager to talk publicly about his experiences. He figured the U.S. press would be interested in Bermúdez's thievery, in the rebel army's chaotic leadership, in his own story of CIA manipulation and double-cross, but two days after his exile began, two CIA agents drove to Villagra's temporary lodgings in Kendall, a Miami suburb. Joe Fernández, the forty-six-year-old agent who had helped recruit the FDN directorate a year earlier, had flown from Langley. Donald Winters, the Tegucigalpa station chief, had flown from Honduras. They invited Villagra out for a Coke.

The two men were concerned about the FDN's shoddy leadership, they told Villagra. They knew Villagra had been one of the army's top commanders, and they wanted to hear his own complaints firsthand. They, too, were upset with the corruption and other anomalies; they were working to set things right. Washington was interested, too, in hearing Villagra's complaints firsthand. Would he be willing to fly up to Washington to complain about the anomalies to the CIA directly?

Of course he would, said Villagra. Great, we'll arrange it, they said. Furthermore, they'd be glad to help smooth out any problem Villagra might be encountering with U.S. immigration authorities. In the meantime, Fernández said, there was another important detail: It would be better if Villagra didn't talk to any newspeople about his experiences.

Villagra flew to Washington at CIA expense. A young agent with a legal pad met him at a restaurant near the airport for a long lunch, scribbling down all of Villagra's complaints, his brow furrowed with concern. Back in Miami, Villagra maintained his silence and waited to see the impact his complaints would have on the FDN. Months passed.

Eventually, Villagra realized he'd been had. There were no changes; the CIA was backing Bermúdez.

"It was all just to neutralize me," Villagra said. "Just to keep me quiet."

Meanwhile, in Tegucigalpa, Bermúdez, Lau, and Sánchez were waging their own counteroffensive within the FDN. Lau issued word that he couldn't be responsible for the safety of anybody challenging the FDN command, and he drew up murder lists. Since Lau had just weeks earlier arranged the elimination of Suicide and his staff, no one doubted his threats.

Some commanders who had voiced opposition to Bermúdez went into hiding. At the Támara clinic, the doctors of the FDN medical corps had made their loathing for Bermúdez and his hirelings clear. Fearing an armed attack by Lau's assassins, the head of the medical corps ordered the Támara medical staff onto twenty-four-hour guard duty. Doctors were sleeping in shifts, clutching AK-47s.

Bermúdez and Sánchez handed out more grease, meeting with commanders who had signed anti-Bermúdez documents, smoothing over the anger. Bermúdez huddled with officers at La Quinta. Sánchez invited others to Tegucigalpa night spots for whiskey and *churrasco* steaks. Bermúdez and Sánchez offered many officers onetime cash bribes to prove that there were no hard feelings; they raised the monthly "family aid" payments to others. Soon the latest American "reform" effort came to a close, amid a torrent of CIA cash.[18]

6

The Cutoff

The U.S. Congress barred further U.S. military aid to the contra army in April 1984 after the CIA mined Nicaraguan harbors, but the Reagan Administration flouted the ban over the next two and a half years, setting up a clandestine finance-and-supply network to support the contra army. The period eventually came under intense American scrutiny during the Iran-contra investigations.

Seen from Washington's point of view, the change from control of the rebel army by the CIA to control by National Security Council aide Oliver North was all-important; it set up a constitutional conflict within the U.S. government. But seen from the Nicaraguan contras' perspective, the switch brought few striking changes. The quality of supplies dropped and military coordination deteriorated, but in most respects, North's administration of the contra army followed patterns established by the CIA.

North continued to view the rebels as so many U.S. "assets." He tailored rebel political activities to events in Washington, rather than in Nicaragua, and backed Bermúdez and the other salaried leaders originally installed by the CIA.

In contrast, important changes came to the contra army and the war it waged. During the war's first three years, Mike Lima and other ex-Guardsmen had fought like a conventional army, invading Nicaragua for

132

destructive campaigns, then retreating to Honduras. But in 1984 many of the ex-Guardsmen withdrew permanently to Honduras to run the rebel army's lucrative rear guard with Bermúdez.

Meanwhile, a handful of commanders like Jhonson, civilians, many of them onetime Sandinistas who had won the respect of their fellow fighters, fought the war. They marched deeper into Nicaragua, stayed longer, and developed more popular backing than any contra forces before them, demonstrating that the rebels were capable of a different kind of war. They forged a social base with peasant farmers through a vast strip of farm country extending from the Honduran border south through nine provinces all the way to Costa Rica, and they attracted thousands of new volunteers.

Late 1983 through April 1984

Jhonson's Special Operations commandos failed miserably in mission after mission during his final months with the unit in 1983 and early 1984. It was a humiliating period, a time of mounting depression and debacle. Most embarrassing were the unit's attempts to destroy Nicaragua's most strategic bridge, across the Paso Caballos estuary to the mainland from the country's largest port, Corinto, on the Pacific coast.

Three times the CIA sent Jhonson's men to blow up the bridge. They left in six-man teams, packed into little wooden fishing boats, from a secret base on an island in the Gulf of Fonseca. Each time, they were to navigate south; beach and hide their boats on the Pacific coast just north of Corinto; hike across a peninsula to the estuary; then, under cover of darkness, swim two kilometers through the waters of Paso Caballos clutching inner tubes for flotation; attach explosive charges with time detonators to the bridge, and retreat.

But things went wrong. Boat motors failed; radios gave out; and, finally, the estuary was simply too well-lit and too heavily guarded. Each time, Jhonson's men had to abort their mission.[1]

The frustration of repeated failure and the isolation of life in the secret unit finally overwhelmed Jhonson. Though his wife lived just half an hour away in Tegucigalpa, he went for months unable to see her. Finally, he persuaded FDN officers to transfer him out of the special forces unit, along with sixteen of his men. He left Lepaterique, visited his wife and kids, and reported to the FDN's new Strategic Command camp in the Las Vegas salient along the Nicaraguan border.

Jhonson's departure came at a time when the CIA was growing increasingly irritated at rebel failures. The Agency was eager for quick, spectacular combat victories.

In the fall of 1983, amid American naval maneuvers, the CIA stationed a spy ship off Nicaragua's Pacific coast, equipped with attack helicopters and a force of mercenaries recruited in Honduras and other Latin countries to fight under CIA command. Using the mother ship as a base, the CIA saboteurs began attacking important industrial and commercial targets along the Nicaraguan Pacific coast. Other CIA mercenaries in the Caribbean hit targets on the Atlantic coast.

In early September 1983, the CIA mounted its own attempt on the Paso Caballos bridge, sending its sappers to shore in speedboats and using sophisticated diving gear to approach the bridge through the estuary. But the CIA team fared no better than Jhonson's men had. An underwater attack by CIA divers a few days later, however, temporarily crippled a submerged pipeline at Puerto Sandino, the country's main petroleum terminal. In January 1984, CIA Hughes 500 helicopters attacked the northern port of Potosí, and a few weeks later, more CIA helicopters participated in an attack on the Caribbean port of San Juan del Norte. The most devastating strike came on October 10, 1983, when CIA attackers operating in speedboats hit large fuel-storage tanks at Corinto with cannon fire. The tanks exploded, forcing the evacuation of several thousand civilians. During the same period, CIA divers mined the harbors at Corinto and Puerto Sandino.[2]

By early 1984, these dramatic attacks were drawing international criticism, and in their wake, rebel officials got an early taste of how the CIA would attribute responsibility for aspects of the Nicaraguan war that aroused public outcry.

John Mallett, the tall, near-sighted American agent who had coached the FDN's newly recruited political leaders before their first press conference in Ft. Lauderdale, was working as the CIA's deputy station chief in Honduras. One morning in early 1984, Mallett woke Edgar Chamorro, the FDN spokesman, at his Tegucigalpa safe house and handed him a statement that the CIA agent himself had written, saying that the contras were taking responsibility for the mining of the Corinto harbors. The contras had neither participated in nor been consulted about the attack, but Chamorro hurried to the September 15 Radio studio to broadcast the statement—in the name of the FDN.

The speech was necessary because the U.S. Congress had grown increasingly wary, disturbed by numerous reports of contra brutality as well as the mounting destruction and scale of the CIA's "covert action." By 1984, the CIA reported to Congress that the force it had originally described as a five-hundred-man arms interdiction unit had swelled to some ten thousand men, and President Reagan was urging Congress to approve funds to expand it to fifteen thousand.

Then the CIA's mines began to explode in Corinto Harbor, damaging five ships from Panama, the Netherlands, Great Britain, Japan, and the Soviet Union. Congress voted to prohibit the CIA from spending any more money for military or paramilitary operations in Nicaragua.[3] Even Republican lawmakers began to say the CIA attacks had irreparably doomed congressional support for the covert war.

"It's over. It was a mistake. They never should have done it," said Senator Ted Stevens, Republican of Alaska.

Mid-1984 through 1985

Jhonson led a small rebel column south into Nicaragua in mid-1984. It was his first experience at the head of a combat unit other than the CIA's Special Operations commandos, and he learned quickly the rebel army's potential as a guerrilla force.

He had no formal plan, but he wanted to contact old friends, to see what they were thinking and what kind of support they could offer. He trekked south to the hills around El Cuá, the first time he'd been back since he'd fled into exile three years earlier, and received an enthusiastic welcome. Many had heard that Luis Fley had joined the contras, but because he had been operating with the special forces on the Pacific coast, no one had seen him. Now word spread through the hills that Fley was back.

During his first weeks in the area, Jhonson set up a command post at a hacienda called The Laurel Trees, on a meadow atop a small mountain ten miles west of El Cuá. The hacienda belonged to Victorino Estrada, whom Jhonson had known when he was a poor dirt farmer, just setting up his farm in the early-1970s. Back then, Estrada had made it his custom, whenever he came through El Cuá, to stop at Luis Fley's store to drink a beer and chat. Now Estrada had built up a herd of fifteen hundred steers. He welcomed his friend back to the region by putting them at Jhonson's disposition.[4]

There was not only plenty of beef, but the terrain made the hacienda almost impregnable. On all sides, the farm plunged down steep, broken slopes that made all approaches difficult, except along Estrada's approach lane, itself ideal for ambushes. Estrada's hacienda overlooked the main thoroughfare bearing traffic north from Jinotega. Soon Jhonson had scores of old friends ferrying supplies to him: flashlight and radio batteries, candy, food, medicine, cigarettes, even the Managua newspapers.

Out of the spontaneous contacts with his old neighbors, Jhonson fashioned a network of collaborators who began to provide him with reliable and timely intelligence. He pieced together a picture of the enemy forces in his zone: The garrison at El Cuá that had been overseen by just a dozen or so men before his 1981 Pedernales del Cuá ambush had become a formidable walled outpost defended by a permanent force of three hundred Sandinista soldiers. Just three miles to the north of Estrada's hacienda, at the village of Pita del Carmen, a Sandinista army platoon was based. Another Sandinista battalion operated out of Abisinia, six miles to the south, and two more Sandinista companies were based at Planes de Vilán, six miles to the west. Cuban military officers were advising their Sandinista army counterparts at every garrison.

At first, Jhonson sought to avoid combat altogether. Instead, he kept his men on the move, and he encouraged them to go to Mass and to the evangelical church services, to talk with people and show their support for religious expression. He instructed his men to share their medicines with the sick.

After several months in his old terrain, he began to set ambushes. When a Sandinista army convoy was to pass near his task force, Jhonson would virtually always receive word an hour or more before its approach. It was plenty of time to pick a deadly curve, to stake out the high ground, and deploy the snipers. Jhonson's men repeatedly bloodied army forces along the roads leading north out of the provincial capital, while taking few casualties themselves. But, uncertain about replacing the munitions for his grenade launchers and other heavier weaponry, Jhonson avoided major risks. Mostly, he visited farmers, asked questions, listened to peasants' views. He found many farmers angrier than ever at the Sandinista authorities. Northern Nicaragua was ripe for rebel organizing.

Sandinista organizers had targeted what had once been a popular farmers' marketing and credit cooperative known as "La Perla" as the seed of counterrevolution in Jinotega province, jailing several of its leaders and pressuring many of its members to resign their memberships. In its place, the authorities had stepped up pressure on farmers to join the Sandinista-controlled National Agrarian Union. Farmers were still forced to sell their crops to the government at below-market prices, even though the economy was starting to deteriorate and inflation was rising faster than at any time in memory. The peasants blamed the government for the decline.[5]

Little of this was new to Jhonson. He believed the Sandinistas had always seen peasants as politically backward, too uneducated for their views to be taken into account; this arrogance had forced his own break with the revolution.

For months, though, the government had been gearing up for a no-holds-barred counterinsurgency war, which had created new conflicts with country people. On all sides, Jhonson encountered farmsteads that the revolutionary government had confiscated from peasants accused of being contra collaborators.

The Interior Ministry's State Security Directorate, the secret police agency, had established an extensive network of agents in the zone. Prowling Jinotega province's back roads in Soviet-made jeeps, State Security agents were acting as a law unto themselves, seizing farmers by the score, tying them with rope and dragging them to confiscated haciendas that State Security had converted into interrogation centers. Some were beaten, others dunked repeatedly in vats of cold water. But, generally, the Sandinista interrogators were leaving no scars; most of the complaints trickling out of the secret prisons focused on the long periods that detainees were held in little closetlike hotbox cells, incommunicado, often deprived of food, water, and sleep between questioning. Many of the detainees were in fact collaborating with FDN forces, but many weren't, and, once taken, they had little hope of defending themselves. After weeks, or in many cases months, of detention, detainees were dragged before the Popular Anti-Somocista Tribunals, the kangaroo courts that the government had set up in May 1983 to try accused contra collaborators. The trials were summary and conviction rates extraordinary. In 1985, the tribunals heard 235 cases involving 559 accused contra collaborators. Only one person was acquitted.[6]

Some farmers were complaining to Jhonson of even worse Sandinista abuses. He gathered the names of half a dozen men from the hills around El Cuá who had been accused of being contra collaborators, then quietly "disappeared" by State Security men.

To the west, Sandinista security authorities had become especially vicious in the wake of Mike Lima's October 1983 attack on Pantasma. Sandinista State Security agents, army soldiers, and militias there had murdered several dozen residents, a number of them evangelical Protestants. After a Protestant minister with ties to the government confirmed several of the murders and complained to Sandinista authorities in Managua, they mounted their own secret investigation, which culminated in the arrest of forty-one soldiers. Twelve soldiers and police were subsequently tried and convicted of rape, torture, and murder. After the trial, the government publicized the convictions to demonstrate its determination to suppress revolutionary abuses.

But Jhonson heard reports of killings by Sandinista authorities around several other northern towns as well.[7]

Thus Jhonson didn't have to spin elaborate visions about what the rebels were fighting for, or make extravagant promises in order to find widespread backing. His message was simple: After the contras win the war, he said, farmers would be able to market their crops freely. They would be able to buy their food and clothing wherever they wanted. Farm confiscations would end; there would be no more State Security agents nosing about the countryside.

Most of all, he said, there would be no military draft. Jhonson had found the draft, which the Managua government had instituted in September 1983, to be the most abrasive of all revolutionary policies to the peasantry.[8] Ever since the Sandinista revolution, most peasants had wanted to be left alone. The Sandinista draft represented the most severe intrusion yet on their lives, a demand that all peasant men choose sides in the war, that they risk their lives to defend the revolution.

Across Nicaragua, tens of thousands of young men who had aspired to remain neutral in the conflict no longer had that luxury. Sandinista recruiting teams grabbed many, but others began to hide, fleeing their farms whenever Sandinista soldiers approached. Many joined the contras.

Scores of young draft evaders flocked to Jhonson's task force. By early 1985, Jhonson had enough recruits for a second hundred-man task force—and then a third. Upon returning to Honduras, he formed a Regional Command, the 15th of September, and became its commander.

Throughout 1984 and 1985, Jhonson proved that the contras, armed as a conventional army by the CIA, were able to wage guerrilla war. The Sandinista government was in trouble with its people, and Jhonson moved in to take advantage of the Sandinistas' difficulties. He forged hundreds of relationships with farmers who became active collaborators with his unit, paid attention to his supporters' problems, and became a good guerrilla cadre, a valuable insurgent field leader.

Key to the work was showing respect for Nicaraguan civilians. This seemed to be common sense, but an incident during one of Jhonson's earliest operations illustrated how enforcing discipline among rebel forces could bring outright confrontation with the ex-Guardsmen in the FDN. Jhonson's men coordinated operations briefly with a two-hundred-man task force led by Francisco Ruiz Castellón, a former Guard lieutenant with the pseudonym "Renato." After one joint attack, their two rebel columns stopped to rest, camping at a rural chapel. Jhonson's men bought a few hens and some fruit from a farmer, then cooked dinner and passed the night. The men of Renato's task force camped at their own site nearby. In the morning, several of Jhonson's commandos reported that Renato's intelligence aide, an ex-Guard sergeant, had put a pistol to the neck of a young woman at the farm site, dragged her into the brush, and raped her. Jhonson confronted Renato.

"This kind of thing hurts our cause. People don't like this," Jhonson said. Renato complained to his aide, who huffily denied having touched the woman. Jhonson went back to his men. They were sure about the rape; they'd seen Renato's aide with the woman, and they'd talked to her after the man had left her.

"All right, pack your stuff up," Jhonson ordered his men. He went back to Renato. "Look, we're pulling out. I don't feel comfortable with people that operate like this."

Jhonson was not the only commander attempting to stop brutality by the ex-Guardsmen. Other former civilians were provoking similar confrontations.

One was Tirzo Moreno, a onetime cattle merchant who had taken the war name "Rigoberto" and had risen to head one of the four regional commands named after Jorge Salazar, a prominent opposition coffee grower killed in 1980 by the Sandinistas. Rigoberto's men, marching along a road near the town of Siuna, captured three Sandinista soldiers, young peasants. Rigoberto gave them sacks of sugar to carry and turned them over to aides. When he arrived at his unit's camp for the night, he found that the three prisoners had been lashed to a tree.

"Why are these men tied?" Rigoberto asked. "Just keep an eye on them." But his aides said they were tired; it would be easier to leave the prisoners bound. Rigoberto went to sleep, but a cacophony of screams and blows woke him.

"What the hell is going on?" he shouted. Through the darkness, he saw that two former Guardsmen in his unit had begun to beat the prisoners. They had already broken one prisoner's nose. The prisoners were sobbing and bleeding, pleading for their lives.

"Look," Rigoberto said, "this kind of shit is not permitted in my unit."

"Why are you defending these Sandinista dogs?" one of the ex-Guards shot back.

"Fuck you! We're not torturing prisoners in the Jorge Salazar," Rigoberto said.

Traveling with the prisoners for two weeks, Rigoberto had a chance to talk with them. They told him they had been drafted away from their families, and pleaded to be released. He freed them. A year later, Rigoberto met one of the men he'd captured and released, now fighting in one of his own Jorge Salazar companies. The soldier had returned home, only to have local Sandinista authorities accuse him of being a contra collaborator.

"That was a political lesson for me," Rigoberto recalled later.

The work of Jhonson and nearly a dozen other commanders was enough to give the rebels a good operational base inside Nicaragua,[9] but it wasn't enough to move forward fast in what had become a very political war. For that, the rebel army needed good top leadership, men able to articulate the dreams of the army's rural backers into a military and political strategy.

1984 and 1985

In Honduras, Colonel Bermúdez was in way over his head. Throughout the war, he had followed instructions—from the CIA, from the Hondurans, from the Argentines—but events in 1984 demanded that he exert real leadership.

Riveiro, Villegas, and the other Argentine military advisers were gone, recalled to Buenos Aires, where a new civilian government had taken power. On March 31, Bermúdez lost another mentor when disgruntled Honduran Army officers deposed Armed Forces Commander Gen. Gustavo Alvarez, forcing him into exile. Relations between Bermúdez's FDN and the Honduran military chilled considerably.

Moreover, when Congress cut off U.S. aid, it barred the CIA from further involvement with the rebels. The station chief in Tegucigalpa, Donald Winters, left for a new posting,[10] and the man who arrived to replace him was Vincent Shields, an overweight Irishman in his forties from Brooklyn. Shields had considerable paramilitary experience, having served in the late 1960s during the CIA's war in Laos as the deputy chief at Long Tieng, the main base for the Agency's army of forty thousand Laotian peasants, but neither Shields nor his base chief, Ray Doty, could direct Bermúdez's work as the Agency had in the past. Legally, the CIA could now only collect intelligence information from the rebels. Dozens of CIA men left Honduras.[11]

Oliver North emerged as the Reagan Administration's emergency administrator of the contra army. With the secret counsel of CIA Director William Casey and the winking approval of President Reagan, North established his clandestine contra support network for the contras. Reagan Administration officials arranged more than $32 million in secret funding for the FDN, most of it deposited by the Saudi Arabian government into bank accounts controlled by contra political leader Adolfo Calero.[12] North put the rebels in touch with two former U.S. military officers, Air Force General Richard Secord and Army General John Singlaub, for help with arms purchases. Eager to improve on the performance of Bermúdez's hapless FDN air force, North paid Secord to establish a secret air-supply operation for the contras, based at El Salvador's Ilopango Air Force Base.[13] North even tried to coordinate FDN military activities, ferrying battle maps and messages from his headquarters in the Old Executive Office Building to the FDN camps in Honduras via couriers. But there was only so much North and his makeshift team could do. There was a command vacuum.

This gave Bermúdez the opportunity to emerge as a true commander, but instead, he proved utterly incapable. For two years, Bermúdez allowed the war to drift. Surrounding himself with a new circle of mediocre yes-men, he frittered away much of his time in womanizing and petty scheming.

In the wake of the CIA's late 1983 housecleaning of the FDN leadership, Bermúdez needed to appoint officers to a new general staff, calling them his "Strategic Command assistants." The men he appointed reflected the calibre of his own leadership. They were all ex-Guardsmen, and in several cases, even less impressive than the thieves and drunks the CIA had purged.

As his logistics chief, Bermúdez appointed Armando "The Policeman" López, a former Guard lieutenant who had built a bloody reputation in the war's first years as commander of an FDN base in southern Choluteca province. Bermúdez named a war-crippled former Guard second lieutenant, Harlie "The Deer" Duarte, as his personnel officer. As his operations aide, he named a former second lieutenant with no command experience at all: Denis "Benny" Pineda.

As his top intelligence officer, Bermúdez appointed Juan José Zelaya, "Little Zelaya," who in the National Guard had worked as the personal secretary to Gen. Samuel Genie, the head of Somoza's Office of National Security. On Genie's team of interrogators and hitmen, Zelaya had been a glorified typist who shuffled files and prepared intelligence forms. After Somoza's fall, Colonel Lau had brought Zelaya into the FDN as his own secretary. For Lau, Zelaya was a go-fer, a nobody. Now Bermúdez appointed him to the critical post of intelligence chief.

For his part, Colonel Lau had become the focus of controversy. Public awareness was mounting about his unsavory past—especially the speculation about his alleged involvement in the 1980 murder of El Salvador's archbishop. As the spotlight intensified, Lau resigned from his FDN intelligence post in 1983, but Bermúdez kept him around.[14]

The "disappearances" that had become routine during General Alvarez's rule had provoked growing outcry in Honduras. Seeking to quiet the clamor after Alvarez's ouster, the new Honduran military commanders appointed a panel of colonels to "investigate" the 247 unsolved political murders and disappearances that had taken place during General Alvarez's four-year rightist crusade. In the course of their probe, the Honduran officers studied Colonel Lau's role in many of the disappearances. They picked Lau up and brought him to Armed Forces headquarters for questioning.

"Lau just told us, 'I've done a few little jobs for the Armed Forces,' " one of the Honduran officers who participated in the probe said later. At the end of their interrogation, the Hondurans told Colonel Lau that he was no longer welcome in the country, and although they do not seem to have pressed him, he eventually moved to Guatemala. Bermúdez, however—whether to placate his friend or to buy his silence—arranged for Lau to stay on the FDN's payroll for years after his departure.[15]

But Lau was only part of Bermúdez's problem. With an international scandal brewing over the FDN death squads, Bermúdez had to hide Lau's henchmen, too. One of the most notorious was Armando López, Jr., the son of Bermúdez's new logistics chief, "The Policeman," and a young killer who had adopted the nom de guerre "The Beast." López, Jr., had become a special liability because, when drunk, he had begun to boast to FDN drinking partners about his homicidal exploits and about the pleasures of killing with a sharp knife. Bermúdez arranged for López, Jr., to travel into exile, reportedly to the United States.[16] Bermúdez hid other members of Lau's assassination squads in various obscure FDN posts. One moved to a new counterintelligence job; another, Bermúdez installed in command of a road maintenance group at Las Vegas; a third, Bermúdez put in charge of bookkeeping at his Strategic Command.

At Las Vegas, Bermúdez enjoyed the trappings of command, the little routines that reminded others of the old National Guard life. He had a stooped old former Guardsman wake him each morning, offering him his pressed uniform, newly shined boots, and a military salute: "Good morning, señor! How did the commander sleep?"

As Bermúdez dressed, his aide-de-camp would run down the camp gossip: which commander had slipped off to Danlí the night before to go whoring, which officer had talked badly of Bermúdez at dinner, which task force leader had been drinking.

As his personal secretary, Bermúdez appointed Ernesto "Sherman" Ortega—no apparent relation to the Nicaraguan president—a former sergeant from Somoza's elite force, the EEBI. Ortega took notes and arranged Bermúdez's schedule. He also introduced Bermúdez to an important contact: his sister. Ortega's mother, in exile, had founded a makeshift beer parlor in a rented house in a lower-middle-class barrio near Toncontín Airport on the outskirts of Tegucigalpa. Drinking there one afternoon with Ortega, Bermúdez met Ernesto's younger sister Rina, a pretty woman in her early twenties, married to a Honduran Army lieutenant. Ernesto arranged for Bermúdez to meet with Rina privately, at one of the FDN's safe houses. Soon Bermúdez had begun his latest affair.

Bermúdez wanted companionship when he was working at Las

Vegas. He began sending his chauffeur to drive Rina Ortega back to the camps in his Land Cruiser. Rina told her husband, the Honduran lieutenant, that she was visiting her brother Ernesto. Sometimes Rina's mother came along on her trips to Las Vegas, to ensure the appearance of a family visit. Bermúdez liked to take Rina horseback riding through the hills, then retire to his Strategic Command headquarters for drinks and dinner.

With Bermúdez himself entertaining lovers in his personal quarters at Las Vegas, the other members of the staff saw no reason to maintain propriety at the rebel army's military headquarters. Armando López's logistics office became a revolving door for young female commandos. Harlie Duarte, the personnel officer, also brought female commandos and whores to the Strategic Command. [17]

None of it would have mattered if amid all the philandering, Bermúdez and his men had offered some vision to their aimless army. But since Bermúdez had no plans of his own, men with wild ideas could persuade him to carry out theirs. Among the wildest were the right-wing activists from the Decatur, Alabama–based group, Civilian Military Action (CMA). At the time of the U.S. aid cutoff, Adolfo Calero authorized his younger brother, Mario Calero, to purchase supplies for the contra army. Mario soon thought he could help the army out with private military advisers, too, and he brought the first CMA men to Las Vegas, a dozen or so gung-ho anticommunists.

The CMA men knew almost nothing about Nicaragua, but they were full of advice. Soon after arriving in Las Vegas in mid-1984, they discovered the FDN's Hughes 500 observation helicopter and immediately decided to use it for rebel parachute training. Bermúdez approved the idea. On the third training jump over Las Vegas, one rebel fighter heaved himself out the side of the helicopter, drifted in the wind, and crashed down through the tile roof of the FDN's main cooking shed. That ended the paratroop training—but not the CMA's enthusiasm.

In late August, James Powell, thirty-six, a former U.S. Army helicopter pilot from Memphis, Tennessee, came to Las Vegas with Mario Calero and a new CMA "training team." With him was Dana Parker, a thirty-six-year-old Huntsville, Alabama, police officer. Both were Vietnam veterans. The day Powell, Parker, and Mario Calero arrived, they had a long session with Bermúdez over beers at the Strategic Command. Calero began to needle Bermúdez about how the FDN was losing the initiative in the war.

Earlier in the year, the CIA had delivered to Bermúdez a list of Sandinista military targets for rebel attack, one of which was the Apali army training base at Santa Clara, between the towns of Ocotal and Jalapa, just ten miles south of the Honduran border. Over drinks, somebody came up with the idea of attacking the Apali base with the three Cessna O-2 observation planes, armed with air-to-ground rocket pods, which the CIA had given the FDN. Bermúdez approved the idea.

Powell didn't speak Spanish, but somebody filled him in on the drift of things. Send the Hughes 500 helicopter, too, Powell said. Armed with rockets, the Hughes 500 could be a powerful weapon. Bermúdez approved that idea, too.

On September 1, 1984, FDN officers helped install a cumbersome rocket pod on the Hughes 500 and armed it with fourteen rockets. Parker climbed into the helicopter's rear seat with an M-60 machine gun and seven hundred rounds of ammunition, hoping to shoot some Communists from the air. Powell, the pilot, only vaguely knew where the Apali was and couldn't even talk to his Nicaraguan copilot, Marco Pozo, who knew little English.

"Don't worry about it. They're pilots. They'll understand each other," Parker told one FDN officer just before their Hughes 500 took off from Las Vegas for the attack. The helicopter rose sluggishly, its normal maneuverability severely reduced by the heavy drag of the rocket pod and its full load.

The three small O-2s, piloted by FDN pilots, took off from Aguacate, flew south across the border to Santa Clara, and rocketed the Sandinista base. The attack was inconsequential, militarily. One rocket slammed into the camp kitchen, killing four civilian cooks; no soldiers were harmed.

Powell, Parker, and Pozo straggled in after the O-2s. Angry Sandinista antiaircraft gunners, waiting for further attacks, blew their helicopter out of the sky. Powell, Parker, and Pozo all died.

In the smoking wreckage of the FDN's only helicopter, the Sandinistas found maps and other documents linking the Hughes 500 to Aguacate Air Base and other CIA-run installations in Honduras. The attack became a major international incident.

The Honduran Army was furious with Bermúdez. Top officers demanded that from then on, Bermúdez request Honduran permission before every rebel flight, even simple supply flights within Honduras. The CIA, accused in Congress of having ordered the flight, was also furious. No Agency men were out at Las Vegas when the contras dreamed up the Santa Clara attack, but once the news broke, an agent flew out to demand an explanation. The Agency ordered Bermúdez to expel the remaining CMA men from Las Vegas.

Bermúdez was embarrassed and shaken. Mike Lima talked with him at the time: "Bermúdez almost cried. 'How did I let myself be deceived by these gringo idiots? I'm a fool,' he said."[18] But even in the wake of this debacle, he developed no plan or strategy of his own.

For the rebel operations room, the CIA had provided the FDN with large-scale topographical maps of Nicaragua. Bermúdez's operations staff followed rebel combat operations with colored markers on the map. Bermúdez's leadership of the war at the time consisted mainly of a periodic visit to the maps to make sure the terrain was well-covered with markers—and hence, with plenty of combat. Sometimes the map looked bare to Bermúdez.

"What the hell is going on?" Bermúdez would demand of his men. "Isn't anybody fighting?"

1984 and 1985

Mike Lima was wounded badly, twice in five months.

The first wound was an accident. On November 26, 1983, Lima was test-firing an 82-mm. mortar tube he'd captured from the Sandinistas, but using Chinese-made 82-mm. recoilless rifle shells. A recoilless rifle is a small cannon, with barrel walls of tooled steel an inch thick, allowing its shells to be packed with far more explosive propellant than mortar projectiles. Fired from a mortar tube, a recoilless rifle shell explodes like a fragmentation bomb.

Mike Lima, young and overconfident with weaponry, dropped three shells in a row into his mortar tube. Nothing happened. On the fourth try, the shell exploded. Pieces of steel mortar casing the size of dinner plates shredded in all directions, killing four of Lima's men instantly.

The blast sliced off Lima's right hand halfway up his forearm and gashed a six-inch hole in his thigh. He seized his bleeding stump with his left hand, wandered, dazed, more than thirty yards from the wreckage, then collapsed.

Contra paramedics rushed him to the Las Vegas clinic for first aid, and the same day, a CIA helicopter evacuated him to the main rebel hospital at Aguacate for surgery. Just a month later, he was flown to Miami to be fitted with a prosthetic arm.[19] In Miami, Mike Lima expressed the psychological trauma over the loss of his hand in a frantic drive to get the prosthesis fitted quickly and get back to the war. He cut through every delay, harassing the medical technicians incessantly. Just three weeks after his arrival in Miami, he flew back to Honduras, and in late March—just sixteen weeks after the mortar explosion—he marched south into Nicaragua at the head of his Diriangén Regional Command.

The Sandinistas, still bitter over the Pantasma attack five months earlier, developed good intelligence quickly on Lima's movements. Sandinista army battalions coordinated an "area ambush," in which several units position themselves around a piece of terrain through which an enemy unit is expected to move, then pound the area with artillery. On April 18, 1984, Mike Lima was leading his three hundred men through a valley, when mortar shells began to scream in on the Diriangén from all sides.

One shell landed practically on top of Lima. The concussion blew him off the ground, wadded him like a piece of scrap paper, and hurled him back to the earth. His left leg was shattered and torn, his good hand was broken, shrapnel had torn into his eye. Amid the barrage, his men laid him in a hammock strung beneath a long pole carried by two commandos, shot their way through the Sandinista lines with machine-gun fire, and began a torturous evacuation north, running night and day for nearly a week. Lima lost a lot of blood along the way, but survived. He was rushed again in a wheelchair to Miami, where a CIA agent came out to whisk him past the immigration and customs lines at Miami International Airport. Microsurgery repaired his eye; therapists strapped a temporary brace on his leg to keep it from buckling under his weight. Two months after his arrival in Miami, Mike Lima again flew back to Honduras.

"I realized at that moment that my glory days were over," Mike Lima recalled later.

He was just twenty-five, full of youthful energy, and head of the Diriangén, but the hands-on command of the unit would have to pass to others. Mike Lima would have to take up other work—but what?

In his first weeks back at Las Vegas, he began to adjust. Soon he shed his leg brace. He was wearing a prosthetic metal hook on his right arm, but clutching a lightweight, AR-15 rifle in his now-mended left hand, he learned to fire off a clip of ammunition. He picked a handsome white horse from an FDN herd and began to ride the hills around Las Vegas.

The rebel army had grown with stunning speed. Just two years earlier, during 1982, his own recruiting efforts with Tigrillo had built the rebel army to more than three thousand men. Now it was nearly four times that large—more than twelve thousand troops. More than six thousand of them were camped at Las Vegas. It was a vast army settlement, sprawling down several valleys and over half a dozen wooded ridges, a smoky warren of troops and huts, dogs and weaponry, fire and mud.

As a result of the flood of new recruits, most of the commandos were strangers to Lima. That frightened him. There was too much disorder. Many commandos, just fooling around, were firing their weapons into the air. The regional command camps stank of marijuana. Some rebel officers chalked up the disarray to the rapid incorporation into the army of hundreds of untrained peasants. Lima, however, had another interpretation. He believed Las Vegas was jammed with spies.[20]

Lima went to Bermúdez, warning about the need to crack down on Sandinista infiltrators. He scoffed at Juan José Zelaya, Colonel Lau's aide from the National Guard's OSN whom Bermúdez had appointed intelligence chief.

"It's embarrassing that Zelaya is heading intelligence," Lima told Bermúdez. "That son of a bitch doesn't even know his own name."

"You want the job?" Bermúdez asked.

Mike Lima became the FDN's intelligence chief. Like his predecessor, Colonel Lau, Lima confused the information-gathering and analytical roles of the intelligence officer with the police role of the counterintelligence chief.

Formally, the army already had a counterintelligence chief. After Lau's resignation, Bermúdez had named an old buddy from the Guard, ex-Maj. Donald "The Bull" Torres, then forty-eight, to the post. Torres had taken some intelligence courses in the Guard and had worked with the CIA during the first years of the war, trying to organize an "internal front" inside Nicaragua. But he spent most of his time in Tegucigalpa, drinking at a dingy downtown bar where whores danced nude sixteen hours a day. Mike Lima considered Torres a bum.

As a start, Mike Lima persuaded Bermúdez to create the rebel army's first military police unit, men who could enforce order in Las Vegas. Bermúdez went along, naming an ex-Guard sergeant, Mariano "Leo" Morales, as its chief. Leo had been a barber in the Guard; now he became a jailer. He and Mike Lima set up a makeshift prison and began to arrest commandos. They picked up marijuana smokers and drunks and insubordinates, men who talked back to their commanders.

Then Lima began what he considered his more important work: recruiting intelligence staff officers to serve in every one-hundred-man rebel company in the army. It was the FDN's first real intelligence staff, but rather than setting up an organization geared toward collecting information on the Sandinista army, Lima recruited a network of informants to spy on the FDN's own ranks.

Lima's informants started accusing rebel commandos of being infiltrators, and Leo's military police began seizing them. At the same time, rebel units were bringing back a few captured Sandinistas to Las Vegas. When he took control of the intelligence section, Mike Lima had inherited three full-time "intelligence officers." One was Ramón Peña Rodríguez, "Z-Two," the forty-five-year-old former Guard corporal who had been Mack's main henchman at La Lodosa. Soon there were quite a number of prisoners to question.

Mike Lima, untrained in counterintelligence, angry about his successive defeats, became a brutal interrogator.

He would start by beating the suspected spies at the beginning of an "interview," accusing them as infiltrators between the hail of blows. Z-Two would help him. Some of the suspects ended up saying what Lima wanted to hear, in order to stop the beating—others didn't. There were some very prolonged, bloody sessions.

Lima was doing this rough work at the intelligence offices at Las Vegas, and a number of the ex-Guardsmen hanging around the Strategic Command learned about the torture sessions. They also figured out that prisoners had begun to "disappear." How many?

"A lot of people," said Walter "Toño" (pronounced TONE-yo) Calderón, a former Guard lieutenant who worked closely with Mike Lima at the time.

"I guess maybe a dozen," said Guillermo Gasteazoro, a former Guard lieutenant who worked at Las Vegas as a radio scanner.

"Some prisoners that were brought to Honduras, Mike Lima just erased them off the face of the earth," Gasteazoro recalled. "There were just some people you couldn't convince . . . . We'd just dust them."

Mike Lima and his FDN driver would load prisoners into his pickup truck, drive them away from the Strategic Command camp, shoot or knife them, then throw their bodies into the Coco River, Gasteazoro said.[21]

Lima's tenure in the intelligence post was short—only two or three months. Several of his colleagues said that because the abuses and disappearances from the intelligence section soon became widely known in the rebel camps, Bermúdez removed him. Toño recalled an encounter he had with Mike Lima and Bermúdez at the Strategic Command headquarters:

"Bermúdez said to Mike Lima in front of me that if he was going to do something, that he shouldn't do it personally, but that he should send someone else to do it," Toño recalled. "He was referring to some guys who had 'disappeared,' and to several others who Mike Lima had tortured right in the offices. So Bermúdez told him in front of me that he was taking him out of that post."[22]

Early in 1985, Bermúdez named another ex-Guardsmen, Rodolfo Ernesto Ampie, to replace Lima. A lieutenant in the EEBI at the time of the 1979 Sandinista triumph, Ampie had been turned over to revolutionary authorities by the Red Cross, given a peremptory trial, and jailed. In late 1983, he escaped from the Modelo Penitentiary outside Managua and fled to Honduras. Joining the FDN, he took the nom de guerre "Invisible." He would hold the intelligence post until 1988.

Mike Lima filled in, for a time, as Bermúdez's operations officer, then as the personnel officer. He helped Mack train recruits. But formal posts were secondary in the FDN. Leading the army was a clique, centering on Bermúdez and Aristides Sánchez, a circle of former Guards whom Bermúdez and Sánchez trusted to do whatever needed doing. Mack belonged. Leo belonged. So did half a dozen other ex-Guards. Mike Lima was a charter member.

Mike Lima quietly maintained his network of informants. He remained the contra army's self-appointed disciplinarian, on the lookout for troublemakers and subversives.

Summer 1984 through summer 1985

The United States was locked in passionate debate about the Nicaraguan war, and one of the gringos who arrived in Honduras to experience the contra struggle firsthand was Frank Wohl. The rebels knew him by his nom de guerre: The Killer Rat.

Wohl was a hard fellow to read. An athletic, fair-haired twenty-one-year-old, he was, when he began his tempestuous affair with the contras, working on a major in psychology at Northwestern University. It wasn't clear to Wohl's friends what exactly in his past in North Miami Beach, Florida, had first bred his fascination with far-right causes, with war and weapons, but at Northwestern, Wohl soon got his name in the papers. Campus authorities discovered that he had an AR-15 automatic rifle in his dorm room, that he was posing for photographs with the weapon in the hallway, that he was spending long hours at a shooting range. Around campus he wore a T-shirt that read "KILL THEM ALL, LET GOD SORT THEM OUT." These things naturally aroused the ire of campus leftists, but Wohl's views soon alienated even many campus conservatives.

"People thought of him as a kook," recalled Tom Holt, a college friend who later became assistant editorial page editor at the *Richmond Times Dispatch.*

When, in early 1984, Wohl heard a campus speech by contra leader Fernando Chamorro, he immediately found the rebel war too alluring to resist. While other students were enrolling in junior-year-abroad programs, heading off to Europe, Wohl called Adolfo Calero at his suburban Miami home, got names of rebel contacts in Tegucigalpa, bought a 35-mm. camera, and flew to Honduras. He told the rebel spokesmen he met at the FDN's public-relations office that he was a free-lance photographer, but he observed none of the rules of journalism. He voiced unabashed sympathy for the contras. He bought a long commando knife and made it the centerpiece of a string of weird jokes—Wohl pretending to stab his new contra friends, Wohl pretending to slash his own throat.

Few professional journalists were getting FDN cooperation in visiting the rebel camps at the time, but Wohl finally begged a ride to Las Vegas with contra acquaintances. There he donned an FDN uniform and took his pseudonym, "Rata Asesina." Soon, Wohl had struck up a friendship with Mack, who invited him to La Lodosa. Wohl spent the entire summer with Mack and his men, traveling inside Nicaragua for weeks with a rebel patrol. There, he got a severe case of diarrhea; the rebels had to nurse him back into Honduras on mule-back.

Wohl returned to Northwestern at the end of the summer bursting with enthusiasm over the contras and their war. Albert Veldhuyzen, a conservative pre-law student who was his best friend, sat up late listening to Wohl's gush of experiences. Wohl was so thrilled that he dropped out of his winter term and returned to the contra camps, spending November 1984 through January 1985 with Mack and his commandos.

This time, however, he returned to Northwestern disillusioned. To his friend Veldhuyzen, he criticized the rebels' commanders. They weren't even fighting in Nicaragua, he said, instead hanging back in the camps, saving their own skins. He'd seen sloppiness, Wohl told Veldhuyzen. Told to distribute propaganda literature in Nicaraguan towns, rebel troops instead just dumped bundles of leaflets in the woods. Rebel patrol leaders were claiming the destruction of targets never attacked.

Then Wohl took out his photographs. He'd shot dozens of rolls, but there was one sequence of thirty-two color slides he wanted Veldhuyzen to see.

"I've got something kind of rare," he said.

Veldhuyzen held the slides, one after the other, up to the light of an overhead bulb in Wohl's apartment.

The photos showed an old gray-haired man with a goatee, clad in a brown sports shirt, digging a shallow grave. Two or three photos further in the sequence, apparently taken minutes later, the man lay flat on his back in the earth. A man in a green uniform stood over him, binding his wrists, the blade of a long knife protruding from his hip pocket.

Then the photos became a torrent of blood; they appeared to have been shot in quick succession.

One showed a second figure crouched on the old man's stomach, slashing the man's throat. The victim's face was contorted into a grimace; his legs and feet jerked upward in a spasm of pain. In the next photo, the killer had leaned his weight forward into the blade, plunging it through the old man's neck.

In the final exposure, the old man's head hung limp, his eyes glazed, staring to the right, his neck gushing blood. A young Indian-looking boy leaned above his body, stabbing a long blade through the man's heart.

Veldhuyzen stared through the color transparencies, stunned.

Wohl told him his story. He said he had taken the photos in January 1985, near the end of his stay with the contras. He'd been with a rebel column inside Nicaragua, near the town of San Juan in the northern province of Madriz, about forty miles southeast of La Lodosa. The rebels had seized the man after villagers had denounced him as a Sandinista informer, Wohl told Veldhuyzen. Then the rebels decided to kill the man.

Wohl wanted to take pictures. He'd left his camera at a nearby base camp, but a contra friend had run back and brought it in time for Wohl to accompany the execution squad up a hill, where they set the old man to digging his own grave. The rebels didn't seem to mind the photographs, Wohl told Veldhuyzen. Some contras even wanted to pose in the photos during the execution—even showing their faces. They allowed him to stand within a couple of yards of the killing itself, so that the extraordinary images filled an entire frame of his 35-mm. camera.

Wohl told Veldhuyzen he wasn't sure what he was going to do with the photos. He knew that they were very sensitive—they could hurt the contras—but he had an idea. The CIA was recruiting at Northwestern. He'd always wanted work in intelligence, and his experiences with the contras had convinced him that this was his calling. He would apply for a job and offer to turn his photos over to the CIA.

During March and early April 1985, Wohl interviewed three times with CIA agents. The first encounter, at the CIA's Chicago-area field offices, went well, he told Veldhuyzen. The CIA scheduled a second interview at a Chicago hotel, this time with an Agency recruiter who flew out from Langley. Wohl, feeling confident, wanted to show that he already had experience in Central America. So at his second encounter, he showed the agent his photos. "What would you like me to do with these?" Wohl asked.

The agent was taken aback. "I don't want to have anything to do with this," the CIA agent told Wohl. He said the Agency would get back to Wohl.

Nonetheless, Wohl thought things were going well. Then he got bad news. An agent sent him an icy letter to inform him that he wasn't in line for further consideration. Wohl was devastated. He called his CIA contact back.

"What about my photos?" Wohl asked.

"Do whatever you want with them," the agent said.

Wohl was shocked at the CIA's attitude, he told Veldhuyzen. They were supposed to be concerned about national security, and yet they didn't care about his photos. Well, he believed there was one thing he could do with his photos—sell them.

"If that's the CIA's attitude, why should I forego a lot of money?"

Ever since the Congress had cut off U.S. military aid to the rebels amid the mining controversy the year before, Reagan Administration officials had been maneuvering for approval of new assistance. In the fall of 1984, Congress had turned back one proposal. Now a showdown vote was nearing on another, a $14 million request for new aid. The White House was going all out.

The contras are "the moral equivalent of our Founding Fathers," President Reagan told one conservative audience. "These are our brothers, these freedom fighters."[23]

With the President hammering on the theme at every opportunity, the contra war was big news throughout April. Wohl's instincts about his photos proved correct. He contacted New York's Sygma photo agency, and his photos sparked a bidding war. *U.S. News and World Report* flew Wohl to Washington, D.C. He went to *Time,* then jetted to New York. *Newsweek* finally bought his photos for fifteen thousand dollars.

March and April 1985

In Honduras, Jhonson returned to Las Vegas with more than a hundred new volunteers, most of them young draft dodgers. Jhonson had been fighting at the head of his own unit inside Nicaragua for a year, and his stature within the rebel army was building.

In the United States, the FDN's domination by ex-National Guardsmen was proving to be a major political handicap, and Bermúdez was now under pressure from the Americans to promote former civilians like Jhonson to command positions.

Now a new congressional vote over contra aid was looming, and Bermúdez was assembling a delegation of four rebel commanders to fly to Washington for display to U.S. congressmen as "freedom fighters." Even though his staff was still composed, to a man, of former Guardsmen, Bermúdez decided that three of the four would be former farmers. Oscar Sobalvarro, known as "Commander Rubén"—one of the contras from Tigrillo's original band—was going. So was Rudy Zelaya, "Commander Douglas," who had attacked the northern Nicaraguan town of Quilalí with Pedro Joaquín González in one of the earliest anti-Sandinista uprisings in 1980. Rodolfo Ampie, "Invisible," the new intelligence chief, would represent the ex-Guardsmen.

Jhonson would go, too. Orlando Montealegre, the rebel force's paymaster, told Jhonson that he was on the list for the trip. Montealegre gave Jhonson his plane ticket and the equivalent of $350. "Buy some new clothes," he said.

For Jhonson, the trip meant culture shock: He had never been outside of Central America. In the course of just a few days, he marched out of Nicaragua, drove to Tegucigalpa, boarded a commercial flight at Toncontín Airport, flew to Miami for a quick stopover, and continued on to Washington, D.C.

A young middle-class Nicaraguan exile working for the rebel organization in Washington met Jhonson's plane and drove the commanders downtown, checking them into the hotel where Adolfo Calero was staying. It was the most luxurious place Jhonson had ever seen, with rococo furniture and glittering chandeliers. He and the other commanders felt uncomfortable, and quickly realized that their daily expense stipends weren't enough to cover Calero's style of luxury. The following morning, the four commanders checked into a more reasonable hotel.

Shortly after their arrival, the commanders were driven to the office of Bosco Matamoros, the FDN's Washington spokesman. Then thirty-eight, Matamoros was a short, bald man from a wealthy family with ties to the National Guard. That morning, April 22, 1985, Matamoros was upset.

He held up a copy of *Newsweek* for Jhonson and the others to see. The magazine had hit the newsstands just hours earlier, featuring four of Frank Wohl's grisly photos.

"Look at the problems we've got," Matamoros told the commanders. "My phone is ringing off the hook. I've been fighting this thing all morning."

Seeing Wohl's photos, Jhonson knew instantly that the killings had been done by Mack's men, and as it turned out, so did all the other commanders. Everybody remembered the Killer Rat, how unlike other American journalists he'd worn a contra uniform, how he'd been friends with Mack. Obviously, the ugly photos just showed what everyone knew about the men at La Lodosa. And now they'd been stupid enough to let the Killer Rat take their pictures!

"This is that kid that was at Las Vegas, and then Mack took him over to La Lodosa," Matamoros said. Heads nodded.

"You guys are definitely going to get hit with this thing too," Matamoros said. "Let me handle it. But if you really get pressured, just say you don't know where the photos came from. Tell them that it looks to you like they're just another propaganda trick arranged by the Sandinistas."

Jhonson felt uncomfortable. He'd been excited about coming to Washington, ready to make his pitch for U.S. aid, to talk about the widespread support among Nicaraguan peasants for the rebel cause. These photos were spoiling his day, too.

Matamoros divided the commanders into two groups: Jhonson and

Rubén, and Invisible and Douglas. The first pair was sent in a cab with a translator and a guide to a stone office building near the Capitol where they were ushered into a string of congressional offices for chats about the rebel army, the war, the Sandinista repression. The lawmakers and their staffs asked mostly softball questions; nobody asked about the Killer Rat's photos.

There were only a couple of hints of the trouble the rebels were in. One Democratic representative, E. (Kika) de la Garza, a Mexican-American from Texas, refused even to let Jhonson and Rubén into his office. Later, when they had some free time—it was a gorgeous spring day—the two took a walk on the mall by the Washington monument. They came upon several thousand opponents of Reagan's Nicaragua policy in a rally staged to protest the upcoming contra aid vote. It took a few moments for the reality to sink in on Jhonson—he and Rubén had stumbled into an angry crowd.

"It was huge," Jhonson recalled later. He figured the protesters might grab him and Rubén and tear them apart if they realized they were anti-Sandinista commanders. The two retreated to Matamoros's office. There, Matamoros was talking with someone over the phone, apparently a Spanish-speaking reporter. Jhonson heard Matamoros accuse the Sandinistas of dressing up as contras and killing an innocent peasant.

"These photos are phony. This is a Sandinista setup!" Matamoros said. He seized on the blue uniforms worn by the killers. "Our men don't even wear those uniforms anymore, we've switched to olive-drab," Matamoros said. "And why weren't the killers carrying canteens?"

Jhonson and the other rebels flew to Miami, where on Wednesday, April 24, they heard the news of the contra aid vote. The House had rejected the Administration's request by the widest margin of any rebel aid vote to that point, 248 to 180.

Administration officials like Otto Reich, the State Department's Coordinator for Public Diplomacy at the time, were blaming the defeat on the shocking impact of Wohl's photos. It wasn't the first time contra abuses had caused a political stink in Washington, and Reagan Administration officials had made it routine practice to reject accounts of rebel atrocities as unfounded or to attempt to discredit those reporting the abuses.[24]

Now Reich, parroting Bosco Matamoros, challenged the authenticity of Wohl's photos and suggested that they had been staged. Among a dozen other details in Wohl's photos, Reich questioned why the contras' uniforms appeared so clean. A Pentagon official pushed Reich's argument even further. Not only were the uniforms too clean, the killers were wearing boots. "But most freedom fighters actually fight barefoot!" the official told reporters.

Another U.S. official attempting to discredit Wohl was Oliver North. In his briefings for conservative fund-raisers at the Old Executive Office Building, North called Wohl "the purported student that took the pictures," portraying him as a Sandinista sympathizer, insinuating that he had faked his photos.[25]

All of this left Wohl in some emotional distress. A fierce anticommunist, he now found himself under attack from the entire conservative establishment. But he defended the authenticity of his photos—even as he tried to justify the assassination. He argued repeatedly that the old man could have turned in other civilians who would have themselves been murdered unless the informant were silenced.

"This is not an atrocity," Wohl told the Associated Press. "We execute murderers in the U.S."

Mainly, however, Wohl was cashing in. "I'd like to talk to you," he told a reporter for the *Chicago Tribune*, "but my agent says that the *New York Post* is willing to buy the photos for fifteen hundred dollars, and that would include an exclusive interview. So if the *Post* is willing to pay fifteen hundred, you have to understand where I'm coming from . . . I try to get as much as I can. That is capitalism."

Wohl eventually earned some $35,000 from his photo royalties.

Of all those attacking Wohl, Adolfo Calero—who had greased Wohl's way into the rebel camps in the first place—sounded most aggrieved. In interview after interview, Calero pushed the line: "It's a fake, it's part of a smear on us." But Calero promised a thorough investigation.

In fact, there was an investigation within the FDN, because the Americans, from Oliver North down to the Agency's men in Honduras, were furious. Angry CIA agents met with Bermúdez, demanding an investigation and an explanation. Their anger was not over the killing . . . but over the photos. Who had authorized the photographer to visit Las Vegas? Hadn't anybody checked his credentials?[26]

Jhonson was curious, too, about how the killing had happened. Back in Honduras, he asked around. Wohl had always maintained that the killing had taken place inside Nicaragua, in Madriz province, but men from La Lodosa gave Jhonson a different version. The old man wasn't a Sandinista informant, they said. He was just some hapless peasant who had fled Nicaragua north into Honduras, passing by La Lodosa, and like so many others, Mack's men had grabbed him.[27]

Bermúdez did look into the killing, and soon figured out that it had been Mack's men. But Bermúdez never announced the results of his investigation, and he did nothing to Mack. Instead, the commander protected Mack so that his name would not emerge publicly. In fact, Bermúdez promoted him, naming Mack to head the rebels' Center for

Military Instruction, a new centralized boot camp under construction near Las Vegas, modeled on the National Guard's training center. Mack would be responsible for thousands of recruits.

Although Bermúdez had quickly established otherwise, the contras maintained for months their claim that Wohl's photos had been staged. Then, in the fall of 1985, Bermúdez gave an interview to CBS Television correspondent Jane Wallace, inviting her to La Quinta. Wearing a camouflage uniform with a service revolver strapped to his hip, Bermúdez tried to cut the part of a guerrilla commander for Wallace's cameras. Perhaps because he was feeling cocky, Bermúdez was the first contra to concede that Wohl's photos were genuine.

Wallace asked Bermúdez what he thought about Wohl's photos of the throat slashing.

"Well, I think it was unnecessary to do it in the way he did it," Bermúdez answered, staring at the camera.

"Not necessary?" Wallace asked.

"Not necessary, because they could be shot. That's all, not to do it like that."

"But you have no problem with people being murdered on the whim of the troops?"

"He was a spy," Bermúdez said. "And in war, spies have to be punished in that way."[28]

Late 1984 and 1985

For the first time, the Sandinistas were hurting the rebels. If, when the contra war began in 1981, the Sandinista army still betrayed its ragtag guerrilla origins, by late 1984 it was fast becoming a modern military force.

In January 1984, the Sandinista army began drafting young men aged eighteen to twenty-five into the army for two years of "patriotic military service." The measure allowed the army to field tens of thousands of new regulars, in addition to the thousands of detachments of local militias it had heretofore been throwing at the rebels. By 1985, the Sandinista army numbered at least 60,000 troops, and some 150,000 other Nicaraguans carried rifles in militia or reserve units.[29]

Most of the draftees were deployed in light, mobile counterinsurgency units, called Irregular Warfare battalions, or BLIs. As often as not, the recruits got little training before being dispatched into the countryside to chase contras, but experience was its own teacher, and the Sandinista soldiers fought with great initiative and courage. The contras knew it better than anyone else.[30]

While the counterinsurgency BLIs were the units most often in direct combat with the rebels, the Sandinista army was also beefing up its regular forces, deploying brigades and battalions in new garrisons throughout rural Nicaragua. They were well armed.

The Soviet bloc channeled astounding quantities of weaponry to the Sandinistas throughout the war—some $550 million in military aid during the first six years of the revolution alone, and by 1985, the investment was making itself felt. At the base of the arsenal were the ubiquitous AK-47 assault rifles, hundreds of thousands of them. East German troop-transport trucks, jammed with recruits, were traveling every major thoroughfare. Sophisticated Soviet radar scanners perched on strategic ridges along Nicaragua's coasts, listening to rebel communications. Strategic crossroads and installations across Nicaragua bristled with heavy artillery, and there were few havens into which the Sandinistas couldn't hurl shells if they located a rebel column. Overhead, everywhere, the skies clattered with transport helicopters.[31]

Rebel casualties were mounting, especially from the terrifying artillery barrages. Six months after Mike Lima was wounded in April 1984, a Sandinista rocket caught his old rival, Tigrillo, north of El Cuá, nearly tearing his knee off. Tigrillo's men carried him, bleeding, on a hammock strung from a pole, for a week through the mountains to a Honduran border airstrip. From there, an FDN helicopter airlifted him to the burgeoning hospital at Aguacate.

Tigrillo accepted his crippling wound with stoicism. His brother Dimas saw him a week after he arrived in the Aguacate hospital. "He didn't say anything, just that I shouldn't worry, because this was part of war," Dimas recalled. "He said he had faith that soon he'd be ready to continue the struggle." Later, Tigrillo was flown to New Orleans for surgery.[32] He lost all mobility in his knee, though doctors saved his leg.

Tigrillo's ordeal was not unusual. The Sandinista army campaign that gave them the initiative in the war brought extraordinary bloodletting on both sides. Hundreds of rebels were killed, and just as many were dragged off the battlefield bleeding. Although the medical system the CIA had established in Honduras for the rebels was adequate, rebels wounded deep inside Nicaragua routinely faced days or weeks of agony.

One rebel with the nom de guerre "Sergeant" took a bullet in the knee and had to hole up in a farmer's hut. Without medical attention, he developed gangrene. To survive, he cut the dead flesh away from his leg with his own knife. Eventually a doctor arrived—but there was still no anesthesia. The rebel stomached the pain of amputation, fully conscious. His story was only one of hundreds like it during the period.[33]

By early 1985, the war was going so well for the Sandinistas that they began to carry their attacks into Honduras to the rebel camps. Years of patient Sandinista road building—the trailblazing that CIA-directed sabotage against Construction Ministry warehouses had tried to forestall—allowed government forces to deploy into remote areas. One new road network enabled Sandinista units to tow heavy artillery—including their awesome, racked BM-21 rocket launchers—right to the southern edge of the Las Vegas salient. The BM-21 can lob a rocket more than thirteen miles, and several of the Sandinistas' border emplacements were just ten miles from Las Vegas. In late January, the Sandinistas began slinging rockets into the rebels' headquarters camp.

For several months, the contras sought to defend the Strategic Command by launching bloody, conventional counterattacks on the rocket emplacements, but the Sandinistas had moved up a half dozen infantry battalions to protect their positions, and the rebels lost many men for nothing. The Sandinista rocketing peaked in May and was accompanied by an advance of several hundred Sandinista infantrymen—backed by helicopters—into Honduras toward Las Vegas. In one three-day period, thirty Sandinista rockets crashed down on top of Mike Lima's Diriangén regional command camp alone, killing four fighters and wounding many more. The Sandinista bombardment also killed a Honduran corporal and several other soldiers in the salient, forcing hundreds of civilians to flee the zone.

The Honduran military had had enough. They ordered Bermúdez to abandon Las Vegas, and sent Honduran Air Force jets to cover the rebels' disorganized retreat. Bermúdez set up his new Strategic Command at Yamales, several miles to the north, well out of range of the Sandinistas' big guns.

The Sandinistas were also pounding La Lodosa, and a few months later, the artillery barrage forced Mack to move his Nicarao regional command over to Yamales, too.[34]

While Sandinista soldiers overwhelmed the rebels on the battlefield, the revolutionary government in Managua adopted a new carrot-and-stick approach with Nicaragua's peasants, aimed at rewarding cooperation with the government while punishing rebel collaborators.

The carrot took various forms. Starting in 1984, the government began to pay significantly higher prices for basic grain crops, so although many farmers continued to resent the government monopoly on crop marketing, at least their incomes began to rise, albeit slowly. The government also reversed its longtime agrarian reform policy. Before 1985, the Sandinistas had discriminated against individual families with its distributions, preferring to channel most of the land parcels to Sandinista-controlled cooperatives. Starting in 1985, the government recognized that that had been a political error, reversed course, and began large-scale handouts of land to individuals. That year, the government distributed 6,204 land titles to private families—almost three times as much land and more than six times as many land titles as in the previous three years combined. Later, government officials pointed to significant improvements in its relations with peasants as a result of these measures.[35]

Against those peasants considered to be rebel allies, though, the government wielded the stick: detention, resettlement, and bombardment. Arrests of accused contra collaborators accelerated drastically in 1985, especially after October, when State Security agents seized not only masses of peasants but rounded up hundreds of religious, labor, political, human-rights, business, and professional activists as well. The program continued into 1986, when some government figures suggest that the number of arrests actually quintupled. Late in 1986, more than five thousand political prisoners jammed government jails.[36]

But if the detentions were massive, the Sandinistas' resettlement program in 1985 and 1986 was truly draconian. President Daniel Ortega and top officials from the army, Interior, and several civilian ministries working as part of a resettlement commission identified dozens of rural zones where too many peasants were considered rebel collaborators, then sent in soldiers to herd farm families out to state-run "settlements." In many cases, homesteads were burned or leveled to prevent peasants from returning. The pace of these evacuations was so frantic that the soldiers were rounding up an average of nearly two thousand farmers a week during the first months of 1985. By late 1986, the government had herded nearly 200,000 people into at least 145 settlements nationwide.[37]

The settlements were themselves exercises in social engineering. Many farmers were relocated to "self-defense cooperatives" established near highways or other strategic points. There, the military authorities brought in families of Sandinista supporters, often from Managua or other cities, to live among, and supervise, the resettled hardscrabble farmers. Militia units were conscripted from among cooperative "members" to patrol the environs looking for rebels.

It was a classic counterinsurgency tactic, designed to separate contra "fish" like Jhonson from the "sea" of peasants in which they had been swimming. Jhonson discovered just how effective the relocations had been when he returned to Nicaragua in July 1985 from a resupply trip to Honduras. Moving south through once-friendly valleys populated by scores of farmers, Jhonson and his men marched for days without seeing a single peasant.

When Jhonson got to the strategic east-west road leading from Matagalpa toward the Atlantic coast, he found that the government had seized farms belonging to many of his friends and had trucked in Sandinista militants from several Pacific coast cities to establish a line of armed settlements along the highway. It had once been hospitable territory; now Jhonson kept encountering hostile militia units. He had to fight his way across.

The Sandinistas' idea in evacuating the farmers was not only to deny the rebels their support population, but to create free-fire zones, allowing government troops to use their artillery without concern for civilian casualties. As it worked out, the evacuations were not complete in many zones; farmers were reluctant to leave their hard-won homesteads and found ways to elude soldiers during the clearing operations. Nonetheless, the Sandinista army often declared these zones "cleared" anyway.

"I kill any peasant I see in that zone, because they're all contras," one government army officer told Alan Bolt, a Sandinista researcher who visited eastern Matagalpa during the period and subsequently helped write a controversial report criticizing army abuses.

"I told the officer—he was a cousin of mine—that there were loads of peasants living in there still," Bolt recalled.

The officer was unmoved.

"We've taken everybody out," the officer replied. "Anybody in there is a contra."[38]

In the wake of the relocations, and with Sandinista artillery bombardments mounting throughout rural Nicaragua, Jhonson found—for the first time in the war—his relations with peasants growing tense. Arriving at homestead after homestead, he found hitherto-friendly farmers now fearful, urging him to leave.

"Please go away! If you stay, we'll pay the consequences," one farmer in a hamlet near El Cuá told Jhonson. A year earlier the man's son had joined Jhonson's rebel unit; now the man pleaded with Jhonson to pull his men off the farm. "If the Sandinistas see you here, they'll shell our home."

Jhonson left. Days later, his bleak situation plunged into tragedy. His two younger brothers-in-law—Douglas, nineteen, and Henry, seventeen—were fighters in his rebel unit. With his men bivouacked near El Cuá, Jhonson sent his two relatives to scour the valley for any peasant who would sell them a steer to feed his troops. While they were gone, a Sandinista BLI discovered his camp, a firefight broke out, and the two teenage boys were cut off from Jhonson's unit. During the combat, automatic-rifle fire cut them down. His men found the two the following day, lying dead in a roadside ditch. Jhonson wept over their bodies.

Throughout the war, the Sandinistas had been quietly building up their fleet of troop-transport helicopters, and by late 1984, they had acquired their first Mi-24s, the armored gunships that are among the most lethal in the Soviets' counterinsurgency arsenal. The first time the Sandinistas used them in a true air-mobile combat operation came in August 1985.

Weeks before, Bermúdez had traveled to Miami, where he and Calero met with Oliver North, then administering the contra army. In the meeting, North emphasized the importance of cutting highways and moving the war into Nicaragua's cities. Bermúdez returned to his Strategic Command headquarters and ordered the rebels' largest attack since Pantasma.[39]

"We need a spectacular attack at any cost!" Bermúdez announced.[40]

Bermúdez targeted La Trinidad, a town with a population of eight thousand straddling the Pan American highway seventy-seven miles north of Managua, as well as several nearby bridges, for coordinated attacks by some two thousand rebel troops. On August 1, the rebels hit La Trinidad at dawn, fighting their way into control of the town by mid-morning. But they were unprepared for the Sandinistas' immediate aerial counterattack: More than a dozen helicopters and planes—including at least one Mi-24—roared overhead before the rebels had time to mount an orderly retreat.

La Trinidad sits astride a steep, jagged canyon through an escarpment dividing the lowlands near Lake Managua from the broad highland valley to the north, surrounding the provincial capital of Estelí. As the rebels' northward retreat led them out of the canyons, they found themselves without cover, and the helicopters strafed them from overhead. Some two hundred contra fighters died under the phosphorus rockets and withering fire of the helicopters' mini-guns.[41]

At the time, Jhonson was ordered to ambush an army convoy north of Pantasma in order to draw government forces away from La Trinidad, but instead of driving into the rebels' line of fire, the Sandinista officer in charge of the convoy sensed trouble and sent down scouts to scour the hills for ambush. Drawing fire from Jhonson's troops, the Sandinista called in air cover. Soon several helicopters were screaming over Jhonson's men, who were caught in an open pasture. Flying low—just a few hundred feet off the ground—the choppers pounded out an enormous volume of machine-gun fire.

"We'd never seen or heard one of those monsters," Jhonson recalled later. In reality the helicopters didn't cause that many casualties—one killed and three wounded among Jhonson's eighty-man column—but at first, cowering under the thunder and scream of the rotors, the whine and crash of the rockets, Jhonson's men were utterly terrorized.

Two of his men had been lugging two SAM-7 antiaircraft missiles, each one forty-six pounds of equipment, all the way from Honduras. Amid the terror, first one missileman, then the other, sighted their rockets and shot. Neither rocket would fire . . . they were duds. The helicopters continued their dizzying circles until dark, then Jhonson's men crept away.

In the months that followed, enemy helicopters always seemed close by. Anytime rebel troops engaged a Sandinista patrol, they could expect to hear helicopters within half an hour, ferrying in Sandinista reinforcements or thundering overhead to lay down air cover for the government forces.[42]

Outgunned and outnumbered, their supplies dwindling, their peasant supporters fearful, most rebel commanders limped back to the Honduran camps during 1986. Thousands of rebel fighters streamed into the Yamales Valley. Jhonson himself pulled most of his September 15th Regional Command.

Even regional commanders who had been operating in central Boaco and Chontales provinces—in some cases for more than a year—came out. They had been fighting inside Nicaragua longer than any other commanders, but now hundreds of men, along with scores of starving civilians, straggled into Honduras under the command of Tirzo Moreno, "Rigoberto," after a month-long trek northward. They had run out of supplies and been forced to eat their own mules to survive. Eighteen men had died along the route, some of hunger-related diseases, others of battle wounds.

Rigoberto recalled his own first encounter with Bermúdez at Yamales.

"God, you look like a cadaver," Bermúdez said.

"Well, we've seen a lot of combat, and we didn't have much food," Rigoberto responded.

"Well, what are you thinking of doing now?" Bermúdez asked.

"What are my orders?" Rigoberto responded.

"Why don't you go to Tegucigalpa and have some fun?" Bermúdez said. "Okay? Let's keep in touch." And that was that. Bermúdez walked away.

"He showed no interest in conditions in my operating zone," Rigoberto said, "nor in how people were reacting to us, how troop morale was holding up, how our recruiting was going. He left all that to the Americans."

Two CIA officers, "Captain Steve," a blond Vietnam veteran of about thirty, and "Major Thomas," an athletic agent about twenty-six whom the rebels believed to be of Mexican or American Indian descent, invited Rigoberto into the CIA's new bunker at the Yamales Strategic Command camp. They said they had been following Rigoberto's long campaign inside Nicaragua with some interest and wanted to hear every detail. They debriefed him for two days with a tape recorder running, writing meticulous notes.

Summer 1985 through June 25, 1986

With the Sandinistas making such military gains, it was clear to the Reagan Administration that the contras would make no more progress until the Congress approved new official U.S. aid. The Administration made important progress toward that goal on June 12, 1985, when the House appropriated $27 million to fund the contras.[43] It was an important turnaround, and it came partly because days before the vote, Nicaraguan President Daniel Ortega traveled to Moscow to request new Soviet aid, embarrassing Democratic congressmen. But the Administration victory was also the result of clever packaging: The White House dubbed the aid bill "humanitarian" because it allowed the provision of food and medicine while barring the purchase of weapons and other lethal equipment. Over the next year, this "humanitarian" aid, along with the aid for lethal weapons provided by Oliver North's secret network and new CIA intelligence support legalized in November 1985, helped the contras to survive.

And yet at the same time it was obvious that even with all this jury-rigged aid, the contras could never advance. So in February 1986, the White House requested $100 million in military aid for the contras, knowing full well that Congress was never going to vote such a decisive package until the rebels' image changed; the army's abuses had become too widely known. Frank Wohl's photos had done a lot of damage, but they were only a small part of the problem. In March 1985, José Efrén "Moisés" Mondragón Martínez, a former Guard sergeant who had been one of Colonel Lau's hitmen, deserted from the contra army, and after fleeing Honduras for Mexico, began talking to reporters. He said that Bermúdez had ordered him killed, and he accused Mack, Zero-Three, Z-Two, The Policeman, The Beast, and several other FDN officers of being serial murderers. During the same period, Americas Watch and other rights monitors issued withering reports on FDN abuses. Few centrist congressmen could stomach a vote for rebel aid.[44]

But the abuses weren't the only problem. Moderate congressmen had grown suspicious of the FDN leaders themselves, especially Calero, who was receiving $1 million a month from the Saudi government. Calero was wearing expensive suits, jetting from speech to speech, hobnobbing with America's wealthiest conservatives. Lawmakers could see what this "rebel leader" really was—a glad-handing businessman.

As a result, U.S. officials decided to create a new political front. Three years after the CIA had installed the FDN's first political directorate in Miami, the Agency—led by Alan Fiers, the CIA's new Central America Task Force chief, a former CIA station chief in Saudi Arabia—was again involved in setting up the new rebel leadership.[45] But this time Oliver North took the lead role. The process boiled down to the same thing, however: U.S. officials recruited the contra leaders and paid their salaries. The new front, known as the United Nicaraguan Opposition (UNO), would have three members: Calero, Alfonso Robelo, the opposition politician whose 1982 rally Jhonson had attended before his arrest by Sandinista police, and Arturo Cruz, a banker. North brought the men together in a Miami hotel room in January to draft a unity statement, and in March he hired a Washington public-relations firm to orchestrate the UNO's public unveiling in a San Salvador press conference.

From a public-relations standpoint, Cruz was an especially effective counterpoint to Calero on the new rebel front. A provincial banker who went to Washington during the 1970s to work at the Inter-American Development Bank, Cruz felt a disgust for Somoza that had led him to endorse the Sandinistas, and after their victory he took several posts in the revolutionary government. When he finally broke with the Sandinistas, he was Managua's ambassador to Washington.

This background gave Cruz extraordinary credibility as a Sandinista critic, and after his recruitment, he began receiving a secret seven-thousand-dollar monthly stipend from North.[46]

Yet Cruz never seemed comfortable posing as a rebel political chieftain. He was more of an absent-minded professor, his glasses always slipping down his nose, and he was no good at lying. From his first involvement with the contras, Cruz was embarrassed by their abuses and began to fight with Calero and Bermúdez, pressing for changes.

Cruz's complaints set off institutional squabbling in the U.S. government that would continue, in various forms, through the end of the war. State Department officials, fed up with Calero and Bermúdez, backed Cruz. The CIA backed the old FDN clique, while Oliver North played both sides, promoting Cruz and Robelo to win votes in Congress while channeling his money and arms to Calero.

The CIA considered the State Department to be hopelessly romantic; the Agency was trying to run a war. One of its operating rules was to remain loyal to an obedient asset, and whatever the neophytes at State had to say about them, Calero and Bermúdez had been obedient. Tony Feldman, the CIA officer who had lured Calero into exile and installed him as the president of the FDN directorate, defended Calero most fiercely and ridiculed Cruz most savagely as a mercurial idealist. One early 1986 meeting in Washington erupted into an angry screaming match between the CIA's John Mallett, who had worked for years with Bermúdez and Aristides Sánchez in Honduras, and Robert Kagan, a twenty-eight-year-old State Department officer working to unseat Bermúdez and Calero.

Cruz's calls for reform brought some cosmetic changes. For instance, Calero installed an old lawyer friend from his Coca-Cola plant in Managua, Carlos Icaza, to revise the contras' Code of Conduct and to set up a new FDN Office of Legal Affairs to sanction rebels accused of abuses.[47] But mostly, Cruz's pressure just aroused infighting in the rebel ranks. Over drinks at one of the FDN's Tegucigalpa safe houses, Bermúdez warned several field commanders that Cruz and his backers were Communists. On another occasion, Bermúdez circulated a petition denouncing Cruz among the rebel commanders. When Cruz toured the camps, Bermúdez ordered a rally by FDN troops on his own behalf, with preordained cheering for his own speech and stark silence after Cruz's.

Cruz's reform campaign and the upcoming contra aid vote focused tremendous attention in Washington on the contra army during the spring of 1986, and dozens of congressional delegations visited the Yamales Strategic Command during this period. Bermúdez developed a formula for entertaining them. He would start with a twenty-minute war situationer in front of a wall-sized Nicaraguan map, take the Americans on a helicopter trip to the FDN boot camp, then fly back to Yamales to the rebel hospital for a few words with the war wounded, move on to the civilian clinic and a plea for humanitarian aid, and return to the Strategic Command for a tour of the staff offices. Bermúdez learned to stress his commitment to human rights in these encounters. But his men were still committing abuses.

Leo, the former National Guard barber Bermúdez had installed at the head of the FDN's military police, was expanding his fledgling prison system. Until 1984, there hadn't been any FDN jails; they weren't taking prisoners in battle, and suspected spies were just chained to trees. At

Las Vegas, Leo had built a small lockup as part of Mike Lima's attempts to impose order. Once established, Leo's military police had detained so many commandos that Leo decided to expand. His opportunity came after the rebel army moved to Yamales. Hidden behind a hill across from the Yamales Strategic Command headquarters, Leo and his men built three barracks-like stockades: timber walls, dirt floors, and a plastic roof, all cocooned in barbed wire. It wasn't long before Leo was tending nearly a hundred prisoners at Yamales and coercing the female prisoners into granting him sexual favors.[48]

At the rebels' basic training camp, known as the CIM, located in the hills five miles east of Las Vegas, Mack was in charge, and his instructors were old chums from the Guard, some of the most brutal men in the FDN. One was Britolde Cruz, "X-Seven," who had helped to strangle Commander Krill on Mack's orders in 1983. Another was Francisco Laríos, "Jersey," who had been with Mack at La Lodosa. The training regimen was punishing. From before dawn until after sundown, Mack had recruits sweating through calisthenics and racing up and down the steep hills ringing the base. The rigors would have been fine, but food at the CIM was always scarce. The result was chronic sickness. Rebel doctors complained to Bermúdez that Mack was selling the CIM's food on the Honduran black market, but Mack was never sanctioned. And there were more serious abuses.

Tirzo Moreno, known as Rigoberto, the head of the Jorge Salazar Regional Command, sent hundreds of recruits to the CIM for training in April 1986 after a long incursion. His commandos had been marching for weeks with little food, but at the CIM, Mack's men maintained rigid rules. When eight commandos failed to report for morning calisthenics on time, Mack's instructors searched the camp and found them sick in their plastic shelters. Amid kicks and blows, the eight were herded down to the parade ground where the other recruits were sweating through the morning push-ups. There, Mack ordered four of the latecomers to climb a tall spruce tree overlooking a ravine—and a fifth to cut it down. Crashing down into the precipice, three of the commandos died. Another was critically injured.

"This is an example to the rest of you," Mack told the other recruits. "You've got to learn what it means to be soldiers."

Dozens of the rest of the panicked recruits waited until nightfall, then fled the base. The next morning Mike Lima, in his informal role as FDN counterintelligence coordinator, came looking for the "leaders of the rebellion." He and his aides pulled out four of those who had fled, beating and kicking them in full view of other commandos.

And there were other horror stories, too, for despite Cruz's reform campaign, Bermúdez's clique was still in charge.[49] But even if Cruz and his aides failed to bring significant change to the contra army, their lobbying campaign to renew U.S. military aid proved effective. They worked, one-on-one, to persuade the several dozen lawmakers who had voted on both sides of the contra issue in the past to support the $100 million package, and in the final House balloting on June 25, 1986, enough congressmen switched their votes to approve the package. The vote was 221–209.

The appropriation included $70 million for weaponry. To pacify congressional worries, the Administration earmarked $3 million in the legislation for human-rights training. The law also allowed the CIA to work directly once again with the contras, not only providing them with intelligence and advice—legal since November 1985—but planning rebel strategy and directing military operations. It was an extraordinary Administration victory.

Representative Buddy Roemer, a Louisiana Democrat who voted for the aid, expressed the view that finally was to carry the House: "Are the contras perfect? Of course not. But neither are we."[50]

7

The $100 Million Offensive

July 1986 through February 1988

The $100 million contra aid package appropriated in the summer of 1986 amounted to a tremendous commitment of American support to the contra army. For the first five years of the conflict, a divided Congress had sputtered and fought against the Reagan Administration's obsession with the rebels, first restricting, then cutting U.S. aid altogether. The $100 million vote was a watershed: Congress reversed course. For the first time, the entire American government signed on to the anti-Sandinista war.

One hundred million dollars was an enormous amount of money for a twelve-thousand-man army—it amounted to nearly ten thousand dollars for every contra fighter. U.S. officials used the money for a sweeping overhaul of what had become a very ragged force. The CIA rebuilt the insurgent air force with Rhodesian mercenary pilots, Spanish planes, and a secret bivouac on a Caribbean isle. Dozens of U.S. agents transformed Aguacate Air Base into a vast intelligence center bristling with CIA antennas and an air-supply hub humming with night flights to Nicaragua. CIA technicians trained elite rebel units in the subtleties of the Redeye heat-seeking surface-to-air missile. CIA purchasing agents bought whole container ships packed with the basics: explosives, guns, and bullets. And there was still plenty of money left over.

"The one hundred million meant we could train the rebels directly," recalled one State Department official working with the rebels at the time. "That meant we could change not only the way they fought, but also the way they looked and talked and even thought. It was a great opportunity."

It was a view that guided Washington's entire Central American policy during the 1980s: Just fund a little U.S. training, policy-makers argued, and Americans could remake the isthmus and its people in our image. Most of Bermúdez's Strategic Command aides and scores of rebel field commanders were flown to the United States for direct training by Green Berets. They were not only taught hard military skills, but also rushed through a course designed to raise their political consciousness.

"The field commanders sensed that they didn't have a good political message," recalled one U.S. official. "They knew they needed it, and they knew they didn't have it."

U.S. officials renamed the contra army—it became "the Nicaraguan Resistance"—and created an integrated political message for it.[1] The Americans thought of this a little like putting together an advertising campaign. The $100 million was paying for a propaganda radio, Radio Liberation, with studios in Miami and transmitters in El Salvador. The officials at State wanted the political directors to carry the same message in their U.S.-funded political tours. And now the rebels were taught to bring the same political message to the battlefield. "Why couldn't the Resistance spray-paint political graffiti on walls in towns they attacked, like the rebels in El Salvador?" one official asked.

When, after months of preparation, ten thousand rebel fighters trudged south to war in the steam of the 1987 rainy season, the results of the U.S. effort to remake the rebels were mixed.

On one hand, it was obvious that the U.S. training had brought changes; the rebels fought more like soldiers and less like hooligans. Within months, insurgent missilemen had knocked down nearly half the helicopters in the Sandinista air force. American military officers resumed control of the rebel army, and in two CIA-directed battles, thousands of rebel fighters converged to overwhelm half a dozen rural towns, seizing Sandinista missile stocks and destroying Soviet radar installations. And the rebels won wide support among Nicaraguan peasants. Many civilians interpreted the $100 million program as an overwhelming and unequivocal U.S. commitment that brought thousands of Nicaraguans into the war on the contras' side, as recruits and collaborators. Many put themselves at the contras' service as they never had before.

On the other hand, back in the base camps in Honduras, Bermúdez's ex-Guardsmen were brutalizing young fighters—especially young women—with the same ferocity as ever. And inside Nicaragua, too, there were many abuses committed by rebel fighters during the year.

Still, the U.S.-backed rebel offensive brought dramatic results. The accumulation of ambushes and sabotage over the course of 1987 put enormous pressure on the Sandinista government. Eight months into the rebel offensive, Nicaraguan President Daniel Ortega sued for peace, committing his revolutionary government to democratic rule and leading it into direct peace talks with the contras.

These were all dramatic developments, yet America hardly noticed. On October 5, 1986, just weeks after Congress voted the $100 million, Sandinista soldiers shot down a C-47 cargo plane operated by Oliver North's secret supply network. North's two-year program of illegal aid became public, and the Iran-contra scandal began to unfold. The Reagan White House, fearful that the scandal could lead to impeachment, began to concentrate on damage control. The Congress that had voted the $100 million only weeks earlier turned its attention to the scandal.

While in Nicaragua, an entirely new phase of the war played itself out during 1987, in the United States, Americans were glued to their television sets, watching the Iran-contra hearings. Eventually, Congress changed its mind—again.

October through December 1986

In late October 1986, Jhonson and sixty other contra commanders climbed onto a U.S. C-130 military transport plane at Aguacate Air Base for a flight to Eglin Air Force Base in the Florida panhandle for seven weeks of training.[2]

Participating in the course were most of the leaders of the FDN's thirty-two regional commands, as well as some two dozen prominent task force leaders. Some, like Jhonson, were civilians; others, including Mack, were ex-Guardsmen. Fighters from the CIA's Miskito Indian army, as well as from another rebel force based in Costa Rica, were also flown in from Central America.

The Americans treated the training itself like a covert operation. After a three-hour flight, the rebels deplaned at a deserted airstrip, ringed with pine forest. American agents urged them onto two buses with blacked-out windows for a drive along a bumpy dirt road to what appeared to be a military school, where the rebels were lodged in—in fact confined to—two modern dormitories, bunking eight to a room. To Jhonson, the classrooms were ultramodern; when the outside air turned chill, there was central heating.

The curriculum for the rebel training was the product of an often stormy debate between officials from the CIA, the State Department, and the Pentagon. The rival agencies quarreled over how the rebels should fight, how supply lines should be organized, what kind of weapons they should fire, and how long the war should last. It was a strictly American debate, fought in Washington. Bermúdez and other contra leaders didn't participate.

Some officials wanted to turn the Nicaraguan conflict, once and for all, into a true guerrilla war. Their position amounted to a variant of the "prolonged war" strategies advanced by guerrilla theorists from Mao in China to Salvador Cayetano Carpio in El Salvador. They argued for the slow, careful organization of an internal base among Nicaragua's people, for the patient knitting together of a logistical network based on civilian supporters. They advocated training and more training so that the rebels themselves could increasingly assume true leadership of the war. Supplies and ammunition, they said, should be carried on mules or captured from the enemy—not dropped from planes.

Others believed that time was running out for the contras. The rebels needed to reestablish their military credibility through spectacular attacks within a year or so, these officials argued. To achieve this, they advocated central direction of the war by U.S. military officers. Oliver North's air-supply force had fallen apart; now the officials argued for reestablishment of a new, professional air-resupply system, based on a mercenary air force.[3]

By late 1986, this latter vision had carried the day. As a result, when Jhonson and the rebels began their training, the main focus was on hard military skills: They learned to deploy soldiers, read maps, sight artillery, staunch wounds, blow things up.

The instructors were Green Berets, working on contract for the CIA, loaned from other assignments. They used pseudonyms: Lizard, Scorpion, Tiger. "Don't ask me my name, and I won't ask you yours," they told the contras. Several instructors soon considered Jhonson one of the best students.

"He was a quick study," recalled one U.S. official involved in the training. "He came to classes well-prepared, he grasped it all quickly. He already understood how to organize guerrilla combat in a region."

In addition to the military instruction, the U.S. instructors conducted a series of "psychological operations" seminars, to carry out a kind of political sensitivity training. By day, the rebels would learn hard military skills; by night, they would gather in a classroom to discuss political warfare. It seemed like a sound idea, but few of the instructors had prior experience with the contras. And they didn't know Mack and the other ex-Guardsmen.

One evening a few weeks into the course, the American instructors decided to focus on the relationship between human-rights abuses and international isolation in guerrilla war. To get the discussion going, they beamed Frank Wohl's slides of Mack's executioners slashing the old man's neck. With the contras watching the slide show, one of the U.S. trainers read a Spanish translation of the *Newsweek* article on the killings.

"The point of it was to show them, 'This is your image,' and ask them, 'How are you going to change it?' " a U.S. military officer involved in the training recalled.

Then the Green Berets encouraged their contra "students" to discuss the incident. What had been the impact of these photos? The Americans wanted a theoretical discussion. They didn't realize that the very commanders whose men had carried out this and scores of other casual murders were sitting in front of them.

None of the contras knew quite what to say. Then one of Mack's friends argued that it had been necessary to kill the old man; otherwise, he could have betrayed the rebels' location, endangering the security of the contra column. That provoked discussion. If the contra column was in danger, somebody said, then the old man could just have been held prisoner for a time until the danger passed, then lectured and released. Jhonson supported that view.

Killing the old man was stupid, somebody said, and it had been completely idiotic to allow a photographer to look on while the terrified captive dug his own grave and lay down in it to face the knife, others added.

Mack himself changed the argument. That whole incident was staged anyway, he said. What's the use of discussing it? The Sandinistas had dressed up like contras and killed a prisoner in a propaganda display. His vehemence quieted the argument. Quite a few of the contras agreed that the Sandinistas were capable of, well, anything.

Then Mack's ex-Guardsmen took the offensive. This whole discussion is bullshit, a premeditated personal attack on certain individuals, they said. The gringos are trying to defame the name of soldiers who have fought in our struggle for years. What had seemed to the well-meaning Americans like a sound idea turned into an ugly stink.

"It created a major crisis," recalled a U.S. military official. "The trainers were just floored. They tried to explain that they hadn't wanted to defame anybody, but the incident soured the rest of that training cycle. Certain instructors just didn't have any credibility left."

Word of the incident spread back to Washington, where the CIA used it as ammunition in the Agency's fight with State. See what we mean? Agency officers said. The State Department is already screwing up the

Recruits at the contra training center, the Centro de Instruccion Militar.

Enrique Bermúdez.

Luis Fley; "Jhonson."

Gritolde Cruz

Salapa - 1998

Isaac Samuel Blake Hurtado;
"Israelita."

Britolde Cruz; "X-Seven."

Sentries guard the Quilalí Regional Command camp during a 1989 torture-murder investigation.

Israel Galeano; "Franklyn."

Rebel troops in parade formation during a review in the Honduran mountains.

(Left to right) Bermúdez and José Benito Bravo Centeno ("Mack").

Contras rest during training at the Centro de Instruccion Militar.

(Left to right) Armando "The Policeman" López, Juan Ramón "Quiché" Rivas, and José Benito "Mack" Bravo Centeno.

Aristides Sánchez.

Luis ("Mike Lima") Moreno and his two children.

On the road to disarming, contras at dawn ride in Soviet IFA trucks on their way to El Almendro, where they handed over their weapons to the UN forces. The Sandinistas transported the combatants under stealth of night to the disarming locations in 1990.

training. This is going to slow the production of military combat leaders. The training cycle limped to an end.[4]

October 1985 through May 1987

The 1987 offensive was more complicated and technically more sophisticated than any previous rebel campaign. It involved new computers, missiles, radios, decoders, and a hundred other U.S. innovations. The American intelligence agent who put all of it together was James Adkins, the chief of the Agency's Honduran base during the crucial year after Congress voted the new aid in June 1986.

Adkins's work in Honduras had begun months earlier, in late 1985, after Ray Doty, turning sixty and facing mandatory retirement, had flown home. Doty and his men hadn't done much with the contras for over a year anyway, due to the U.S. aid cutoff. Adkins, in contrast, arrived just after Congress loosened the 1984–1985 ban on CIA contacts with the rebels.

During the course of his twenty-month tour, Adkins would first reestablish close CIA intelligence relations with the rebels and then, after June 1986, engineer the Nicaraguan rebels' most ambitious offensive of the war.

Adkins was a long-faced, clean-shaven man, fifty years old, trim and just six feet tall. Born in Huntington, West Virginia, he still spoke with a bit of a drawl, and said things like "You bet your butt!" Coarse brown hair, clipped short along the peak of a high forehead, was beginning to show gray. Framing his steel-blue eyes were lines betraying the stress of earlier Agency postings.

In the 1950s, before he was a CIA agent, Adkins had enjoyed a brief but unsuccessful career as a pitcher in the Milwaukee Braves farm system, then served a seven-year stint as a state trooper in West Virginia. He had returned to college at Marshall University in Huntington when a CIA campus recruiter interviewed him in 1966. The recruiter was impressed. Adkins signed on.

A year later, when Adkins was thirty-three, he flew to Bangkok, beginning a two-year tour in Southeast Asia. The Agency had prepared him little for the experience. He'd never seen anything like Thailand, and during his first weeks, he was completely disoriented. The assignment became only more exotic when the Agency shipped him to Laos. There—like Ray Doty, whom Adkins got to know—he advised the forty-thousand-man Laotian peasant army that the CIA had recruited to fight North Vietnamese regulars moving arms through eastern Laos. Adkins was flown into remote northern Laos and set out with a battalion of guerrillas opening a new border camp east of the Plain of Jars. He spoke not a word of Lao, but with no other Americans within a hundred-mile radius, he learned to make himself understood. For two years, he lived in a thatched hut, ate rice and insects, and carried an M-16 rifle, fighting alongside the peasant combatants.

When Adkins left in 1970—five years before the final bloody rout of the CIA's army of Laotian peasants—Laos had stamped him as had no other experience. When he arrived, he'd been just a good ol' boy with police experience. He flew home an expert in paramilitary war, a man who knew how to coordinate air-supply drops, plan sabotage campaigns, and manage peasant armies.

After Laos, Adkins switched cultures. He joined the Agency's Western Hemisphere division, took some Spanish classes, and, a year later, flew south. He spent the next decade bouncing around Latin America under diplomatic cover, first as a political officer in Santo Domingo, then as an economics officer in Santiago, then as the chief of station in Guyana. Adkins arrived in Georgetown just in time for crisis duty during the November 1978 Jonestown mass suicide of more than nine hundred followers of the American cult leader Jim Jones.

In the early 1980s, Adkins was reassigned to Langley. With his paramilitary background and his extensive Latin American experience, he was a sure bet for recruitment for service in the Reagan Administration's new paramilitary project in Honduras. But he wasn't in the mood. His wife was happy in Washington, and Adkins himself smelled trouble from a suspicious Congress. He resisted, but in late 1985 his boss finally handed him a ticket and ordered him onto a plane south. He was the new Honduras base chief.[5]

By this time, Congress had decided to allow the CIA to provide the contras with advice and intelligence information, which opened wide opportunities for new Agency initiatives. Adkins sensed that the quality of intelligence reporting to Langley from Honduras had been poor, and eager to bring himself up to speed on the nature of rebel operations inside Nicaragua, he began helicoptering to the rebels' border bases at Banco Grande and Yamales to debrief rebel commanders returning to Honduras. Bermúdez wasn't doing it, and Adkins knew that many of the CIA men in Honduras were paramilitary trainers—"knuckle-draggers," he called them—incapable of writing a coherent intelligence report. Adkins did the debriefings himself, grabbing rebel commanders, sitting them down under a tree at the edge of the Banco Grande helicopter pad, and peppering them with questions: How many men did they have inside Nicaragua? What Sandinista units were they fighting? What Sandinista tactics were they facing? How were Nicaraguans reacting to the

rebel forces? Where were the Sandinistas' radio intercept stations located? What were the common routes flown by Sandinista helicopters?

Adkins also oversaw the development of the rebel army's first serious
intelligence collection system. When Congress loosened the ban on CIA
contacts with the rebels, lawmakers also authorized the CIA to provide
the rebels with $4 million worth of radios and other electronic spy gear.[6]

Contra communications security had, until then, been poor. The
rebels had been using obsolete "code pads"—a secret list assigning number sequences to each letter of the alphabet—to scramble their radio
messages. Used just once, the pads offered a secure, if cumbersome system, but the rebels were transmitting with the same pads over and over.
East German, Bulgarian, and Cuban communications experts in
Nicaragua were routinely breaking rebel codes.

All that changed with Adkins's arrival in Honduras. With him came
a horde of new CIA communications men, who brought dozens of computerized keyboard scramblers for rebel use. The scramblers worked on
the same principle as the code pads, assigning number sequences to each
letter, but the new machines could spit out coded messages in a fraction
of the time, and they constantly changed their own codes. The communications men also brought dozens of sensitive radio receivers and
antennas; working with the rebels, they set up little intercept camps on
Honduran ridges all along the Nicaraguan border. From those peaks, the
rebel antennas began to listen in on the daily radio conversations
between Sandinista military units all over Nicaragua. Employing new
computers, the advisers taught contra analysts to collate hundreds of
intercepted radio messages for use in identifying Sandinista military
units, tracking their movements, and guessing their intentions.[7]

While Adkins's work with the rebels went fine, his relations with the
Honduran military were rockier. Adkins smelled drug corruption.

During the first years of the contra war, the CIA had handled all arms
purchases for the rebels directly, but with the 1984 U.S. aid cutoff, control over arms purchases passed to amateurs like Calero and North.
With millions at stake, numerous arms traders reached for the action.
The cooperation of the Honduran military was necessary to move any
supplies to the rebels, and a group of top Honduran officers had been
reaping a bonanza from payoffs they demanded on every shipment.

Into this environment, one Miami-based arms company muscled in
most forcefully. The company, R M Equipment Inc., was run by Ronald
Martin, a former Marine, in partnership with retired Lieutenant Colonel
James L. McCoy, the defense attaché at the U.S. embassy in Managua
during Somoza's final years. Developing close contacts with Honduran
military officers through a Miami-based Cuban exile, Mario Dellamico,

Martin and McCoy cut several lucrative arms deals during the U.S. aid cutoff period. Then, in early 1986, Martin and McCoy began to position themselves for the bonanza they saw developing as the Reagan Administration proposed spending $100 million on the contras. They invested between $15 and $20 million to ship hundreds of tons of weaponry and munitions to Honduras—including millions of AK-47 rounds—storing them at a weapons dump at Aguacate Air Base, controlled by the Honduran military.

The idea was to have all the arms in place so that when Congress passed the $100 million, CIA procurement men could just walk across the airstrip at Aguacate and shop for weapons as though it were . . . a supermarket. That, in fact, is what Martin and McCoy's project was called: an "arms supermarket."

To Adkins and other CIA men, the whole thing stank. Where had the venture capital come from? It smelled like drugs. In October 1986, as Adkins and his procurement aides began to purchase arms with the $100 million, he refused to buy from Martin and McCoy, despite the fact that Honduran military officers who had financial interests in the transactions tried to force the CIA to buy its weaponry from the arms supermarket.

At one meeting, Honduran Commander-in-Chief General Humberto Regalado decreed that the CIA could bring no further arms of the type already stockpiled by Martin and McCoy into Honduras. Adkins exploded. "Don't try to pull any of that cheap shit on me," he said, and he stalked out.

There was a tense silence. Regalado looked around. "One more performance like that and he's out of the country," he told other CIA men.[8]

Fortunately, Adkins had a new aide, a smooth and diplomatic U.S. Army officer with excellent ties to the Honduran military, Army Colonel Jerry Clark, forty-five. Nearly half of Clark's twenty years of Army service had been spent in Honduras by the time he was detached to the CIA in late 1986 as the operations chief for the $100 million program. His Honduran postings had been highly visible: head of the U.S. military group, military attaché. A native of Puerto Rico, he spoke excellent Spanish and had an easy temperament and a whole knot of close friendships with top Honduran Army officers.[9] Clark smoothed things over for Adkins with the Hondurans.[10]

Perhaps because of his experience in Laos, Adkins, like Doty, emphasized the need for an efficient air-supply system. With the October 1986 shooting down and capture of American cargo handler Eugene Hasenfus over Nicaragua, the El Salvador–based air-supply organization created by Oliver North fell apart. The FDN still had its own "air force," the clique of former Somoza-era pilots headed by Bermúdez's crony, ex-National Guard Colonel Juan Gómez, but Adkins looked them over and judged them useless—corrupt, lazy, inept. If the new air-supply system were to be serious, the CIA would have to start over. Adkins's men recruited Rhodesian mercenary pilots and procured new resupply planes: two Spanish Caza 2-12s and two DC-6s.[11]

But where to base the new air wing? The logical place was Aguacate. It had changed a great deal since the early days when the CIA first rented the "base" from the Honduran military in 1983. Over the years, U.S. military engineers and the CIA had built Aguacate into a sprawling base with a virtual industrial park of warehouses and aviation maintenance hangars, a three-hundred-bed hospital, and an eight-thousand-foot runway busy with C-130 traffic. The problem, in fact, was that Aguacate was too busy. Journalists and opposition Honduran politicians were harping constantly on the rebel presence at the base. There was no way the CIA could add the hundreds of new supply flights it was planning over the next months to Aguacate.[12]

Instead, the CIA built a new supply center on Swan Island, a tiny dot 119 miles off the Honduran coast on the turquoise waters of the Caribbean, four square miles of sand, palm trees, a few houses, and a grid of roads. Technically, it was Honduran, but the CIA had long enjoyed its use. During the 1961 Bay of Pigs invasion, the CIA had set up a radio transmitter on Swan to broadcast propaganda to Cuba. In 1987, Swan became a busy arms transshipment center. A CIA freighter ferried containerized supplies from Texas and Florida ports to the Swan docks, where CIA agents used a hydraulic derrick to unload the containers, and tractor drivers towed them into place along the island's 3,500-foot all-weather runway. So great was the cargo traffic at the height of the offensive that nearly 150 containers lined the runway. The CIA assigned some 130 Nicaraguans to work on Swan, sorting cargo, packing bundles, folding parachutes, and loading planes. The Nicaraguans lived cheek-by-jowl with the mercenary pilots, but the Rhodesians didn't socialize on Swan. Instead, after every few flights over Nicaragua, the Rhodesians flew northeast to the Cayman Islands to deposit their salaries and buy whiskey.

In charge on Swan was a CIA agent the rebels knew as "Major John," an American of about thirty who liked to lift weights and shout orders. He spoke not a word of Spanish, dealing with the Nicaraguans through two interpreters, a Puerto Rican man named "Frenchy" and a woman named María. He was in command of more than a dozen other CIA agents based on the island.[13]

The Hondurans were impatient, not only about the rebel presence on

Aguacate, but about the rebel encampment at Yamales. During 1986 so many contras and their families had streamed into the Yamales salient that Hondurans began calling it derisively "New Nicaragua." The contra camps had displaced a number of Honduran coffee farmers, and intermittent visits by journalists to the base camps kept the insurgent presence in the headlines. With the passage of the $100 million program, the Hondurans saw relief: With the thousands of rebel fighters retrained and rearmed, they could abandon their Yamales bivouac for Nicaragua.

And yet that would still leave Bermúdez's Strategic Command at Yamales. Dozens of new CIA agents were working with the rebel forces and the Americans were taking increasingly direct control, but in the CIA's view, Bermúdez and Sánchez were still key leaders. A myriad of tensions were by now tearing at the rebel army from within: Former National Guardsmen distrusted former Sandinistas; frontline combatants resented rear-guard logistical officers; unpaid soldiers envied the officers with their salaries and pickup trucks. The men in Honduras were beginning to view the contras' new headquarters in Miami as a swamp of overpaid bureaucrats. Whatever their limitations, Bermúdez and Sánchez knew the rebel officers and their families and they understood the subtleties of their conflicts. They were to maintain cohesion. The CIA gave them an ample budget to dole out to commanders or their girlfriends as little favors, or as outright bribes, when necessary. In a way, Bermúdez and Sánchez were simply glorified guidance counselors, probation officers, and personnel agents, but they were central to the CIA's plans.

The Hondurans wanted Bermúdez's Strategic Command, along with a series of other rebel facilities—a clinic, a supply dump, a weapons tent, Mack's training center, Leo's prison—moved out of the Las Vegas salient. But where to? The Americans pressured Bermúdez to set up his Strategic Command and the rest of the rebels' Honduran operations at San Andrés de Bocay, a jungle hamlet on the Honduran banks of the confluence of the Bocay and Coco rivers, fifty miles to the northeast of Yamales. The rebels were already using San Andrés as a staging area from which to infiltrate troops into Nicaragua, and if Bermúdez moved there, the rebels could claim, for propaganda purposes, to have their headquarters inside Nicaragua. Furthermore, San Andrés was isolated from unauthorized journalists.[14] So, in the spring of 1987, hundreds of troops trudged for more than a month, herding mules laden with tents and supplies, east through the Honduran wilderness to San Andrés. Bermúdez helicoptered in and out of San Andrés, overseeing the move.

Unfortunately, in May 1987, the Sandinistas reacted almost immediately with a major attack on the new rebel base. President Daniel Ortega called it his government's largest operation ever. Inside Nicaragua, there were no roads north to San Andrés, so the Sandinista government used thirty-six helicopters to deploy some three thousand of its troops into position. After several days of fighting, the Sandinistas forced the rebels to withdraw.[15]

Bermúdez seized on the opportunity to install his Strategic Command at Aguacate, in a circle of U.S. Army campaign tents about three hundred yards east of the main rebel hospital. He and his aides were not reluctant about leaving the border. They'd found San Andrés utterly disagreeable—steaming hot, humming with mosquitos—and at San Andrés, the Danlí bars and Tegucigalpa restaurants to which Bermúdez's men had grown accustomed were totally inaccessible. At Aguacate, Bermúdez had Colonel Gómez and the rebel air force handy. They weren't flying any missions over Nicaragua; Bermúdez and Gómez could fly to Tegucigalpa on weekends—or further, to San Salvador or to Guatemala City.

The CIA needed to keep in touch with Bermúdez. Jerry Clark, the CIA's operations chief, helicoptered out to Aguacate periodically to consult with Bermúdez, but Clark had a lot of responsibilities in Tegucigalpa. With the new Strategic Command installed at Aguacate, the CIA needed a military team there to relay orders to Bermúdez from the CIA base in Tegucigalpa. The CIA's man at Aguacate became Don Johnson, a Green Beret colonel from Texas. At forty years old, Johnson was a muscular man, six feet two inches tall. His gray hair was receding, but his high forehead, large, deep-blue eyes, straight nose, and wide mouth made him a handsome man. In all, an impressive figure.

A Vietnam veteran who had been in Central America for nearly a decade, training government soldiers in El Salvador and Honduras, Johnson was getting tired of what military men called the "cucaracha circuit." But he'd had a lot of good times, like the Christmas he spent in El Salvador in the field with the grunts from the Salvadoran Army. He needed to get food to some troops bivouacked in the wilds, and the only way he figured he could do it was by air. Johnson herded a few cows into the bay of a cargo plane, flew them bawling and shitting over the army camp, then shoved them out the door to plunge hundreds of feet to the ground. Their leathery skin held them together, more or less, Johnson would say with a grin. The meat was really tender.

Central America had wrecked his marriage. His wife finally left, Johnson would tell friends at parties in Tegucigalpa, after he deep-sixed three microwave ovens during a single home leave in El Paso. He just couldn't remember about the metal: He tried to boil water in his field canteen, and wrapped foil over a casserole. The ovens blew up.

Back in Honduras after the breakup, he began taking his workouts and running more seriously. He'd pump iron and then go down to the bars in his torn jeans to chat up the girls from the Peace Corps, or the young American foreign-service officers getting their first taste of the Third World with a posting at the Tegucigalpa embassy. Johnson was older, but he held his own because he was such a character, always telling stories, always yucking it up. His shenanigans around Tegucigalpa became well known. One pizza parlor even renamed one of its concoctions—the one with extra onions and potatoes the way he liked them—"Pizza Don Johnson–style."

Johnson spoke good Spanish, so the Pentagon detailed him to the CIA for the $100 million program. From then on, the fun was only on weekends—and sometimes not even then. Johnson moved to Aguacate into a new, air-conditioned house with sleeping quarters, a suburban-style kitchen, and a "situation room" arranged around a rack of field radios and big topographical maps of the Nicaraguan war zone.[16]

Throughout early 1987, the pieces came together—newly delivered weapons, newly trained troops, newly recruited air force, newly established bases. When some ten thousand troops marched south into Nicaragua during the first months of 1987, they were newly trained and equipped. They wore smart-looking new camouflage uniforms and carried sophisticated new computerized radios in their new backpacks; some were even carrying video cameras to film the action. The American-financed offensive was under way.

May through August 1987

When Commander Jhonson and his regional command staff joined the trek south for the $100 million offensive in May, they were carrying their usual supplies, weapons, and ammunition, but this time they had a special payload: a Redeye antiaircraft missile, twenty-nine pounds and nearly twenty thousand dollars' worth of lethal firepower.

Jhonson wanted to hunt for a Sandinista helicopter immediately. During the preceding days, the Sandinistas had mounted their attack on Bermúdez's fleeting border headquarters at San Andrés, and dozens of Sandinista helicopters were ferrying troops back south, flying several missions each day between their forward camps along the Honduran border and Jinotega's provincial capital. Jhonson saw his chance: Four Mi-17 transport helicopters flew by in a line toward the north one morning and didn't return in the afternoon. Jhonson figured they'd be back the following day. Before dawn, he had his men remove the Redeye from its canvas bag and readied its three-thousand-volt batteries. He told one rebel carrying video equipment to get his camera ready, too.

Weeks earlier, Jhonson's missileman had been flown to Swan Island for instruction by CIA agents on how to launch the Redeye (in military parlance, a "shoulder-fired, infrared homing antiaircraft missile," manufactured by the U.S. firm General Dynamics). On Swan, the CIA men set up a computerized firing simulator that allowed the students to practice locking the heat-seeking eye of a practice missile onto a lit cigarette one hundred yards distant. Now Jhonson set his ambush carefully, putting his missileman on a slope overlooking the broad valley through which the helicopters had passed.

Jhonson's unit had new U.S.-supplied radio scanners, and his radio operators had some luck. They tuned in the cockpit conversations of pilots in several Sandinista helicopters who were revving their motors on the airstrip miles to the north at one of the Sandinistas' forward bases.

"This bird is smoking a lot," one of the pilots said.

"Don't worry, it'll stop when it gets warmed up," another pilot radioed back.

Listening, Jhonson could hear the pilots chatting while three of the helicopters loaded up with soldiers and a fourth took on more than a dozen officers—apparently staffers who had directed the Sandinista drive against San Andrés.

"Let's move out," one pilot said. The radio crackled out the sound of several helicopters taking flight. Minutes later Jhonson could hear the helicopters fly into earshot, approaching down the valley from the north.

"Get ready!" Jhonson called to his missileman. "Go for the last one."

The missileman was inserting the Redeye's cylindrical batteries, each the size and shape of a long flashlight. Jhonson watched the helicopters come into view, four Mi-17 transports, flying in a column some thousand feet above the valley floor about a mile away.

"The last one is yours. Make it good," Jhonson said.

Holding the missile on his shoulder like a bazooka, the missileman sighted in on the last helicopter, then activated the Redeye's electronic sensors. The grip buzzer began: *Beep . . . beep . . . beep.* When, a few seconds later, the missile picked up the heat of the helicopter's turbines, the beeping melted into a continuous shriek.

The missileman fired. The Redeye's booster motor—the first of two propellant motors—kicked in, sending the missile wobbling about twenty feet into the air. Since Jhonson had never seen one fire, he thought its initial, unsteady path signaled a misfire, but then the sustainer motor kicked in, and the rocket streaked in seconds to a speed of nearly a thousand miles an hour.

Suddenly the helicopter was smoking.

Jhonson gazed, transfixed; those moments would remain frozen in his mind forever. As the helicopter burst into flames, its forward motion slowed. It began to arc toward the ground, gliding slightly at first, then picking up speed, plunging earthward finally like a semi-truck to explode into flames on the ground about a mile away.

On the scanner, the Sandinista radio traffic turned to panic.

"Jesus, wait, something's happened to the rear helicopter," one of the three remaining pilots said.

"Fuck, it looks like it crashed. It's sending up smoke below," the pilot said.

"Let's go back," another said.

Two helicopters began to circle, and a third returned to hover above the crash.

"I'm seeing just pieces," the first pilot radioed. "Everything's ripped apart. We'll have to go down and see if there are any survivors."

"I can't, I'm just carrying wounded," another answered.

"Then call for reinforcements out here!" the first pilot answered.

"A missile did this," another pilot said. "There must be Guardia down there."

"Then we have to shut up, we can't talk on the radio anymore," one pilot said. The communication stopped.

Jhonson wasn't carrying another Redeye, or he would have shot down a second helicopter. Instead, he watched for a while. After a time, two other helicopters arrived, landing near the crash site and unloading infantry. Jhonson and his men marched about a mile to the south, set up their radios, and transmitted a message to the Strategic Command: "Our Redeye took out a Sandinista helicopter!"

Hours later, the Defense Ministry issued a communiqué. "Mechanical problems" had caused an Mi-17 to go down near El Cuá, killing all fifteen soldiers and crew members aboard. But Jhonson's aide had taped the entire shootdown with the video camera; Jhonson was able to confirm his claims by sending the video back to Honduras.[17]

Over the next months, the Redeyes proved extraordinarily deadly. Jhonson's unit alone shot down two more helicopters during the course of the year, and the entire rebel army destroyed more than two dozen helicopters—nearly half the government's total force. The helicopter destruction robbed the government of the tremendous tactical air advantage it had enjoyed for two years, while on the ground the rebels were stretching the government's military control to the limit.

By mid-1987, some ten thousand contra troops were fighting inside Nicaragua, dispersed in platoon-sized units across thousands of square miles of Nicaragua, from the coffee slopes of the north to the cattle plains of the southeast. They were ambushing army convoys, blowing up electrical towers, and attacking farm cooperatives, while U.S.-trained paratroop sapper squads were dropping into remote areas to blow up generating plants and microwave towers.

It was not a war of large, coordinated attacks, but rather a shifting mosaic of hundreds of isolated, killing engagements, each rebel unit operating largely on its own, taking its own initiatives. That was the CIA strategy: Escalate a war of erosion throughout the year, force the Sandinistas to wear themselves out in constant pursuit of rebel forces. Attacks on major cities would come later.

Jhonson, moving south, set up operations in his own local theater of the war, in eastern Matagalpa province. He established his command post in the hamlet of Ubú, a clearing on a forested plateau with a good water supply about thirty miles east of the provincial capital and a few miles south of the rushing waters of the Tuma River. Just as during earlier years when he had operated in the hills overlooking his own former farmstead near El Cuá, now in Ubú Jhonson was only a day's march from his father's farm, where he was born. It was the zone whose hills he had traversed as a teenage fumigator for the Health Ministry.

His command post wasn't much; just a circle of hammocks strung from trees around a cooking fire. It lay at the center of a triangle formed by his three hundred-man task forces, one some ten miles to the northeast, one ten miles to the southwest, and another eight or ten miles toward the rising sun.

In a typical day, Jhonson and his men were up well before dawn to gulp sweet coffee for breakfast; then, after the fog had lifted, Jhonson would crank up his long-range solar-powered radio. Amid a lot of squawking, he would communicate in code with the Strategic Command at Aguacate, more than one hundred miles to the north, reporting his and his task force commanders' locations. He'd run down any recent combat and pass along supply requests to the rebel logistics officer, who would be preparing an airdrop to Jhonson's unit. With CIA-installed radio scanners along the border intercepting Sandinista communications, often the Strategic Command would warn Jhonson that the Sandinistas had located one of his units. In that case, Jhonson would radio a warning to his task force commanders.

Almost every afternoon, local farmers would trek in to talk to Jhonson, many bringing information on Sandinista troop movements. Hundreds of peasants, amid the mounting desperation of Nicaragua's economy—and sensing that Washington was more firmly behind the rebels than ever—were flocking to join rebel collaboration networks.

Jhonson received twenty CIA airdrops during 1987, out of 470 the Agency orchestrated to all rebel units during the year.[18] The resupply flights, flown by the CIA's mercenary pilots, came at night, and they took a lot of Jhonson's time. The bundle-packers on Swan needed a precise list of Jhonson's supply requirements; the operations officers at Aguacate needed intelligence information about nearby Sandinista forces to gauge the risks of the drop; the mercenary pilots on Swan had to know his exact compass coordinates. It all required hours of radio work before each night drop, when Jhonson's men would light the signal bonfires for the planes droning in through the inky darkness over the treetops, dumping parachute bundles and ammunition crates. Under this scheme of warfare, Jhonson, like other regional commanders, spent far more time coordinating airdrops than he did directing combat.

Nationwide, however, there was plenty of fighting and it eventually wore the Sandinistas down. The economy told the story most dramatically: It moved during the year from decline to disorder to downright chaos. Government military spending was already gobbling more than 50 percent of the national budget, and through the year the country's streets, markets, and other infrastructure—already eroded by years of wartime austerity—crumbled into ruin. The government was financing its operations by printing worthless currency, and inflation surged from 700 percent early in the year to 15,000 percent at its close. With prices spiraling out of control, industry collapsed, farms stood idle, living standards plummeted. More than a thousand of the sixteen hundred laborers at one state-owned textile factory quit to take up street commerce, as speculation became more profitable than production. In a state-run store at midyear, the price of a small imported refrigerator was the equivalent of eighteen years' salary for the clerks selling it. Begging children clogged Managua's streets. Hospitals had no anesthesia, pharmacies no aspirin, groceries no food.[19]

As the disaster deepened, the government never lost military control, but by midsummer the Sandinista leaders realized that they could not survive long if the war-related economic hemorrhage continued unchecked.

August 1987 through January 1988

On August 7, 1987, Nicaraguan President Daniel Ortega signed a regional peace agreement that committed his government to democratic reforms in exchange for pledges by his four Central American counterparts to end their behind-the-scenes support for the contras. The accord, signed in Guatemala City, contained provisions aimed at ending guerrilla conflicts in El Salvador and Guatemala as well, but it most closely addressed the specifics of the war in Nicaragua. Ortega's pledge to carry out fundamental reforms toward democracy reversed years of Sandinista intransigence, underlining his government's extraordinary vulnerabilities amid the contra offensive. In effect, the Sandinistas sued for negotiated peace.[20]

At the agreement's heart was the commitment by regional governments to lift restrictive emergency laws, release political prisoners, begin peace talks with their armed opponents, and hold free elections. At the same time, the accord rejected armed struggle as a tactic for political change.

The accord threw the Reagan Administration, whose regional strategies were centered on military buildup and force, into confusion. Bermúdez, aware that the pact put the contras on the political defensive and threatened further U.S. military aid, was furious. He was still so angry a month after the agreement was signed that he pounded his fist on a table and shouted in fury when discussing the peace agreement with three American journalists.[21]

Honduras became especially vulnerable to international pressures. With support for the contras now outlawed, Honduran authorities panicked when a multinational inspection team asked to visit Aguacate Air Base in December 1987. Frantic Honduran Army officers ordered contras stationed there to change into civilian clothes and to clear the base of supply planes. Air-worthy planes were flown away, but several damaged aircraft remained as evidence of the contra presence. CIA agents ordered the excavation of a vast pit at one end of the Aguacate airstrip, and the aircraft were bulldozed in and blown up with explosive charges.[22]

For their part, the Sandinistas launched a political offensive on a dozen domestic and international levels. Eventually, they opened face-to-face peace talks with the contra leaders, but in the first weeks after Ortega signed the Guatemala agreement, they mounted an ambitious psychological operation aimed at persuading individual contra field officers to surrender or to break with Bermúdez's Strategic Command.

Against no rebel commander did the Sandinistas wage their campaign more vigorously than against Jhonson, partly because he had three brothers in the Sandinista army, and partly because of his sizable peasant following. The Sandinista army's psychological warfare experts stalked Jhonson for weeks. They assigned all three of Jhonson's brothers from their various Sandinista army posts to the Matagalpa Army Brigade headquarters: Lieutenant Francisco Fley, thirty, a logistical officer, from the Matiguás garrison; Lieutenant Enrique Fley, twenty-nine, a teacher, from Jinotega's Tomatoya military school; and Lieutenant Jorge Fley, twenty-seven, a communications officer, from a listening post in the town of Cuapa, in Chontales province. All began working full time, plotting a strategy for persuading Jhonson to defect. State Security agents began visiting Jhonson's mother Teodora, sixty-seven, and his father Federico, eighty-two, at their Matagalpa home, attempting to enlist their support.

In early September, a peasant messenger brought Jhonson a note from a Sandinista lieutenant based at a garrison near the hamlet of Cuskawas, not far from Jhonson's camp. The lieutenant wanted to talk. Suspicious yet curious, Jhonson dispatched five aides to hear the lieutenant out at a nearby farm; he warned his men to cut no deals and accept no favors. Jhonson's emissaries reported back that the Sandinistas were friendly: They were offering medicine and food to Jhonson's unit, and they said Jhonson's brothers wanted to talk to him.

Jhonson was amused. He wasn't afraid of ideological infection from the Sandinistas, and, in fact, he did want to see his brothers. He sent his men to several further encounters. Eventually, Jhonson was convinced that his initial suspicions were correct: the Sandinistas were just trying to use his brothers to trick him. If the Sandinistas really wanted to negotiate seriously, they should meet with the Resistance's top leaders. This idea of opening peace talks at the local level, he concluded, was just to divide the rebels.

Having met successfully several times with Jhonson's men, the Sandinistas were devoting most of their radio traffic between the Matagalpa Brigade and Sandinista field units in eastern Matagalpa to orchestrating the encounters. Naturally, the CIA-directed radio scanners along the Honduran border were intercepting the communications and relaying them to Bermúdez and his Strategic Command at Aguacate.

There, Bermúdez, Invisible, Mike Lima, and the other ex-Guardsmen flew into a fury. "He's dealing with the Sandinistas! He's a traitor!" Bermúdez and his men were saying of Jhonson. Bermúdez fired off a radio warning to Jhonson: cut off the contacts with the Sandinistas.

Jhonson, irritated, radioed back to Bermúdez explaining how the contacts had begun, trying to reassure him obliquely that he was not double-dealing. Then he decided to teach the Sandinistas a lesson. He sent them a new message, suggesting a time and place for a meeting with his brothers.

The encounter that followed was fraught with the ironies of all wars throughout the ages that have pitted brother against brother. Lieutenant Francisco Fley, the Sandinista, hiked into the Matagalpa hills to meet

Luis "Jhonson" Fley, the contra. Francisco, accompanied by another Sandinista soldier, Lieutenant Enrique López, carried a walkie-talkie to keep in touch with a Sandinista army captain following a few miles behind with seventy troops. Jhonson came at the command of one of his hundred-men task forces.

When he walked forward to greet his brother and López in a clearing, Jhonson felt like weeping. He and Francisco had been close enough in age to share their boyhood, and they had fought together as Sandinista guerrillas. When the Sandinistas had jailed Luis, Francisco had gotten him out. Now long war years had taken their toll on Francisco; he looked old to Jhonson.

"It's good to see you, buddy. How's the family?" Jhonson said.

"They want the war to end," Francisco said. "Let's talk about reconciliation."

Just what Jhonson had expected. His brother was a decoy, sent by superiors to confuse him with family nostalgia. Francisco was to try to persuade him to defect, so the Sandinistas could parade him as a propaganda trophy. In reality, Francisco's wasn't a friendly visit.

"Look, this war isn't going to be solved by us, talking here as brothers," Jhonson told Francisco and Lieutenant López, feigning righteous indignation. "It'll end when the Nicaraguan people have their grievances met. I think you're being used for political ends. That makes you a target. I'm sorry, you're my brother, but I have to forget that for the moment. You are now prisoners of war."

Jhonson turned to armed aides. "Search them. Take their radios," Jhonson said.

"This wasn't the agreement," Francisco sputtered.

"There wasn't any agreement," Jhonson shot back. "You're coming with me."

Jhonson led the two prisoners away with his men, setting a fast pace toward the north. He could hear Sandinista officers calling Francisco frantically through the walkie-talkie: "What's going on?"

For the rest of the day and through the night, Jhonson marched his column fast and hard and long. He knew the government had helicopters nearby, and he had to put distance between his men and the Sandinista forces backing Francisco's mission. Francisco, recalled from a desk job for the mission, wasn't in shape, and when Jhonson at dawn the next morning told his column to rest, Francisco was exhausted.

When Francisco woke up hours later, the glowing coals of a rebel campfire were sizzling with the hot grease of a recently slaughtered steer; Jhonson was preparing a feast to entertain his captives. Francisco got a chance to see a string of peasants marching up to their friend Jhonson, bringing vegetables, cigarettes, and bits of helpful information on recent Sandinista activities in the zone. Soon the two were talking as brothers again. Francisco brought Jhonson up to date on years of family gossip.

For eight days, Jhonson marched his two Sandinista prisoners at a now-leisurely pace through a string of rural hamlets. In a brotherly gesture, Francisco offered to carry Jhonson's pack. Jhonson offered to get Francisco a visa to move his family to the United States; Francisco urged Jhonson to leave the contras and return home. Both brothers clung tenaciously to their own convictions.

More than a week later, Jhonson released his brother and Lieutenant López in a little ceremony before a backwoods preacher and a gathering of villagers. Lieutenant Fley returned to duty at 311th Brigade headquarters. Jhonson slipped back into the hills dominated by his contras.[23]

Jhonson's resistance to the attempts to induce his defection became a major psychological victory for the rebels. The Sandinistas never acknowledged publicly the drubbing Jhonson had given them, but they tempered their early optimism about triggering the contra army's collapse, and within less than a month Ortega announced peace talks with the top contra leadership.

In late November 1987, Jhonson received a radio message from Bermúdez: He had been named to a rebel commission that was to negotiate with the Sandinistas. Jhonson marched out of Nicaragua as a rebel combatant for the last time.

In Honduras, Bermúdez, the CIA men directing the rebel offensive, and other U.S. officials greeted Jhonson as a hero. His record as a commander had proven to be one of the best: Not only had he embarrassed the Sandinistas, but all year long he'd proven the popularity of the rebel cause, winning hundreds of new collaborators in Matagalpa. His forces had shot down three helicopters during the year, and the destruction of the helicopters spread Jhonson's fame—especially because of the videotape he'd sent back to Honduras of the Redeye missile knocking down the first. The video had been reproduced, and copies were circulated among Resistance supporters throughout Central America and the United States.

Jhonson was even invited to an awards ceremony at a luxury hotel in Miami where U.S. Assistant Secretary of State Elliott Abrams praised Bermúdez and several anticommunist "freedom fighters" from Angola, Afghanistan, and other U.S.-backed rebel movements. At the ceremony, Jhonson stood before twelve hundred Cuban and Nicaraguan exiles, who cheered as they watched a new screening of his video.[24]

Jhonson came away from the awards banquet with mixed emotions.

The praise had been gratifying, but rather than emphasize to Jhonson the agenda he shared with the U.S. officials, the Cubans, and the other exiles, the ceremony left him feeling distant. What did these cheerleaders know about the hardship of civil war? For them, the Nicaraguan war was just an idea, a distant struggle between "communism" and "freedom." For Jhonson, the stink of the war hung too close for him to turn easily to platitudes.

He stayed with his family in Miami for a time after the banquet, and one afternoon, when he returned to his cramped apartment off West Flagler, his wife, Magda, grabbed him at the door.

"Luis, they say Enrique died in an ambush!" Magda blurted out.

Jhonson grabbed the phone and called one of his sisters-in-law in northern Nicaragua.

"Luis, it's true!" the woman shouted over the crackling phone line. "Enrique drove into a contra trap on the highway between Matagalpa and Jinotega last week. I'm sorry." She had few details. She could bring Jhonson's mother to the phone the next morning; his mother could explain, she said.

Jhonson hung up and sat down, staring. He had been fighting against Enrique and his other two brothers for five years—but he'd never really thought of it that way. Seven years younger, Enrique was Jhonson's favorite brother. Jhonson admired Enrique because he helped their mother around the house after his own work, because he was always devouring some Rubén Dario poem or absorbed in a book, because he looked after their younger siblings. Enrique was a kid without vices.

Jhonson had driven the road between Jinotega and Matagalpa a thousand times. He could see its foggy curves now, climbing up over the mountain rib separating Jinotega from Matagalpa. Which contra unit would it have been? Jhonson began to imagine just how he would set an ambush along that road himself. He reeled in horror from the thought. Whose troops had killed his brother?

As Jhonson sat staring at his apartment's dirty walls, he felt the shock erode, leaving just pain.

"Enrique! I miss you already!" Jhonson said to himself.

At nine the next morning, he dialed Nicaragua. His hand shook as his sister-in-law put his mother on the line. He hadn't spoken to her since 1982.

"Mother, can you hear me?" Jhonson shouted.

"Luis! Is it you?" she shouted back.

"Yes, Mama, it's me. What happened to Enrique?"

"Oh, Luis . . . Well, Enrique was coming very early last week in one of the military trucks from where he was giving classes, you know, at the military school up past Jinotega," she said. His mother's voice sounded shaky, older, but she told the whole story. Jhonson just listened.

"There was a report that there were armed men in the road, but you know how Enrique was, Luis, he never wanted to be late, so he insisted: 'I'm going on.'

"They say he was in the cab," she went on, "and that nine or ten of his students—recruits, you know—were riding in the back. And when they got to the lane leading into the Fundadora Hacienda, well, the contras were waiting for him. There he was. They attacked his truck."

Jhonson just couldn't help himself. He was sobbing, covering the phone receiver so his mother wouldn't hear.

"The contras shot out the tires, and he died there, Luis. Oh, Luis, they say they hit his truck with a rocket. They say Enrique was totally destroyed . . . But we didn't get to see him. The army gave his body back to us two days later, but nobody could see it, you know, the wooden box came inside a sealed metal coffin.

"Maybe that was God's will, Luis," she said. "You know this has hit your papa real hard. He just lies in bed. He won't come out of his room. He's not eating, Luis.

"I just believe we have to trust ourselves to the will of God.

"Luis, can you hear me? I don't want it to continue like this. I don't want any more of my sons to die, I can't bear it. I don't want you brothers killing each other, you hear me?

"Luis, get out of this. Get out of it . . ."

Jhonson could just barely pull his voice together to answer.

"I am out, Mama. I'm here with my family now. Don't worry about me, Mama, I'm out of danger," he said.

"Will you come home, Luis?" she asked.

"Someday, Mother, someday," he answered.[25]

March through November 1987

In May 1987, just weeks into Jhonson's incursion into Nicaragua, U.S. and contra officials announced the discovery of an extensive Sandinista spy ring, said to have infiltrated agents into nearly every contra facility in Honduras. It was a sensational, if double-edged announcement: alarming because rebel secrets were said to have been thoroughly compromised; encouraging because the roundup appeared to demonstrate that with U.S. help, the insurgents' counterintelligence system was improving.

In fact, however, all that had changed was that the rebels were seizing larger numbers of suspects—and that American officials were working in closer coordination than ever with the ugliest aspect of rebel operations. CIA officers trained rebel interrogators, loaned U.S. helicopters, administered polygraph tests, monitored the developing investigation, and finally accepted and trumpeted its conclusions.

Whether the Resistance and CIA interrogators succeeded in neutralizing genuine infiltrators remains unclear. The claims made at the time about the case remain questionable, not only because of the contras' record of paranoia over infiltration, but also because most of the conclusions drawn in the investigation were theories suggested to suspects under torture, then "confirmed" through their acceptance by the victims.

"At first they deny their participation, but when we grab them and pressure them in a significant manner, we succeed in confirming things," Mike Lima, one of the interrogators who participated, said of the investigation.

After the passage of the $100 million U.S. aid package, CIA agents trained the rebel intelligence chief, Rodolfo Ampie, "Invisible," as well as several of Bermúdez's interrogators, in counterintelligence methods, according to a senior CIA officer working in Honduras at the time.[26] Within weeks of the CIA training, the rebel agents put their lessons into practice in a joint U.S.-rebel counterintelligence sweep, perhaps the first of the war.

Analyzing captured Sandinista documents, rebel agents developed suspicions that several contra commandos working at Aguacate Air Base were infiltrators. They secretly seized and interrogated several commandos, and the questioning hardened their suspicions.

The early suggestions of enemy penetration alarmed everyone. Both Bermúdez and Calero told Invisible they wanted to be kept closely informed of the investigation's progress,[27] and the CIA was extremely concerned as well. Agency polygraph experts who flew down from Langley tested many of the suspects, and as the probe widened, the Americans dedicated at least one CIA helicopter to the hunt for suspects. As prisoners under interrogation named new suspects, Resistance counterintelligence men helicptered to Aguacate, Yamales, and Tegucigalpa, rounding them up. Many commandos at Aguacate were called into Strategic Command offices, then quietly seized to prevent members of the alleged ring from warning one another, loaded aboard a helicopter, and flown away for interrogation. The suspects were questioned at the rebels' military police center, established two years earlier at Yamales.[28]

Invisible led the investigation, but his interrogators—several of whom weeks earlier had received CIA instruction—included the rebel army's most brutal ex-Guardsmen: ex-Major Torres; Torres's right-hand man, known in the Resistance as "Julio"; José Zepeda, known as "Joel," who would become the head of the counterintelligence center; César Tijerino, known as "Six-Seven," a former lieutenant and interrogator from Somoza's secret police agency, the OSN; and Ramón Peña Rodríguez, "Z-Two," who had been Mack's interrogator at La Lodosa and was now attached to Invisible's intelligence section.[29]

The questioning was predictably brutal. Many of the detainees described their ordeal to investigators twenty months later, when GAO auditors and human-rights investigators inspected rebel prisons. One of those questioned was Rogelio Centeno Chavarría, a twenty-one-year-old rebel helicopter mechanic who said he was among some twenty prisoners seized at Aguacate, bound, blindfolded, and flown to the Yamales Military Police center. There, interrogators lashed his hands behind his back, then hung him by his wrists. Dangling from a beam, Centeno was beaten and his body was scorched with burning cigarettes. He finally broke when his interrogators tied a rubber hood, cut from a U.S. Army rain poncho, over his head. They told Centeno that when he wanted to admit his guilt, he could wiggle his foot.

"When I was just about asphyxiated," Centeno recalled, "I raised my foot. But if you continued to deny the accusations, they'd put the hood back on. Since I couldn't take any more, I had to tell lies."

Held for thirty-six days, Centeno and other rebel suspects were fed only rice and beans tossed to them onto the earthen floor.[30]

Several of the prisoners claimed that Mike Lima himself, then a sort of utility officer to Bermúdez's Strategic Command staff, had participated in the brutality, in one case riding over a bound prisoner on a horse, and another time beating a suspect with an iron bar.[31]

Former Guard Lieutenant Guillermo Gasteazoro, a rebel who worked closely with the CIA and with Bermúdez as an interpreter, said he used his friendships with several members of the counterintelligence section to participate in some of the interrogations. Gasteazoro said he did it for his own entertainment.

"I'd play cat-and-mouse with the prisoners," Gasteazoro recalled. He described one May 1987 interrogation session in which he helped Z-Two and Six-Seven question several bound and blindfolded rebel detainees.

"They were doing the dirty end—I was playing good cop, they were playing bad cop," Gasteazoro said. "They were beating the living shit out of one of them with black jacks . . . hitting them in the testicles, in the stomach and lower backs—not in the face. It was a typical military interrogation, like in 'Nam."[32]

The rebel probe lasted nearly two months while Resistance and CIA agents compiled hundreds of pages of interrogation transcripts and other investigatory documents. Rebel counterintelligence officers eventually wrote a fifty-page report piecing together the accumulated "evidence" into a complex and alarming portrait of Sandinista infiltration dating to the rebel army's first days.

The ringleaders, the rebel report said, were two intelligence agents sent to infiltrate the rebel force by Sandinista Army Brigade 40-10, based in Nicaragua's northeastern Chinandega province. The first, José Wilson Jackson, was seized and tortured by rebel investigators early in their probe. He eventually "confessed" to his involvement and named a number of his recruits. The second alleged Sandinista agent was never captured.

According to the report, Jackson came to Honduras in 1982. After joining the fledgling FDN army and adopting the nom de guerre "Wilson," he began sending secrets back to Nicaragua from La Quinta, Bermúdez's Strategic Command at Las Vegas, and other sensitive rebel installations to which he had access. In early 1985, Wilson began to work at Aguacate in one of the "kicker" teams that packed parachute bundles and flew in the cargo bays of rebel supply planes. At Aguacate, he began to receive money and other logistical help from the second Sandinista agent, Carlos Andrade Espinoza, who had taken up residence in Catacamas, the town nearest to the Aguacate base. Wilson recruited more than a dozen collaborators among the rebels working at Aguacate, establishing spy rings in the aircraft maintenance hangar, the electrical plant, among the nurses and paramedics in the Aguacate hospital, and at the Aguacate warehouse. Wilson also recruited spies to work at the rebel hospital and supply center at Yamales, as well as at the rebel army's main Tegucigalpa warehouse.

The Resistance report attributed a number of mysterious accidents to the alleged spy ring. In September 1986, an unmarked C-47—one of the cargo planes purchased for the rebels by Oliver North—flew from Aguacate to Guatemala, loaded up with boots purchased from the Guatemalan Army, then flew back toward Aguacate. Over Teupasenti, thirty-five miles northeast of Tegucigalpa, the plane developed engine trouble and crashed. Honduran soldiers recovered the rebel cargo. The report blamed the crash on sabotage to the aircraft's engine by Wilson's alleged spies.[33]

In March 1986, a wounded rebel died in the Yamales hospital as a result of a lethal overdose of penicillin. The report called it murder by one of the spies. The report also cited the loss of numerous supply bundles over Nicaragua as a result of sabotage to parachutes by alleged spies working in the Aguacate cargo warehouse.

In May 1987, the nose tire on a rebel DC-6 blew out as the plane was taking off from the Aguacate runway. The cargo plane veered out of control and crashed. There were no injuries, but the plane was a total loss. The Resistance investigators concluded that saboteurs had placed a board pierced with nails on the runway, causing the crackup.[34]

The secret report from the counterintelligence section's investigation was never released publicly, but U.S. officials accepted and disseminated its major conclusions.

"It was a systematic sabotage operation in effect since 1983," one American official told the *Los Angeles Times* in May 1987. "It was extremely sophisticated, very well done, and done over a long period of time."[35]

Given the rapid expansion and decentralized organization of the contra army, it wasn't surprising that the Sandinistas infiltrated some spies into contra ranks. Nicaraguan government officials boasted of their espionage successes throughout the war.[36] Many doubts remain, however, about the conclusions drawn from the 1987 investigation, including some later expressed by Bermúdez.[37] Alfonso Sandino, a Nicaraguan lawyer who interviewed most of the imprisoned infiltrators when they were released twenty-one months after their initial interrogations, concluded that many of the incidents of alleged "espionage" had been simple accidents.[38]

U.S. officials appear to have accepted the report's conclusions because CIA agents were monitoring the interrogations. There is no evidence that the Americans actually participated in any torture, but the lie detector tests that CIA agents administered to numerous suspects about pivotal questions were a key element in the credibility eventually given the overall investigation. Air Force Commander Gómez wrote a secret memo to Bermúdez on May 18, 1987, reporting that Wilson "has not satisfactorily passed two polygraph tests. In the second test, more specific questions were asked about whether he had collaborated with the Sandinistas, passing them information. This is where he failed."

"There will be a third test," Gómez added, "and I request instructions for action, since the USA advisers in Washington are asking what we are going to do with him."

Bermúdez inked a handwritten note to the memo and passed it on to Invisible: "Invisible, to me it seems that we have to seek punishment for this man."[39]

The brutality meted out during this investigation has never been publicized. How much the CIA agents knew of it at the time remains unclear. A former official who discussed the 1987 investigation with

CIA officials at interagency meetings in Washington concluded that "CIA officers in the field turned the other way" when faced with evidence of rebel brutality, "or simply discarded rumors that may have been more than rumors."

Bermúdez certainly knew about the brutality, because in the fall of 1987 he orchestrated an elaborate maneuver to hide the victims of his army's worst abuses from public view.

The Central American Peace Agreement, signed in August 1987 in Guatemala, called for the release of political prisoners throughout the region. Honduran authorities reacted by demanding the dismantling of the Resistance prison at Yamales. The Americans urged the Resistance to orchestrate a public prisoner release as a propaganda exercise, to show that they were complying with the regional accords and to prove that they were a humanitarian force.

At the time, the Resistance was holding at least 110 prisoners, perhaps more.[40] About eighty were prisoners of war, captured during combat inside Nicaragua, who had suffered no ill-treatment. About thirty others, however, were accused infiltrators who had been tortured. If released, these prisoners would describe the torments they had endured to the international press.

Under the noses of American officials, the rebels divided the prisoners into two groups—one, a "public" group, that would be released, the other a group who could be expected to denounce abuses if freed.

The release of the first group came in mid-September 1987. Eighty prisoners were collected at Aguacate, then flown south to Liberia, Costa Rica, for delivery into the custody of local Costa Rican government officials who had offered to facilitate the release. The Resistance's winnowing process worked well; none of those released complained of abuses during confinement.[41]

A different fate awaited the approximately thirty detainees whose release the rebel leadership considered too dangerous. Bermúdez assigned Leo to build a new, clandestine detention facility in a place so remote as to be inaccessible to the international inspection teams expected to begin touring the region to verify compliance with the peace accord. Leo and some fifty of his military policemen helicoptered to the rebels' border base at San Andrés, hiked from the main installations several hours north into the rain forest, hacked out a clearing, and built a new log-and-barbed-wire prison compound. When the new facility was ready, the rebels' thirty remaining prisoners—a group that included Centeno, Wilson, and most of the others rounded up during the counterintelligence investigation—were bound, blindfolded, flown to San

Andrés, and shoved into the rude jail. There they would languish, ill-fed and poorly clothed, until their release fifteen months later in December 1988.[42]

June 1986 through November 1987

What had begun as a secret war had become one of the most public and heavily reported conflicts in the world. Yet Bermúdez, Sánchez, and their ex-Guardsmen were still trying to keep many violent secrets hidden.

That is why they came to hate Marta Patricia Baltodano so intensely. Baltodano was the lawyer the State Department hired to clean up the rebel army's human-rights image, and she proved to be a dogged investigator. Scrapping her way into the inner workings of the rebel army, she began to document their abuses in greater detail than any outsider before her.

Baltodano was just twenty-eight, a short woman with curly hair and a wide smile, when she began her work with the contras in 1986. The oldest daughter of a middle-class Nicaraguan accountant, she had studied law at Managua's Jesuit-run University of Central America. As a student during the Somoza regime, she'd done volunteer work for Managua's main opposition watchdog group, the Permanent Commission on Human Rights, filing habeas corpus petitions, searching for government critics Somoza's security men had "disappeared."

As the National Guard was fighting its last, door-to-door battles with the Sandinistas in Managua, Baltodano was completing her law studies. After the Sandinista triumph, she passed her bar exams, then sought a post with the Sandinista Foreign Ministry, but, seeing evidence that the abuses she'd hoped would end with Somoza's fall—summary executions, mistreatment of prisoners—were in fact continuing under Sandinista rule, she decided instead to pursue her human-rights work with the Commission full time.

Within months, the Sandinistas turned on the Commission, first trying to take it over from within, then failing that, targeting its leaders for harassment. In 1981, the Commission's director, José Esteban González, traveled to the Vatican to complain about Sandinista rights abuses. Revolutionary authorities mobilized Sandinista activists to the Managua airport to protest his return, and the crowd turned violent. The mob caught Baltodano, who was at the airport to meet González, beating her, spitting on her, and tearing off her blouse, while police looked on. After a harrowing fifteen-day detention and repeated threats, González fled into exile; Baltodano, just twenty-three, rose to head the Commission.

For four years, she battled the revolutionary state and watched Sandinista abuses shift from revolutionary excess to counterinsurgency repression during the first years of the contra war.

In late 1985, Baltodano went into exile, and by mid-1986 she had cut a deal with the State Department to head its contra human-rights reform drive. Baltodano's reasons for making the dramatic shift were complex. She had a baby and was reluctant to raise it in Sandinista Nicaragua, but most important, by mid-1986 Baltodano—like many Nicaraguan opposition activists—believed that with Washington's backing, the contras would drive the Sandinistas from power. If the contras were to one day rule, Baltodano felt, it was more important for Nicaragua's future to try to reform their movement than to fight a sterile battle with the Sandinistas at home.[43]

Marta Patricia Baltodano realized from the beginning that her reputation was at stake. "This is one of those adventures in which you risk losing everything, but in which you can, perhaps, make an impact," she said shortly after making her decision to head the human-rights drive.[44]

In August 1986, Baltodano flew to Washington and met Cresencio (Cris) Arcos, the State Department official who was working out the details of the human-rights program. A Chicano who grew up in south Texas, Arcos had joined the U.S. Information Service after getting his master's degree at Johns Hopkins University. He served in the late 1970s in the U.S. consulate in Leningrad, and then had been posted as press attaché in the Tegucigalpa embassy. There, calling on his native Spanish and quick humor, Arcos made himself far more important than his post, charming the often-irascible Honduran President Roberto Suazo Córdova, back-slapping his way into the good graces of a suspicious Honduran officer corps, and winning the confidence of Bermúdez, Sánchez, and other contra leaders. Just as important, Arcos ingratiated himself with an otherwise hostile American press corps. In mid-1985, the Reagan Administration had appointed Arcos deputy director of the Nicaraguan Humanitarian Assistance Office, established to channel $27 million in nonlethal aid to the contras, a post that put the details and secrets of Washington's contra war at the center of his daily agenda. When Baltodano came to see Arcos, then forty-two, he was the State Department's deputy coordinator for public diplomacy, assigned the task of persuading Congress to back Reagan's agenda in Central America.[45]

Arcos explained the origin of the Administration's contra human-rights program. Past rebel atrocities had so alienated Congress that when lawmakers passed the $100 million military aid program, they set aside $3 million of it to finance a cleanup. The Reagan Administration had not requested the money, but Arcos and other State Department officials had assembled a program to educate fighters about human-rights principles, to monitor their behavior, and to investigate atrocities. Naturally, some abuses would continue, Arcos said—that was inevitable in a guerrilla war—but the Administration needed to be able to say that the army was evolving.

After Baltodano agreed to head the State Department's project, she worked with Arcos and government lawyers to establish the Asociación Nicaragüense Pro-Derechos Humanos (Nicaraguan Association for Human Rights), insisting that it be independent from the contra army and that it control its own funds. The $3 million turned Baltodano's association into the second most generously funded rights group in the world. Only Amnesty International, monitoring 128 countries, had more money.[46]

Upon flying to Tegucigalpa to flesh out her organization, Baltodano discovered that even if she had plenty of money and State Department backing, she also had plenty of enemies.

In Honduras, Everett Ellis Briggs, known as Ted, was the new U.S. ambassador. Though he understood clearly that supporting Baltodano's work had become the price of doing business with the U.S. Congress, he was not enthusiastic. At fifty-two, Briggs was one of the Foreign Service's most influential officers. The son of a Yankee patrician who had himself been a distinguished diplomat, Everett took up the diplomatic life right out of Dartmouth College in 1956, and over his thirty-year career, he served in U.S. missions in La Paz, Berlin, Lisbon, Luanda, Asunción, and Bogotá. Back at Foggy Bottom in 1981, Briggs had been a deputy assistant secretary; immediately before he arrived in Tegucigalpa, he'd been ambassador in Panama. During the Reagan years, Briggs had quietly nurtured a reputation as one of Washington's most conservative envoys. Many who dealt with him found that his political views combined unpleasantly with his personality: The perquisites of his upbringing and career had made him a haughty man. He was domineering with staff, contemptuous with reporters, overbearing with seemingly everyone.[47] "You couldn't tell whether Briggs was smelling you or looking at you," recalled one State Department colleague.

Arriving in Tegucigalpa in the fall of 1986, Briggs was to represent the State Department in a country where the CIA was running one of its most ambitious paramilitary operations. State, conscious of mounting congressional opposition to the contra program, considered Baltodano's effort a priority. The CIA saw the human-rights program as a peripheral nuisance; they had a war to fight. Briggs took a middle path, accepting Baltodano's role, but begrudgingly. He wasn't openly hostile, but embassy officials quickly made clear to Baltodano that they wanted her to keep a low profile.

Like the CIA, Briggs saw how Baltodano, by poking around in the hitherto-secret contra world, could complicate his life and slow the war effort. Briggs's views also reflected the Tegucigalpa embassy's relation with the rebel army. The embassy's view of the Resistance was essentially that of the Bermúdez clique, and Briggs himself quickly forged cordial personal and working ties with Bermúdez. Naturally, Bermúdez, Sánchez, and the ex-Guardsmen saw Baltodano's work, from the start, as a threat. "They saw her as one part of a larger Communist conspiracy," one U.S. official recalled.[48]

During Baltodano's first weeks in Honduras, she pulled together a staff, established a computer-equipped office in a large Tegucigalpa residence, and began recruiting a network of some fifty rebel commandos who would double as human-rights "delegates," reporting from every level of the army. The generous U.S. funding allowed Baltodano to offer seventy-five dollars a month to each "delegate," and she stationed several aides in an office at the Yamales camp.

First on Baltodano's agenda was to investigate several alleged contra atrocities that had been fouling the rebel army's reputation for years. One was what had come to be known as the Cuapa case, named after the village eighty miles east of Managua, seized by rebel forces on August 2, 1985. The *Washington Post* reported after the contra attack that the rebels had executed eleven Sandinista prisoners during the Cuapa siege. Jemera Rone, an attorney for the New York human-rights monitor Americas Watch who mounted her own investigation in Cuapa days after the contra attack, confirmed the execution reports.

Reagan Administration officials repeatedly denied that the atrocity had occurred, and President Reagan himself sent a report to Congress claiming "there is no reliable information to confirm that military prisoners have been executed by Resistance forces" at Cuapa, suggesting that the publicity about the case had resulted from a Nicaraguan "government press story," though it was the *Washington Post* that broke the news.

Bosco Matamoros, the contra spokesman in Washington, had been parroting the Administration line, perhaps hoping the controversy would go away. Instead it festered throughout 1986. Both Americas Watch and Amnesty International wrote Secretary of State George Shultz, demanding an explanation, but by early 1987 nearly two years had passed, neither Bermúdez nor any other rebel official had carried out a serious investigation, and many U.S. congressmen were angry.[49]

Baltodano quickly demonstrated what she could do. By putting out feelers throughout the contra army, she was able to identify rebel commandos who had witnessed the Cuapa incident. In taped statements, the witnesses told Baltodano how Leonte "Atila" Arias, a contra unit commander who fought at Cuapa, had ordered Sandinista prisoners dragged to a gully outside the village and shot. Atila, a former Guard lieutenant, was a member of Bermúdez's inner circle. Baltodano's quick investigation corroborated the international charges, proved that Reagan Administration officials had been wrong, and made rebel officials—especially Bermúdez—look stupid. Baltodano had shown how easily Bermúdez or Sánchez could have identified the guilty party themselves, had they wished.[50]

Worse, Cuapa was just one of a string of embarrassing cases. Baltodano was overseeing multiple, parallel investigations, and by April, she had pulled together information on a dozen other controversies, including the forced recruitment by rebel commandos of eight Mennonites and the murder of five Baptists in Matagalpa. Baltodano demanded, in writing, that Bermúdez set up tribunals to try the rebels implicated.

Baltodano's quick call for action enraged Bermúdez and Sánchez. Never before had they been forced to deal seriously with allegations of abuses by their men; they were used to brushing aside accusations as "Sandinista lies." Furthermore, they realized that Baltodano was picking up clues to the cheap manipulation that had become their style. She had learned how they routinely bribed rebel commanders to keep them in line and how they had conspired together against the would-be contra reformer Arturo Cruz. "It was a Mafia like I'd never seen," Baltodano recalled.[51]

Finally, Bermúdez exploded. Seizing upon a trivial dispute with one of Baltodano's Yamales aides, he flew into a fury, ordering his men to expel Baltodano's entire staff bodily from the Strategic Command camp and remove all of the Association's office equipment.

Bermúdez told Richard Chidester, a thirty-six-year-old political officer in the Tegucigalpa embassy who helicoptered to Yamales to mediate the ensuing crisis, that he believed the State Department had sent Baltodano to Honduras to dig up evidence against him personally. "This is a maneuver to discredit me, so the State Department can get rid of me," Bermúdez said.[52]

Arcos, now Baltodano's principal State Department supervisor, flew from Washington to Tegucigalpa in order to help her. Meeting in a Resistance safe house near the Tegucigalpa airport with Arcos, Baltodano, Chidester, the CIA's John Mallett, and several others, Bermúdez, Calero, and Sánchez attacked Baltodano. Calero accused her of leaking damaging stories to the international press. Sánchez and Bermúdez accused her of recruiting a staff made up of closet Sandinistas. The CIA's Mallett nodded in agreement.

Arcos defended her. "Look, Enrique," he said. "Marta's role is critical. Congress wants to know that even though there's a war going on
and abuses will occur, there's a mechanism to punish those responsible."

Baltodano herself stood up. She looked a little out of place, a fuzzy-
haired woman of twenty-nine facing down a ring of older men.

"I'm doing this work because I'm a patriot," she said. "I want a new
Nicaragua as much as any of you do. But the Nicaragua I'm fighting for
isn't a Somoza-era replay. I'm not going to front for someone who wants
a public liar to say everything is fine inside the Resistance."

Finally, Bermúdez backpedaled. There'd been a misunderstanding, he
said. He'd never thrown Marta out of the camps. Of course Marta Patricia could work at Yamales, he said.[53] It was decided that the Resistance
would appoint a "legal adviser" to help Bermúdez coordinate his work
with Baltodano. The man chosen was Donald Lacayo, who had worked
as Calero's principal lawyer at Coca-Cola in Managua until he left
Nicaragua in 1982.[54]

On the surface, the meeting seemed to solve Baltodano's problems.
Bermúdez allowed her people back into Yamales, but that turned out to
be of little use, since the contras were vacating Yamales for Aguacate
and San Andrés, and Bermúdez and his people began making it difficult
for Baltodano to get onto Resistance helicopters.

There were other angry meetings. In one encounter at Aguacate
between Baltodano and Aristides Sánchez, Bermúdez, Mike Lima, and
other rebel commanders, the contra clique turned emotional. Crowded
around Baltodano in one of the Strategic Command tents by the airstrip,
they began to hurl insults.

"You don't understand what this war is about!" Sánchez shouted.
"Of course there are abuses. You better believe that if some Sandinista
kills my wife and daughter, I'm going to take revenge."

"What are you doing here, anyway? You're an ex-Sandinista!" Mike
Lima screamed.

Baltodano kept her composure. "Contras who commit abuses are
confusing the whole world," she said. For the good of Nicaragua, she
was going to go after the bad apples. They need to be exposed, punished,
expelled, she said.[55]

Never before had any independent woman spent any length of time
in the rebel camps. Now Baltodano began to uncover the systematic sexual abuse that had become part of daily life in the rebel world.

A case that provided an initial education for Baltodano in mid-1987
was that of a young woman named Berta Díaz, a twenty-year-old commando who contacted one of Baltodano's aides in Yamales, saying she

wanted to deliver a written report on a series of "anomalies" that had befallen her over the preceding months at the José Dolores Estrada regional command camp, headed by former National Guardsman Marcos "Black Dimas" Navarro. Baltodano suspected that Díaz had been raped. Bermúdez's counterintelligence agents intercepted the complaint, and the next thing Baltodano knew, the young woman was detained at Leo's military police stockade at Yamales. Baltodano's aides tried to interview Díaz, but Leo's military police blocked the way. They always had an excuse: Berta was sick, Berta was out bathing, Berta was away. After Baltodano's Yamales investigators began favoring Leo's prison guards with little bribes like chocolates, cigarettes, and cassette tapes, they got to see Díaz.

When Díaz was led in, she seemed frightened, trembling. She no longer wanted to discuss the "anomalies." Baltodano's investigators had to cajole her story out bit by bit, emboldening her into bursts of candor before she retreated back into silence. It took hours.

Bullies in the José Dolores Estrada camp, she said, had accused her of being an infiltrator. They stripped her naked and shoved her into an earthen pit. Over a period of days, they tortured her by tying a rubber hood over her head until she was asphyxiating, and by holding her head under water in a trough. Then, one of her tormentors sexually abused her in a prolonged, three-hour rape in front of a group of commandos.

After Bermúdez's counterintelligence people intercepted the complaint she'd written for Baltodano's human-rights people, Díaz said that Invisible, the Resistance intelligence chief, had interrogated her. Why had she tried to file the complaint? Didn't she see how something like this could hurt the Resistance?

Now, however, Díaz insisted that she was pleased to be inside the military police stockade. She was Leo's "partner," she said, and she wanted it that way.

"I feel it's better to be detained than to be free, in comparison to what I was living outside," Díaz said.

Hearing of the interview, Baltodano concluded that Díaz was still in danger; her relation with Leo had too many coercive implications. Baltodano went to Leo to request Díaz's release. Only on Bermúdez's order, Leo said. Bermúdez was traveling outside Honduras at the time, and on his return, Bermúdez told Baltodano that Díaz had been transferred to a new rebel detention area at San Andrés de Bocay.[56]

During the same period, Baltodano interviewed another woman, Yorlin María Ubeda, whose story suggested that Díaz's was not an isolated case. An attractive, fair-haired young woman, Ubeda had been dragged into the Yamales counterintelligence area in November 1985 and accused of being an infiltrator. Then just nineteen, she was immediately blindfolded, stripped naked, splayed out on a rubber poncho with her hands and legs tied to stakes, and raped repeatedly by a series of interrogators. As far as Baltodano could gather, Ubeda's "interrogators" never followed any coherent line of questioning. Ubeda was held for months, merely for the sexual gratification of her captors. Ubeda said that virtually every night drunken counterintelligence men stumbled into the stockade to stare at her, to curse her, to pinch her thighs and pubis, and eventually to rape her. Ubeda provided Baltodano with their pseudonyms: "Six-Seven," "Chino Eighty-Five," "Julio," "Joel." They were the regular counterintelligence interrogators, the men American officials were crediting in the newspapers with rolling up a major Sandinista spy ring.

Ubeda told Baltodano that one evening she even heard a rebel officer named Pincho radio her jailer, asking that she be "loaned out" for a time. The request was approved, Ubeda said. Pincho showed up at the stockade and marched her away with him to his hut, where he threatened to kill her if she didn't have sex with him.

Charged as an infiltrator, Ubeda was eventually put before a "tribunal," consisting of three ex-Guardsmen in a musty tent. She was convicted and sentenced to a year. Ubeda said she was not the only woman who faced this treatment in the rebel jails. She provided Baltodano with the names of half a dozen young women she had met in the Yamales stockade whose ages ranged from fourteen to twenty-four. All had been raped and abused, Ubeda said.[57]

Everywhere she went, Baltodano heard stories about mistreatment in the Yamales jails. One of the women tortured there was Jacqueline Murillo Castillo, a diminutive twenty-year-old whom Baltodano had first met when Murillo was working as Bermúdez's secretary at his Strategic Command. Baltodano learned her story almost by chance.

Baltodano had flown out to Aguacate on some business for the human-rights association. While there, she decided to visit the hospital. Strolling through a recovery hall crammed with scores of wounded contras, Baltodano saw Murillo in one of the beds.

"What are you doing here?" Baltodano asked. She remembered Murillo as a cheerful, blue-eyed woman with a striking smile. Now she looked pale.

"I'm sick," Murillo said. "Can we talk for a few minutes before you leave?"

Baltodano led her out of the Aguacate hospital, away from prying ears. The two women sat down under a tree.

"They hurt me, Marta," Murillo said.

She'd been accused of being an infiltrator and detained. Held for about a week, she was blindfolded, stripped naked, bound, and beaten. At one point, her interrogators suspended her by her hands from a rope. Murillo said that while she was strung up like that, naked, Guillermo Ortega, a video cameraman from the rebel army's Tegucigalpa public-relations office, had entered the interrogation area and tormented her, handling her genitals and scorching her legs with burning newspapers.

Telling her story, Murillo began to cry.

Baltodano had known Ortega, the cameraman, from her university days in Managua. The story seemed weird; how would a married cameraman from Tegucigalpa have gotten involved in torture in Yamales?

"But it was him, Marta," Murillo said. "I saw him, he put his hand in my vagina, he hung me up and beat me." She said that after she'd begun to hemorrhage badly, her tormentors had called in one of the U.S.-trained paramedics, who recommended that they send her to the Aguacate hospital. Once Murillo had recovered the strength to stand, she went, furious, to see Bermúdez, she told Baltodano.

"Look what they did to me!" she had shouted at Bermúdez. "You had something to do with this, didn't you!" Murillo said Bermúdez just walked away.

It was the first time Baltodano was certain that Bermúdez had known about torture and done nothing to intervene. She was furious.

Back in Tegucigalpa, Baltodano typed up Murillo's statement and went to see Lacayo, the Resistance's "legal adviser." She wanted a tribunal to investigate the case. Lacayo flew to Aguacate, talked to Murillo himself, and obtained a medical statement from the doctor who had examined her, certifying that she'd been tortured and burned. Lacayo interviewed Ortega, Murillo's accused tormentor, and then he recommended to Bermúdez, in writing, that he call a tribunal to investigate. Bermúdez consented—but a series of Bermúdez's aides immediately warned Lacayo to treat the case "with supreme care."

"I began to think there was something dark there, something they were trying to hide," Lacayo said later. Eventually, according to Lacayo, Bermúdez himself asked that he discontinue his prosecution of the case.

"Find a way to arrange this thing legally," Bermúdez told Lacayo.

Months of delays followed. Eventually, Bermúdez permitted a panel of rebel commanders to try Ortega, although he never ordered Ortega detained. Instead, during the trial, Baltodano was stunned to find that Ortega had been granted a U.S. visa and had fled Honduras to Miami. That, she knew from experience, could only have happened with the complicity of American officials.[58]

At the end of eighteen months of U.S.-financed work, Baltodano's results were mixed. She had confronted Bermúdez and his clique; she had challenged them. But she hadn't changed them.[59]

October 1987 through February 1988

The contras' 1987 campaign, their most important of the war, culminated with a December strike by thousands of rebel troops against Nicaragua's largest mining complex. The surprise raid, conceived, planned, and coordinated by dozens of CIA agents and led by rebel commanders, proved that the contras had learned much from their American trainers. The CIA wanted the attack to be a spectacular climax to an offensive that had been going well, militarily, all fall. Contra forces were killing and wounding scores of Sandinistas—more than one hundred dead per month—and rebel rocketeers carrying U.S.-supplied Redeye missiles had already shot down more than twenty Sandinista air force helicopters. But U.S. funding for the rebels was running out, and Reagan Administration officials knew they would face a tough congressional contra aid battle early in 1988. They needed more sensational attacks.

CIA planners considered the copper, silver, and gold mining triangle formed by the towns of Siuna, Bonanza, and Rosario a perfect target. Located about 160 miles northeast of Managua and about 100 miles southeast of Aguacate, the mines were pumping $23 million a year in gold revenues alone into Sandinista coffers. CIA strategists, eager to tighten the war's stranglehold on the Nicaraguan economy, wanted to cut off the flow. Furthermore, Soviet technicians had established a major radar center at Siuna to track CIA supply flights. That made the town an even more appealing target.[60]

Because the attack was so important, it would be meticulously planned and coordinated by the CIA. Higher-ups at Langley suggested the attack, producing the "overheads," the satellite photos of the mining complex and nearby garrisons, as well as a torrent of other relevant intelligence. Then CIA men at the Tegucigalpa base created an entire battle plan, which Don Johnson reviewed with Bermúdez and Invisible out at Aguacate.

An important aspect of the attack was to be diversionary ambushes elsewhere in Nicaragua, to put Sandinista forces off balance, followed by simultaneous strikes on the three towns by more than three thousand rebel troops. To supply the rebel forces for the attack, CIA flight dispatchers kept the Swan Island mercenary crews busy from early November on, with multiple cargo drops every night. In mid-November, Johnson had Bermúdez order some two thousand rebels to start marching north from Nicaragua's central provinces to get into position around the mines. Another one thousand began a six-week trek south through the jungles toward the mines from bases in Honduras. Leading the troops were several well-known regional commanders: Diógenes Hernández, known as "Fernando," and Tirzo Moreno, known as "Rigoberto," were in charge of two of the Jorge Salazar units; Francisco Ruiz, "Renato," an aging ex-Guard, led another. The Americans even pressured Mack, who hadn't been inside Nicaragua for years, to participate. To maintain secrecy, the rebel forces marched silently, without using their field radios.

Johnson worried about secrecy at Aguacate, too, especially in the wake of the discovery of the spy ring there earlier in the year. He told Bermúdez that in order to keep the attack secret, the formal command post for the attack would not be Bermúdez's "Strategic Command" tents, but rather Johnson's own CIA quarters. Johnson ordered all the main rebel field radios brought to his own office.

Late in the third week of December, rebel forces began radioing Aguacate to announce that they were converging on dozens of points specified in the CIA's battle plans as staging areas: hills overlooking the mining towns, nearby military garrisons, and ambush points along the only roads through the region.

The rebels attacked all three mining towns before dawn on Sunday, December 20. Once the combat was under way, the rebels radioed Aguacate with regular reports. Rigoberto's men had fought their way into control of Siuna, a town of ten thousand, seizing two military warehouses, as well as the Siuna airstrip. Outside town, rebel troops located the radar installation, a parking area jammed with several Soviet-built truck trailers containing electronic equipment, and they destroyed it with C-4 explosives. They also blew up Siuna's main gasoline storage tank. Upon finding a government food warehouse stacked with canned goods, they urged local residents to sack it. What was left they burned.

Some twenty miles to the northeast, rebel fighters under Renato seized the town of Bonanza and its airstrip. They destroyed the nearby Siempre Viva! hydroelectric generating plant, used to power the mines. They also found and looted a housing settlement usually occupied by Czech mining engineers—they were away for Christmas—smashing the East-bloc radios and televisions with special glee. At Rosario, Fernando's troops met fierce Sandinista resistance—thirty rebel fighters died during the initial battles for just two neighborhoods—and although they damaged the Rosario airport, his troops had to abandon the attack. To the east, along the main road to the Atlantic coast, rebel sappers blew up two bridges.

At Aguacate, Victor Sánchez (Aristides's younger brother), who was then the rebels' acting operations officer on Bermúdez's Strategic Command, at first had no idea the attack was under way, since Johnson had ordered the command post moved into the CIA quarters. Sánchez was puzzled by the apparent commotion inside the CIA house.

"What's happening in there?" another rebel officer asked him.

"I don't know," Sánchez answered. "Let's go see."

"So we went up to the house of the gringos," Sánchez recalled later, "and there were all the radios, and Johnson had taken complete charge of everything."

Johnson was in his jogging shorts, pacing in front of his maps, elated.

"He was arranging everything on his maps," Sánchez said. " 'Let's try this! Now let's move them here!' It was like a party, in his own house, as if he were playing with lead soldiers. Don Johnson was really excited, reporting to his superiors by radio. It was like it was a big game."

For the CIA, the enthusiasm was unavoidable. For once, the rebels were fighting like skilled soldiers! All the Americans' work seemed to be paying off. But Sánchez and several other contras had a different reaction. Watching the CIA men orchestrate the combat, Sánchez and others began to wonder: "Whose war is this, anyway?"

"That's when we saw that Johnson was giving direct orders to Bermúdez," Sánchez recalled. " 'Colonel, sign this for me!' he'd tell Bermúdez. And he'd hand Bermúdez an order, already typed up. 'I'm going to do this troop movement.' He wasn't even consulting. And Bermúdez was signing."

Perhaps it was the excitement or tension, but it was one of the few moments in the war when CIA agents allowed anyone to watch them issue direct commands to top contra leaders. It proved to be a major mistake, causing indignation that spread through much of the contra officers' corps.[61]

Another detail sparked anger as well. The CIA felt it was critical to exploit the attack's propaganda possibilities—if U.S. journalists didn't report the attack, it might as well not have happened. Johnson ordered several rebels to radio press bulletins from Aguacate to rebel spokesmen for media distribution.

"Remember, we need some heroes!" Johnson said. He and the other CIA agents especially liked Invisible, the rebel intelligence chief who had helped more than any other rebel to refine the attack plans. Never mind that Invisible didn't participate in the attack itself—Johnson recommended that Invisible be portrayed as one of the heroic commanders responsible for the rebel victory.

Unfortunately, Invisible was vacationing in Miami during the actual fighting. When word spread through the rebel army that the CIA had ordered press communiqués crediting Invisible with the attack, many fighters were livid—especially Rigoberto, Fernando, and other rebel officers who had spent nearly three months trudging through the jungle to carry out the attack.

At the same time, the CIA was also trying to arrange a rendezvous between Bermúdez, "the supreme commander of Resistance forces" during the attack, with U.S. reporters.

Originally, Johnson had hoped to fly Bermúdez into one of the captured mining towns and then helicopter in journalists to interview him. In Tegucigalpa, rebel press spokeswoman Adela Icaza began calling selected journalists early Monday, the morning after the initial attacks. She told one reporter that he'd be flown into Nicaragua "to see Bermúdez eating hamburgers on Siuna's main street." But after reporters converged on Toncontín Airport, they waited for hours, until mid-afternoon, before being told to climb into a waiting Huey helicopter for departure.

At Aguacate, Johnson had had to downgrade his plans. Monitoring the battle reports, he saw that Sandinista reinforcements were converging on the mining complex, and he realized he'd have to settle for second-best: a press encounter with Bermúdez at the contras' river base at San Andrés, on the Honduran-Nicaraguan border. San Andrés had little to do with the attack on the mines, but the CIA men figured its remote jungle location would add a touch of tropical adventure to a journalist's interview with Bermúdez.

The helicopter bearing reporters for Reuters, the *Washington Post,* the *Chicago Tribune,* NBC, and several other U.S. media finally touched down at a small clearing in the thick jungle canopy at San Andrés just before dark on Monday. Bermúdez's CIA Bell helicopter was parked at the edge of the clearing. At the end of a twenty-minute hike up a trail, the reporters met Bermúdez, dressed in his combat fatigues.

"Where are we?" somebody asked.

"This is the new Strategic Command," Bermúdez answered. He ushered them into a roomy wooden hut and, with rebel aides stoking kerosene lanterns, started an initial briefing on the rebel attack. He still held out hope that the reporters would be flown into Siuna, but he conceded that the chances were slim; the Sandinistas were airlifting reinforcements to the town. Bermúdez sat up late, telling the circle of journalists old anecdotes about the war, but he seemed distracted, completely disconnected from the battle still raging at the mining complex. He never issued any orders; he wasn't conferring with aides. For an officer guiding his troops through their finest hour, the journalists thought, Bermúdez seemed utterly demoralized.

Tuesday morning, Bermúdez met the journalists with a grand announcement. "I've ordered the troops to retreat," he told them. He produced two teletype printouts of "his" command, which had been radioed to the troops. He told the journalists that they would be flown back to Tegucigalpa, but there was time for one-on-one interviews for all of them. He brought out his Plasticine-covered battle maps for another briefing, and aides produced a tape recorder to play back intercepts of Sandinista army radio communications—recorded at the CIA's scanning posts at Aguacate—to show that the Sandinistas had been confused by the rebels' diversionary attacks. The photographers shot dozens of rolls of Tri-X: Bermúdez sitting in a jungle clearing, Bermúdez pointing at his combat maps, Bermúdez reading the printouts. Then the Huey helicoptered the journalists back to Tegucigalpa in time to file, before deadlines for Wednesday's papers, their interviews with "the commander of the Northern Front of the Nicaraguan Resistance."[62]

None of the stories mentioned Don Johnson, or Aguacate, or the CIA role in the attacks.

With a new contra aid vote scheduled for early February in the U.S. Congress, the CIA wanted to follow up the rebels' propaganda victory at the mining complex with another spectacular operation. CIA agents began calling for an attack on Juigalpa, the capital of Chontales province, in central Nicaragua eighty-five miles east of Managua. Don Johnson ordered an increase in supply flights to rebel troops outside the town, but the region was saturated with Sandinista combat troops, and rebel officers at Aguacate warned against the airdrops. There just wasn't enough separation between rebel forces and the enemy, they argued.

"We have to go ahead. We need the propaganda," Johnson shot back, and he sent three flights in three days to drop mortar shells and other supplies around Juigalpa. The third day's flight fell to a Nicaraguan DC-6 crew, based at Aguacate, piloted by Donaldo Frixione. The fifty-one-year-old flyer was a former commander of Somoza's Air Force whom the CIA had recruited in Miami months earlier. Over Juigalpa, two contra special forces troops parachuted from Frixione's DC-6, carrying battle plans for the attack the CIA had ordered on Juigalpa. Minutes later, a Soviet-made C2-M rocket slammed into Frixione's plane. The DC-6 crashed about eighty miles southeast of Managua; Frixione and at least two of his crew died in the wreckage. Hours later, Frixione's seventeen-year-old son Alex answered the phone at home in Miami. A man's voice identified the caller as a CIA representative and announced that Frixione had been shot down. Inside Nicaragua, the best that the hard-pressed rebels around Juigalpa could muster was a mortar strike on the town on January 20.[63]

While the CIA was straining to impress the Congress with the contras' new fighting prowess, Washington hardly noticed. In mid-November, the congressional Iran-contra committees had released their report, blaming the White House for "secrecy, deception, and disdain for the rule of law." Although the contras had been only peripherally involved in North's "enterprise"—which is about the extent to which they'd been involved in most of the direction of the war—they suffered its political consequences.

Even more damaging to the contras' chances for further aid had been the peace negotiations gaining momentum since August. Even while the fighting had been under way at the mining complex in December 1987, Sandinista and contra delegations had been negotiating, indirectly through mediators, from separate hotels in Santo Domingo. In mid-January, the two sides held their first face-to-face talks in San José, Costa Rica.

Reagan Administration officials ignored the signs, pushing stubbornly for passage of an ambitious new military aid package for the contras: $36 million, to be spent over just four months. Several key congressmen said later that they couldn't understand why the Administration had pushed such an unrealistic package when the political climate was so unfavorable. In any event, a number of Democratic representatives who had voted before for contra aid switched their votes on February 3, 1988, when the bill came to the House floor. The Administration request went down 219–211.

"Today's vote is the end of a chapter," said House Majority Whip Tony Coelho, the California Democrat who led opposition to the package. "The contra policy is past."[64]

8

Back
in the Camps

February through November 1988

The rejection in February 1988 by the U.S. Congress of any new military aid for the contras threw the rebel army into turmoil. Contra units streamed out of Nicaragua into Honduran base camps, some ordered back by Bermúdez, others returning on their own. In early 1988 cease-fire talks with the Sandinista government, contra negotiators drawn from the latest CIA-recruited political front signed an accord with the Sandinistas and then, bickering like teenagers, said they wished they hadn't. A group of dissident officers openly challenged Bermúdez's control of the army. The "supreme commander" held on to his post only when the CIA intervened forcefully on his behalf.

The Americans were in disarray, too. With Administration policy collapsing, top CIA officers who had been involved in the program for years quietly retired. The State Department and the Agency for International Development took over direct administration of the rebel army. It was a presidential election year, and by summer, Washington's main goal was to keep the contra army, a mounting political liability, out of the news.

February through April 1988

The latest U.S. aid cutoff was not like earlier congressional setbacks for the contra project. This time it was final. The cutoff convinced rebel negotiators to sign a cease-fire agreement with the Sandinista government just seven weeks later. Two encounters with American officials dramatized to rebel leaders that Washington was finally giving up on the Project.

The first was the resignation of Alan Fiers, the senior CIA official who had coordinated Langley's participation in the contra war since October 1984 as the Agency's Central America Task Force chief. Fiers had barely survived 1987 and the Iran-contra hearings; newspapers had reported several times during the year that CIA Director William Webster was likely to fire him for his role in the scandal. Fiers was never forced out, but in December, Webster gave him a "serious reprimand." After Congress slashed the contra program on February 3, Fiers called it quits.[1]

He began to say his good-byes. In a White House meeting of the restricted interagency group that brought State Department, CIA, and National Security Council officials together to discuss the Nicaraguan Project, Fiers turned to Assistant Secretary of State Elliott Abrams and said, "It's time for us to get out of this, time for new blood."

Days later, at a Miami meeting with the rebel directorate and other functionaries—to whom he was known as "Cliff"—Fiers broke down and wept. "He talked about how attached he was to the fighters," recalled Marta Sacasa, a Resistance spokeswoman at the time. "He said that when he was at home with his barbecue, he couldn't stop thinking of the commandos in the field."

Fiers's performance left a dramatic impression on Calero, Sánchez, and other contra leaders. The war was really over; Fiers, the man who had run it, was leaving.

Two weeks later, packed into a meeting room at their headquarters in an industrial park adjacent to the Miami airport, rebel officials met several State Department officials who had flown down from Washington. They included Special Ambassador Morris Busby; Cris Arcos, the urbane Chicano diplomat overseeing the contra human-rights program; Robert Kagan, Elliott Abrams's young Yale-educated deputy; the CIA's John Mallett, and others. If the contra leaders were still entertaining hopes for more military aid, Busby, Kagan, and others now laid out the bad news: There won't be any more, they said; not during the Reagan Administration, probably never.[2]

Despite the cutoff, equipment shortages were not the rebel army's immediate problem. Nearly two hundred ship containers packed with munitions, uniforms, and other supplies—enough for months of continued rebel operations, all bought and paid for—were backed up along the airstrip on Swan Island. The problem was how to get the supplies to the troops once the CIA airdrops ended; the CIA had money and legal authorization to continue its supply flights only until the end of February 1988.

Suddenly the CIA was forced to confront the shortsightedness of its own high-technology supply delivery system, based on container ships, forklifts, and airplanes. The airdrops had allowed the rebel army to operate across Nicaragua, but once the CIA planes stopped flying, the rebels would be stranded. Suddenly everyone was wishing the Nicaraguans had developed a more down-to-earth logistical trail, based on mules and trails and canoes.

It was a little late, but the CIA decided to offer the rebels what it could: Don Johnson offered a technical briefing for Bermúdez on how to set up a ground-and-water supply delivery system. Men at the Tegucigalpa base got the briefing materials together fast, drawing up maps of Nicaragua's waterways and mountain trails, estimating the tonnage that could be moved on mule-back, offering suggestions for dividing the force into burden-bearers and fighters, like other guerrilla armies did.

Bermúdez wasn't interested.

"*No somos Chinos*," he told Johnson. "We're not Chinamen. Our peasants won't accept this kind of thing. They're willing to fight, but they won't carry a bag of rice on their backs."[3]

Bermúdez's haughty attitude angered Johnson. "Even if we get more money for this program later," he told other U.S. officials, "I won't work with Bermúdez again."

Despite Bermúdez's lack of interest, there was no other logical thing to do with the supplies on Swan except fly as much as possible to the Honduras-Nicaragua border, where it would be available for troops marching out of Nicaragua. CIA planes began flying day and night south over the Caribbean to the rebel base at San Andrés, parachuting armaments for storage in several weapons stockpiles.

Meanwhile, the Honduran military—long jealous of the sophisticated weaponry the CIA had been channeling to the contras—attempted an audacious power play. Traveling to Swan Island, a Honduran Army officer attempted to seize the dozens of Redeye missiles stored there. "Major John," the CIA agent in charge on Swan, had to intervene.

"These missiles are U.S. government property," he told the Honduran through an interpreter. "Keep your hands off."[4]

On February 29, when the CIA airlift ended, a lot of supplies were still on Swan, but the CIA had succeeded in dumping some three thousand metric tons into San Andrés.[5]

The Sandinistas saw their chance. If they could take out the contras' new border supply dumps at San Andrés, they would deal a critical—

perhaps killing—blow to the rebel army. Early in March, the Sandinistas sent company-sized intelligence units on reconnaissance missions into Honduras, conducted air strikes against the rebel camp, and finally deployed six Sandinista battalions—roughly 4,500 troops—to the border to attack the rebels' riverbank installations at San Andrés. Bermúdez ordered the 1,500 rebel troops in the area to defend the base, then fled to Tegucigalpa by helicopter. Both sides took scores of losses in the protracted mortar duel that followed, but by March 16, the Sandinistas overran the base as the rebels, outnumbered and outgunned, retreated farther into Honduras.

Frantic U.S. officials, convinced that the Sandinistas were about to capture the rebels' only remaining stockpiles, went to the President. Reagan ordered 3,200 U.S. troops from the 82nd Airborne and 7th Infantry Divisions flown to the U.S. air base at Palmerola, Honduras. Faced with the potential for clashes with U.S. troops, on March 17 President Ortega pulled his troops back into Nicaragua, ending the Sandinista drive.[6]

Just thirteen weeks had elapsed since the contra army had won its greatest military victory. Four days after the battle of San Andrés, a battered rebel army's negotiators opened new peace talks with the Sandinistas at the southern Nicaragua border village of Sapoá. The force was cut off from further U.S. military aid, its payroll was threatened, its long-term handlers were leaving the Project, its base camps were in disarray.

But the Sandinistas were facing a crisis, too. The Nicaraguan economy was in collapse. Sandinista labor leaders were angry; many militant revolutionaries were desperate for peace. This serendipitous combination of pressures forced both sides to shed their longtime intransigence during the three-day encounter at Sapoá.[7] The two sides forged a surprising cease-fire agreement that offered several formulas for national reconciliation.

Spring 1987 through April 1988

The men who would negotiate for the rebel army were the central figures in the latest political front group, recruited and funded by Washington a year earlier. The previous directorate, the UNO triumvirate of Cruz, Robelo, and Calero, had crumbled in February 1987 after Cruz resigned, unable to stomach his alliance with the old FDN clique any longer.

U.S. officials had agreed that the new Resistance directorate should represent the major Nicaraguan political parties. At White House meetings in the weeks after Cruz's resignation, the Americans tossed names around: Calero could represent Nicaragua's Conservative Party, everyone agreed. Aristides Sánchez could move to Miami and represent Somoza's old Liberal Party. Pedro Joaquín Chamorro—the son of Nicaragua's martyred publisher—could represent the Social Democrats and add his colorful name to the Resistance directorate. But who would represent the Social Christians? The Agency suggested Azucena Ferrey, a Christian Democrat activist still living in Managua. She agreed to go into exile to join the directorate.[8] The Agency also liked Alfredo César, the thirty-six-year-old former head of Nicaragua's Central Bank. César had admirers throughout Latin America and liberal friends in U.S. Congress. He was an attractive, articulate politician, an independent thinker. "The Agency men said they knew the game with him: 'You didn't buy César, you rented him,' " recalled Robert Kagan, a State Department official who helped put the Resistance directorate together.[9]

The Resistance was more extravagantly funded than any earlier rebel directorate. Assistant Secretary of State Elliott Abrams advocated secret U.S. funding to build a Resistance political bureaucracy that he hoped could one day mature into a Nicaraguan government-in-exile. Under the plan, each Resistance director, representing a political *tendencia*, was to publish a newsletter, travel widely for public speeches, sponsor forums, or carry out other initiatives aimed at building opposition to the Sandinistas. This would cost money.

The CIA was authorized to channel nearly $1 million per month to fund Resistance political activities. Part of those secret political funds were what became known as the *tendencia* payments: $15,000 a month to each of the Resistance directors, a total of $180,000 per year per director!

Reagan Administration officials imposed virtually no accounting demands, and as a result, the lavish funding soon brought the proliferation of a Resistance bureaucracy comprised of some four hundred Nicaraguan exiles. The contras established U.S.-funded offices not only in Miami but in Madrid, Paris, Caracas, Mexico City, Guatemala City, Tegucigalpa, San Salvador, and San José. Notwithstanding the international outreach, the Resistance directors were picked because American officials believed they would appeal to the U.S. Congress.[10] But the new directorate's main role turned out to be not lobbying but negotiating a peace agreement.

Calero, César, and Sánchez, three of the five members of the directorate, negotiated for the Resistance at Sapoá. Two field commanders, Diógenes Hernández, known as "Fernando," and Walter "Toño" Calderón also sat with the rebel negotiating team but were rarely consulted. A parallel team of State Department and CIA officials traveled with the Resistance party.

The site of the talks was the Sapoá customs post, a sheet-metal building just inside Nicaragua, north of the Costa Rican border. On March 21, the first day of the talks, General Humberto Ortega—the president's brother, the Defense Minister, and head of the Sandinista delegation—waded through a crowd of journalists and Sandinista security agents to an open-air podium to announce that the government had ordered its troops into an immediate, unilateral truce. Hours later, the rebel delegation arrived at Sapoá after driving north from its base in the Costa Rican town of Liberia and reciprocated the Sandinista gesture by ordering rebel troops to observe their own truce. In retrospect, that cease-fire—ordered before the Sapoá talks even got under way—proved of more lasting importance than the formal Sapoá peace accord itself; despite initial skepticism, both sides stopped the war, and neither side ever began it again in earnest.

After two days of negotiating, the two sides stunned nearly everyone when the Ortega brothers and other Sandinista officials joined Calero, César, Sánchez, Toño, Fernando, and other rebel officials on a wooden stage in front of the Nicaraguan flag to pen their names to the Sapoá agreement.

It provided a simple formula. During a temporary cease-fire, both sides would make concessions designed to build mutual confidence. Rebel combatants would move into rural enclaves, the government would release some 3,300 political prisoners held in government jails, and exiled Nicaraguan leaders—including the rebel directorate—would return to Managua for a continuing dialogue with the Sandinistas about conditions under which the rebels would lay down their arms for good.

For the contras, the accord offered tangible gains at the end of a war they had failed to win: in short, peace with dignity. For the Sandinistas, it meant the revolution's survival after a protracted counterrevolution. Over the next weeks, however, the accord fell apart, the victim of sabotage by both sides. Bermúdez began to sabotage the cease-fire process even while the two sides were still meeting at Sapoá. In Tegucigalpa, fuming over the reports of progress toward an agreement, Bermúdez called in reporters from Costa Rica's Radio Impacto to tape a tirade, broadcast across the isthmus just as negotiators were signing the Sapoá accord, that challenged the rebel negotiators' authority to sign any agreement. He insisted that his men would never lay down their arms until "final victory."

After the negotiations, Sánchez, Fernando, and Toño flew from Costa Rica to Honduras to report back to other contra officers on the cease-fire's terms. Bermúdez called in all the rebel officers who were handy in Tegucigalpa—Jhonson was there, along with Mike Lima and a dozen or so ex-Guardsmen—to rail against the agreement and at Fernando and Toño for signing it. Aristides Sánchez, who had also signed at Sapoá, stayed out of sight.

Bermúdez had loathed Calero ever since the CIA had installed Calero in 1983 as the contra army's civilian "commander-in-chief," and now Bermúdez accused Calero of selling out the contras at Sapoá. He stirred Mike Lima, Mack, and half a dozen other officers to anger, then flew them to Miami to unload on the peace accord.[11]

In Miami's Nicaraguan and Cuban exile communities, there was bedlam. Most of the Cuban-owned radio stations were denouncing the accord, and Bermúdez took to the airwaves to add his voice. The tension climaxed on March 26, the weekend following the Sapoá talks, in a Resistance assembly at the Viscount Hotel north of the Miami airport. As Calero and other Resistance directors entered the hotel, angry exiles booed and heckled.

"Traitors!" the exiles shouted. "You've betrayed us!" One angry Nicaraguan exile activist punched Enrique "Cuco" Sánchez—Aristides's brother and Calero's brother-in-law—in the jaw, knocking him down.

Inside, Bermúdez, Mack, Mike Lima, and others stomped into a hotel meeting room. Some who watched said it reminded them of an old-time Nicaraguan military coup, like the Guardia marching in to seize the civilian government. Bermúdez took the podium to attack the Sapoá accord in a long speech, directing most of his vitriol at Calero. Bermúdez urged the formation of an exile committee to "monitor" the Resistance negotiators, to ensure they would make no more blunders like Sapoá.[12] The contra haggling continued, behind the scenes, during two weeks of Sandinista-Resistance technical negotiations back at Sapoá, aimed at drawing the boundaries of rebel enclaves and writing the rules under which the zones would operate.

With the fighting stopped and the contras divided, the Sandinistas responded by quietly reinterpreting the Sapoá accord. When Calero, César, and some forty other Resistance officials flew to Managua on April 15 for the first cease-fire talks in the Nicaraguan capital, the Sandinista negotiators laid down unreasonable new demands for quick and total rebel disarmament. They argued that the Sapoá accord contained an "implicit" requirement that the contras lay down their arms. The document called for nothing of the kind, but having maligned the accord themselves, the Resistance negotiators were now in no position to enforce strict Sandinista compliance with it.

Another development, however, proved more damaging to the contras' negotiating prospects. Fernando and Toño failed to arrive in Managua for the new talks. They were in Tegucigalpa, denouncing corruption and secret violence in the contra army and calling on Bermúdez to resign. There was rebellion among the rebels.

February through June 1988

Fernando and Toño became two of the key leaders in the dissidents' rebellion partly out of anger at Bermúdez's criticisms of their role in the peace talks, but the challenge to Bermúdez that emerged in the spring of 1988 went deeper than that. It became an outpouring of rebel dissatisfaction with Bermúdez's leadership and with his servile obedience to the Americans, one of the few attempts during the war by the contras' own commanders to chart their own course. The CIA crushed it.

Toño's sudden opposition to Bermúdez surprised many contras. Toño had been a standout National Guardsman; like Mike Lima and Invisible, he was the top cadet in his Military Academy class. In the rebel army, Toño had enjoyed close ties with Sánchez and Bermúdez and had even helped suppress the first dissident rebellion in early 1983. But Toño began to see things differently in the fall of 1987, when he joined the rebel negotiating commission. Thrust into a whirl of hotels and restaurants, airports, and interviews, he discovered how Bermúdez's leadership had tarred the rebel movement with a neanderthal image. His detractors pooh-poohed Toño's insubordination as a sign of the sudden vanity that gripped him as he moved as a rebel negotiator through the international spotlight. And there was some evidence for that: Overnight, Toño traded his combat fatigues for jacket and tie, started lifting weights in a Tegucigalpa health club, and began a series of affairs with several glamorous female TV correspondents. Nonetheless, he was bright, and many of the criticisms he leveled at Bermúdez found wide resonance in the contra army.[13]

Fernando, the son of a rancher, had been a twenty-three-year-old seminarian when he joined the rebel army in 1982, a handsome student with long eyelashes and delicate features. Over several years of combat, he had risen to head one of the contras' most successful combat battalions. Yet his popularity with the troops seemed to derive as much from the decency he projected—his soft-spoken manner, his evangelical Protestant sensibilities—as from his battlefield prowess. As a student, Fernando had learned the rhythms of sermonizing, and his ability to frame the rebel struggle in Christian terms had made him a favorite of American officials. When John Mallett, the CIA's deputy station chief in Honduras, was transferred back to the United States, Fernando had stood up at a going-away party in Tegucigalpa to eulogize Mallett, comparing the agent's work with the contras to Moses's efforts to lead the Israelites into the Promised Land.

From his earliest days in the rebel army, however, Fernando had seen things that didn't square with his beliefs. Once, patrolling the Honduran border as a foot soldier in 1983, he was stunned when he stumbled across several rebel bodies. Fernando discovered that they and numerous other commandos—perhaps dozens—had been murdered for casual reasons by their FDN commanders: Armando López, then forty-seven, the former Guard police lieutenant with the pseudonym "The Policeman," and César Tijerino, a former Guard lieutenant known as "Six-Seven," who had been an interrogator from the National Security Office. Fernando discovered that Tijerino and López had gone on a homicidal rampage, murdering commandos after minor provocations. In one case, Tijerino had strangled several commandos just because they had developed diarrhea.[14]

When Fernando began to work at Bermúdez's Strategic Command headquarters at Yamales in 1986, he saw more brutal treatment of young commandos. He also saw thievery—and Bermúdez's servility to the Americans. In a late 1986 Yamales meeting with several U.S. agents including James Adkins, the CIA base chief, Fernando and other rebel officers disagreed with the Americans, who were urging the rebels to send several rebel units into Nicaragua immediately. It wasn't a hostile encounter, but Fernando felt the Americans were wrong. He and other rebels complained to Bermúdez, but he just shrugged it off. "The CIA has never permitted me to take decisions," Bermúdez said. In 1987, Fernando was transferred along with Bermúdez's Strategic Command from Yamales to Aguacate. There he saw that the rebel "air force" was really just a glorified air taxi service, flying Bermúdez and his ex-Guards back and forth to their homes in Tegucigalpa, and often to the region's whorehouses. By early 1988, Fernando was fed up.

The third dissident conspirator was Tirzo "Rigoberto" Moreno, thirty-three. Like Fernando, Rigoberto had been a civilian before the war, a mustachioed cowboy who traveled northern Nicaragua in a pickup truck as a livestock trader. As a field officer, Rigoberto had demonstrated an uncanny battlefield acumen.

"He was a brilliant commander. An absolute general," said one CIA officer who monitored Rigoberto's performance. It was Rigoberto's military prowess, in fact, that eventually led to his break with Bermúdez. Having watched Bermúdez's handling of the war over several years, Rigoberto concluded that Bermúdez had neither strategy nor vision.

The discontent over Bermúdez's command mounted in the weeks after the February 3 U.S. aid cutoff. Rebel battalions were retreating across the border, angry and harassed, dragging their wounded. Many commanders came back confused about the cutoff and the cease-fire negotiations. It wasn't even clear where the army's main base camps were to be now: San Andrés? Yamales? Some new site?

The troops wanted answers, but amid the chaos, Bermúdez wasn't around. Nobody could say where he was. Finally, however, the commanders began to solve the mystery.

For more than two years, Bermúdez had been carrying on an affair with María Eugenia Ortez, a slender commando in her early twenties with an ivory complexion and flaxen hair, the daughter of affluent Nicaraguan farmers. Bermúdez had set Ortez up in a cozy house in the village of El Paraíso, south of Danlí, and in 1987 she had borne Bermúdez a son, whom she named Enrique II—although Bermúdez already had a teenage son named Enrique living in Miami. To look after her, Bermúdez moved out of his Ciudad Nueva safe house on Tegucigalpa's outskirts, brought Ortez into the city, and set up housekeeping with her in a secret new residence in Tegucigalpa's Prado neighborhood, a walled mansion along a quiet boulevard overlooking the Choluteca River. Now, his army in chaos, Bermúdez was spending his time in Tegucigalpa with his lover and child, and he wasn't giving out his phone number.[15]

Word got around, and it made the field commanders mad. One angry leader was Tigrillo, now thirty-one and limping on his crippled knee. Several thousand rebel commandos still considered Tigrillo their top commander, and as they poured into Honduras, they needed food and medicine. Tigrillo, like other commanders, wanted to talk to Bermúdez, "but he was hiding from us," Tigrillo recalled. Finally, Tigrillo and several other rebel commanders drove to Tegucigalpa and stomped into the Resistance finance office. They scrawled out a message for Bermúdez, demanding a meeting. Somebody got it to Bermúdez, who set a date for an encounter at the rebel medical clinic in Danlí. Toward the end of February, when Bermúdez arrived at the clinic for the evening encounter, more than sixty rebels—commanders, fighters, wives, screaming babies—had packed into the long, windowless shed facing one of Danlí's clay streets. Bermúdez faced a clamor of complaints and questions, but instead of bringing answers, he had brought an attaché cash stuffed with five thousand Honduran lempiras, the equivalent of $2,500. By doling out cash as little favors—fifty lempiras to this commander, one hundred lempiras to that fighter's wife—he hoped to lubricate the squeaking wheel.

This time, however, it wasn't enough. During the meeting, several commanders told Bermúdez they wanted to change the army command structure, abolishing his "Strategic Command." Bermúdez would remain the top commander, but they wanted to elect a formal general staff. Bermúdez finally agreed.[16]

In late February the thirty or so top commanders met with Bermúdez in one of the staff tents at San Andrés—amid the CIA's final airdrops to the base—to elect the new staff. Bermúdez brokered the meeting. He arranged the election of former Guard Sgt. Juan Ramón "Quiché" Rivas as chief of staff. A short and slender man of Indian parentage, Quiché was a capable combat commander, but many rebels found him too taciturn, given to brooding silences—he lacked the social skills to lead a whole army. It was clear he would never threaten Bermúdez's own control.[17]

Mack replaced Invisible, the intelligence chief whom many rebel commanders resented because of the way the CIA treated him as a favorite. Mike Lima became counterintelligence chief, replacing Donald Torres, whom virtually everyone except Bermúdez had come to loathe for his binges and brutality.

Instead of silencing Bermúdez's critics, though, the general staff election angered them. Toño, despite a long absence from the battlefield, had nursed his own ambitions to become the contra chief of staff; Quiché's election embittered him. Rigoberto, too, was disappointed when Bermúdez made him the staff's civilian affairs chief, the post responsible for attending to rebel refugee families. It offended Rigoberto's commander's pride. "I'm going to be delivering milk?" he asked.

In the weeks after the general staff election, Toño, Fernando, and Rigoberto began to grumble, and in early April the three commanders cut an alliance of convenience with three Resistance bureaucrats, all aides to Calero, who'd been working in Tegucigalpa. One was Orlando Montealegre, a relative of Calero's who had been the rebel army's paymaster. Another was Donald Lacayo, the lawyer who had been Calero's counsel at Managua's Coca-Cola bottling plant before the war and whom Calero had installed in the Resistance legal office in Tegucigalpa. A third was Calero's brother-in-law, Enrique "Cuco" Sánchez.

With the bonanza of U.S. funding drawing to a close, these bureaucrats were likely to lose their Resistance posts anyway and thus had little to lose by challenging Bermúdez. Calero, drawing on his wartime profits, began channeling funds to them in Tegucigalpa.

The dissidents' first move reflected the dynamics of power in the rebel army: Fernando, Rigoberto, and Toño met with Richard Chidester, the embassy political officer who, for nearly two years, had been one of the contra army's main American contacts in Tegucigalpa. They laid out their criticisms of Bermúdez, and asked for a meeting with the CIA.

The rebels knew the station chief as "Terry." They had met him a few times when he had helicoptered out to Aguacate to talk to Bermúdez. Terry was fifty, but with his thinning white hair and creased face, he looked older. He had a distinguished CIA career, stretching back more than two decades. A 1960 graduate of the University of Pennsylvania, Terry had started in the CIA with a tour as a paramilitary agent in Laos, when the Agency was still recruiting and training its forty-thousand-man peasant army. Beginning in 1965, he operated under diplomatic cover all over Latin America: as an economic attaché in Buenos Aires, a political officer in Santo Domingo, and in other later postings in La Paz, Caracas, and Lima. During the 1980s, Terry was back at Langley, climbing through the headquarters bureaucracy. He was deputy chief of the Operations Directorate's Latin America division when the Agency sent him to Tegucigalpa during the $100 million offensive.[18]

Like his predecessors, and like Ambassador Everett Briggs, whose embassy he was joining, Terry developed a close working relationship with Bermúdez. The three men were of the same generation, and they worked well together. The two Americans helped Bermúdez do his job, and he helped them do theirs, too. Both Terry and Briggs respected Bermúdez, who was an honored guest at many embassy functions.

These tight relations with Bermúdez became a factor when Chidester reported back to the embassy about the dissident challenge. Several days after the dissidents' first meeting with Chidester, Fernando got a phone call at his rented home in Tegucigalpa. It was Terry; he wanted to talk.

The meeting came days later, one morning in April 1988, at Chidester's Tegucigalpa home. Fernando, Toño, and Rigoberto, wearing civilian clothes, took positions in the stuffed chairs in Chidester's living room. Terry, Chidester, and several other U.S. officials sat on the sofa. As Chidester's wife ferried in coffee and cookies, the rebels laid out their complaints.

Fernando had set up the meeting, so he broke the ice, summarizing their complaints: They felt Bermúdez was militarily incompetent and politically inept, and his aides were thieves. Toño and Rigoberto joined in. Bermúdez had never once entered Nicaragua to fight—how were field commanders to respect a phony like him?

Fernando recalled the 1983 murders by Armando López, "The Policeman," of young rebel commandos. He'd seen the bodies. Had Bermúdez ever punished López? No, Fernando said. Where was López at that moment? Working on Bermúdez's supply staff, on the American payroll. Rigoberto reminded everybody that Mack had murdered several of his own recruits during 1986 basic training. Toño told the Americans what was common knowledge in the rebel army, that for years now Bermúdez's logistics officers had been shaking down Honduran truckers for bribes in exchange for contracts to deliver goods to Yamales. Toño had brought in documents to prove his point.

"We told Terry everything," Fernando recalled later. The dissidents went on for a little over an hour. Then Fernando moved to the bottom line: They wanted Bermúdez to leave Honduras and move to Miami, to join the contras' political directorate. In his place, a junta of rebel commanders would run the army.

There was a pause. Terry glanced around at the other Americans, then leaned forward in his chair.

"We'll be frank—we're not going to support you," he said. "The position of the U.S. government is to support Enrique Bermúdez."

"Well, we're going to change him anyway," Fernando said. "We wanted you to know up front. No misunderstandings."[19]

What the dissidents attempted was, essentially, a military *golpe*, but instead of proclaiming their rebellion Latin-style, from the base camps, entrenched behind their troops, they adopted a remarkably un-military strategy, based on petitions and persuasion. That probably reflected the influence of Calero's civilian advisers. With Calero and associates paying the bills, the plotters rented a suite at Tegucigalpa's Alameda Hotel to set up an informal headquarters. There, Tigrillo joined their campaign, and on April 16, using a borrowed typewriter, they hammered out a five-page manifesto that compared Bermúdez to Somoza, blaming him for "autocratic" leadership and abuses against rebel fighters in Honduran base camps. It concluded with a call for Bermúdez's replacement by a commanders' junta.

The dissidents fanned out to all the rebel enclaves in Honduras, seeking signatures for their manifesto. The campaign climaxed on a weekend in April at the Hotel Granada in Danlí, where the dissidents rented several rooms and lobbied wavering commanders with liquor and cash. Twelve of the army's thirty-two regional commanders and a few dozen other influential fighters eventually signed the anti-Bermúdez petition.

At the same time the dissidents were working to unseat Bermúdez, however, Bermúdez and the embassy were organizing a counterattack. Bermúdez seized the dissidents' CIA-paid vehicles, cut off their salaries, and expelled Fernando and Toño from the rebel negotiating team. The same weekend the dissidents were in Danlí, U.S. officials arranged a pro-Bermúdez rally at Honduras's Sixth Army Battalion, the pine-shaded garrison near Danlí which had always been a staging area for Honduran Army cooperation with the contras. Several hundred rebel fighters and their families were trucked in for an afternoon of pro-Bermúdez speeches and free food. With several CIA agents watching, Bermúdez accused Toño and the other dissidents of having defected to the Sandinistas during the peace talks. To prove his point, he held up to the crowd poster-sized blow-ups of a photo taken at Sapoá showing Toño embracing his cousin, an official in the Sandinista Interior Ministry. It had been only a cordial family greeting after years of war, but Bermúdez offered it as betrayal. The following week, Bermúdez relieved the dissidents of all rank.

Circulating their own petition denouncing the dissidents for "favoring Sandinismo," Bermúdez's people were also distributing cash. He raised the monthly salaries of officers who appeared to be wavering, and eventually nineteen regional commanders signed the Bermúdez petition.

By the last week of April, Toño sensed that the winds were blowing against the dissidents. He called together several journalists, and, for the first time publicly, on-the-record, denounced Bermúdez. "He's a dictator just like Noriega or Castro," Toño told the reporters.

The dissidents were going for broke. They moved from the Hotel Alameda to the much more expensive Maya, preferred by journalists, and two days after Toño's first sensational interview, he was joined by the rest of the dissidents for a virtual press conference with a number of reporters, including correspondents for *Newsweek* and the *Washington Post*. The following morning, May 4, Honduran security agents detained all the principal dissidents except Fernando and Tigrillo in their Maya Hotel suite. Hours later, they picked up Tigrillo in Danlí. (That same day, Bermúdez, Calero, and other contras were meeting in Washington with Secretary of State George Shultz.) The Hondurans held the dissidents at secret police headquarters in downtown Tegucigalpa, waiting for the U.S. embassy to arrange their travel documents. Two days later, the seven dissidents were shoved onto an Eastern Airlines jet and deported to Miami.

Fernando escaped. Warned by a young rebel just as he was arriving at the Maya Hotel on May 4, he drove east to the Yamales camps, skirting several Honduran military checkpoints. With units still streaming in from Nicaragua, the base camps were in chaos, and there was plenty of confusion about the dissident campaign. Many troops were surprised to see Fernando, since they had heard from Bermúdez's people that he had defected to the Communists. Now he visited his own Jorge Salazar units, and was received with *abrazos*. He radioed staff headquarters with a message: Dissident units would no longer obey Bermúdez's orders and Bermúdez loyalists were barred from dissident camps. Fernando called on members of the Resistance political directorate to travel to Honduras to hear the case against Bermúdez.

The standoff lasted three days and brought the only bloodshed of the rebellion. Troops loyal to Bermúdez fired on several dissident troops bumping along a road from one camp to another in Fernando's jeep. Two were wounded.

In Miami, the dissidents' deportation aroused outrage among staff employees at the Resistance offices on the northern edge of Miami International Airport. Fernando and Rigoberto were well known in Miami as two of the army's best commanders. Were Bermúdez and the Americans just going to pitch them into the street?

Two members of the Resistance's five-person directorate, Azucena Ferrey and Pedro Joaquín Chamorro, flew to Honduras, supposedly to mediate in the continuing showdown between Fernando and Bermúdez. There, however, they encountered a predictably hostile reaction from CIA officials when they outlined suggestions for conciliation. Chamorro told one CIA agent that he believed the civilian directorate enjoyed the institutional power to replace Bermúdez if it so decided.

"I admire your idealism, but let's be realistic," the agent responded.

CIA and Honduran authorities used the directors as bait to entice Fernando away from his troops and end the rebellion definitively. Three Honduran military officers drove to Yamales and told Fernando that the contra directors were waiting for him at the Sixth Battalion base. Fernando climbed into their jeep—and soon realized he had been detained. He was taken to Tegucigalpa, held for three days, and deported to Miami. He was never even allowed to change his clothes. Honduran military officers told Chamorro that "the allies"—their euphemism for the CIA—had demanded Fernando's expulsion.[20]

The deportations effectively ended the rebellion, but the CIA's heavy-handed tactics brought further embarrassment to Bermúdez and the CIA in Miami. Chamorro returned to Miami embittered, and met with the dissident commanders at the Resistance offices. When an angry CIA agent called him to complain that the dissidents shouldn't be visiting the contra headquarters, Chamorro blew up.

"They kicked you out of Honduras," he said to the dissidents. "Now they want to kick you out of our offices."

Chamorro drafted a proposal to remove Bermúdez and to replace him with Fernando, presenting it to the rest of the directorate in a meeting at Resistance headquarters. Aristides Sánchez looked it over, then stalked out of the room. He called John Mallett, his longtime CIA handler—then based at Langley—and returned to the meeting room with a speaker phone. Mallett phoned the Miami headquarters, and Sánchez read Chamorro's proposal aloud to the agent over the phone.

Mallett launched into an angry diatribe against the directors, especially Chamorro. He called Chamorro "stupid . . . an imbecile," and said that the contras deserved no more U.S. aid. The directors sat speechless while the agent blasted away for more than twenty minutes. Chamorro slumped into a couch.

"We don't respond to insults," Calero said when the agent finally paused. The meeting broke up.

The dissident rebel officers had arrived in Miami virtually penniless. Tigrillo's situation was particularly bleak; illiterate, limping on his war-damaged knee, he couldn't adjust to the American way of life. For a time, he got work picking lemons as an illegal laborer on a south Florida migrant farm, and months later he returned illegally to Honduras. The Hondurans detained him, then deported him to Guatemala. Toño found work as a surveyor. Fernando tried to make ends meet selling life insurance. Rigoberto applied for political asylum, but a year later found that his application—routinely approved for Bermúdez loyalists—was stalled. He still couldn't work.

Months after their challenge to Bermúdez, the three dissidents got the number of the Miami CIA station and a young, blond agent came out to their bleak apartment block to talk. He listened to their complaints about Rigoberto's asylum petition and their requests for economic help in getting started, then said he'd get back to them. He never did.

May and June 1988

With American help, Bermúdez held on to his command of the contra army, but the dissident challenge had torn at Resistance cohesion during a crucial moment. Now, for the first time, Bermúdez took direct leadership in the cease-fire talks.

Publicly, the Resistance's main negotiator in the final 1988 cease-fire talks was Alfredo César, who for his own obscure political reasons had backed Bermúdez against Calero during the dissident rebellion. César was a bright tactician, smooth at the negotiating table, glib with the press, but Bermúdez, his power consolidated, now had a direct veto over any agreement.

Bermúdez was taking his political advice from a little-known adviser, Harry Bodán. During the 1970s, Bodán had been Somoza's vice foreign minister. After Somoza fled Managua on July 17, 1979, jeering exiles nicknamed Bodán "July 16th" because of stories circulating about how even as Somoza was packing his bags in the bunker, Bodán had been whispering to the dictator: "No, my General, everything's okay." In those final days, Bodán laid dubious claim to the post of Nicaraguan Foreign Minister, but only for a few hours. When Bermúdez took him on as his main adviser in 1987, Bodán used the same sycophantic approach, always putting forward as advice that which he thought Bermúdez wanted to hear. By late spring 1988, Bermúdez wanted more than anything for Washington to reverse course and vote new military aid to the contras. As Bermúdez traveled to Managua twice in two weeks for final cease-fire talks with the Sandinistas, Bodán advised Bermúdez not to sign any agreement. Don't tie your hands, he said, the Americans will eventually vote more military aid.

So, instead of fighting to preserve the gains they had already won at Sapoá, Bermúdez and César laid out sweeping new demands. They called for a rewriting of the Nicaraguan constitution, the suspension of the draft, the unilateral release by the Sandinistas of all political prisoners.

"It's all negotiable," César told reporters. But it wasn't. In the afternoon hours of the final cease-fire talks on June 9, the Resistance presented an entirely new package of impossible demands. Bermúdez called for the mass resignation of the Nicaraguan Supreme Court, the repeal of Nicaragua's communications and public security laws. They demanded that the Sandinistas allow the Resistance to open an office in Managua.

This time, the peace talks that had begun with so much promise eleven weeks earlier at Sapoá broke down completely. It was clear that Bermúdez had no way of improving his army's military position—his forces would only get weaker. Sapoá was as good as Bermúdez and the Resistance were going to get.[21]

April through October 1988

Sometime after its disastrous February defeat in Congress over rebel aid, the Reagan Administration finally gave up on its contra Project. Some officials had accepted the reality earlier, some held out longer, but by late spring, there was a fundamental shift in the relations between Washington and its Nicaraguan army. Once the most-favored instrument of American foreign policy, suddenly the rebels found themselves to be the unwanted legacy of a now-discarded military policy.

The evolution of Washington's new relations with its contra army began in late March, when Congress voted $17.7 million to supply the rebels with food, clothing, and other survival supplies.[22] The new funding brought a major bureaucratic shift. Starting April 1, the State Department's Agency for International Development (AID), a civilian agency normally devoted to development projects, began taking over administration of the army from the CIA. That meant the wholesale replacement by new AID functionaries of scores of CIA agents who had worked in Honduras to administer the $100 million offensive. The CIA base in Tegucigalpa lost most of the agents assigned to it, and at the embassy, where many of the agents maintained diplomatic cover, men assigned or contracted to the CIA during the rebel offensive spent April packing their files, cashing out of the commissary, and saying their good-byes.

In their place, dozens of bureaucrats—secretaries and purchasing agents, accountants and contract pilots—from AID's new Humanitarian Assistance Task Force were moving to Tegucigalpa. Throughout April, the CIA's logistical agents, the men and women who had supervised the purchase and transport of food and other goods for the rebel army, were turning over their lists of Honduran suppliers, truckers, and contractors to the new AID people. It was an awkward process; what had been a covert program was, in the space of a few weeks, turning public.[23]

Contrary to widely held belief, CIA funding of the rebel army did not end completely. The Agency was legally authorized to continue "sharing intelligence" with the Resistance, and in practice, payments continued for at least two years after the March 1988 U.S. military aid cutoff, money used to fund the Resistance's intelligence and counterintelligence operations, secretly paying for vehicles, safe houses, and other supplies used by Mack, Mike Lima, and their clandestine rebel agents. The CIA also continued to secretly fund the exile politicians serving on the Resistance directorate, paying each of them fifteen thousand dollars per month until July 1989.[24]

Nonetheless, after March 1988, AID officials took over many aspects of the rebel army previously administered by the CIA, and they were forced to make sensitive decisions. Should they begin paying for Bermúdez's safe house? They decided they shouldn't. What about the salaries the CIA had been paying to the contra officer corps? Should AID begin to fund them? They decided they should; AID called the payments "family assistance."[25]

From the first days after the February 3 aid cutoff, rebel units had been streaming north to Honduras, at first into San Andrés, and later back into Yamales, which once again became the new headquarters camp. By mid-April, when the AID food deliveries began reaching Yamales, at least four thousand rebels and thousands of other camp followers were again turning Yamales into a sprawling contra settlement of campfires and plastic-and-stick huts. Hundreds more were arriving every week.[26]

Journalists visiting with contra units in rural camps inside Nicaragua were puzzled by the exodus. Most contra commanders inside Nicaragua at the time were expressing confidence about their ability to hold their positions comfortably for months: They had access to plenty of food, and since the cease-fire had begun, they weren't using ammunition. Few wanted to return to the Honduran camps.[27]

But Bermúdez ordered them back to Honduras, arguing that without supplies or ammunition, they were facing "annihilation" inside Nicaragua. That didn't square with the commanders' own views of their prospects. Why was Bermúdez ordering them out?

The mystery deepened in July and August, when contra units marching back to the rebels' border base at Banco Grande, on the Coco River northeast of Yamales, began dragging thousands of civilians with them, the messengers and other collaborators who had been key to rebel successes in 1987. Some six hundred trudged into Banco Grande from Estelí province in July and in early August, nearly twelve hundred more dragged in after a month-long trek from south-central Chontales province. Weeks later, another one thousand appeared, also famished. Most were young men, though there were plenty of women and children, too.

Their trek had been precipitous and ill-planned. Lacking supplies or adequate clothing, many had been forced to eat flowers and roots along their route in order to survive. Some arrived with bleeding feet; others wore only underwear. In one group, thirteen people had starved to death along the way. More than a hundred required immediate emergency medical treatment at Aguacate.

AID task force officials who helicoptered to Banco Grande to meet them were stunned at their condition. As the Americans unloaded large plastic bags of raw beef from the AID helicopters, some of the refugees fell upon the food sacks in desperation. Clawing through the plastic, they ate the meat raw, then, unable to digest the sudden protein, they vomited the food back up.[28]

Why had they come? The civilians said rebel field commanders had ordered their evacuation. The commanders said the orders had come from Bermúdez: Round up your civilian support networks and march to Honduras. Bermúdez offered the same explanation he'd given for ordering his reluctant field commanders back to Honduras, arguing that the civilian supporters had been "exposed." They were facing Sandinista retaliation, Bermúdez said. But the civilians themselves said they'd only come because they'd been ordered to.

Finally, Bermúdez's motives began to dawn on several U.S. officials. Sensing that the Reagan Administration was finally pulling out of the war, Bermúdez was looking for leverage. By piling up troops and peasant supporters in the base camps, he thought he could pressure U.S. officials more effectively for more military aid.[29]

For his part, Bermúdez wasn't planning to stay in the camps; he wasn't even planning to spend much time in Tegucigalpa. He was moving to Miami. His wife, Elsa, aware of his philandering, had been pressuring him to come home, but there were compelling financial incentives as well. When AID officials took over the rebel army's payroll from the CIA, the "Family Assistance Program," Bermúdez was receiving $2,750 per month. (U.S. officials conceded the likelihood that Bermúdez was also receiving other secret CIA payments.)[30] There were, however, even more generous funds available in Miami. There, the CIA was paying $180,000 per year to each Resistance director. Supposedly, these funds were to finance each director's political initiatives, but since Reagan Administration accounting demands were loose, some directors were spending the funds on new cars and fine wines. Miskito Indian Director Wycliffe Diego used his funds to purchase a new air-conditioning system for his home in Honduras. Director Azucena Ferrey had even bought a mink coat with her political funds during the $100 million offensive. Calero was building a new home in Costa Rica, and channeling investments into electronics firms in Guatemala and Miami.[31] Bermúdez found the incentives too generous to resist. In August 1988, he engineered his own election to the Resistance directorate and moved to Miami.

April through October 1988

In late April 1988, Jhonson became the Resistance army's top legal officer, and his life changed dramatically. He moved from the base camps to Tegucigalpa, and gave up his rifle and troops for an office and staff. His men ribbed him a bit about his desk job, about the new U.S.-funded jeep he'd been given, about his new soft life. But Jhonson's new post brought him more difficulties than anything he'd ever faced in the field.

His formal title was "legal adviser to the Resistance Army of the North." State Department officials had established the Legal Office in 1987, funding it with a twelve-thousand-dollar monthly budget to pay for an office and a staff of lawyers, clerical help, and investigators. The post gave Jhonson responsibility for investigating human-rights abuses committed by Resistance troops and for prosecuting suspects before commanders' tribunals.

As the legal adviser, Jhonson was to head the Resistance's primitive legal system, an unwieldy and often contradictory structure adapted from the systems of military courts-martial used by Somoza's National Guard as well as by the U.S. Army. In reality, there was nothing "legal" about the Resistance's legal system. Neither Honduras nor any other government except the United States considered the Resistance army's internal deliberations to have any validity. Within the Resistance, however, the post gave Jhonson important powers, and he brought his own good intentions to their use.

Bermúdez appointed him to the post to replace Donald Lacayo, the longtime Calero associate whom Bermúdez had fired for joining the dissident rebellion. Bermúdez would doubtless have preferred to install one of his own clique, but State Department officials wouldn't have signed off on that. Furthermore, Bermúdez believed he could control Jhonson; the Resistance legal system gave the commander-in-chief great influence over Jhonson's work.

On the other hand, the Resistance structure envisioned close cooperation between the legal adviser's office and Marta Patricia Baltodano's Nicaraguan Association for Human Rights. An informal division of labor had evolved, loosely analogous to the relation between police detectives and prosecutors in the U.S. justice system. Baltodano's staff of human-rights investigators generally functioned as the detectives, investigating abuse reports, then turning over evidence of wrongdoing to the legal adviser, the equivalent of a state's attorney. If the legal adviser thought the evidence warranted, he could recommend formation of a "Military Court of Justice" to hear the case.[32]

Jhonson, then, was to work *for* Bermúdez, while working *with* Baltodano, but by late April 1988, Baltodano and Bermúdez were on a collision course. Bermúdez was blocking Baltodano's work at every turn. She was starting to feel used, as though her human-rights work was just putting an acceptable face on a brutal system.[33]

Complicating matters further were Jhonson's relations with the Americans. As the legal adviser, Jhonson for the first time came into routine, often daily contact with U.S. officials. His main U.S. embassy liaison was Timothy Brown, fifty, a fleshy man with receding sandy hair who headed the Special Liaison Office, set up to coordinate embassy contacts with the Resistance. Born in Kansas and schooled in Nevada, Brown had served as a Marine Corps guard in the U.S. embassy in Somoza's Managua in the late 1950s. In the foreign service, he had been posted to Saigon and Thailand during the U.S. war in Southeast Asia. He joined Briggs's embassy in Tegucigalpa during the contras' CIA-directed $100 million offensive. Jhonson found Brown humorless and severe, but they got along. For their meetings, Jhonson would go to the walled U.S. embassy compound, built like a bunker into an imposing hill overlooking downtown Tegucigalpa, or Brown would drive in one of the embassy's armored vans to Jhonson's Comayagüela office.[34]

In his discussions with Brown and other U.S. officials, Jhonson began to learn why the State Department had erected the Resistance's curious legal system: to persuade Congress to vote additional aid for the rebel force. When contra troops were accused of new abuses, Administration officials could point to the work of the legal adviser and to the rebels' system of disciplinary tribunals as evidence that, despite occasional errors, the army was evolving in a progressive direction. This objective surrounded the system with ambiguity and not a little hypocrisy. It was as much a system of public relations as it was a system of military justice.

Yet individual U.S. officials brought contrasting agendas to their work. In addition to dealing with Brown, Jhonson was also expected to report directly, by phone, to the State Department in Washington, generally to Bert Charneco, the Air Force colonel on loan to the State Department to oversee the contra human-rights effort. Charneco and other State Department officials were much more forceful about the human-rights issue, pressing Jhonson to pursue rebel abuses aggressively. Jhonson soon figured out why he was expected to report his activities twice: State Department officials didn't trust the embassy's reporting.[35]

All of these factors complicated Jhonson's work throughout 1988 as he tested his new powers as legal adviser. He tried to bring common sense to the job, and he had his own agenda. Not pretending to know much about Washington politics, he didn't see his work solely as an effort to influence U.S. lawmakers. He knew the madness that could result when commanders abused the life-and-death powers their American weaponry gave them, and one side of him also harbored a certain eagerness to settle accounts with contra commanders whose brutality he'd watched over the years.

The "office" Jhonson inherited was just a house with filing cabinets and desks cluttering the living room. Jhonson moved a cot into one of the bedrooms, hung his clothes in the closet, and made it his home. His staff included two middle-aged Honduran secretaries and two Nicaraguan exile lawyers who helped acquaint him with his workload and the backlog of pending cases. Jhonson spent his first weeks reading through the seemingly endless files, trying to get a sense of where to begin. He was alarmed to find that he had inherited 284 current investigations of rebel crimes, ranging from robbery to marijuana distribution to murder.

Jhonson found as he went through his files that his predecessor, Lacayo, had produced reams of pedantic legal documents, and he'd brought quite a few cases to trial—thirty during the last half of 1987—but hadn't accomplished much. Most of Lacayo's tribunals dealt with minor camp crimes; few of the cases he'd tried had involved the kind of serious battlefield abuses about which international human-rights monitors were complaining.[36]

Jhonson proved more effective than Lacayo. Under Lacayo's administration, a number of commandos accused of rights abuses had simply refused to return to Honduras from Nicaragua to face charges. Lacayo had prosecuted and convicted several in absentia. Jhonson knew how the base camps worked. He went to the general staff and said he wanted official messages radioed into Nicaragua ordering these men back to Honduras to accept their punishment. The messages were sent and the men came out and submitted to punishment, so he became assertive in other ways.

"Jhonson took on the world," a State Department official recalled later.

One early achievement was the joint visit Jhonson and Baltodano made to the Resistance prison at San Andrés. Baltodano had asked Bermúdez, without success, to visit the prison at San Andrés ever since she had learned of its existence in late 1987. Usually, Bermúdez or Mike Lima just told Baltodano there was no room on the helicopters, and although Baltodano asked Tim Brown and other American officials at the Tegucigalpa embassy, they didn't help either. Relations between Baltodano and Brown became downright unfriendly; Baltodano didn't feel welcome in the scowling American's embassy office.

Baltodano complained to Washington, and her backers in the State Department began sending cables to Tegucigalpa, urging Briggs's embassy to help her get to the San Andrés prison.

"We'd always get the message back: 'Bad timing blah-blah-blah, logistics problem blah-blah-blah, helicopter shortage blah-blah-blah,'" recalled a State Department official who read the cables. Repeated delays from the embassy eventually led State Department officials to believe that Briggs and Terry, the CIA station chief, were backing Bermúdez in his efforts to keep Baltodano out of the prisons.

"They'd never just say, 'Look, we don't want these human-rights people out there,'" the official recalled. "But the bottom line is that Briggs and his embassy were overtly hostile to Baltodano and her work."[37]

Baltodano began complaining to Jhonson. She was worried about the condition of the prisoners at San Andrés. Jhonson concluded that Baltodano was right and he proposed they visit them together. Jhonson's cooperation helped Baltodano immensely; she didn't have to feel like she was sneaking in behind the Resistance's back, and suddenly space on a Resistance helicopter was available.

Jhonson had never been to the new stockade either, and when the helicopter touched down at the rebels' San Andrés base camp, he had to ask among the commandos to learn the prison's exact location. After the U.S. helicopter had clattered away for Tegucigalpa, Jhonson found that the prison camp was several miles distant from the San Andrés helicopter strip—over rough, jungled terrain. They had to walk, and it was a tough march for Baltodano. She didn't have good boots, and she fell repeatedly in the mud along the way.

Upon arriving at the prison camp, Jhonson introduced himself to the rebel guards. They wanted to argue. The tour hadn't been authorized, they said. Jhonson just pushed his way in.

"I'm Commander Jhonson, the Resistance's legal adviser, and it's my job to visit the prisoners. That's what we're going to do," he told the guards.

Inside several rough timber-and-barbed-wire cell blocks, Jhonson and Baltodano found sixty-six embittered detainees. A few were Sandinista prisoners of war, but most were rebels who had been accused of being infiltrators in the counterintelligence investigation that had begun at Aguacate a year earlier. The prisoners complained that food was scarce, and one of the women said she'd been raped at the time of her detention. Several of the prisoners complained that they didn't even know what they were accused of, and others mentioned an especially alarming complaint: One of their fellow detainees, a Sandinista aviation mechanic whom the rebels had captured after shooting down his helicopter inside Nicaragua in mid-1987, had disappeared. Counterintelligence agents had arrived one night and taken him away. The prisoners were demanding to know what happened to him.

Jhonson and Baltodano had no idea what had happened to the prisoner. For the time being, they decided that they should try to get some of the prisoners released right away. After hiking back to the San Andrés camp, they found Mike Lima waiting. They insisted that there were a number of obviously innocent people at the prison, and they wanted them released. Mike Lima backed off; he said he didn't know much about the prisoners, since they weren't his responsibility. But he agreed to the immediate release of ten of them.

Back in Tegucigalpa, Jhonson got a glimpse of the close working relationship between the Resistance's counterintelligence interrogators and the CIA when he asked Bermúdez about the missing Sandinista mechanic. Bermúdez said the counterintelligence section had turned the prisoner over to CIA agents weeks earlier. The Americans were questioning him about Sandinista helicopter maintenance. Later, Baltodano expressed her concern over the prisoner's fate to the U.S. embassy. CIA agents arranged an interview for her with the prisoner of war at a Tegucigalpa safe house used by Americans to interrogate rebel prisoners. Baltodano found the twenty-two-year-old Sandinista prisoner in good health. He had agreed to provide intelligence information to the CIA in exchange for help in obtaining a Canadian visa.[38]

Jhonson brought the same open-minded attitude he had demonstrated with Baltodano to his relations with journalists. Seeing no reason to keep reporters away, he began issuing letters authorizing them to visit the Yamales camps. That infuriated Tim Brown, his embassy liaison, and after an article Brown didn't like appeared in the U.S. press, he complained about Jhonson to Bermúdez and other Resistance officials. Jhonson wasn't reliable, Brown said.

Jhonson ignored Brown. He continued his work, organizing tribunals, working to reduce the backlog of abuse investigations. Over several months in the summer and fall of 1988, he obtained convictions in a series of camp discipline cases. State Department officials were elated at Jhonson's progress, and the Resistance army's image improved a great deal during his tenure. But despite his good intentions, Jhonson finally proved no more successful at reforming the army than his predecessors had been. Bermúdez and his clique had too many ways to influence the outcome of tribunals, even while seeming to cooperate.

Jhonson saw the duplicity during the course of one of his first tribunals, set up to consider murder charges resulting from the rebels' August 1985 attack on the town of Cuapa, during which a contra unit had executed ten Sandinista prisoners. The affair had turned into one of the most controversial cases of the war.[39]

More than a year earlier, Baltodano had located several rebel fighters who had fought at Cuapa and who said that former National Guard Lieutenant Leonte "Atila" Arias had ordered the killings. Jhonson knew Atila. During the early years of the war, as a unit commander fighting intermittently inside Nicaragua, Atila had been a pillager, a commander who preferred to loot the countryside and rape women rather than engage the enemy. Atila hadn't set foot in Nicaragua for several years, instead hanging back at Strategic Command headquarters with his friends.

Early in 1987, Baltodano had turned over the evidence implicating Atila to Lacayo, then the legal adviser, who called for a tribunal. But Atila threatened Baltodano's witnesses until several refused to testify, and Baltodano herself began receiving threatening phone calls during the trial from male callers saying they knew where her little boy went to school. When a panel of commanders met in Lacayo's legal affairs tent at Aguacate to hear the Cuapa case in September 1987, Atila helicoptered in more than a dozen of his own "witnesses," commandos he'd rounded up in the base camps who testified that they'd been at Cuapa and "knew" the accusations against Atila to be lies. Atila and his witnesses argued that the case was a Sandinista fabrication; no prisoners had been executed at Cuapa, they said.

Atila was acquitted of all charges, but days later one of Atila's witnesses confessed to Baltodano that Atila had coached him about what to say in his testimony. Baltodano, calling the verdict a "notorious injustice," appealed the case to the Resistance directorate in Miami, and under pressure from State Department officials, the directors overturned Atila's acquittal in January 1988.[40]

Jhonson inherited the case two months after he took over his legal post, and he convened a new tribunal. Baltodano produced a new witness, but the new tribunal also acquitted Atila of the murder charges. This time, though, there was a minor consolation. Jhonson's tribunal caught Atila in a lie. In his 1987 testimony, Atila had denied that the execution had even taken place, but this time he acknowledged that eight prisoners were executed at Cuapa, blaming the killings on other commandos—all of them fighters who had since died in combat. Jhonson's tribunal convicted Atila of perjury, sentencing him to three months' imprisonment.

Baltodano was outraged. After the tribunal's verdict, she questioned the performance of Jhonson's prosecuting attorney before the tribunal, accusing Atila of making payments to the lawyer. Jhonson had his own complaints against the prosecutor who had been Somoza's former consul in Tegucigalpa, and Jhonson fired him.[41]

Still, the Cuapa case underlined one of the critical flaws in the Resistance legal system: Prosecution of crimes depended on the testimony of witnesses who were often the victims of the abuses at issue, and who, in the violent atmosphere in and around the rebel camps, remained vulnerable to retaliation. This proved to be a central issue in a controversial new case that Baltodano turned over to Jhonson in the fall of 1988.

For more than a year, Baltodano had been taking statements from commandos—most of them young women—who complained that they'd been tortured and sexually abused by Resistance counterintelligence interrogators. Baltodano had become aware of the prison brutality during the 1987 investigation she carried out after finding Bermúdez's twenty-year-old secretary, Jacqueline Murillo Castillo, burned and injured by interrogators, in the Resistance hospital at Aguacate Air Base. She'd learned more through her involvement in the case of Berta Díaz Arteta, the young commando whom Bermúdez's men had jailed, supposedly for her own protection, after she reported that she'd been raped in the base camps. From another abused woman, Yorlin María Ubeda, Baltodano had collected more stories of sexual abuse, and of barbarities committed against the male prisoners, too. Ubeda told Baltodano how laughing interrogators had stripped one male teenage prisoner naked and forced him down on all fours, ordering him to grunt like a pig while they rammed a pole into his anus.

Baltodano collected names of other young women who had been raped and abused by Resistance interrogators. Several had later been released, and Baltodano succeeded in locating them in Danlí and Tegucigalpa. They all told similar stories: During their detention as infiltrators, the women said they were held naked, generally in isolation, during weeks of "questioning" by Resistance interrogators that invariably involved rape and torture. The women all named the same group of counterintelligence interrogators as their tormentors, Baltodano realized. The torture and sexual coercion were routine.

The problem for Baltodano was that in order to bring formal charges for these abuses, the women would have to testify about their experiences before one of the Resistance tribunals. Not surprisingly, the women were afraid. Nonetheless, by mid-1988 Baltodano had persuaded a handful of women to testify before a tribunal, and she drew up her most controversial case.

Baltodano accused the rebel army's interrogators of systematic torture and rape. She named Donald Torres, Bermúdez's former Military Academy student, former counterintelligence chief, and friend. She named Leo, the contras' longtime jailer, a man so close to the rebel army's top commander that when Bermúdez's mistress, María Eugenia Ortez, went into labor in 1987 with Bermúdez's child, he dispatched Leo to drive Ortez to the doctor and to arrange other birthing details. Baltodano accused nearly a dozen other longtime interrogators as well, men whose brutality dated to the first days of the rebel army.[42] It was the most explosive case she had ever investigated. When she turned it over to Jhonson in August 1988, the case confronted him with his sharpest conflict to date: She was asking him to prosecute several of his commanding officer's closest associates.

But that was only one of the conflicts Jhonson was wrestling with at the time. While he and Baltodano were pressing the Resistance army to punish rebel human-rights violators, Jhonson knew that Sandinista soldiers and security agents were committing more serious abuses than ever before against rebel supporters inside Nicaragua.

During the six months since the cease-fire had begun at Sapoá, a small contingent of Jhonson's rebel troops had remained in the mountains of eastern Matagalpa province, where he had operated during the 1987 $100 million offensive. Jhonson knew hundreds of farmers in the zone, and he liked to read the radio messages his troops were sending back to rebel headquarters at Yamales.

During the summer of 1988, the rebels were reporting a surge of local murders as Sandinista security agents sought out peasants collaborating with contra forces and quietly executed them. Local Sandinistas had been eliminating contra collaborators sporadically throughout the war, but now, with the main body of the rebel army in Honduras and their peasant supporters unprotected, the murders had increased dramatically.

Jhonson did what he could to publicize the Sandinista assassinations. At the end of an August reporting trip to the Yamales camps by *Washington Post* reporter Julia Preston, Jhonson detailed several of the latest Sandinista murders to her over dinner in a Danlí restaurant. A week later, Preston followed up the leads during a trip to eastern Matagalpa. Visiting the farms of several peasants whose names Jhonson had provided, and talking with missionaries and other local sources, she discovered that Jhonson's allegations were not only accurate but were part of a much wider pattern of Sandinista atrocities.[43]

The murders of peasants he had recruited as Resistance collaborators made Jhonson feel extraordinarily helpless and, for a time, ambiguous about his efforts to punish rebel abuses. Many times, he had listened to Bermúdez, Sánchez, and other rebel officers use reports of Sandinista atrocities to justify lenience toward contras guilty of crimes. "This isn't a party in some girls' school!" Sánchez shouted at Jhonson on one occasion. "This is war!"

But Jhonson drew a different conclusion. He'd taken up arms against the Sandinistas precisely because of the injustices he'd seen revolutionary authorities commit. Seeing contra fighters carry out similar abuses angered him, hardening his resolve to see them punished. When Baltodano passed along her case against the counterintelligence interrogators, Jhonson, following procedure, took the documents to Bermúdez, whose authority was necessary to approve the formation of an investigatory tribunal. Bermúdez studied them for several days. At their next meeting, Jhonson asked Bermúdez about the case.

"*Comandante*, Marta Patricia and the Association have presented evidence for a trial against Leo," Jhonson told Bermúdez. "I'll have to begin an investigation and tribunal."

"Don't do anything. Leave this case alone," Bermúdez ordered Jhonson.

Stunned, Jhonson didn't know how to react. Then he typed up a resignation letter and handed it to Bermúdez. A day or two later, Bert Charneco called Jhonson from the State Department.

"I can't let you resign," Charneco said.

"Well, Colonel, I can't continue in the post if they aren't going to let me investigate," Jhonson replied.

"But there's nobody that can take your place," Charneco said. "Wait a while. Let me talk to Bermúdez."

Several days later, Bermúdez called Jhonson, authorizing him to move ahead with a probe of Baltodano's latest charges. Jhonson and Joshua were taking statements from Leo and others involved in the counterintelligence case when, in November, Joshua found a series of anonymous notes in the legal affairs tent at Yamales that interrupted their work.

The notes reported a murder in the Quilalí camp.

February through November 1988

In the fall of 1988, Mack and Mike Lima carried out the rebel army's biggest anti-infiltration dragnet, a series of frantic sweeps involving the detention and torture of hundreds of young rebel fighters.

Bermúdez had appointed the two ex-Guardsmen as the Resistance's intelligence and counterintelligence chiefs in February. Their posts gave Mack and Mike Lima a special new relationship with the CIA. Because of the two sections' involvement in intelligence gathering, the CIA had assigned them special budgets; Mack and Lima became the only two rebel officers, besides Bermúdez, to whom the CIA assigned direct CIA liaison agents. Mack's liaison officer, who introduced himself as "Roberto," was to oversee the use of the intelligence section's U.S.-funded headquarters facility at Yamales, its U.S.-funded safe house in Tegucigalpa, its U.S.-funded vehicles, including a jeep for Mack's personal use, and the U.S.-funded salaries paid to the section's staff. As his deputy, Mack named Ramón "Z-Two" Peña, now fifty, the hunched former Guard corporal who'd been his interrogator during the early days at La Lodosa.

Mike Lima found that the CIA had assigned two liaison officers to work with him and the dozen agents on his staff at counterintelligence headquarters in a four-bedroom Tegucigalpa safe house. One CIA agent, born in Venezuela, concerned himself with direct oversight of Resistance counterintelligence activities. The other, an American of Greek descent, was an Agency auditor responsible for ensuring that a series of CIA-financed computers—along with the rest of the section's monthly budget—were put to good use.[44]

Lima named Noel "Trickster" Castillo, a former Guard lieutenant, as his deputy in Tegucigalpa. As his deputy in Yamales, Lima named José "Joel" Zepeda, a former Guard sergeant who'd been a contra interrogator since the early days of the war.[45]

Mack and Lima's first joint initiative came in the weeks after the dissident rebellion, when they offered Bermúdez crucial assistance in reestablishing control over an army in turmoil. More than a dozen regional commanders had at one point joined the rebellion, calling into question the loyalties of thousands of troops. Bermúdez, Lima, and Mack worked together to reorganize the contra units whose commanders had wavered. By midsummer, the dissident turmoil was subsiding, but there was a new threat.

Thousands of fighters were returning from Nicaragua. Many were fresh recruits: Some were volunteers, some were forcibly conscripted, all were untrained and undisciplined. They turned Yamales into a smoky warren of huts and mud, of latrines and fire.

The disorder alarmed Mack and Lima. Suspicious of the strange new faces crowding rebel ranks, alert to the danger of Sandinista infiltration, they began to equate demoralization with conspiracy. A helicopter flying above Yamales took an AK-47 round in the fuselage. To Mike Lima, this was not a chance misfire, this was hostile ground fire. One fighter died suddenly of mysterious causes; this was not food poisoning, this was murder. Radios were damaged and rifles left in the rain to rust. This was not negligence, this was sabotage.[46]

Mack and Lima both alerted their agents to be on the lookout for suspicious behavior. Soon Mike Lima's Yamales deputy, Joel, detained a handful of newly recruited commandos for questioning with the hood and the ropes, then fanned back out through the camps to seize suspects whom the first detainees had accused as infiltrators. Soon dozens were detained, then scores.[47]

One day in late summer, as the dragnet was just getting under way, Lima and Mack were chatting in Mack's intelligence tent at the general staff camp when Isaac Blake, a twenty-nine-year-old commando with the pseudonym Israelita, walked into the tent and saluted. Mack offered Blake a seat. Both Mack and Lima knew Blake well. When Blake first joined the contra army in 1984, he had been based at La Lodosa; Mack was his first commander. Mike Lima met Blake during a training course later the same year. Now Blake told the two commanders that he had just returned from Nicaragua, where he claimed to have received information about a network of Sandinista infiltrators operating in the rebels' Quilalí Regional Command.

Mike Lima had counterintelligence agents working in most of the regional commands, but none in the Quilalí, so he decided to put Blake to work, pursuing spies. The same day, Lima went with Blake to Commander Denis, the personnel officer, and arranged Blake's transfer to the Quilalí camp. Blake built a hut at the edge of a swamp near the Quilalí camp and began to recruit helpers. A couple of months later, he began to detain suspected infiltrators, and two weeks after that, young Isaac González was dead.[48]

Later, U.S. officials would try to portray Blake's abuses as an isolated case, the work of one deranged individual,[49] but they weren't. When Mike Lima sent Blake to the Quilalí camp in early September, the Resistance was holding about eighty prisoners: about sixty at the San Andrés prison, and a couple dozen at Yamales. Over the next three months, Blake seized and interrogated about thirty commandos. During the same period, Lima, Mack, and their agents detained and tortured more than three hundred.[50]

In his work at the Quilalí camp, Blake followed the methods that had become routine in Resistance interrogations over several years and that were being practiced on a much larger scale during the same weeks just across the hills of the Yamales Valley at the counterintelligence section: Prisoners were tied, beaten, kicked, hung, hooded, and sometimes slashed.

Mike Lima and Mack were the principal officers leading the mass detentions, but they frequently called Bermúdez, still the army's commanding general, in order to keep him informed.[51] Bermúdez betrayed his own awareness of the abuses in mid-October when he suddenly barred Marta Patricia Baltodano from visiting the prisons. At the time, hundreds of detentions were turning the rebel jails into virtual concentration camps.[52]

After Blake's November 14 murder of Isaac González, Lima, Mack, and others on the general staff tried to cover it up. And although he consented to Jhonson's investigation, Bermúdez tried to keep the crime quiet, too.

One day in early December, Jhonson encountered Mike Lima on a sidewalk in Tegucigalpa in front of the Resistance Communications safe house. Mike Lima said he'd just returned to Tegucigalpa from a meeting of the general staff in Yamales.

"Hey, look, Luisito," Mike Lima said to Jhonson. "About that kid that died out in the Quilalí. Can't we just keep this thing to ourselves, so that it doesn't come out?"

Jhonson told him to forget it.

9

The Quilalí Tribunal

December 1988 through March 1989

Throughout his 1988 presidential campaign and in a news conference the day after his election, George Bush vowed to fight for a renewal of military aid to the contra army. But behind the scenes, his Administration was from its first days developing a new Nicaragua policy, based on diplomacy, not war, that left the future of Washington's army of Nicaraguan peasants very much in doubt. It was a dramatic policy reversal. Secretary of State James Baker III negotiated the new approach with the Democratic Congress secretly, and there was virtually no public hint of the shift until late March 1989.

During this twilight period—the final months of the contra policy—Jhonson's Quilalí investigation and tribunal became the focus of attention for the rebel army itself and for the feuding American bureaucracies administering it. Coming at the end of the eight-year war and centering on the abuses that had been, perhaps, the U.S.-financed force's central flaw, the tribunal assumed significance within the contra force well beyond that of the individual guilt or innocence of the commanders Jhonson brought to trial. The tribunal became a kind of referendum carried out by the rebel army itself on its own top officers and their leadership throughout the war. For the first time, young rebel officers, led by Jhonson, found the confidence to challenge the crimes of corrupt higher-ups. For the first time, top contra officers were called to account for crimes they had made their trademark.

The discovery of the November 1988 murder of Isaac González in the Quilalí camp threw the American officials who knew of it into virtual panic, sparking new recriminations in the already suspicious relations between officials at the State Department and their rivals at Ambassador Briggs's embassy in Tegucigalpa. Neither bureaucracy wanted to be blamed in a last-minute contra human-rights scandal. After Jhonson's investigation was well under way and it had become clear that word of the murder was circulating in Washington, Briggs's aides called Jhonson into the Tegucigalpa embassy and encouraged him to undertake a thorough investigation. They even offered to assign him U.S.-paid bodyguards, guessing that he might feel threatened by higher commanders in his own army. Jhonson was grateful for the offer, and pleased to see the belated embassy support, yet over the next weeks, a series of unexplained mysteries—witnesses who dropped from sight, unexpected deportations—left him with the belief that the embassy and the CIA were quietly undercutting his efforts. State Department officials shared his view.

For their part, embassy officials accused their rivals in the State Department of manipulating the Quilalí tribunal to purge the contra force of its most prominent ex-Guardsmen. That, to Briggs and others, seemed a cheap betrayal after the loyalty to American goals the Guardsmen had shown throughout the war.

Mack, Mike Lima, and other ex-Guardsmen went further. Slow to grasp their unfolding predicament, they finally reacted with an attempt at crude cover-up. They tried to subvert Jhonson's tribunal, then challenged its results, calling his entire investigation a State Department conspiracy aimed at dismantling a no-longer-wanted proxy army. They accused Jhonson and the younger officers who sat on his tribunal of being American puppets.

U.S. officials pressured Jhonson to pursue the tribunal, but he followed his own impulses as well. Like any competent investigator who has uncovered wrongdoing, Jhonson had a personal stake in seeing his probe continue to its logical consequences. He wanted justice. Although the tribunal posed considerable risks, Jhonson took them, challenging the CIA's ex-Guardsmen. As it turned out, Jhonson got burned. The tribunal brought the end of his war.

December 1988

When the Honduran government learned of the murder in the Quilalí, it reacted by demanding that the Resistance dismantle its prisons—immediately.

The brutality itself was not what outraged President José Azcona and the army high command, whose views shaped virtually all of Azcona's policies. Through army liaison officers working directly with the contra force, the Honduran military had known about and tolerated similar abuses by Bermúdez's men for years. The problem now was that the crimes were becoming public, and at a bad time.

Honduras had suffered prolonged international criticism for its own human-rights record ever since General Gustavo Alvarez had established his network of army-run death squads to "disappear" arms traffickers and government critics when he controlled the military from 1981 to 1984. But in July 1988, that criticism assumed a tangible and costly new form when the Inter-American Court of Human Rights, a Costa Rica–based tribunal sponsored by the Organization of American States, condemned Honduras for its "policy of disappearances directed or tolerated by the government." Army killings in Honduras had never been as numerous as those committed by military regimes in Guatemala, El Salvador, Argentina, or Chile, but the Inter-American Court's ruling, the first of its kind in Latin America, was an embarrassing blow to the Honduran government, already badly isolated internationally for its long cosponsorship of the contra army with Washington.

The Azcona Administration was forced to admit that Honduran military agents had kidnapped and executed dissidents, and it had to promise to make hundreds of thousands of dollars of indemnity payments to relatives of the victims. In the months following the ruling, Honduran authorities, both military and civilian, were fed up with human-rights criticism. The last thing they were ready to accept was new international blame for abuses committed by the contras.[1]

Throughout the contra war, the Honduran military retained tight control over the Tegucigalpa government's relations with the rebel army. Civilian officials—most of whom opposed the contra presence—were excluded from both the formulation and execution of policy. But in the fall of 1988, during the final days of the Reagan Administration's tenure in Washington, things were changing in Honduras. One sign of the shifting Honduran position came when civilian authorities, with military acquiescence, began exercising new initiatives. In early October, Foreign Minister Carlos López Contreras called on the United Nations in a General Assembly speech to establish a multinational force to supervise Honduran borders, to expel both Marxist guerrillas from neighboring El Salvador as well as the Nicaraguan contras. It was a signal to Washington of Tegucigalpa's mounting dissatisfaction. Weeks later, when López Contreras learned of the Quilalí murder, he sent a terse letter to Secretary of State George Shultz, calling the existence of the clandestine contra jails an intolerable infringement on Honduran sovereignty and demanding their quick dismantling.[2] Washington had little choice but to agree.

Throughout December, Tim Brown, together with William Meara, Briggs's twenty-nine-year-old aide, and other U.S. officials, worked behind the scenes to coordinate the release of all contra detainees to Honduran authorities. It would bring an end to the detention system that Bermúdez, Mike Lima, and Leo had been building since 1984.

Jhonson, as the legal adviser, represented the Resistance in numerous meetings with U.S. and Honduran officials to work out details. Taking the lead for the Honduran Foreign Ministry was Virgilio Galvez Madrid, a respected career diplomat who had been Honduras's Minister of Foreign Relations during the mid-1970s and had served as Honduras's ambassador to Chile and several other Latin countries. By the time Jhonson met him, Galvez was nearly eighty, a wizened aristocrat who had rankled throughout the Reagan decade under the arrogance of American officials in Tegucigalpa. One dispute in an early meeting that brought Jhonson and Tim Brown together with Galvez showed the mounting level of Honduran anger.

"How many prisoners are you holding?" Galvez asked Jhonson. The Honduran military had provided Galvez with a list of nearly three hundred contra prisoners; Jhonson carried a list, which he had obtained from Mike Lima, of only about one hundred. The discrepancy arose because Mike Lima's agents were reporting to the Honduran military when they detained commandos for investigation, but were not following up to report releases. As a result, the Honduran military's list just kept growing. By the time Jhonson met with Galvez, the Hondurans had the names of nearly two hundred "detainees" whom the contras had already released; nobody could understand the discrepancy.

"What have you done with the other two hundred?" Galvez demanded.

"I really don't know which two hundred prisoners you're talking about, sir," Jhonson answered meekly.

Galvez dealt Jhonson a tongue-lashing, reprimanding the contra army for abusing Honduran hospitality. Then he nodded toward Brown.

"But neither you nor I are responsible for this mess," Galvez told Jhonson. "These North Americans are to blame. But they don't want to accept any responsibility. We matter nothing to them."

The prisoner delivery was set for December 24. The Honduran anger spilled into public view shortly before the release when the Foreign Ministry issued a communiqué saying it had recently discovered Nicaraguan Resistance jails holding "a considerable number" of prisoners, and calling the jails "an intolerable offense to the dignity of our country." The communiqué announced that the Honduran government would "rescue" the prisoners and turn them over to the Honduran Red Cross.[3]

There was a lot to do in order to arrange the release. The Americans were concerned that the prisoners not appear battered or starved when released, so American officials bought exercise warm-up suits to clothe them and helicoptered plenty of rich food out to Yamales to help restore their health. The prisoners had to be brought together. Some eighty prisoners held at the remote jungle camp at San Andrés, including most of the rebels accused of being infiltrators during the 1987 roundup at Aguacate, had to be transported fifty miles southwest along the Coco River to Yamales. Using AID's two contract helicopters, Mike Lima and William Meara began ferrying human cargo from the barbed-wire San Andrés stockade to four new plastic-roofed shelters constructed on the hill at Yamales called Los Congos. Lima's men were marching dozens of other detainees rounded up in recent weeks as infiltrators to Los Congos from Joel's counterintelligence interrogation center and the adjacent Military Police stockade.

Since mid-October, Bermúdez had refused to allow Marta Patricia Baltodano or anyone else on the staff of her Nicaraguan Association for Human Rights to visit Resistance prisons. Now with preparations under way for the mass release, Bermúdez suddenly reversed course; he urged Baltodano to visit the detainees. Baltodano dispatched Alfonso Sandino, forty-one, an attorney who had recently become her top aide, and three others from her human-rights staff to Yamales on December 22.

After climbing out of an AID helicopter and wading through the backwash of the rotors at Los Congos, Sandino and the other Association interviewers made their way into the new AID-constructed shelters. They found 123 prisoners; 96 were accused infiltrators or Sandinista prisoners of war, the rest rebels serving time for common camp crimes ranging from murder to robbery. They were the same detainees whom GAO auditors had interviewed three weeks earlier. As Sandino and his staff selected prisoners at random for interviews, it became obvious why Bermúdez had for so long denied Baltodano's staff access to his detention centers. The detainees told the same stories the GAO had heard three weeks earlier: The male political prisoners had to a man been tortured, the women had all been raped. Though the majority had once been rebel fighters, all of the prisoners wanted out of the Resistance; forty-four of the ninety-six political prisoners said they wanted to return to Nicaragua. In late afternoon, Sandino helicoptered back to Tegucigalpa, drove straight to see Jhonson at his office, and laid out the grim story. Jhonson listened, then decided he wanted Bermúdez and Tim Brown to hear Sandino's unsettling account directly.

Tim Brown, stern-faced as usual, presided over the encounter the following morning at Jhonson's office. Bermúdez—who loathed Sandino because of his ties to Baltodano—stomped in with barely a greeting, then listened in stony silence as Sandino summarized his findings. The image the Reagan Administration had carefully knit together about contra human-rights improvement was about to unravel.

"Who do these prisoners claim tortured them?" Bermúdez asked Sandino.

Sandino repeated the names of the interrogators he and his aides had gathered from the prisoners: Mike Lima, Donald Torres, Joel, Leo, Z-Two, Julio, Chino Eighty-Five, Six-Seven—the same names that Baltodano had included in the case she had lodged two months earlier.

Now Sandino turned to Jhonson. "Dr. Baltodano wants to know what happened in the case involving Leo and the counterintelligence section," Sandino said.

Bermúdez interrupted. "Aw, that's an old case of no importance," he said. "Forget about it."

Jhonson got up from the table, went to his cabinet, and brought Bermúdez the file containing the case against Leo.

"No, *Comandante,* he's referring to this case," Jhonson said.

Bermúdez glanced through the papers, then put them aside on the table. "These are old incidents from the past," Bermúdez said.

Tim Brown brushed the discussion aside. Men who specialize in counterintelligence are, by definition, tough and dumb, he told Sandino. The problem was what to do about the soon-to-be-released prisoners who'd been tortured. What could be done to keep them from complaining about their abuses publicly?

It was too late, however, to worry about that. The release was scheduled for the next morning, Christmas Eve, and there was still great confusion about who was to be released.

Throughout the preparation of the prisoner release, Jhonson had encountered difficulties with the prisoner lists given him by Mike Lima. Several days earlier, Mike Lima had given him a list including 111 names; a day later, Lima had replaced it with a new list of 104 names. Now Sandino had a new count. According to Association records, the Resistance was holding more than 150 prisoners, Sandino said. Yet during his Yamales interviews, he'd found only 123 prisoners, including some 22 common prisoners. At least 30 prisoners were missing, Sandino said.

Brown didn't hide his impatience. He wheeled on Bermúdez. "By tomorrow morning, I want everybody handed over!" he snapped.[4] But after the meeting, Bermúdez flew off for Christmas in Miami, leaving Jhonson to oversee the prisoner release.

When, after a five-hour drive, Jhonson pulled his jeep into Yamales past the general staff headquarters to the Military Police camp at Los Congos, he found that Pastor "Denis" Meza, the Resistance's personnel officer, and José "Joel" Zepeda, the Yamales counterintelligence chief, had already begun moving the prisoners. A crowd of detainees in their new AID-purchased sweat suits were climbing aboard two trucks for transport to the nearby village of La Fortuna, where they were to be delivered to the Honduran Army.

Jhonson found the general staff headquarters virtually deserted. Mack, Mike Lima, and the other staff members were in Tegucigalpa or Miami for Christmas. There were other surprises. Along the road, Jhonson saw Jesús "Pinares" Gómez, a rebel who had been sentenced to seven years' imprisonment for the 1986 murder of five men in the central Nicaraguan village of San José de Las Mulas. Pinares was drunk and jubilant. "They let me go," he said, grinning at Jhonson.

Farther along, Jhonson saw a rebel with the pseudonym "Rolando" who had been sentenced to prison for kidnapping four Nicaraguan schoolteachers. Rolando, too, smelled of rum and was wandering loose.

Jhonson understood that Joel and Denis had released a series of rebels convicted of human-rights abuses. He checked his list of 104 prisoners; neither Pinares nor Rolando were on it. This was supposed to be a release of prisoners of war, not common criminals.

When Jhonson pulled his jeep up in front of the tent encampment in La Fortuna, six miles to the north, Honduran Army officers were matching names with prisoners, checking off their list. Sitting with a group of detainees who had already passed into Honduran control, wearing a new sweat suit and a smile, was Isaac Blake.

Jhonson hadn't seen Blake since their encounter at the counterintelligence center ten days earlier, when Joel had brought out Blake briefly to introduce him to Jhonson. Joel had been too busy then to allow Jhonson to interview Blake. During the ensuing days, Joshua, Jhonson's investigative deputy, had gone several times to interview Blake, but Joel had always been too busy. Neither Jhonson nor Joshua had ever taken a formal statement from Blake about his role in the Quilalí murder.

Jhonson again grabbed for his list of 104 prisoners. Blake's name wasn't on it. Jhonson saw Denis.

"What's Blake doing here?" Jhonson asked him. "And how come Pinares and Rolando are wandering around loose?"

"Don't blame me," Denis answered. "It was a decision of the whole general staff."

Jhonson walked to the table where the Honduran officers were checking off prisoners' names. Their list, like his, numbered 104 prisoners, but differed substantially from the 104-name document that Mike Lima had given him days earlier. On the new list—which Denis had apparently turned over to the Hondurans hours earlier—prisoner number 104 caught Jhonson's eyes: Isaac Blake.

Jhonson began to see what was happening. He recalled a conversation he'd had weeks earlier with Mike Lima in Tegucigalpa in front of the Resistance safe house that served as a communications office. Lima had said he'd just returned to Tegucigalpa from a meeting of the general staff in Yamales, and had asked Jhonson if there wasn't some way that they could arrange to cover up Isaac González's murder. Jhonson had told him no. Now it was looking as if Mike Lima, searching for a way out of his mess, had seized on the prisoner release as a way of solving a lot of problems, and Denis made it sound as if the entire general staff was involved.

Two days later, on December 26, the Honduran authorities turned over the 104 newly released prisoners to the United Nations High Commission on Refugees. Sixty, including Blake, elected to stay in Honduras and were sent to a UN refugee camp; the other forty-four prisoners requested to return to Nicaragua and were immediately repatriated.[5]

At his Tegucigalpa office during the last week of December, Jhonson spent time comparing prisoner lists before he finally thought he understood what had happened. The general staff had sorted through the scores of detainees and arranged the release to suit their own interests. They'd sent more than a dozen battered detainees—including most of the prisoners whom Blake had seized at the Quilalí—back to their regional command camps and, in their place, had released to the Hondurans some fifteen prisoners condemned for crimes ranging from murder to rape. They had turned more than a dozen other common criminals loose in the rebel camps. By releasing the convicted criminals, the general staff had reversed more than two years of human-rights work, dismantling at a stroke the Resistance's entire system of judicial sanctions. And, finally, they'd turned Blake over to the Hondurans. That got rid of a man Bermúdez and the general staff no longer wanted around.

Herding detainees here and there, the general staff had turned the prisoner release into a burlesque, and they'd made Jhonson look like a fool since he was the Resistance official technically in command of the delivery.

So it was with more than a little irritation that Jhonson turned his attention to the eleven typed statements in the Quilalí case that had backed up on his desk. While Jhonson had been focusing on the release, Joshua had continued to interview witnesses to Blake's Quilalí abuses as well as victims. Most of the new statements were from the gang of young peasant bullies Blake had recruited to help him with his interrogations.

Working alone in his dark Comayagüela office, Jhonson read the statements through several times. They told of the terror in the Quilalí camp from different perspectives, but they agreed on the important points: Blake and his men had tortured Isaac González to death on November 14; at least two women had been repeatedly raped; Blake had claimed to be carrying out his "investigation" on orders of Mike Lima, who had visited the Quilalí camp and talked to Blake three days after González's murder; Mack and Franklyn had also visited the Quilalí camp and spoken with Blake during the reign of terror.

Jhonson grabbed a pen and scribbled a long memo to Juan "Quiché" Rivas, then the Resistance chief of staff. Technically, Quiché had the power to form investigative tribunals, although Jhonson knew that in practical terms, Bermúdez's influence would still be crucial. When he was done with his memo, Jhonson called in Julio César Delgado, a young exiled Nicaraguan lawyer who was his State Department–funded staff prosecutor, to clean up the language, but it remained a blunt statement of the evidence implicating not only Blake and his bullies but Mike Lima, Franklyn, and Mack.

Jhonson called on Quiché to form a tribunal to investigate his own general staff.[6]

January and early February 1989

In mid-January Alfonso Sandino and several other Association human-rights workers visited the UN refugee camp known as Las Vegas de Jalan near Teupasenti, sixty-two miles northeast of Tegucigalpa, where Blake and the fifty-nine other ex-prisoners had been located in the days since their release.

The camp was a bleak settlement of miserable Nicaraguan exiles living in scorching tents amid screaming children and hungry dogs. Sandino found Blake standing over a cooking fire, stirring a simmering cauldron of carrots and rice. Blake, at first apprehensive at Sandino's arrival, stroked his goatee, appraising Sandino carefully through narrowed eyes. Then he turned friendly and offered Sandino a bowl of his stew.

Blake agreed to an interview about the events at the Quilalí camp, and Sandino began taping. For a few minutes, the questioning proceeded uneventfully. Then Sandino asked, Who were you working for? Blake waved a finger at the tape recorder. Sandino switched it off.

"I'll tell you if you don't tape. They'll kill me," Blake said. "I was working directly for Mike Lima and Joel in counterintelligence. They sent me on that mission." He went to the entrance of his shelter and grabbed a heavy cudgel. "I stay on guard at night. They're going to send someone here to kill me."

That same day, Sandino and the other Association staffers interviewed many of the other fifty-nine former Resistance prisoners now settled at the UN refugee camp. Most of them had been interrogated in Joel's counterintelligence center, and the human-rights workers collected dozens of new accounts of torture.

Several of the former prisoners had experienced Blake's terrors and were not pleased to be living alongside him now as a fellow "refugee." Several young women complained that Blake had begun threatening them. After hearing Sandino's report, Marta Patricia Baltodano alerted UN authorities in Tegucigalpa, who agreed that Blake's continued presence in the camp was unacceptable and petitioned the Honduran authorities to take custody of him. Honduran soldiers detained Blake, taking him to the Army's Sixth Battalion headquarters at the village of Ojos de Agua, near Danlí.[7]

The Honduran authorities do not appear to have considered prosecuting Blake for the murder he committed on their territory, perhaps because they had never before prosecuted any member of the rebel army for similar crimes. Instead, Blake was held for three weeks, first at the Sixth Battalion base in a cell he later described as a "dungeon," and later for a few days at another detention facility in Danlí. On or about February 10, 1989, he was driven south to Las Manos, the border post perched on a pine-shaded mountain ridge just fifteen miles north of the Nicaraguan town of Ocotal, and quietly deported. Sandinista State Security agents detained Blake for questioning, but he appears to have convinced them that he had been kidnapped and forced to join the contras four years earlier and had suffered abuses himself while in contra hands. The Sandinista police arranged for him to tell his sad story to Jilma Rodríguez, the stringer in Ocotal for *Barricada*, the Sandinista party organ, then released him. Blake made his way to Managua, where he joined a gang of ruffians intimidating the residents of the working-class neighborhood of Don Bosco.

Blake's sudden deportation was highly unusual; no other contra fighter in memory had been deported to Nicaragua. It prevented punishment of a rebel agent who had murdered one rebel fighter and had tortured dozens more. It also, of course, made him unavailable for embarrassing testimony before Jhonson's impending tribunal that would have incriminated Mike Lima, Mack, Franklyn, and perhaps other members of the general staff.

Whether or not American officials questioned Blake during his Honduran detention or influenced his sudden and unusual deportation remains unclear. But the CIA liaison agents working with rebel counterintelligence demonstrated ravenous curiosity about Blake during the period, questioning the section's chief, Mike Lima, virtually every day. Who was Blake? How long had Blake been working for counterintelligence? Lima repeatedly insisted he had no ties to Blake, but his denials weren't convincing. No sooner had the CIA liaison officers reported Lima's latest denials than higher-ups back at Langley were bouncing reply cables off the satellite to Tegucigalpa asking for more information. "They were pestering me every day," Mike Lima said.[8]

A spokesman for the U.S. embassy in Tegucigalpa said U.S. officials neither debriefed Blake during his detention nor influenced the Honduran decision to deport him. But why not? Given their extraordinary powers in Honduras, U.S. officials could have prevented Blake's deportation. Were U.S. officials, like Mike Lima and the general staff, eager to see Blake far away?

For his part, Blake said in an interview a year later that "an American adviser," wearing civilian clothes and sunglasses, arrived at the jail where he was being held in Danlí in early February 1988. Accompanied by several Honduran authorities, the "American adviser" drove Blake in a Toyota Land Cruiser from Danlí to the Las Manos border post to deport him, Blake said.[9]

Ambassador Briggs, during an interview six months after Blake's deportation, echoed an argument used by Bermúdez, insinuating that Blake's return to Nicaragua showed he was a Sandinista infiltrator. The murder of Isaac González, Briggs said, "was a terrible, terrible incident. And the screwball that ran that particular show hightailed it back into Nicaragua and showed up on the Sandinista side."[10]

January through February 11, 1989

After Jhonson issued his written call for a tribunal, the initiative was left with Bermúdez, and the Quilalí investigation stalled. Jhonson and Joshua kept taking statements, but they weren't going to learn much that was new until a tribunal began questioning higher commanders. Given Bermúdez's continuing role as army commander, Jhonson knew Quiché, the chief of staff, would only order a tribunal when Bermúdez told him to. But Bermúdez and his general staff stalled as long as they could, perhaps hoping that with Blake gone, the Quilalí controversy might just blow over. Eventually, facing mounting American pressure and seeing no other way out, Bermúdez ordered the general staff to form a tribunal and get on with a trial, but not before rival American views of human rights and the contra army had erupted into a peppery behind-the-scenes showdown. State Department officials pressed for a quick showcase trial; U.S. diplomats in Tegucigalpa sought to protect Bermúdez and his men from what they viewed as a vendetta by Washington liberals. For six weeks, American quarreling gave Bermúdez the excuses he needed to do nothing.

Both rival American bureaucracies were in a thankless position. Honduran officials were increasingly cold to U.S. diplomats in Tegucigalpa, and the diplomats at numerous other foreign missions in Tegucigalpa barely disguised their contempt for the American role in Honduras. Throughout Reagan's last year, there was no clear mandate for the U.S. mission to execute. The policy was in a shambles.

Conditions were no better at the State Department. Since CIA administration of the rebel army had ended nearly a year earlier, a half dozen overworked officers had been baby-sitting a policy and an army none of the major players in American politics even wanted to think about anymore. Now Ronald Reagan was packing his bags for California, and the cluttered workspace they shared on the Department's fourth floor seemed to symbolize the end of the glory days for the Project. The glamour jobs that once had embodied the prestige of Washington's anticommunist adventure in Central America had become an exhausting march of long days and unpleasant choices. Everyone was gobbling lunch at their desks, staying late, working weekends. Empty pizza boxes littered the floor, ashtrays overflowed, phones rang incessantly with no secretary to answer them.

One of the officers was Bert Charneco, to whom had fallen the task of monitoring the Resistance investigation of the Quilalí murder. At forty-six, Charneco was the Puerto Rican–born U.S. Air Force colonel assigned since late 1987 to oversee the State Department's contra human-rights program. He considered the murder of Isaac González to be a major disaster. Like most of his associates, Charneco was a conservative and a believer in the contra cause. In July 1988, on a trip to Managua to escort a U.S. congressional delegation and meet with Nicaraguan government human-rights officials, he had seen Sandinista police use tear gas and clubs to suppress an opposition rally. It had reinforced his view that the Sandinistas were changing little despite the democratic rhetoric they had adopted since opening cease-fire talks with the rebels. In contrast, Charneco believed that Baltodano's human-rights work had improved rebel behavior significantly. Throughout 1988, the future of the U.S. relationship with the contras was murky, but one thing was absolutely clear: If the Resistance didn't handle the Quilalí case correctly and move to punish those accused as torturers, the rebels' enemies in Congress would end U.S. support, once and for all.

There was a bottom line written into the legislation governing the U.S. humanitarian aid. Known as "Section 204," the language barred the provision of aid to any group found to be systematically violating human rights. In Charneco's view, the widening revelations of prison torture had begun to make the abuses sound discouragingly systematic. As the weeks passed in January and the Quilalí investigation seemed to be going nowhere, Charneco grew increasingly impatient.

In contrast, the cables reaching the State Department from Ambassador Briggs's Tegucigalpa embassy minimized the gravity of the situation. The killing in the Quilalí camp had been an "isolated act," according to the cables; the torture of contra prisoners had not been widespread, and Bermúdez was handling the case with admirable candor. Some embassy messages hinted at irritation with so many Department inquiries about human-rights questions. The messages insinuated that the Department was merely pursuing a spiteful purge, and protested that there was little cause for this harassment of Bermúdez's ex-Guardsmen.

Briggs and his officers seemed to be telling State not to micro-manage embassy affairs,[11] but by January 1989, Charneco and other State Department officials had long since grown skeptical of the reporting on Resistance affairs from the Tegucigalpa embassy, especially on human-rights issues.

Charneco had gotten his first taste of the attitude that seemed to prevail at the Tegucigalpa mission during his introductory meeting with Ambassador Briggs in the envoy's office during his first visit to Honduras in late 1987, after taking the State Department human-rights post. Briggs virtually chewed Charneco out, even questioning his credentials. "Why are you involved in this human-rights program?" Briggs had asked him.

Charneco had extensive military experience. He'd begun as an Air Force navigator in 1967, flying 225 combat missions over Vietnam, and finished as a full colonel, the top officer at the Torrejon Air Base in Spain, with more than four thousand U.S. airmen under his command. Along the way, he'd tackled many tough assignments, including heading one Air Force self-inspection program during an earlier stint at Torrejon where he was expected as a matter of routine to tell his commanding officer what his boss was doing wrong. By 1987, he had a lot of confidence. Charneco told Briggs he could carry out any assignment.

"But what do you know about human rights?" Briggs insisted. Pacing behind his embassy desk, his voice rising, Briggs criticized the State Department's human-rights program as ill-considered and amateurish,

and he barely disguised his hostility for Marta Patricia Baltodano's organization, suggesting that Baltodano's rights investigations were aimed
merely at discrediting Bermúdez and his ex-Guardsmen.[12]

That was just one of many similar encounters between officers at
Briggs's embassy and State Department officials working the contra program back at Foggy Bottom during the last year of the Reagan Administration. Throughout 1988, mutual suspicion mounted. State
Department officials observed that the Tegucigalpa embassy's cables
invariably seemed to reflect the views of Bermúdez or Aristides
Sánchez, which were almost invariably those of the CIA. Embassy officers, on home leave in Washington, began to quietly complain to State
Department officials that they felt they would run into career problems
if they tried to report contra abuses they encountered in the field.

"Embassy officers were telling us that when they came across allegations involving the Resistance, they were strongly discouraged from
looking into them," recalled one State Department official. "Their feeling was that if they tried to report these things, one, the cables would
never get out of the embassy, and two, they would have faced some kind
of in-house reprimand. Anyone who reported against the party line was
ostracized."

As a result, embassy cables generally painted a far rosier picture of
Resistance affairs than the officials at State believed. But if there was
skepticism about the embassy's reporting before, the mission's tardy
reporting of the Quilalí murder and the other contra prison abuses com-
pounded the mistrust. Isaac González died on November 14, 1988. Jhonson learned of the murder and notified William Meara, Briggs's personal
aide, on November 22, but the embassy first reported the murder to
State by cable on December 14, five days after Jhonson had informed
Charneco of the crime directly by phone.

"In the Quilalí case, embassy officers walked a fine line between
willful ignorance and intentional obstruction of the Department's
attempts to investigate," one State Department official recalled later.

As the weeks went by in January, with no action by Bermúdez, the
State Department's impatience mounted. By then, all the key
Democrats in Congress knew about the pervasive torture in the rebel
prisons because the GAO auditors who toured Bermúdez's stockades at
the end of November, before the prisoner release, had briefed key lawmakers. More lurid details were reaching Congress after GAO auditors
returned to Honduras in January for more prisoner interviews at the UN
refugee camp at Las Vegas.

Meanwhile, Baltodano's interviewers, talking to the released prisoners, were piling up their own extensive reports on contra torture. Alfon-

so Sandino, Baltodano's aide, had accumulated so many detailed accounts of torture by mid-January that they formed a nine-inch stack of typed transcripts on his desk. In order to make sense of who'd been abused and by whom, Sandino had to develop a card catalog of torturers and victims.

For their part, Jhonson and Joshua continued to interview commandos based at the Quilalí camp, piling up more accounts from witnesses and victims, but little new emerged. Higher commanders were clearly involved in the case, but the only way to assign guilt and innocence was to question the general staff members themselves, who refused to cooperate. Further progress depended on the formation of a tribunal.

State Department officials finally decided to send Charneco to Honduras. They cabled the Tegucigalpa embassy, outlining an agenda for Charneco's proposed six-day visit, centering on an evaluation of Jhonson's Military Prosecutor's office. But in reality, the whole idea was for Charneco to pressure the Resistance to get on with the tribunal. State's cable requested that the host ambassador, in this case Briggs, grant Charneco "country clearance" for his trip, a routine formality when Washington-based officials visit foreign countries.

In a display of the extraordinary rivalry between the bureaucracies, Briggs refused to allow Charneco into Honduras. Briggs's cable, which reached the Department the Friday night before Charneco's scheduled Sunday flight, said that the embassy was simply too short-staffed at that time to accommodate the visit. State Department officials read another meaning to the cable. "The embassy didn't want anybody from Washington down there running around finding out what had been going on," as one official put it.

After Charneco was blocked from Honduras, the carping became an angry behind-the-scenes dispute, with nasty cables fired back and forth across the diplomatic wires and terse phone exchanges between Briggs and Cresencio Arcos, the State Department official who had been an architect of the human-rights program and was now the newly appointed deputy assistant secretary of state for Central America. The law was on State's side: If the Resistance didn't form a tribunal, "Section 204" of the aid legislation would force U.S. investigators to open their own probe into the Quilalí murder. Finally, Briggs sent David E. Lindwall, the embassy's smart young new liaison officer, to Yamales to urge the general staff to get on with a tribunal.

Meanwhile, Charneco, blocked temporarily from Honduras, got to Bermúdez anyway. Upon flying to Miami, Charneco went to dinner with Bermúdez and his wife, Elsa, at their suburban Kendall home. Over steak and rice, Charneco politely twisted Bermúdez's arm. He recalled a recent speech in which Bermúdez had denounced the Sandinistas' human-rights abuses. "But, Enrique, you don't have any credibility now. Your people are doing the same thing," Charneco told Bermúdez.[13]

Eventually, Bermúdez got the message. Back in Honduras the second week of February, he traveled to Yamales and met with his general staff. Minutes later, Commander Denis, Bermúdez's personnel officer, radioed from Yamales to Jhonson in Tegucigalpa.

GENERAL STAFF OF THE RESISTANCE ARMY
11 February 1989

Message

To Commander Jhonson:

I need you to come immediately, to begin the trial in the Quilalí case.

Tell us when you are coming, says Commander Bermúdez.

He wants us to do it as rapidly as possible.

Commander Denis[14]

After weeks of stalling, Bermúdez was suddenly in a hurry.

February 1989

Four days after Commander Denis's breathless message, seven contra field commanders in U.S.-issue camouflage filed into the Resistance's "Hall of Justice," a U.S. Army campaign tent under a stand of eucalyptus trees some two hundred yards down the slope from the contra general staff headquarters at Yamales. After unstrapping their service revolvers and slinging them over the backs of wooden chairs, they sat around a rough table. Deliberations were under way.

The commanders were nervous. With the rebel army idle and its future uncertain, the Quilalí case had become a focus of great rumor and speculation. Virtually every peasant fighter in each regional command the length of the Yamales Valley knew about the killing of Isaac González. Attention had been building for more than two months, as Joshua called witnesses from the Quilalí camp to headquarters for questioning. Stories were circulating about the involvement of higher-ups. Most younger commanders assumed that only the lowest-ranking fighters implicated in the case would ever be punished, but there were signs that this case might go further, and that had many of the army's top officers upset.

Resistance tribunals had always been three-member panels, but mindful of the political delicacy of this case, Jhonson had expanded this one to seven.

He was pleasantly surprised at the commanders the general staff chose to sit on the panel. There were no ex-Guardsmen; they were all field commanders in their mid-twenties, men with decent reputations. One was Santos "Wilfredo" Zeledón, twenty-five, the onetime farmboy who had been Jhonson's executive officer and had taken command of Jhonson's troops when Jhonson became the legal adviser. The tribunal president was Eddy "Fernando" Midence, the commander of the contras' tiny artillery unit. With curly dark hair and a peach-fuzz mustache, Midence looked younger than his twenty-five years, but he'd seen plenty of combat during the 1987 offensive. Midence spoke up even before Jhonson had time to swear in the panel.

"Are we just supposed to convict 'Israelita,' and that's it?" Midence asked, referring to Blake by his pseudonym.

"What do you mean?" Jhonson asked.

Midence said he and the other six commanders had just come from a meeting at general staff headquarters with Commander Denis. As personnel officer, Denis had earlier radioed messages to each of the commanders' camps, notifying them of their participation on the tribunal and ordering them to his office that morning to receive "instructions."

Midence said with some bewilderment that the "instructions" had amounted to a lecture by Denis, speaking in the name of the general staff, warning the tribunal to limit its inquiry to Blake and his men at the Quilalí camp. The tribunal was not to get bogged down in some widening search for guilt by others. Blake had killed a prisoner; this was to be a tribunal about Blake.

"Is this tribunal supposed to get to the bottom of this, or are our powers limited?" Midence asked Jhonson.

"Forget what Denis told you," Jhonson told the panel. "Your job is to look at all the evidence and decide for yourselves who's guilty of what. You are the ultimate authorities on this matter. Don't let yourself be influenced by anybody—not even by Commander Bermúdez."

Jhonson swore in the commanders. Then he explained that there would be no presiding judge. The commanders themselves were the tribunal "magistrates." Jhonson, as the Resistance's legal adviser, would merely administer the proceedings by supplying documents and calling witnesses. His two U.S.-paid attorneys, both Nicaraguan exiles—one a prosecutor, the other a defense attorney—could advise the tribunal and counsel witnesses.

During a two-month investigation, Joshua had collected thirty-two typed statements from victims, fighters, and staff officers at the Quilalí, Jhonson said, pointing at the documents stacked on the table. Those materials would serve the tribunal as preliminary evidence. The tribunal members were to read the statements, then call in any Resistance member they wished for further testimony. They were to take as long as they needed—days or weeks—and they were to use their own collective common sense to decide who was guilty of what crime.

The commanders divided the depositions among themselves and set to work. They read all day, and when it got dark, Jhonson rigged one bare light bulb so that it hung glowing over the table in the night air, powered by a distant, droning gasoline generator.

At the end of their first day, the commanders had identified fifty-two commandos they considered to be involved in the case. They decided to call two dozen in for questioning, starting with the teenage girls whom Blake had detained and tortured. Released in December after their ordeal, the seven girls had been sent back to the Quilalí camp. In mid-January, they had told their stories to Joshua, but Jhonson was worried about how their testimony would go before a tribunal. Would the women be too fearful to testify?

It went fine. Called from the Quilalí camp by radio, the girls hiked over to the general staff camp together the next morning and, one after the other, marched into the legal affairs tent to tell their stories. A sixteen-year-old commando known by the pseudonym "Sandra" was one of three sisters who testified. Fernando, the tribunal president, questioned her after she'd taken a seat before the tribunal.[15]

"Your name?" Fernando asked.

"Magdalena Ortez Rivera."

"Date and place of birth?" Fernando asked.

"May 3, 1972, in the hamlet Valley of Cortez in Quilalí, Nueva Segovia province."

"Education?"

"Third grade."

"Why did you join the Resistance?" Fernando asked.

"Because I was having problems with my family," Sandra answered.

"Do you have brothers in the Sandinista army?" Fernando asked.

"Yes, I have a brother, Pablo José Ortez. He belongs to the 32nd Battalion, based at La Reforma, Quilalí."

"What Sandinista organizations did you belong to before you joined the Resistance?" Fernando asked.

"I was just a member of the Anselmo Díaz cooperative," she said. "I worked there on the land with a machete."

"Did you get any training from the Sandinista army?" Fernando asked.

"No. My mother wouldn't let me," Sandra said.

Jhonson, listening, recalled the picture of Sandra and her two sisters, Otilia and Rosa, that he'd pieced together from his reading of their statements to Joshua. After the revolution, when the three sisters were just toddlers, the Sandinistas had herded their family onto the state-run Anselmo Díaz cooperative farm outside the town of Quilalí. None of the sisters had more than three years' schooling. Instead, they grew up toiling in the revolution's corn and bean fields, alongside their mother. During the 1988 cease-fire, contras from the Quilalí Regional Command camped nearby. All three sisters, falling in love with rebel commandos, had followed them back to the Yamales camps. Probably they'd hoped for something better than the misery they'd experienced under the Sandinistas. Instead, seized as infiltrators within months of their arrival in Yamales, they'd found nothing but savagery.

"What happened to you in the Quilalí Regional Command?" Fernando asked Sandra. She told her story, referring to Blake by his pseudonym, Israelita.

Well, Israelita and his men arrived at my hut on October 30, late at night, and they told me to get up.

"Where are you taking me?" I asked.

"You'll find out," one of them said. They tied my hands behind me and took me to Israelita's hut. He told me: "Tell the truth."

"What truth do you want me to tell?" I asked.

He said if I didn't tell the truth, he'd put a hood filled with wet ashes over my head. And since I had nothing to tell him, he put the hood on me for five minutes, until I was gagging. Then he blindfolded me, tied my hands, and stuffed a rag in my mouth. He took me to a swamp he called "Acapulco." He put his knee on my head and forced my face into the water and didn't let me out of there until I was drowning. . . . The next day they didn't ask me anything. They just put me in a pit covered with some wood. . . . Once when he took me out of the swamp, he tried to light my hair on fire with a cigarette lighter. But since my hair was all muddy it wouldn't light.

Fernando interrupted. "Sandra, did they sexually abuse any of the prisoners?"

"Well, in my case," Sandra answered, "Israelita told me that if I didn't live with him, he'd send me to the Pit of the Serpents. I said, 'No,

I couldn't.' So he said he'd have to send me back to Acapulco. And that upset me because when you're drowning there in the water, it's sad. So I said yes."

The tribunal next questioned Sandra's twelve-year-old sister Rosa, whom Blake had also taken as a concubine, and Otilia, the oldest sister at seventeen. Otilia told the tribunal she was four months' pregnant when Blake dragged her in:

> They took us to Israelita's hut . . . and Israelita began to accuse me of being an infiltrator.
> "You pregnant whore, I'm going to kick that little monkey right out of you," Israelita told me.
> And Juan, his helper, said, "Should I put the hood on her?"
> "Yes," Israelita said. So they put the hood on me for fifteen minutes. And I was in great pain, because before arriving at the hut, Israelita had thrown me against a pile of firewood. And I began to hemorrhage. . . .

As she lay weeping in Blake's pit after one long beating several days into her detention, Otilia told the tribunal, she lost her child.

The tribunal had heard several references to photographs that Blake and his men had taken of the girls during the torture sessions. They questioned Carmenza Cruz, a fifteen-year-old commando known as "Mirna," about the photos. Tall, slender, and quick-witted, she had joined the Resistance with several of her male cousins in mid-1988, and though she drew a lot of male attention in the camps, her cousins had protected her for a time. But they'd returned to Nicaragua with other contras when the counterintelligence men detained her.

"Do you know about any photographs taken of some of the prisoners?" Fernando asked Mirna when she took her seat before the tribunal.

"They took about four of me . . . naked," she said.

"What was the point?" Fernando asked.

"Israelita pushed me inside his hut, and he told me to take off my boots. And since I didn't want to, he called Gangman, the prisoner he had helping him.

" 'Take the boots off this bitch,' he said. Gangman tore off all my clothes, and then Israelita put his knife to my neck.

" 'Now, whore, you're going to do what I say,' he told me."

Alí brought in a camera with a flash, Mirna told the tribunal, and with half a dozen of Blake's young bullies standing around smirking, Blake forced her with his knife to adopt various degrading poses. Alí shot pictures.

Listening to this part of Mirna's testimony, Jhonson recalled his own anger a month earlier, when he'd first learned of the incidents. He had caught the officer who liked to be called "Robespierre" passing Mirna's photos around to a group of snickering commandos in the Yamales camps. Jhonson's anger flashed, and he grabbed the photos. The next time he saw Alí, the ambitious little intelligence officer who had taken the pictures, Jhonson's anger flared again.

"I saw your photos, you little asshole," Jhonson had said. "Very professional investigation you fellows carried out with those poor peasants."

February 1989

The next day, the tribunal called several more commandos from the Quilalí. They were all young peasant boys, and there was no way to distinguish between them, Blake's victims, and the bullies who'd helped Blake as aides. Seventeen-year-old Luis "Vidal" Maldonado, however, proved he was a victim by hiking up his pants leg to display a five-inch gash across his knee left by Blake's knife.

By the afternoon of the second day, Jhonson noticed that several tribunal members appeared tense. They weren't questioning witnesses; they just sat in their seats. One reason, Jhonson guessed, was that one of the commanders on the tribunal was Denis "Johnny" Galeano, the younger brother of Franklyn, the general staff operations officer implicated in the case. Jhonson and everyone else assumed that Johnny was reporting every detail of the tribunal's proceedings to his brother and to the rest of the general staff. In several testimonies, witnesses, both women and men, had mentioned the general staff's involvement. One witness recalled how Blake repeatedly said he was working for Mike Lima. Another referred to the visit paid to the Quilalí during Blake's torture by Mack and Franklyn.

Jhonson understood the tumult the tribunal was provoking when Juan "Quiché" Rivas, the army's chief of staff, met with the Nicaraguan exile attorney acting as Jhonson's prosecutor to offer a deal. Quiché said he wanted the tribunal to suspend its proceedings. In exchange, he offered to accept sole responsibility for Isaac González's murder and for the other crimes committed at the Quilalí camp. The prosecutor came to Jhonson. Was this arrangement possible?

Jhonson was stunned. How can somebody accept sole responsibility for crimes committed by more than a dozen men?

"No, we can't do that," Jhonson told the prosecutor.

But the young commanders on the tribunal lost their nerve. Perhaps the tribunal, which had not yet called any general staff members, had come to see the need to question higher officers and was unsure of its powers. Jhonson guessed the general staff had begun to pressure the tribunal members. Midence talked to Jhonson privately.

"Commander," Midence said. "There are higher-ups involved here. I don't know if we have the power to question the general staff. I don't think we can continue."

"Hold on. You men are the maximum authority," Jhonson said. "To form your judgment, you can question anyone you like."

But Midence was afraid. Would the general staff heed the tribunal's dictates? After less than a week of testimony, the tribunal simply stopped meeting.[16]

Jhonson tried to get the proceedings under way again, with no success. Over a weekend, he drove into Tegucigalpa with the tape recordings of the proceedings to date and set his secretaries to transcribing them. Then he returned to Yamales on an AID helicopter.

When Jhonson walked into the general staff camp, there was a meeting under way in the staff operations tent of the Council of Commanders, the body that included the contra general staff and all the regional commanders. Mike Lima, Mack, and most of the army's other ex-Guardsmen were packed into the tent as well; more than thirty top officers sat facing Jhonson.

Jhonson faced an angry interrogation. Quiché, the chief of staff, was in charge, but a lot of officers were asking questions. "Why aren't there any ex-Guardsmen [on the tribunal]?" piped up Colonel Gómez, the air force chief who had once been Somoza's pilot. "It's all civilians. Is this some kind of war between the ex-Sandinistas and the ex-Guardsmen?"

Jhonson tried to keep calm amid the badgering. Who named the tribunal? The general staff named the tribunal, he said. Ask them why there aren't any ex-Guardsmen. Who appointed the legal adviser? Colonel Bermúdez appointed me, Jhonson said.

The questioning became insulting. Who was Jhonson working for, the CIA? The State Department? Was he a contra or a gringo?

Mack stood and faced Jhonson.

"What are you trying to do to me?" Mack asked. "I've been in the Resistance from the beginning. Are you trying to throw away all my years of struggle?"

Jhonson, beleaguered, took refuge in the Resistance Code of Conduct. The army had a Code, and he was just trying to enforce it, he said. He wasn't picking on anyone.

That set off several diatribes by the ex-Guardsmen about the Code of Conduct. Who'd written it? Let's get rid of it.

The only commander who came to Jhonson's defense was Midence, the tribunal's president. He said he'd read the Code, and Jhonson was right. As far as he could see, Jhonson had only tried to enforce the Resistance's own rules.

But Mack and the other commanders interrupted to hurl more insults at Jhonson. Finally Jhonson got mad.

"We've had dozens of tribunals before," he said. "There's never been any problem with our Code of Conduct. Why now?"

He answered his own question: "Because until now, all the tribunals have gone against little people, never against commanders."

Early March 1989

With the tribunal suspended, Jhonson went to the Americans for help, and so did Marta Patricia Baltodano. The result was the most forceful and candid human-rights pressure Washington had ever brought to bear on the contras.

The embassy sent its young liaison officer, David Lindwall, to Yamales to urge the general staff to reconvene the Quilalí tribunal, but the staff ignored Lindwall's requests. Bermúdez, in Tegucigalpa, supported the staff's intransigence. To friends, Bermúdez was calling the Quilalí case an "old problem" that Marta Patricia Baltodano had dredged up to discredit the Resistance.

Baltodano, whose investigators had carried out dozens of interviews with the Resistance's ex-prisoners during January and February, was shocked to discover the full extent of the cruelty interrogators had dished out to their detainees and was angered by Bermúdez's clumsy attempts to cover up his men's abuses. She shared Jhonson's impatience over the tribunal's suspension, and considered the Quilalí case key to any further rights progress. "I'm tired of these games," she told a reporter. "Bermúdez and his clique are just playing with me."

Baltodano fired off a powerfully worded letter to the Resistance directorate, describing the Quilalí abuses in extensive detail and laying out her suspicions that contra authorities were trying to cover up the crimes. She knew it would eventually circulate in Washington.

During the second week of March, Bermúdez, Aristides Sánchez, Adolfo Calero, and several other Resistance leaders traveled to Washington to meet with Bush Administration officials. During the visit, three congressmen, all longtime contra supporters, invited Bermúdez and the rest of the directorate to the Hill for a chat.

The encounter came in the congressional offices of Rep. Ike Skelton, a conservative Missouri Democrat. Skelton had offered key support to the contras during the 1986 campaign to pass the $100 million aid package, but he also valued Baltodano's views, and her letter about the Quilalí case had disturbed him. It had also upset the other two conservative congressmen whom Skelton had asked to the meeting: Rep. Charles W. Stenholm, a Texas Democrat, and Rep. Rod Chandler, a Washington State Republican.

At the meeting, Bermúdez, Calero, and Sánchez sat on one sofa, facing the congressmen. Half a dozen congressional aides and other onlookers, including those from the contra delegation, listened from the edges of the room.

Skelton began by asking the Resistance leaders for an update on the most recent developments in Central America. After listening to their report, Skelton followed with a blunt recital of his concerns. He'd heard that after all the U.S. money spent on human-rights training, contra commanders were involved in new abuses in the camps. When Skelton finished, Representative Stenholm leaned forward and spoke with equal candor to the contra leaders.

Representative Chandler, a former television anchorman, joined the meeting after it was already under way. Normally jovial, Chandler was, perhaps, angriest of all. He sat down across from the contra leaders so he could fix Bermúdez directly with a cold gaze.

"I've expended a lot of time and taken a lot of political risks for the Resistance," Chandler said. "Now we're hearing about these new abuses. What's going on?"

The new reports, he said, sounded extremely serious, and worse, he'd heard allegations that Bermúdez and others were dragging their feet with their investigation.

"If you're trying to cover this thing up, I'm going to reconsider my support," Chandler said, his voice rising. "And if you were in any way involved in this thing personally, I think it's time for you to step down as Resistance commander."

Bermúdez was at a loss for words. He tried to say that the Resistance was already investigating, but the congressmen brushed his protestations aside. Baltodano's letter had made it clear that the probe was stalling.[17]

The encounter deeply embarrassed Bermúdez, long accustomed to celebrity treatment in the offices of conservative congressmen. When the meeting ended, he raced to the State Department to make a long-distance call to Jhonson in Tegucigalpa.

"They humiliated me in the Congress!" Bermúdez gasped to Jhonson just minutes after the congressional encounter.

Jhonson listened to Bermúdez's account, then composed a message to radio out to the general staff at Yamales.

LEGAL ADVISER TO THE RESISTANCE ARMY
14 March 1989

Message

To: Commander Quiché, Chief of Staff, and Other Members of the General Staff
From: Commander Jhonson

At 1300 hours today Commander Bermúdez called from the State Department in Washington to tell me that an avalanche is falling on us in Washington because of the Quilalí case. Just now they were about to lynch him in the Congress. The situation is very serious for our organization there—the future of the humanitarian aid and the family aid is at stake. We have to do a clean trial that allows for no doubts, no matter who is touched. The only way to save our organization is by carrying out a clean trial. The tribunal has a huge task. Commander Bermúdez wanted me to let you know.[18]

Within hours of Bermúdez's embarrassment in Washington, the general staff reconvened the Quilalí tribunal.

March 14–22, 1989

After leaving the Resistance communications office, where he sent his radio message to Yamales, Jhonson drove his jeep through Tegucigalpa's cobbled streets to Mike Lima's counterintelligence safe house. Now Jhonson figured he could persuade Lima to testify before the tribunal. When Jhonson arrived, Bermúdez had already called from Washington. Lima, meekly accepting the inevitable, climbed into Jhonson's jeep for the trek east to the border camps.

Five hours later, it was dark when Jhonson and Lima pulled up the slope to the general staff camp at Yamales. To Jhonson's satisfaction, they found the young commanders of the tribunal already huddled in the shadowy glow of the legal affairs tent.

The commanders were finishing their questioning of the seventeen-year-old peasant commando called Gangman, who had described with not a little shame how he'd endured Blake's tortures for a time, then joined Blake's interrogators as "chief prisoner."

When Gangman finished, Mike Lima unstrapped his pistol, swore allegiance to the Resistance's fallen heroes, and began his testimony.

He made clear immediately that he had carefully prepared. Various witnesses had told the tribunal before its suspension that Blake, during his reign of terror, had repeatedly claimed to be working for Lima. Now Lima came armed with an alibi: several radio messages that he said proved that he had never authorized Blake's brutal investigation.

Mike Lima said that Roberto "Nolan" Martínez, the Quilalí's young commander, had made inquiries about Blake to Joel, the Yamales counterintelligence chief. According to Lima, Joel, pleading ignorance, had radioed counterintelligence headquarters. Mike Lima held aloft Joel's radio message, then read it aloud to the tribunal:

RESISTANCE ARMY
Message 4

5 November 1988
From: Joel, Chief of Section 6, Zone 2
To: Commander Mike Lima

I need to know if the commando Isaac Blake, pseudonym Israelita, works for counterintelligence, since he says that his work is authorized by you. Commander Nolan wants to know if this is true. I do too.

Mike Lima told the tribunal that he'd been away when Joel's radio message arrived, but he read the reply he claimed his deputy, Noel "Trickster" Castillo, had radioed back.

RESISTANCE ARMY
Message 21

7 November 1988

From: Trickster
To: Joel, Counterintelligence Yamales

Responding to Message 4, I don't know that person. Trickster[19]

"I think I've demonstrated that neither I nor anyone in my section authorized Israelita's work. Not by message, nor orally, nor in any form," Mike Lima summed up as the young commanders passed Trickster's message around.

Jhonson later noted that Mike Lima could easily have printed out the radio messages after the fact, back-dating them in an attempt to build an alibi, but the tribunal gave Lima every benefit of the doubt. They never asked him why he didn't detain Blake for the murder, or why he didn't detain Blake for falsely claiming to be carrying out his investigation on Lima's orders, or what he knew about Blake's mysterious release to the Hondurans.

The following day, the tribunal also handled another top commander, the Resistance operations chief Franklyn, with careful deference. Franklyn, thirty-nine, was one of the most senior Resistance commanders, a former coffee farmer who had been in charge of the Jorge Salazar Regional Command, one of the Resistance's most prestigious units. Franklyn had come to international prominence when his contra unit seized eight pro-Sandinista West German development workers during a 1986 attack on a state farm, holding them for a month before their release, unharmed. Though Franklyn contradicted the testimony of several earlier witnesses, the tribunal didn't challenge his claim that he saw no signs of brutality during his November 1 visit with Mack to the Quilalí camp, nor did it challenge a dozen other contradictions in Franklyn's testimony.

The evidence accumulated suggested that the entire general staff and probably Bermúdez as well participated at least in the attempt to conceal the Quilalí murder. But the tribunal commanders apparently concluded that they lacked the power to convict any but those they considered the most guilty, and they began to see who that commander was after testimony by Alí, the Quilalí intelligence officer.

Alí laid out the most extensive overview of Blake's abuses that the tribunal had heard. His appearance permanently focused the tribunal's inquiry on Blake's ties to Mack.

What caught the tribunal's attention was Alí's account of the visit by Mack and Franklyn to the Quilalí camp. Alí described his own surprise at finding the two general staff members in Blake's hut talking with Blake and his two prisoners, battered and bound.

"Did they see the prisoners?" one tribunal member asked Alí.

"They saw the prisoners," Alí responded.

Alí described how he had immediately handed Mack a written report on the interrogations, including several tapes of the interrogation sessions on which the victims' screams were recorded. He told the tribunal how on November 15, hours after González's burial, he had typed a memo reporting the incident, then carried it over the hills for personal delivery to Mack. But Mack wasn't present at the general staff camp, he said, only Z-Two, the fifty-year-old ex-Guard corporal from La Lodosa whom Mack had appointed as the Resistance army's number-two intelligence officer. Alí said he had handed his report to Z-Two.

"What was Z-Two's response?" the tribunal asked.

"He said, 'Well, he's already dead now. Let's wait and see what measures Commander Mack will want to take,' " Alí said.

"What measures did Mack order?" the tribunal asked.

"I waited for them to send instructions, or to send personnel, or to take some decision," Alí said. "But I never heard anything at all."

The tribunal members paused for a few moments. Alí pulled a copy of his report on González's death from a folder of documents and passed it around the table:

RESISTANCE ARMY
Quilalí Regional Command

15 November 1988
To: Commander Mack, General Staff
From: Intelligence Officer, Quilalí Regional

I'm informing you about the following situation that has occurred in our intelligence section:

At 2010 hours, 13 November 1988, the following subject was captured:

Name: Isaac Iglesias González, "Managua"
Age: 17 years
Civil Status: Single
Place of Origin: Nueva Guinea Province
Date joined Resistance: Mid-May 1988

This subject . . . was arrested and taken to the interrogation office. Under accusation of espionage. During interrogation, he would only reveal the above details.

At 2200 he was interrogated again. He didn't want to give any information.

The analysis we've done on all the reports we have on the prisoners here in this regional command is that these persons come with training: political, ideological, psychological, intelligence, counterintelligence, military secrets, forms of infiltration. This preparation makes them tougher.

At 2400 hours he suffered a sharp rise in blood pressure. (High Pressure) 90/180.

At 2410 hours he died.

The paramedic that attended him concluded that it was the rise in blood pressure that killed him.

At 600 hours he was buried. Only the team of interrogators, the sentries, and Nolan learned of the burial. Given this situation, I'm reporting to you and waiting for suggestions.[20]

"Were you sending reports to Mack on all your work?" one tribunal member asked.

"I reported everything," Alí said. "All the information that the prisoners gave us, I reported to the intelligence section of the general staff."

Alí opened his folder and began to take out documents that he passed around to the tribunal members, mostly messages he had written to Mack—nearly thirty in all—informing him in great detail of six weeks of interrogations. They showed that Alí was still sending memos to Mack about new interrogations in early December, nearly three weeks after González's murder.

Even more surprising to the tribunal were the copies of radio messages that Blake himself had sent to Mack. As the tribunal passed the documents around, Alí explained how in preparing his own testimony he had gathered copies of Blake's radio messages from the files at the Quilalí camp's radio tent, where he knew Blake had communicated frequently with Mack.

Blake had printed his messages out on the little computerized decoders that the CIA had given the contra army two years earlier. In one message to Mack, Blake referred to "the work here that you know I'm carrying out."

Other messages were detailed requests for supplies, such as tape recorders, blank recording tapes, timers, notebooks, pens and pencils, carbon paper, flashlights, batteries.

"Were these supplies delivered?" somebody asked. Yes, Alí said, they were. They were the tools he and Blake had used to record and transcribe interrogations.

The tribunal members studied the documents and finally asked Alí to leave them for further scrutiny. Midence, the tribunal president, dismissed Alí.

Alí and his documents not only confirmed that Mack had known about Blake's work and failed to intervene, but suggested that Blake was working for Mack directly. The documents made it look, several young commanders said, as if Mack had been trying to form his own network of counterintelligence agents. Their discoveries animated the young commanders. Having formed their own hypotheses, they wanted to check them out. New confidence overcame their former nervousness; they wanted to talk to Mack.

Jhonson walked up the hill to the staff camp to get Mack. Bermúdez, rushing back from Washington, had by now arrived in the camps; Jhonson found Mack huddled with Bermúdez in one of the staff tents. Jhonson tapped Mack's shoulder.

"We need your testimony," he said.

Mack didn't hesitate, but the tribunal was stunned and angered to hear how Mack responded to questions that had already been answered by other witnesses.

What did Mack know about the abuses that took place at the Quilalí camp? Midence asked.

"I heard later that there were excesses," Mack said. "But I only found out after everything was finished. . . . Only later. Not before."

Had any member of the general staff authorized the Quilalí investigation?

Mack said he didn't think so.

What about his visit with Commander Franklyn to the Quilalí camp?

That was a "routine visit," Mack said.

Did he see any prisoners?

No, Mack said, just two persons who were being questioned. "There was no sign that they'd been tortured," Mack said. "They just had them off to one side to question them."

Had Alí reported to Mack about the interrogations or about Isaac González's death?

"No." Mack responded in a pedantic tone, then launched into a lecture about military hierarchy. "Alí doesn't belong to my section, he is the intelligence officer of the Quilalí and his commander is Nolan. That's who named him and that's who Alí reported to. He didn't report anything to me about any deaths."

Later the tribunal repeated the question. Had Alí sent reports to him either about the interrogations or about Isaac González's death?

No, no, Mack said.

"Do you have anything to add?" Midence asked.

"Well, I hope you get to the bottom of this thing, for the good of the institution," Mack said. "I want this cleared up as soon as possible—so our organization can keep its immaculate reputation."

Midence dismissed him.

Mack's performance was so transparently false that it hardened the tribunal's resolve about his involvement, and it moved to close the holes in the evidence they were accumulating against him. Mack had denied that Alí had sent him any reports. Perhaps, several tribunal members reasoned, Alí had just delivered his reports to Z-Two, Mack's deputy. Perhaps Mack had never seen them.

Midence, the tribunal president, sent a messenger to the intelligence tent to call Z-Two. Minutes later, the messenger returned, somewhat breathless. Z-Two wasn't interested in testifying, the messenger reported. He had no desire to appear in any tribunal. He had nothing to say.

Midence turned to Commander Wilfredo, who'd been named tribunal secretary. "Write up a note to Z-Two telling him this is not an invitation. It's an order," Midence said.

Word of Midence's quick response was relayed to the Intelligence tent. Minutes later, while Wilfredo was still typing the note for Fernando's signature, Z-Two appeared in the doorway of the legal affairs tent, looking sheepish.

"Did you want to talk to me?" he asked. Z-Two unstrapped his pistol and sat down.

He confirmed that Alí had delivered a report to him in mid-November, at the time of the Quilalí murder, and that he'd passed it along to Mack immediately. But he denied that he'd read it. He even claimed that he hadn't learned of Isaac González's death until a few days before, during the course of the tribunal, four months after the murder.

Several commanders sat shaking their heads through the entire performance.

Finally, Midence dismissed him. Z-Two, mustering a weak grin, turned to one of his acquaintances on the tribunal.

"*Hombre*, I thought that you fellows were just joking when you called me to testify," he said. "I want to cooperate in any way I can."

"Eat shit," the commander shot back.

Other commanders were called. One was Chief of Staff Juan "Quiché" Rivas, who a month earlier had offered to take sole responsibility for the Quilalí abuses. Quiché refused to appear, but the tribunal chose not to attempt to force his appearance. After questioning twenty-five commandos and commanders, the tribunal members felt they'd heard almost enough testimony. But they wanted to question Mack one more time.

Wednesday, March 22, a week after the tribunal renewed its proceedings, the general staff called a routine commanders' meeting, attended by several dozen top officers including Jhonson, Mack, and the tribunal commanders. When the meeting broke up late in the morning, one of the tribunal commanders called Mack to the legal affairs tent to sign the typed transcript of his first testimony.

As Mack looked over the transcript of the testimony he'd given a week before, tribunal member Rolando "Efrén" Rodríguez addressed Mack with unusual candor. A rugged, onetime ranch hand, Efrén still preferred a black cowboy hat to the U.S.-issue camouflage caps worn by other rebels.

"Commander Mack, we're going to be frank," Efrén said. "You were lying to us. We've heard a lot about this case, and you lied to the tribunal. That could cost you."

Mack stood up, startled. He looked around him at the circle of young commanders.

"What do you mean?" he said.

"You lied to the tribunal. And we'll make you pay for that," Efrén said. "But if you want, we'll give you another opportunity. You can modify your testimony before signing."

Mack paused. "You want me to testify again?" he asked. He thought a moment, flustered. "All right, let's do it now," he said.

So the tribunal sat down to question him again. The questioning was tougher this time, but Mack didn't volunteer a confession, and the young commanders had little success prying out straightforward answers.

Midence, recalling the tape recorders and other supplies that Alí said Mack had provided Blake's interrogators with at the Quilalí, asked Mack if he had been directing Blake's work.

No, Mack said, he had nothing to do with Blake.

Jhonson, monitoring the testimony, was worried that the young commanders, failing to pose crucial questions, might later have difficulties coming to a verdict. He pulled aside Julio César Delgado, his young, mustachioed prosecutor, to feed him some new questions to throw at Mack.

Delgado, after an hour of questioning, finally got Mack to acknowledge that Alí had delivered a report to his office about the Quilalí murder.

"Did you read it?" Delgado asked.

"Not necessarily, because in my office I manage a thousand documents," Mack answered.

"Did you read it or didn't you read it?" Delgado insisted.

"Yes I read it, about three days after the subject had died. By then it was all over," Mack said. "I just saw it as one more report for my files."

Midence interrupted. "But you're a member of our general staff, one of the top leaders of our organization. Didn't you have enough initiative to meet with the other commanders to analyze this situation?"

"By then, they were already burying the man," Mack said.

"So after you read the report, what did you do?" Delgado continued.

"The act had been consummated," Mack said. "There was nothing to do."

The questioning continued for more than two hours, and Mack grew irritable. At the end, he was hunched in his chair wearing a sullen glare, hurling insolent answers back at the tribunal. When the questions finally stopped, he turned on Delgado, Jhonson's young prosecutor.

"*Muchacho*, you can be very bothersome. I'd like to catch you—someday, somewhere—other than here," Mack said, half-smiling. He got up and stalked out.

March 22–24, 1989

The Americans wanted a verdict, quickly. In Washington, Secretary of State James Baker was negotiating a new bipartisan accord on the contra policy with Congress, and Bush Administration officials wanted to be able to point to a resolution of the Quilalí murder-torture case. David Lindwall, the Tegucigalpa embassy's liaison officer, was pestering Jhonson, wanting to know when the tribunal would conclude its deliberations. Bert Charneco called Jhonson long distance from his State Department office with the same question every day. Even Bermúdez, after his fright in Congress, wanted a quick decision.

Jhonson also wanted the young commanders to act quickly. It was *Semana Santa*, Holy Week, the week before Easter, when nearly everything in Latin America stops. Jhonson was worried that with no more witnesses to question, the young commanders might postpone their verdict, drift away, and lose familiarity with the case.

"I decided to trap them," Jhonson recalled later. Standing before the young commanders in the legal affairs tent, he told them he was taking them into Tegucigalpa, where they could deliberate in his office without distractions. By early evening, five tribunal members were ready, but Jhonson had already lost two: One went to Miami for a health checkup; another, pleading family problems, slipped off to Danlí. The others piled into Jhonson's red Toyota pickup and set out for Tegucigalpa. After rolling into the capital, dusty and beat, at 2 A.M., they ate takeout Chinese food, then shoved aside the desks in Jhonson's office to sleep on the floor.

Jhonson was up four hours later. He boiled a kettle of sweet coffee and dished up rice and beans for breakfast. His phone was already ringing. The U.S. embassy, Bermúdez, and Charneco called to ask when there'd be a verdict. At nine o'clock, Jhonson sat his men down to work.

"Men, consider these deliberations as though we were in combat,"

Jhonson said. "We're not going to rest and we're not going to run—not until we've defeated this thing. Understood?"

Heads nodded, then the commanders worked for twenty hours straight. Midence led the proceedings, tapping his pencil on the table with nervous energy, steering the tribunal through a consideration of each of the rebels involved in the Quilalí abuses. The commanders consulted their lists of victims and victimizers; they mapped out the role each defendant had played, weighing degrees of guilt and innocence. Finally, they voted, orally.

"You, brother, what do you say?" Midence asked each of his men.

Mike Lima was declared not guilty, and they also cleared Trickster, his counterintelligence deputy. The tribunal's gentle questioning of Lima had left them with insufficient evidence to convict.

Blake, tried in absentia, was found guilty of the murder of Isaac González, of multiple rape, and of mass torture. Because the Honduran government had dismantled the contra prisons three months earlier, the most severe sanction the tribunal could impose was expulsion from the Resistance army. In Blake's case, this amounted to no punishment at all since the general staff had turned him over to the Hondurans in December, effectively expelling him from the Resistance.

Expulsion was, however, a more significant punishment in other cases. The tribunal ruled Gangman, the seventeen-year-old peasant whom Blake had made "chief prisoner," guilty of murder and torture, thereby expelling him from the Resistance army.

As the tribunal voted, they scribbled out the arguments leading to decisions. Jhonson gathered the drafts and coordinated his secretaries and lawyers as they typed up transcripts and corrected the language.

The tribunal worked through the afternoon. After another dinner of rice and beans, the tribunal voted the commandos Rambo and Alí guilty of multiple torture, expelling them, too, from the rebel army.

It was already late in the evening when the tribunal began considering the involvement of the higher commanders: Quiché, the army's chief of staff; Mack, its intelligence officer; Z-Two, Mack's intelligence deputy; Franklyn, the operations chief; Joel, a top counterintelligence officer; and Nolan, the Quilalí's regional commander. Everyone was tired; commanders were yawning as Jhonson ferried in another tray of steaming coffee. Whether it was the fatigue, the strong coffee, or the sounds of the cicadas outside in the Tegucigalpa night, something caused Midence to turn reflective, and he sat forward to speak in sudden earnest about the tribunal's work. The same young commander who had a month earlier suspended the tribunal for fear of retribution now talked with new conviction about its mission. He said the honor of the organization was at stake.

It seemed to Jhonson that everybody understood Midence. Like Jhonson, the young commanders knew the underside of their collective history: Because of a few, much of the world considered the contras to be mere bandits, mercenaries, and brutes, despite their peasant origins and collective sacrifices. Like Jhonson, the commanders also knew who had made the sacrifices, and who had been the brutes.

They made their decisions. Neither Quiché nor Joel had testified. As a result, the tribunal called for further proceedings to determine their status. They were neither convicted nor absolved.

The tribunal also called for a new trial of Z-Two: "The tribunal believes that Commander Ramón Peña Rodríguez, Z-Two, deliberately lied in his statement . . . has committed perjury, and should be tried in a separate proceeding."

The tribunal convicted Nolan, the Quilalí's hapless young commander, of complicity in murder and torture, expelling him from the rebel army.

Then, well past midnight, the commanders turned to Mack. More than one of the commanders wanted to convict Mack of complicity in murder, as the intellectual author of Blake's work.

"Mack is intelligence chief but says he didn't know what was happening out there?" one commander asked skeptically.

Others argued, however, that despite their suspicions, the evidence they'd collected wasn't solid enough to convict Mack of murder. What was clear, however, was that Mack had learned of González's murder within a day of his death and had done nothing.

Somebody quoted Mack's tribunal statements: "By then, they were already burying the man. . . . The act had been consummated. . . . There was nothing to do."

Mack's attitude didn't really surprise anyone. They all knew how he had treated prisoners at La Lodosa, and several could recall the photographs that Frank Wohl had taken during his 1985 visit to Mack's base. Now it was time to call Mack to account. At 5 A.M. March 24, Good Friday, the commanders voted unanimously: Mack was guilty of concealing the murder of Isaac González.

The sun was already lightening the eastern sky over Tegucigalpa. Jhonson napped for half an hour, rose for his morning wash, and began distributing the tribunal's verdict. He phoned telefax copies to Charneco at the State Department and to Bermúdez at his home in suburban Miami. Then he climbed into his pickup and drove to the Tegucigalpa home of David Lindwall, his liaison officer, to deliver a copy for the embassy.

At Lindwall's home, Jhonson also found "Roberto," the American he knew to be Mack's CIA liaison agent, and passed him a copy of the tribunal's decision, too. The decision of most interest to Mack's CIA officer came on page twelve of the tribunal's verdict:

"Although Commander Mack was aware of the serious events that took place in the Quilalí Regional Command," the decision read, Mack never took any action. "That characterizes him as an accessory to murder for having concealed it.

"This tribunal therefore orders his expulsion from the Nicaraguan Resistance Army."

March 27–30, 1989

Three days after the tribunal's verdict, Bermúdez flew into Tegucigalpa to meet with Mack and more than a dozen others at the Resistance communications headquarters. Everyone was angry. Never before had a rebel tribunal convicted a top officer like Mack! One by one, the ex-Guardsmen turned on Bermúdez, accusing him of sacrificing Mack to save his own skin with the Americans.

"Mack's been with the struggle since the beginning," fumed thirty-three-year-old Denis "Benny" Pineda, Bermúdez's onetime operations aide, a man with his own record of prisoner abuses. "Why didn't you protect him?"

"Who else are you going to abandon to the gringos?" asked Francisco "Renato" Ruiz, thirty-seven, by then the Resistance's top paymaster. Half a dozen others fired similar reproaches at Bermúdez. Mack, his face flushed, stared on in silence, then gave vent to his own rage.

"You let them screw me, just for the hell of it!" Mack shouted at Bermúdez, slapping his hand on the table. "You think you're going to wipe your feet on me after all my years of sacrifice? We'll see about that!" He stalked out.

The other ex-Guards continued to excoriate Bermúdez. Six months earlier, Bermúdez had moved to Miami to join the Resistance directorate and to collect the CIA's $180,000-per-director political payments. Now he realized he hadn't been spending enough time in Honduras. He was out of touch—and frightened.

So Bermúdez blamed Jhonson. It was Jhonson who'd pushed the Quilalí case, Bermúdez said. "He's working hand-in-hand with Marta Patricia Baltodano. Jhonson's started thinking like a gringo. He's become a State Department puppet."

What are you going to do about it? the ex-Guardsmen demanded. Why don't you kick him out?

"Maybe you're right," Bermúdez said. "Jhonson's become too obsessed with human rights."[21]

On the street, Mack continued to fume. Noel "Trickster" Castillo had followed him out and heard his angry threats.

"If they take me out, I'll take Bermúdez down with me!" Mack vowed to Trickster. "I know a lot of things about Bermúdez, things he's done. And I tell you, I'm not going out alone."

Over the next weeks, Mack proved that his were not idle threats. For two decades, he had been fighting his way up through an underworld that had begun amid the terrors of the Somoza family's final years and taken new form in the secret bloodshed of the contra war. He'd survived and prospered in a dirty business; he'd accumulated many secrets. Now, down and out, he began fighting his way back.

He started with an immediate assault on the Quilalí verdict. The war had been lucrative for Mack, and he now enjoyed the resources to retain a private Tegucigalpa attorney to file an elaborate appeal of his conviction before the Miami-based panel of CIA-paid Nicaraguan exile lawyers that was the Resistance's "appellate tribunal." But Mack used other methods, too. Antonio "Alí" Herrera, the twenty-year-old intelligence officer at the Quilalí camp, had provided the evidence that was key to his conviction. Mack sent his armed men at Yamales to threaten Alí, seeking to force a retraction of Alí's testimony. He persuaded the general staff, for a time, to defy the Quilalí verdict. He intimidated everyone—including Bermúdez and the officials at Briggs's U.S. embassy.[22]

The same day that Bermúdez met with Mack and the other ex-Guardsmen, Jhonson was working in his office across town when a CIA agent Jhonson knew as "Major Ricardo" phoned. A Colombian-born agent in his mid-forties with graying curly hair, Ricardo was an auditor and information collector for the Agency. He invited Jhonson to dinner, saying that Ambassador Briggs and other U.S. officials were interested in analyzing the evidence against Mack in the Quilalí case.

"They wanted to form their own opinion of Mack's guilt," Jhonson recalled later.

Throughout the afternoon, Jhonson made photocopies of his entire Quilalí case file—the verdict, the messages that Blake and Alí had sent to Mack, the dozens of typed statements his aide Joshua had taken, the trial testimony. That evening, he drove his jeep through Tegucigalpa's twisting cobbled streets up past the soccer stadium, along the glaring fast-food sprawl of Morazán Boulevard, and into the parking lot of the hilltop Hotel Maya. After nodding his way through the usual gauntlet of hissing prostitutes in front of the hotel, Jhonson sat down with Ricardo in the Maya's candle-lit luxury dining room.

Over a two-hour meal, Ricardo questioned Jhonson about the case. What did Jhonson think about Mack's participation?

"He was guilty. He knew what was going on in the Quilalí camp, and he did nothing to stop it," Jhonson told the American agent. Handing over the four-inch stack of tribunal documents, he suggested that the Americans read all the messages to Mack from Alí and Blake.

"The CIA men were worried," Jhonson recalled later. "And they were embarrassed, because the head of the intelligence section they were supporting was involved in this crime."

Briggs and the Tegucigalpa CIA station quickly concluded that Mack had been unfairly convicted, a judgment that clashed dramatically with the reaction in Washington. At the State Department, officials cheered the verdict, and in the ensuing hours they drafted a policy memo halting U.S. AID family-assistance payments to eleven rebel commanders and fighters implicated in human-rights abuses. Five of those suspended were the men convicted of torture, murder, and cover-up by the Quilalí tribunal: Mack, Rambo, Gangman, Nolan, and Alí. The other six suspended were the longtime counterintelligence interrogators whom the Resistance's released prisoners had denounced as torturers in interviews with Marta Patricia Baltodano's investigators: Mike Lima, Joel, Donald Torres, Six-Seven, and two others.[23]

Slashing U.S. aid payments to Mack and Mike Lima—who were, besides Bermúdez, perhaps the two best-known ex-Guardsmen in the contra army—was the most forceful move Washington had ever taken against contra human-rights abusers. Briggs and his embassy were outraged. They considered the suspensions a dangerous overreaction to a minor camp incident that had been aggravated by too much American meddling from the beginning. Some U.S. officials who watched the embassy's reaction to Mack's conviction later argued that there were other reasons the mission defended Mack so steadfastly over the following months.

"Let me tell you a little bit about this culture," one U.S. diplomat who watched Briggs and the CIA react to Mack's conviction said later. "In normal espionage, the handler has leverage over the agent he recruits. But in covert operations, the handler becomes an accessory to the crimes. If I recruit you into the contras and later I say, 'We know you've committed this crime and we want it to stop,' you'll say, 'Don't interfere, or I'm going to tell the press how you've known all about it—and about all the other crimes I've committed.' The blackmail is reversed. There were certain people who had an interest in protecting Mack. They couldn't piss him off and let him go public."

So deep were the embassy's differences with State Department policy that the Department sent a delegation, led by Deputy Assistant Secretary of State Cresencio (Cris) Arcos, to Honduras to make sure that the embassy backed the tribunal's verdict. It was a tense three-day visit.

Arcos, then forty-five, had been working with the contras throughout the decade: as the press spokesman at the Tegucigalpa embassy in the early days, as an administrator of the first humanitarian aid program in 1985 and 1986, and now as the point man for the Project in Washington. Arcos knew how to use his native Spanish and back-slapping charms to persuade often-reluctant Latin leaders to accept U.S. policies. But in the bureaucracy, Arcos wasn't as senior as Briggs, who at fifty-four was nine years older and had punched his own ticket as deputy assistant secretary seven years earlier, before a stint as ambassador to Gen. Manuel Noriega's Panama. Furthermore, class differences played a part in the antagonisms: Arcos was a south Texas Chicano, Briggs an Ivy League aristocrat.

Briggs extended the usual protocol, picking Arcos up at the airport in his ambassador's limousine and lodging him at his sprawling official residence on a hill overlooking downtown Tegucigalpa. But when the arguments began over the Quilalí case, Briggs proved short-tempered.

Briggs told Arcos that Mack had been railroaded. Mack had appeared before the tribunal as a witness, yet at the end, the tribunal had convicted him! The fault lay not so much with Commander Jhonson, Briggs told Arcos, but with Marta Patricia Baltodano. She was pursuing a vendetta against all the former Guardsmen in the Resistance, he argued.

Arcos conceded that Jhonson's tribunal, like the earlier Resistance court-martial, had been no model of jurisprudence, but under the latest humanitarian aid legislation, Arcos said, the contras' enemies in Congress could cut off the entire army from U.S. food aid if they harbored human-rights violators. That's why the Department had suspended Mack, Mike Lima, and the other abusers. "We've got no choice," Arcos told Briggs. "There's clear evidence that these guys have committed some serious crimes. We've got to get it cleared up or we can say bye-bye to the whole army."

As the back-and-forth became more heated, Briggs's aides noticed that the envoy's voice rose half an octave and his jaw muscles began to knot up under his cheeks. Finally, Briggs outlined the heart of his argument, based not on questions of due process but of pragmatism and power. Didn't Arcos see the likely consequences of this verdict? It would erode contra morale and undermine the Resistance's longtime leaders. It threatened to provoke unpredictable turmoil.

Briggs's last point seemed to gain credibility when David Lindwall, the embassy's young liaison officer with the Resistance, burst into the ambassador's carpeted office, still breathless and windblown from his helicopter ride back from Yamales. The rebel general staff was threatening to resign if Mack was forced from the army!

That excited everybody. Nonetheless, Arcos insisted that U.S. policy was clear: Human-rights abusers couldn't be tolerated. The two diplomats were still arguing the following morning, March 30, when Briggs left Arcos and half a dozen other American officials at Toncontín Airport, where they would catch a helicopter to Yamales.[24]

Jhonson was among those waiting on the tarmac for the trip. Arcos greeted Jhonson and took a seat next to him in the helicopter. "Which commanders are threatening to resign if Mack is suspended?" Arcos shouted to Jhonson above the roar of the rotors as the helicopter clattered its way over the hills toward the eastern border.

Jhonson didn't know, and it didn't become clear until they set down at Yamales and walked down the slope from the hilltop landing strip through the eucalyptus trees to the big olive-green general staff operations tent. As Bermúdez and Sánchez rose to greet Arcos, Jhonson looked around. The tent was already packed with nearly fifty rebel field commanders; the entire Resistance medical corps was on hand. Mack was sitting at the front table with the general staff, still wearing his uniform, in defiance of his expulsion by the tribunal.

Bermúdez had just introduced Arcos and the rest of the American delegation when Commander Denis, the personnel officer, stood to read a pronouncement from the general staff directed to the Resistance directorate and the army, as well as to the U.S. embassy and the "USA advisers."

"The general staff has been analyzing the verdict of the tribunal in the Quilalí case," he began, "and wants to make clear the judicial anomalies and violations of Universal Human Rights that were committed in that trial against José Benito Bravo, *Comandante* Mack.

"The right to defense is an inalienable human right . . . and in the Code of Conduct there was no way for Commander Mack to defend himself. . . . The tribunal deliberated secretly, behind the backs of the accused. . . . Every person is innocent until proven guilty.

"These are some of the elements that were not taken into account in this trial." The letter Denis read compared the Quilalí tribunal to the drumhead Popular Tribunals before which the Sandinistas convicted thousands of ex-Guardsmen for war crimes in 1980.

"If we Resistance combatants are fighting to install a process of liberty and social justice in Nicaragua, we can't . . . commit this kind of error against Commander Mack.

"For these reasons, the general staff has decided: One: Commander

Mack will continue in his functions as G-2 of the general staff, since we of the general staff don't consider that he's guilty.

"Two: We accept the tribunal's verdict concerning the persons involved directly as the material actors in the Quilalí crimes. Decreed in the headquarters of the general staff of the Resistance army, March 28, 1989," Denis concluded.

Jhonson saw immediately that the staff had carved out a ludicrous position, challenging the tribunal's methods as unfair to Mack, yet accepting the validity of the convictions of all of Blake's foot soldiers.[25]

When Denis sat down, there was an awkward silence. Finally, Bermúdez stood to introduce Arcos, who walked to the front of the tent. He didn't mince words.

"If you send this letter forward," Arcos said, "you immediately risk losing American support for the Resistance."

He explained the provisions of the latest contra aid legislation that called for cutting off U.S. aid to any groups found involved in human-rights violations, drug trafficking, or other crimes.

"Like it or not, you've got to support your own judicial processes," Arcos said. He shifted to the broader topic of emerging Bush Administration policy on Nicaragua. The struggle is going to be political from now on, not military, he said. He talked for half an hour. When he stopped, hands shot up as a dozen field commanders began firing questions.

"What are you saying? Have you converted us into refugees now? After all our dead and wounded, you're cutting our aid back to just rice and beans?" asked one of the rebel doctors.

"Your struggle has moved onto political terrain," Arcos said. "Forget further military aid. That's been decided already. You won't get any more. The Sandinistas would have to do something extraordinarily stupid before Congress would vote more military aid."

It was the first time that the mass of contra field commanders had heard their situation outlined so bluntly. At the end of the meeting, Arcos called Bermúdez, Sánchez, and the general staff into another, smaller staff tent nearby to repeat his warning about the Quilalí tribunal. If they didn't honor the verdict, there'd be no more aid of any kind.

"You don't understand how it will look in the United States if you have a trial and then refuse to abide by its outcome," Arcos told them. Then he turned to Bermúdez, with Mack and the rest of the general staff watching. "And you better not touch Jhonson."

He looked Mack in the eye. "Nobody's out to get you," Arcos said. "But the tribunal has made its judgment, and we support them. There's an appeals process. If you feel you've been unjustly condemned, then use it."[26]

Mack walked out. Jhonson was standing in the parking area talking to a group of commandos when he emerged.

"Well, you fucked me royally. I hope you're pleased," Mack said to Jhonson. "You shit all over me. What kind of *compañero* are you? What about my future? They've cut off my aid. What about my family?"

"I didn't screw you, Commander Mack, you're mistaken," Jhonson said. "The tribunal judged you. You had the opportunity to defend yourself, to tell your side."

Mack wheeled to walk away. "You have a Sandinista attitude," he shot back at Jhonson in parting.

Inside the tent, the general staff backed down. Aristides Sánchez hurried out to get a typewriter and paper, and the staff drafted a new letter, directed to Ambassador Briggs. It retracted the staff's earlier bombast, agreeing to respect the judicial process. Pending Mack's appeal, he was to remain suspended as intelligence chief, receive no U.S.-financed salary, and stay out of the Yamales camps. The Americans had enforced the tribunal's verdict—for a time.

10

Final Verdicts

February through July 1989

On March 24, 1989, as Jhonson was distributing the Quilalí tribunal's verdict in Tegucigalpa, President George Bush was standing under the glare of television lights in Washington announcing a dramatic shift in U.S. policy on Nicaragua. The new approach, embodied in a bipartisan accord signed with Republican and Democratic congressional leaders, called for new emphasis on peaceful diplomacy instead of military pressure. It reversed the policy that had stood for a decade.

President Ronald Reagan had said his goal in Nicaragua was to get the Sandinista government to "cry uncle." Now, announcing the new approach, Bush said: "We do not claim the right to order the politics of Nicaragua. That is for the Nicaraguan people to decide."[1]

The accord, negotiated by Secretary of State James Baker in weeks of behind-the-scenes meetings with congressional leaders during the Bush transition, marked the public end of the use of the contras as a U.S. military instrument. Instead it committed Washington to keeping the contras alive, but quiet, for a year as the Sandinista government moved toward internationally supervised elections. To keep the contras alive, Democratic leaders agreed to extend the $4.5 million per month in U.S. nonmilitary aid that had already been sustaining the rebels for a year. To keep them quiet, Baker gave Congress the power to end the aid quickly if the rebels launched offensive military attacks or committed more human-rights abuses.

On one hand, the policy offered a promising new way to pressure the Sandinistas politically. On the other, it was a formula for temporarily warehousing an army that Washington no longer wanted. It ended years of partisan warfare over the contra program and brought the new Administration praise. The credit was probably deserved, not so much for any conceptual brilliance as for the unusual humility the policy represented in Washington's relations with other countries in the region. After a decade in which Ronald Reagan's Washington bullied and badgered its Central American allies into cooperation with the contra policy, the Bush Administration now agreed to "work in good faith" to implement the latest peace plan negotiated by the five Central American Presidents.

That plan, drawn up in a February 1989 summit at the Salvadoran resort of Tesoro Beach, laid out the central tradeoff that provided the logic behind the Bush Administration's new policy: contra demobilization in exchange for free, internationally monitored elections in Nicaragua. President Daniel Ortega promised to organize the balloting on February 25, 1990.

Bermúdez, Calero, Sánchez, and several other contra leaders decried the agreement, arguing that no Sandinista promise was worth believing and that only new military offensives could bring political change to Nicaragua. "This is like trying to leash a dog with sausage links," Calero told reporters.[2]

Nonetheless, within a month after the agreement was signed, events were making the old arguments of the CIA-recruited contra politicians sound increasingly stale. In Managua on March 17, the Sandinistas fulfilled an important commitment under the Central American peace plan by freeing 1,894 former National Guardsmen imprisoned since the 1979 revolution.[3]

At the same time as this, events in Eastern Europe were discrediting the hard right's knee-jerk claim that Communists would never cede power peacefully. During the weeks after the Tesoro Beach accord, Soviet President Mikhail Gorbachev pledged not to interfere in the reform movements sweeping the East bloc: Hungary opened its borders with Western Europe, and opposition candidates humiliated Poland's ruling Communists in the first free elections in forty years.

With public attention focused on Eastern Europe, U.S. officials quietly moved to implement the more painful aspects of the new Nicaragua policy. As the political focus shifted to Nicaragua's internal anti-Sandinista opposition, Bush Administration officials saw no more need for the exile politicking of the Resistance directorate, or for the scores of rebel political functionaries working at the Resistance's Miami headquarters.

Two years earlier, CIA agents had been enticing opposition leaders into exile to work with the Resistance. Now Administration officials began urging them to go home.

Some did. One of the first was Azucena Ferrey, forty-three, a Christian Democratic politician who had traveled into exile in 1987 to join the Resistance directorate and who flew home to Managua in May 1989. Ironically, in the hours before she left Miami, her phone rang constantly as angry Nicaraguan exiles called to insult and threaten her. "People were accusing me of having cut a deal with the Sandinistas," Ferrey said. "That's a tremendous lie."

Another former Resistance director who returned to Managua was Pedro Joaquín Chamorro, the thirty-seven-year-old newspaperman whose mother, Violeta Barrios de Chamorro, would soon seek the nomination as the opposition's main presidential candidate. A third who decided to challenge the Sandinistas politically was Alfredo César, the thirty-seven-year-old Resistance director who, with Adolfo Calero and Aristides Sánchez, had negotiated the 1988 Sapoá accord.[4]

But the contra army's three main politicians, the men the CIA had recruited in the Project's early days—Bermúdez, Sánchez, and Calero—refused to participate in the elections.

In 1988, the Resistance headquarters at the northern edge of Miami International Airport enjoyed a $500,000 monthly subsidy; by 1989, even with the U.S. aid policy reversed, the monthly U.S.-paid budget was still $260,000, supporting an office staff of more than fifty employees, and individual directors were still receiving secret annual payments from the CIA of $180,000 each.[5]

Elliott Abrams, the assistant secretary of state in 1986 when Congress voted the $100 million contra aid program, had advocated the secret CIA political funding to nurture political activities that could lead to a Nicaraguan government-in-exile. But long before the Bush Administration reversed U.S. policy in early 1989, some U.S. officials, including Deputy Assistant Secretary of State Cris Arcos, had grown critical of the proliferating corruption spawned by the CIA payments.

Another critic of contra spending was Arcos's boyish-looking aide, Dan Fisk, an Oklahoma conservative with a taste for penny loafers and red suspenders. In 1984, when Fisk was just three years out of Georgetown University and a true believer in the contra cause, he had plunged into the world of Washington contra politicking. As a congressional staff member of the Republican Study Committee, a group of conservative House members, Fisk had arranged Washington lobbying tours for contra fighters like Tigrillo and Mike Lima, and he'd gotten to know the contra political directors. Fisk had developed especially close relations with Calero, and the ties only tightened after Elliott Abrams invited Fisk to work at the State Department in 1986.

Over the years, however, Fisk's enthusiasm for the contra cause dimmed as he watched reports accumulate of Resistance directors spending their CIA political funds on mink coats, new cars, and air-conditioning for their homes. And Fisk's disillusionment increased in the spring of 1989 as some Resistance directors refused to acknowledge the changing political environment in Managua, expressing more concern for their own finances than for the welfare of the thousands of rebel combatants in the Honduran camps.[6]

In a series of often stormy meetings in Miami and Washington, Fisk, Arcos, and other Administration officials informed Calero, Bermúdez, and Sánchez that the Resistance headquarters in Miami would be closed and that the secret political payments to the directorate would end. As the U.S. officials put it: "The time for exile politics is over."

One State Department meeting with Calero, Bermúdez, and Sánchez, chaired by Arcos, turned especially tense.

"We encouraged them to go back and put the Sandinistas to the test," recalled one U.S. official who participated. "We told them, 'Go challenge them.' And that just seemed to take their breath away."

U.S. officials heard a bit of a whimper in the voice of Bosco Matamoros, the contras' Washington spokesman, when he complained, "You make going home to Nicaragua sound so simple. But this isn't some visit to Disneyland."

Other contra leaders began to grumble, too. Finally, "Tim," a CIA agent participating in the meeting, got angry.

"Remember what killed the dinosaurs?" he asked. "They wouldn't adapt to the environment. Now you've got to change, too, or you won't survive either."

"What do you mean by that?" snapped Calero. "Would you repeat that?" Tim repeated his comment. Calero noted it down, and after the meeting rushed to Capitol Hill to complain to his conservative friends.

Meanwhile, Sánchez and Bermúdez gathered with other contra leaders at Bosco Matamoros's apartment near Dupont Circle for an informal session with the press. They told reporters that the Sandinistas were Communists who couldn't be trusted in an election. Sánchez vowed to "support the armed struggle to the end. My perception is that [Bush Administration officials] want to end their relationship with the Resistance. But we're not a package that you can throw away, just like that. . . . If you won't support us, you have no right to lead us into disaster."[7]

If rebel leaders like Sánchez and Calero were suddenly disillusioned with their American handlers, the reverse was also true.

"Did seven thousand contras die so a handful of their leaders could live in Miami, travel first class, and stay in the Ritz-Carlton Hotel? I don't think they did," complained one State Department official. "But that's all we see some of these guys doing."[8]

The tensions peaked in June 1989, when Washington cut the political payments, reducing the Miami office to a telephone receptionist and a caretaker staff. Calero, Bermúdez, and Sánchez complained on Capitol Hill that the State Department was "selling out" the contras. Conservative leaders began to denounce Arcos and Fisk by name in meetings and calls to the White House.

In an attempt to calm emotions, Arcos and Fisk met with several conservative lawmakers and their staffs to explain the Department's point of view. The problem was that to many congressmen, Calero, Bermúdez, and the contras' other English-speaking politicians *were* the contra movement. Few lawmakers had had more than cursory contacts with rebel field commanders or fighters, and now they were confused.

"How can you abolish the Resistance directorate?" one congressman asked Arcos and Fisk. "Wasn't it elected by the Resistance Assembly?"

"Yeah," Fisk answered, according to one of the participants in the meeting. "And the Resistance Assembly is fifty-four Nicaraguan exiles selected and paid for by the CIA."

For conservatives who had revered the Resistance, these were difficult assertions; some had even invited Resistance directors like Calero into their home districts to make speeches. It was a shock when Arcos and Fisk began to detail the seediness that had come to characterize contra politicking.

"You are the ones who told us that these guys were the moral equivalents of the founding fathers," an angry congressman told Arcos in one Capitol Hill meeting.

The cutoff of U.S. political funds sparked more contra squabbling. Resistance directors and employees, losing their salaries, began to haggle over the endowment of the Nicaraguan Resistance Educational Foundation, a nonprofit charity established in Washington by the widow of CIA Director William Casey and other conservative benefactors for the treatment and rehabilitation of the contra army's disabled and maimed. The directorate ordered the Foundation's caretaker, Ernesto Palazio, to begin paying each of them two thousand dollars' monthly salaries from the Foundation's endowment. Palazio refused. Bosco Matamoros, who shared the Foundation's Washington office with Palazio, retaliated by calling in Washington reporters to display checks and other documents he had purloined from Palazio's files, claiming that Palazio himself had spent lavishly at Resistance expense. The squabble ended when Palazio changed the locks on the office to keep Matamoros out.[9]

It was an ugly period. Calero, enraged at what he termed "betrayal" by U.S. officials, launched into an embittered tirade during one meeting with staff aides for several conservative congressmen. Calero enumerated an extensive list of CIA agents with whom he had worked during the war, threatening to expose the agents by making their full names public. "I know who these guys are," Calero told the staffers. "And I'm going to fuck them if they fuck me."[10]

April through August 1989

The back-stabbing and double-dealing following the cutoff of the CIA's secret political funds to the contra bureaucracy in Miami spread into the ranks of the rebel army, too.

In August 1988, Bermúdez had moved from Honduras to Miami to join the Resistance directorate and to get access to the $180,000-a-year *tendencia* budget the CIA was providing for each rebel director. At the time, Bermúdez had given up his position as the rebel army's "general commander," turning day-to-day command over to Chief of Staff Juan "Quiché" Rivas. When Bermúdez learned in the spring of 1989 of the impending cutoff of his CIA funds, he decided to move back to Honduras and reassume his position as "general commander." Quiché, however, was in Bermúdez's way.

In March 1989, however, Ambassador Briggs and his CIA men at the Tegucigalpa embassy suddenly discovered allegations that Quiché had been involved in narcotics trafficking nearly ten years earlier, in the months after the Sandinista revolution, when Quiché had been living in exile in Guatemala. Quiché appears to have worked for a time as a mule, a small-time smuggler moving drugs concealed in personal luggage, working on commission for larger traffickers. Ricardo, the Colombian-born CIA agent, helicoptered to Yamales to break the harsh news privately to Quiché: He would give up his chief-of-staff post immediately or face a full U.S. investigation. Quiché resigned without protest, citing "health problems." With American help, he moved his family to the United States.[11]

The circumstances of Quiché's departure remained secret to all but a few top commanders, but those who knew how the Americans had unceremoniously fired their chief-of-staff were angry. Was it really coincidence that Briggs had used nine-year-old allegations against Quiché at the precise moment when Bermúdez needed Quiché out of the way? They smelled treachery.

Aristides Sánchez encouraged their suspicions. Throughout the war, Sánchez had worked so closely with Bermúdez that each man had seemed to be a virtual extension of the other. But Sánchez, too, was losing his CIA political funds and, like Bermúdez, needed to carve out a new position for himself back in Honduras. With American money drying up and the rebel army's future in doubt, the contra leadership was no longer spacious enough for both men. Sánchez turned on Bermúdez.

A master conspirator, Sánchez honed Quiché's mysterious departure into a weapon against Bermúdez. Whispering to rebel field commanders behind the scenes, Sánchez began accusing Bermúdez of reporting the narcotics allegations against Quiché to the Americans in order to force Quiché out.[12]

True or not, Sánchez's accusations made sense; since he reassumed his former post as general commander, Bermúdez was the main beneficiary of Quiché's sudden resignation. Others also benefitted. Israel "Franklyn" Galeano, the operations chief implicated with Mack in the Quilalí case, was promoted to replace Quiché as chief of staff. In turn, Marcos "Black Dimas" Navarro, the former National Guard soldier, replaced Franklyn as operations chief.

Though Bermúdez was back in command, his position was shaky. Among the army's former peasants, trust for Bermúdez had dwindled in the year he'd spent in Miami with the other high-living contra politicians. Many former Guardsmen blamed Bermúdez for sacrificing Mack during the Quilalí tribunal, and now many commanders heard Sánchez's hints that Bermúdez had fingered Quiché to the Americans. Bermúdez's esteem among the troops had eroded so dramatically that even State Department officials like Cris Arcos and Dan Fisk were alarmed. The Americans had always counted on Bermúdez as an administrator of unquestioned loyalty to U.S. interests, but now Bermúdez's very dependence on Washington seemed a liability.

"Bermúdez appears to be totally dependent on our [CIA] station for guidance," said an internal memo that circulated in the State Department during April 1989. "It's the first place he calls when he arrives and the last he calls before he leaves Honduras. He has his safe house with telephones and telex. His own car, driver, bodyguards. He has a helicopter at his disposal via the embassy. He has an additional aircraft (a Baron) that is flown by his private pilot Colonel Gómez. It is no coincidence that the boys [the CIA] have a special relationship with Bermúdez's intelligence and counterintelligence units; both have always been commanded by a former Guardsman. The combat commanders see this and easily reach the conclusion that Bermúdez is the 'gringos' man.' "

Bermúdez seemed so weak and unpopular with the troops that State Department officials feared that continued American backing for him, when Bush Administration policy was leading to certain friction with the contras anyway, might spark a new officers' rebellion.

"We were going to lose control of the rebel army," one State Department official recalled.

As a result of these fears, Arcos, Fisk, and a handful of other State Department officials quietly orchestrated a coup in July 1989, designed to shift power in the rebel army from Bermúdez to Franklyn and his general staff. The State Department flew Franklyn and other key field commanders to Washington for a secret, two-day meeting at the West Park Hotel in Rosslyn, Virginia, across the Potomac from Foggy Bottom. State Department officials explained the meeting as an effort to develop a rebel political offensive in advance of an impending summit of Central American Presidents, scheduled for early August at Tela, a resort village on Honduras's northern Caribbean coast. But the Department's real goal was to strengthen U.S. ties with Franklyn and his general staff, and to signal to Bermúdez that Washington would no longer allow him to monopolize U.S. relations with the contras nor the Resistance's relations with other governments in Central America.

But Bermúdez still had powerful U.S. friends. In June, Everett Briggs had ended his posting at the Tegucigalpa embassy and returned to Washington to become President Bush's top Latin American adviser at the National Security Council, and "Terry," the CIA's station chief in Tegucigalpa from 1987 through mid-1989, had returned to Washington to head the Latin American Division of the Agency's Operations Directorate. At the last-minute insistence of Briggs and the CIA, the State Department was forced to include Bermúdez in the Rosslyn meeting. Aristides Sánchez was also invited.

Once the meeting began, Bermúdez sensed that he was being undercut, and by the second day he was desperate. He buttonholed Arcos in a hotel corridor to plead to be kept on as rebel commander. Bermúdez assured Arcos that he, better than any other Resistance leader, could help the Americans take the contra army apart, if that's what Washington decided. "You're going to need me if you decide to demobilize the Resistance," Bermúdez told Arcos.[13]

When he returned minutes later to the downstairs room where Franklyn and the general staff had been meeting with other U.S. advisers, Bermúdez realized his pleas had fallen on deaf ears. A commanders' commission had been named to tour Central America at U.S. expense to meet with the region's Presidents in advance of the Tela summit. Franklyn would lead the rebel tour. Bermúdez was not invited.

For the first time, an influential sector of the American bureaucracy had turned on Bermúdez, and Bermúdez began to fight for his survival. Over the next weeks, as the State Department–sponsored commanders' commission toured Central America, shadowed everywhere by Department officers who booked their hotels and flights and arranged press interviews, Bermúdez traveled on his own parallel tour, presenting himself as the rebel army's true commander. The most damaging incident came in El Salvador, where Bermúdez created a nasty public stink, elbowing his way in to meet with President Alfredo Cristiani an hour before Cristiani was to see Franklyn and the State Department–backed commission.

The infighting grew so treacherous that it absorbed most of the attention of the rebel leadership and of their U.S. liaison officials during the period, overshadowing other developments in the rebel army. During the same summer weeks, however, a quiet showdown was developing over the Americans' three-year human-rights reform effort.

Pending a decision on Mack's appeal to a review panel in Miami of his conviction in the Quilalí case, the State Department had ordered him suspended from his intelligence post, barred from the Yamales camps, and cut off from his U.S.-financed salary. Tim Brown and other U.S. officials at the Tegucigalpa embassy protested that the sanctions were too severe. But during several trips to Honduras during the same period, Bert Charneco became more convinced than ever of the need to cut all U.S. ties to Mack.[14]

One commando provided Charneco with an eyewitness account of how, in 1981, when Mack was working as a military trainer with CIA-funded Indian rebels in the Honduran Mosquitia, Mack had arranged the fatal ambush of a rival contra leader. Another contra regional commander described to Charneco how Mack had ordered a series of commandos executed in FDN base camps during 1983 and 1984. The commander offered to pinpoint the clandestine gravesites where more than two dozen of Mack's victims were buried. While Charneco was piecing together Mack's murderous past, a U.S. intelligence cable to the State Department reported that his violence was continuing into the present. The cable linked Mack to a mysterious explosion in Las Trojes, the village fifteen miles northwest of the Yamales camps where he was living during his suspension. Some informants were telling U.S. officials that Mack, angry at one of his Honduran lovers, had detonated a grenade near her home. Other U.S. sources had it that Mack had actually blown up the woman's house with military explosives.[15]

This new information suggested that Mack's involvement in the Quilalí abuses was only one detail in an entire career of unchecked violence, yet the Quilalí case was the only instance in which someone in the Resistance—albeit with U.S. backing—had brought Mack to account. Now, with the Miami-based Resistance appellate tribunal considering Mack's appeal, Sánchez and Bermúdez were portraying him as a victim.

The tribunal's four "magistrates" were all Nicaraguan exiles who for years had been living off the U.S.-financed Resistance payroll in Miami: Evenor Valdivia, an oligarchic lawyer from Somoza's Liberal Party; Marcio Baltodano, an associate of Adolfo Calero's; Harry Bodán, Bermúdez's personal adviser; and J. David Zamora, one of Somoza's Liberal Party senators and a onetime lawyer for the National Guard.[16]

Jhonson had gotten an uneasy feeling about the panel's intentions when the four-man tribunal traveled to Tegucigalpa in June, supposedly to review the Quilalí verdict, and didn't even bother to call him. Instead, the tribunal lawyers spent their excursion to Tegucigalpa interviewing Mack, several other former National Guardsmen, and the general staff. Jhonson began to suspect that the appeals tribunal, in classic Latin fashion, would base its verdict not on any considered review of the evidence but on the desires of the powers-that-be.

Both Bermúdez and Sánchez had made clear that they wanted Mack exonerated. Bermúdez feared Mack's enmity and wanted to patch things up. Sánchez, at once quietly blaming Bermúdez for Mack's conviction and working to reverse it himself, was readying Mack as an ally for the moment, months later, when he would openly betray Bermúdez.[17]

The bad news came late in July when Harry Bodán, Bermúdez's adviser, called Jhonson from Miami to telefax the appeals tribunal's seventeen-page decision to Jhonson's Tegucigalpa office. The original commander's tribunal had expelled five relatively unimportant rebels from the contra army—Blake, Gangman, Rambo, Alí, and Nolan—along with Mack. The appellate tribunal upheld the expulsion of all five foot soldiers, but overturned Mack's conviction for cover-up. The tribunal conceded that Mack had been guilty of negligence, but imposed no sanction.

Depressed, Jhonson sat at his desk in the Tegucigalpa heat, wading through the byzantine legal jargon with which the appellate tribunal had tried to dress up the political expediency at the heart of its decision. The panel argued that Jhonson, upon concluding his initial December 1988 investigation, had recommended the formation of a commanders' tribunal to examine evidence only against Blake. Therefore, the appellate tribunal reasoned, the commanders' tribunal had no right to convict anyone but Blake because no one else had either known they were on trial or had been given the opportunity to prepare a defense.

Digging through his files, Jhonson pulled out his initial investigative report recommending a tribunal and saw immediately that the appellate panel was wrong. His report listed evidence of potential crimes committed not only by Blake but by Mike Lima, Mack, Franklyn, Nolan, and several other rebels. Jhonson found numerous other passages of the appellate panel's decision that could only have resulted from a sloppy or deceitful reading of the trial record.[18]

Three days later, Bermúdez, Franklyn, and the commanders' commission returned to Tegucigalpa after their tumultuous competing Central American tours. It was nine o'clock in the evening when Jhonson drove to the Alameda Hotel, the Resistance's favorite Tegucigalpa hangout, to deliver the appellate verdict. Jhonson went to Aristides Sánchez's room, where he found Bermúdez, Sánchez, Franklyn, Mike Lima, and several other top commanders. Mack was sitting at one side. The contra officials lapsed into a chilly silence when Jhonson entered.

"Here's the appeals tribunal's decision. They declared Mack innocent," Jhonson said, handing Franklyn the document.

"If he's innocent, then we ought to install him back in the general staff," Sánchez said.

Franklyn jumped right in, agreeing. "That's right. If the decision was to absolve him, then we ought to restore Mack to his position right away." Jhonson was outnumbered, but he protested anyway.

"I don't think Commander Mack should get his intelligence post back," Jhonson said. "First of all, even the appellate tribunal admits that he's guilty of negligence that resulted in a commando's death."

"Look, I've had enough punishment," Mack shot back. "For five months, I've been humiliated."

"Sorry, but I don't think it's good for the organization at this point to put Mack back in as intelligence chief," Jhonson argued. "It'll hurt us politically, especially in Washington. I think we should wait on this."

"Fuck the gringos!" Sánchez said, raising his voice. "Mack's innocent, and you want to keep screwing him, unjustly? He should return to his post right now. Where's your lawyer?"

"He's in the office, I guess," Jhonson answered.

"Call him up. Tell him to write up a document restoring Mack to his post," Sánchez said. "Do you agree, Franklyn?"

"Sure. Of course I agree," Franklyn said. Jhonson had no choice. He dialed his office, and when his lawyer answered, Jhonson handed the receiver to Sánchez, who dictated the document he wanted. The lawyer typed it up and delivered it to the hotel the same night. Sánchez and Bermúdez signed it for the directorate.[19] Two days later, Franklyn sent a radio message informing every rebel unit that Mack was again the army's intelligence chief.

The appellate panel's verdict and the military command's decision to reinstall Mack as intelligence chief humiliated Jhonson and the young commanders who had served on his Quilalí tribunal, but the pressures Bermúdez and Sánchez had exerted to reverse the Quilalí tribunal were aimed fundamentally at insulting not Jhonson, but Washington.

U.S. officials had trumpeted the tribunal's original verdict as a triumph for human-rights reform within the Resistance, and it had received widespread press coverage. Representatives Chandler, Skelton, and Stenholm, the three congressmen who in March had pressured Bermúdez and Sánchez for action, had written the directorate two weeks after the tribunal's original verdict to congratulate the Resistance for its "decision to expel a member of the general staff . . . a difficult decision" that the lawmakers said demonstrated the Resistance's "commitment to the principle that no man is above the law. . . . The tribunal's willingness to . . . subject the powerful as well as the weak to a single standard of justice is a tribute to the democratic nature of the movement."[20]

Mack's reinstatement went virtually unnoted in the U.S. press, and neither the Bush Administration nor the Congress voiced any public displeasure over what amounted to a dramatic display of Resistance contempt for Washington's human-rights stance. State Department officials turned down a Resistance request to reinstate Mack's U.S.-financed salary, but the rebel leadership paid no significant price for reinstalling Mack.

On the contrary, Everett Briggs, who had been President Bush's top Latin America adviser at the National Security Council since June 1989, arranged a display of White House appreciation for the contra leadership. Throughout the summer the White House had been under pressure from conservative Republicans accusing Bush of "abandoning" the contras, and by late July the White House wanted to send a different message to the American right. Just five days after Bermúdez, Sánchez, and Franklyn had reinstated Mack as the rebel army's intelligence chief, Briggs arranged for the three to meet personally with President Bush for forty-five minutes in the White House.

The President, Vice President Dan Quayle, National Security Adviser Brent Scowcroft, White House Chief of Staff John Sununu, Assistant Secretary of State Bernard Aronson, and other U.S. officials sat on one side of a table in a White House conference room, while Bermúdez, Sánchez, Franklyn, and several other rebel commanders sat across from them. The President told the rebels that he wished his Administration could help their cause more, but "our hands are tied. And you have both hands tied behind you. But we've got to persist in the struggle together."

"It was a kind of keep-your-chins-up speech," recalled a U.S. official who attended. There was no mention of Mack.

The front pages of the Honduran papers the following morning carried photos of President Bush shaking hands with Bermúdez. Sánchez and Franklyn looked on smiling. Jhonson, back in Tegucigalpa, shook his head. He understood the message: U.S. pressure for human-rights reform had been temporary. Now the Americans had other priorities.

August 1989 to January 1990

The summer of 1989 was a watershed period. Mack's reinstatement in late July was part of the utter collapse of three years of U.S.-financed contra human-rights reform. Then, on August 7, the five Central American Presidents agreed at Tela to work together to demobilize the contra army within ninety days. It was the most stunning political blow yet to the rebel army.[21]

The coup de grace to Jhonson's human-rights work came days later in August with the tribunal that tried Mike Lima, Joel, Leo, and nine other counterintelligence interrogators on torture charges. Marta Patricia Baltodano had assembled the accusations during two years of investigation, and they added up to the most controversial human-rights case ever presented to a Resistance tribunal, alleging that torture and sexual abuse were systematic in rebel jails.

In the fall of 1988 when Baltodano had first presented Jhonson with the four-inch-thick sheaf of interviews documenting the abuses, Bermúdez had warned Jhonson not to pursue the case. When Jhonson discovered the Quilalí murder, he was too busy to focus on the older charges, but during the months after the Quilalí tribunal's verdict, Jhonson and Joshua turned their attention to building the case against the counterintelligence interrogators.

The case threatened the men responsible for the army's worst brutality, and Jhonson and his investigators encountered immediate intimidation. Mack sent Britolde "X-Seven" Cruz—the hard-eyed former Guardsman who had strangled Krill near Mack's Alauca base six years earlier—to circulate a petition through the Yamales Valley denouncing Jhonson as a Sandinista agent. Jhonson shrugged that off, but when a group of armed contras threatened to kill Joshua if he continued to poke around in the case, Jhonson told Joshua to seek protection from the American embassy. There, however, a U.S. official working as a liaison with the contras shrugged his shoulders. There wasn't really much protection the Americans could offer, he said.

Even more intimidated were the witnesses whose testimony Jhonson needed if a tribunal was to convict the torturers. All were ex-prisoners, and most had left the Resistance; some were living in UN refugee camps in Honduras, others were in Danlí and Tegucigalpa. Several were women who'd been raped in contra stockades. Most refused to testify; what protection did they have against reprisals from the defendants who had already tortured them and were still influential within the contra army?

Despite the obstacles, Jhonson was cobbling together a case and a tribunal when Aristides Sánchez pulled him aside in July. Suspend your investigation, Sánchez warned Jhonson, everyone is sick of your meddling. Even the State Department is tired of human-rights crusading, Sánchez said. "Leave people alone."²²

Jhonson called Washington to speak with Bert Charneco, his main State Department liaison. Was Sánchez right? Had the Americans called for him to ease up? Charneco called Sánchez a liar. He assured Jhonson that the Department wanted him to persevere. But Jhonson wasn't sure of American intentions. Ever since Congress had passed the latest contra humanitarian aid law in April, he'd felt none of the fervent U.S. pressure for human-rights action that had been incessant before Congress voted.²³ Then Mack was absolved and reinstated, the Central American Presidents signed their Tela accord, and Jhonson's remaining hopes for the counterintelligence case crumbled. When a commanders' tribunal met at Yamales in the week after the Tela summit to hear the charges, several witnesses failed to appear and the field commanders on the panel summarily acquitted Mike Lima and every other accused interrogator still belonging to the Resistance.

That was the end of Jhonson's investigative work. Within days, he watched his team fall apart as half of the dozen young commandos on Joshua's staff at Yamales deserted from the rebel army, slipping away to travel as illegals to the United States.

Even Marta Patricia Baltodano gave up on her long fight to reform the contras. "We lost the battle," she said at the time and moved back to Nicaragua to return to monitoring Sandinista rights abuses.

It was a demoralizing period. Jhonson learned of hundreds of fighters who were drifting away by requesting weekend passes to Danlí or Tegucigalpa, then heading north toward the U.S. border. He knew that among the deserters were many of the army's brightest, most capable commandos: radio operators, U.S.-trained paramedics, intelligence analysts, young staff officers in the regional commands.²⁴

At the same time, the U.S. embassy in Tegucigalpa was extending to some contras the right to travel to the United States legally, some even with the much-coveted status of refugees. Virtually all were members of

Bermúdez's clique—because only Bermúdez enjoyed the influence to arrange U.S. approval of rebel visa requests. Several contras to whom the Americans extended the privilege to move to the United States legally were well-known killers. Armando "The Policeman" López, Bermúdez's murderous supply officer, moved to Orlando, Florida. César "Six-Seven" Tijerino, whose rebel salary State Department officials had suspended earlier in the year for his part as a torturer, moved to Hialeah. Leonte "Atila" Arias, who in 1985 had ordered Sandinista prisoners executed after a rebel takeover of the Nicaraguan village of Cuapa, moved to Miami. Bermúdez's longtime personal secretary, Ernesto Ortega, moved to West Palm Beach—and with him went his sister Rina, Bermúdez's former lover.

Perhaps the most symbolic move came when Mike Lima flew to Miami and took work as a security guard.

Mack, however, was *not* leaving. Now forty-five, he was back on the general staff. He'd been paying dues in the National Guard and the contras for more than thirty years, he'd learned the subtleties of military command, and now he was nursing new ambitions. After Mike Lima's departure, Mack took over the counterintelligence staff and brought several ex-Guardsmen who had been with him since La Lodosa onto his new payroll. Firing Lima's deputy, he replaced him with Francisco "Jersey" Larios; another of his new agents was X-Seven, his executioner from the old days. Mack used his friendship with Franklyn to extend his powers. Franklyn had never served in a regular army, and as he grappled with the complexities of military administration, he leaned increasingly on his friend Mack. As a result, Mack was able to install his own people in other key command posts.[25]

Mack's main powers, however, continued to derive from his control of the intelligence and counterintelligence operations. That command gave him two CIA-financed safe houses in Tegucigalpa, three CIA-paid vehicles, and the authority to handle two clandestine CIA-funded payrolls. After all that had become known about Mack's violent past, Jhonson was certain the CIA would move quickly to end the Agency's clandestine funding for intelligence and counterintelligence operations after Mack's reinstatement. As the weeks passed, however, Jhonson realized he was wrong. Mack was prospering.

For Jhonson, though, the contras' power struggles seemed increasingly futile. The call by the Central American Presidents for the Resistance's quick demobilization was forcing rebel leaders to make difficult decisions. U.S. influence was waning; Jhonson thought it was time to accept that peaceful avenues of opposition to the Sandinistas were reopening.

In mid-fall, during a visit to Miami, Jhonson had a long discussion with Azucena Ferrey, the former Resistance director who had returned to Nicaragua in June. Visiting Miami to encourage exiles to participate in the upcoming elections, she explained why she was optimistic about the balloting scheduled for February 1990. During lengthy negotiations with the fourteen-party anti-Sandinista coalition, the National Opposition Union (UNO), President Daniel Ortega had agreed to a package of electoral reforms that was sure to make fraud very difficult, and hundreds of international observers were already arriving in Managua to monitor the campaign. Moreover, the nomination of Violeta Chamorro, the silver-haired widow of the anti-Somoza newspaper publisher, had ensured that the opposition would avoid a vote-splitting proliferation of candidates.[26]

It all looked promising, Ferrey told Jhonson. The biggest risk was that the Sandinistas might call off the election—but that only seemed possible if the contras were to flood into Nicaragua and carry out attacks. Ferrey emphasized to Jhonson the importance of participation by some rebel commanders in the vote: They could galvanize support for the opposition, move the country toward reconciliation, and demonstrate that the contras weren't all militarists and would accept a political solution.

Jhonson liked the idea. He returned to Tegucigalpa, drove straight to Yamales, and met with Joshua, his legal staff, and several other close friends in the army to discuss a return to Nicaragua to campaign in the elections. Jhonson's enthusiasm spread to his men, so he walked into the chief of staff's tent and told Franklyn he wanted to lead a contingent of rebels who would fly to Managua to represent the Nicaraguan Resistance in the elections.

"That's a stupid idea," Franklyn responded. Violeta Chamorro? "She's a white, oligarchic bitch," he said. Sandinista victory was certain in the elections; they would rig the balloting. "The Sandinista Front is an armed party. The only way to confront it is with a rifle in your hand."

Franklyn was preparing for prolonged war. In mid-fall, he ordered thousands of commandos back into Nicaragua to put them out of reach of the United Nations monitors who, under the terms of the Tela Accord, were to oversee rebel demobilization. Throughout the war, rebel troops had carried bundles of U.S.-supplied cash to finance food and other supply purchases from local peasants. Now they were marching into Nicaragua with neither cash nor food.

"Learn to survive like guerrillas!" Jhonson heard Franklyn shout at departing troops during one send-off at Yamales. Many commandos considered it unfair, but they saw no other choice but to follow orders.

Jhonson's conversations with the troops reminded him how little democracy the commandos of the contra army had ever enjoyed. Throughout the war, their lot had been to accept orders from above, like so many workers on some tropical plantation. During Bermúdez's long command, anyone who had seriously protested the dictates handed down from the CIA through Bermúdez had faced reprisals ranging from deportation to execution. This had all seemed the natural order of things during a war, but now Franklyn and the general staff were barking out orders in the same autocratic way even though a cease-fire had been in effect for nearly two years, the Sandinistas were organizing elections, and the decisions at hand were no longer military but political.

It made Jhonson angry. One night he typed an indignant letter, protesting the infiltration of commandos into Nicaragua without supplies and without consultation. The time had passed when a handful of leaders should be making choices affecting the lives of thousands of rebels. From now on, Jhonson urged, every fighter in the force should have a chance to participate in the decisions about the army's future. The next day Jhonson, Joshua, and what was left of their legal staff distributed the letter to all the field commanders in the Yamales Valley.

Franklyn's operations chief, Marcos "Black Dimas" Navarro, fired an angry message back at Jhonson, warning him never again to distribute documents unapproved by the general staff. There was personal fury in the message, and Jhonson thought he knew why—war, for Dimas, had been lucrative. Stories had long circulated about his involvement in death squad killings, cattle rustling, and drug trafficking. Jhonson had heard complaints that Dimas was even deploying his troops to pan for gold in the rivers near his border camp. He'd taken to draping his neck and wrists with heavy gold jewelry, he owned a fleet of cars and jeeps, and he had purchased a wood-working factory in Choluteca. His wealth had become an embarrassment to the Resistance.[27]

Jhonson sensed that Dimas's anger was part of a wider unwillingness among the members of the general staff to give up their newly acquired perquisites of power. Feeling defiant, Jhonson sent a message back to Black Dimas: "The Sandinistas couldn't silence me—and you won't either."

Over the next weeks, Jhonson grew only more convinced that he was right and the general staff was wrong. On October 21, contras operating in the south-central mountains used a Claymore mine to ambush a truckload of thirty-two Sandinista reservists on their way to register to vote in the elections. Nine soldiers died. Days later, President Ortega canceled the nineteen-month old cease-fire and seemed close to canceling the elections—using just the rationale about which Ferrey had warned.[28]

The contras reacted by stepping up their preparations for war. In November, Bermúdez, Franklyn, and Mack flew to San Salvador for a meeting at Ilopango Air Force Base with Salvadoran military officers. The Salvadoran Army had captured large stocks of Soviet-made munitions from the Marxist-led FMLN guerrillas during an insurgent offensive in November 1989, and the contra leaders asked the Salvadorans to turn the captured munitions over to them for use against the Sandinistas. Their secret proposal violated the central theme of the two-year-old regional peace accord to which El Salvador was a signatory, and, perhaps fearing new international controversy, the Salvadorans rejected the contra request.

To Jhonson, the entire exercise was a militarist fantasy entertained by men who couldn't see that the world was changing. He'd never felt more alienated from the rebel leadership. "They've made war a way of life," he told a reporter. He called Joshua and a handful of other aides and friends into Tegucigalpa for new talks about the rebels' future. Jhonson could see that they, too, wanted a change, and they decided to return to Managua to participate in the elections without general staff approval. On December 21, Jhonson typed up and delivered a letter to Franklyn:

> We've concluded that the armed struggle is no longer the way for our organization. We believe that the electoral process in Nicaragua is the result of our efforts and the sacrifices of our dead and wounded. Therefore, we've decided to go back to Nicaragua to participate . . . as opposition activists, to continue our struggle for democracy. We expect that some may misunderstand our decision, but we hope you will see that we are betraying neither our organization nor our cause nor our principles. . . . We are going not to Miami, but to Nicaragua.[29]

The next morning, Jhonson, Joshua, and the eight other commandos who signed the letter visited the Nicaraguan embassy in Tegucigalpa to request guarantees that if they returned to Nicaragua, they wouldn't be "interrogated, investigated, detained, imprisoned, harassed, or conscripted." Jhonson was the only high-ranking contra commander who had accepted the government's long-standing invitation for rebel commanders to participate in the elections, and the Sandinista ambassador, Francisco Lacayo, treated Jhonson and the other commandos courteously. He promised to obtain Sandinista government approval for a document spelling out the guarantees Jhonson had requested. United Nations peace-keeping officials, working in Central America at the request of the Central American Presidents, promised to monitor Sandinista compliance and to help with the logistics of the rebels' return. After visiting the Nicaraguan embassy, Jhonson flew to Miami to tell his wife and sons of his decision.

On Christmas Eve, after receiving Jhonson's letter, Franklyn sent a radio message to every unit in the contra army:

> The decision of Commander Jhonson referring to his travel to Nicaragua was personal. It violates the policies of the Nicaraguan Resistance. When he goes to Nicaragua, Jhonson and those who travel with him will cease to belong to our organization.[30]

Jhonson was sitting in his wife's Miami apartment the day after Christmas when the phone rang. It was Joshua's brother, a twenty-five-year-old commando named "Cris," calling from Tegucigalpa. He said that Franklyn had called the general staff and hundreds of troops together for a meeting that morning in Yamales. "I thought you'd want to know," Cris said. "Franklyn said you were a traitor, that you had abandoned the struggle. He said you had deserted from the organization, and that if you returned to the camps, he'd have you detained and shot. He said, 'Traitors don't deserve to live.' "

Later there was another call from Tegucigalpa, from Jhonson's long-time secretary. Jersey, the former Guardsman who was Mack's counterintelligence chief, had driven to Jhonson's office, accompanied by several stone-faced agents. They'd shoved their way into the office, saying they had orders to take an inventory, and were rummaging through Jhonson's legal files. His secretary had gotten a glimpse inside a couple of the men's attaché cases; they were carrying small automatic rifles.

Jhonson told her to go home. He apologized for not being able to help her more, then hung up.[31]

"Sons of bitches," he said to himself. He stomped out of his wife's apartment onto the open-air, second-story hallway. The long, sagging building hugging a fetid canal on Miami's West Flagler Street looked more like a cheap motel than a residence. Leaning his elbows on the railing, Jhonson stared down into the parking area, littered by half a dozen junk cars. Trash was spilling out of an overloaded dumpster in the center of the lot. Down the hallway to his right, someone had discarded a ruined air conditioner. It was blocking the stairs. He turned to lean his back against the rail. Somebody, Jhonson couldn't remember who—perhaps one of his sons—had years earlier stuck a plastic, blue-and-white decal that said NICARAGUA on the apartment door. Now it was peeling away.

"It's time to go home," Jhonson said.

January and February 1990

Jhonson's mother, half a dozen siblings, and scores of friends and journalists were waiting when Jhonson, Joshua, and seven other rebels touched down at Managua's César Augusto Sandino Airport on January 8, 1990. Jhonson hadn't seen his mother for nine years, and when he stepped into the terminal and swept her into his arms, he couldn't control his tears.

"My son!" his mother wept, oblivious to the glare of the television lights. "God brought you back to me."

Jhonson hadn't seen his brother Francisco, now a Sandinista army captain, since he had taken Francisco captive three years before. When Jhonson stuck out his hand, Francisco stared at him sullenly, and there was a moment of tension. Then Francisco cracked a grin, Jhonson broke out laughing, and they, too, embraced.

Several television channels broadcast their airport encounter worldwide as a symbol of the accelerating Nicaraguan peace process. For Jhonson, it was the beginning of a personal reconciliation that over the next weeks proved occasionally exhilarating, sometimes depressing, often difficult, always surprising. Jhonson's war was finally over. After years as Commander Jhonson, he again became Luis Fley.[32]

He hadn't seen Managua for a decade, and as he and the eight other rebels drove in a United Nations jeep to a hotel, he got his first impressions of the destruction wrought on the capital by war and economic erosion. Sandinista campaigners had hung black-and-red party banners from light posts in the median strip of the airport boulevard to dress up the city for foreign visitors in advance of the elections, but Managua was too ruined to decorate. The banners hung limp, seemingly exhausted in the city's foul heat. South of the boulevard, Fley saw a parking lot jammed with the wrecked hulks of Soviet Army trucks sitting on blocks, stripped of wheels and every other salvageable part. Past the Camino Real Hotel, a warren of clapboard-and-carton shacks cobbled together by hundreds of squatters sprawled across a dry creek bed. At a stoplight blocks farther, a barefoot old woman with swollen ankles limped toward Fley's vehicle, leaning on a stick, hand outstretched, begging. A pack of filthy children rushed to Fley's window to hawk newspapers, cigarettes, and chewing gum. Along the earthen path edging the road, even the best-dressed pedestrians looked shabby. Many were in rags. Across a weed-choked railroad siding, crumbling factories and battered warehouses, smeared with a decade's accumulation of revolutionary slogans, stretched through Managua's churning dust into the distance. By the time Fley and his companions arrived at their hotel, they were thoroughly demoralized. Managua was a moonscape, a war zone.

Fley's return to Nicaragua aroused considerable interest among the hundreds of journalists covering the election, and a Dutch television production company decided to produce a half-hour documentary on Fley and his divided family. Fley traveled with the video crew north to El Cuá, the town 145 miles northeast of Managua where he had been living before he joined Tigrillo's contra band in 1981, and along the road Fley stopped to point out the frontier farmhouse he'd built more than a decade earlier. The Sandinistas had long since turned the property over to a peasant supporter. As the Dutch crew filmed, a cattle truck with more than twenty peasants clinging to its rear bed drove by slowly. One of the peasants recognized Fley.

"It was your farm before, you contra son of a bitch," the Sandinista shouted, "but now it belongs to the people." Fley wheeled, but couldn't pick the heckler out of the crowd of faces. Minutes later, along the dirt street running through the center of El Cuá, he saw how the once sleepy village had become a virtual garrison. East German army trucks jammed the street; uniformed soldiers loitered everywhere. Fley found the house he'd built fifteen years earlier, now occupied by El Cuá's Sandinista army commander.

Fley's arrival created a sensation. Dozens of peasants mobbed him, shaking his hand and shouting greetings. Several wives of Fley's former contra combatants approached. Some expressed irritation that Fley, who had recruited their husbands into the contras, had returned alone.

"Why isn't my husband with you?" one woman asked.

"Patience, señora," Fley said. "He'll come back."

Fley had to confirm to a teenager that her father was seven years dead. She went away weeping.

Fley was eating lunch with the Dutch video crew at the town's only eatery when he chanced into his first political debate. "Luis Fley!" a man's voice called out from a nearby table. "Aren't you even going to say hello?"

He turned and saw Nicolás Herrera, thirty-four, the Sandinista political chief in El Cuá. Fley had been friends with Herrera as a teenager, but Herrera, wearing a T-shirt urging Daniel Ortega's reelection to the presidency, was in the mood for an argument.

"So you've decided to give up the war the Americans imposed on us to destroy the revolution," Herrera said to Fley. "What about the other mercenaries? Will they give up too?" Fley listened for a while as a crowd of peasants gathered, and the Dutch crew pushed aside their plates to grab their cameras. Finally Fley interrupted.

"You think I'm a mercenary?" Fley asked.

"No, I don't mean you," Herrera said. "I mean all the other contras that are in Honduras living off the CIA."

"Let me tell you something. They're just peasants," Fley said. "Farmers who had no other choice but to go to war because of government abuses. You Sandinistas tried to impose a system that went against all our idiosyncrasies as Nicaraguans."

"No, no, this was a war of aggression that's cost our country fifty thousand lives," Herrera said. "Now it's time to end it."

"The war can't end by one side imposing its ideas on the other. There's got to be a democratic process. Clean elections. Will the Sandinista Front let the people decide their future freely?"

"Look around, Luis," Herrera said. "That's what we're doing. We've invited thousands of observers so there'll be no doubt about whether we Sandinistas want a true democracy."

"We'll see," Fley said. "Right now I'm going to buy you a Coke." Herrera grinned, and the political discussion ended.

"You took a great step, coming back," Herrera said as Fley departed.[33]

Back in Managua, Fley registered to vote and hit the campaign trail as an activist for the National Opposition Union, the UNO. Fley's first rally was in a Pacific coast village southwest of Managua. As a crowd of straw-hatted peasants awaited the arrival of Violeta Barrios de Chamorro, the publisher of the opposition daily *La Prensa* who was the UNO's presidential candidate, somebody introduced Fley.

"This is Luis Fley, until recently known as Commander Jhonson," the announcer said. "Until now, he's been defending our freedom with weapons and troops. Now he's taken up the civic struggle." Fley was embarrassed, but he climbed up on the platform by the side of a dirt road.

"I've given up the war to come home and participate in this other struggle," he said, "the struggle to democratize Nicaragua. It's the same fight I was waging before."

It was the first of many rallies Fley addressed over the next weeks, traveling in caravans from the cattle ranches of the central hill country to the coffee towns dotting the northern highlands. In the village of Río Blanco, in the heart of the eastern Matagalpa mountains where he'd fought in the 1987 CIA-financed offensive, thousands of peasants trudged through a drizzling rain to rally for UNO, applauding long and loud when Fley was introduced. Days later, Fley stood on a platform alongside the Roman Catholic cathedral in Matagalpa to address some thirty thousand cheering anti-Sandinistas.[34]

At virtually every rally, international election observers mingled with the crowd. Months earlier, the Organization of American States and the United Nations had sent a total of some 670 observers into Nicaragua, and the number was mounting daily as new groups flooded in. (By election day, between two thousand and three thousand foreign observers were in Nicaragua.) Their presence helped Fley overcome his skepticism about the possibility of free elections. He couldn't see any way the Sandinistas would be able to repudiate the results.[35]

At the same time, his conviction that the Sandinistas were going to lose the vote—badly—grew. Tens of thousands of people were out of work, Nicaraguans were sick of the incompetence of the Sandinista bureaucrats, and most of all, people complained of exhaustion with army recruitment and militarism, with war and weaponry. The ground swell for peace was playing against the Sandinistas. The contras had been largely inactive for nearly two years, bivouacked in Honduras or camped quietly inside Nicaragua, and Nicaraguans were blaming the country's continued war-related hardships on the government, which despite the diminished contra threat had refused to reduce the size of the army or end the draft.

At several rallies, however, peasants approached Fley to complain of new contra abuses: Rebel numbers were mounting in the countryside, and some were extorting money from peasants and stealing livestock. Fley could see what was happening: Rebel units ordered into Nicaragua were hungry and were resorting to abuses and extortion to survive. Scattered contra attacks on government units threatened to give the Sandinistas new excuses for canceling the election.

In February, Fley flew to Tegucigalpa to ship his personal belongings to Managua. For security, he stayed at the home of Alfonso Sandino, the forty-two-year-old attorney who was Marta Patricia Baltodano's top human-rights aide, and during the day, he worked out of Sandino's Nicaraguan Association for Human Rights office in suburban Tegucigalpa. The office had become a kind of hospitality center for Resistance fighters visiting Tegucigalpa, and Fley had an opportunity to chat with dozens of commandos there. Several conversations plunged him back into the underworld of violence and conspiracy that had become a distasteful memory since his return to Nicaragua.

One contra leader who had worked for years in the southern Honduras town of Choluteca pulled Fley aside for a furtive conversation.

The man was terrified. His sister had been murdered weeks earlier, he said, amid a wave of assassinations of Nicaraguan exiles in Choluteca. More than a dozen contra fighters had been killed in the preceding four months, he added, several gunned down in the streets, gangland-style. The frightened man told Fley that contra assassins were eliminating rebels who had witnessed crimes earlier in the war.[36]

And yet another conversation with Alfonso Sandino was even more depressing for Fley. He knew he'd been defeated in his human-rights showdown with Mack, but nonetheless Fley believed he'd cleaned up the system. Now Fley learned to his dismay that Mack's counterintelligence section—under Francisco "Jersey" Larios, who had seized Fley's own office six weeks earlier—had again begun seizing and brutalizing commandos.

In mid-January a contra fighter had approached Dr. Ramiro Granera, thirty-two, one of the exiled Nicaraguan physicians serving in the medical corps, at the contras' Yamales hospital. The fighter wanted Granera to come with him to treat an injured commando. Granera drove with the commando several miles to a secluded campsite he'd never before visited: the counterintelligence interrogation center.

The injured commando was Bernardo Rocha, a fifty-year-old former peasant who had been fighting in the rebel army for eight years. Rocha's right eye was cut, his face badly bruised, and his back lacerated with bloody welts. Jersey, Mack's counterintelligence chief, was standing by.

"What happened to this man?" Dr. Granera asked.

"He fell down," Jersey said.

Granera, a traumatologist, could see that Rocha had been beaten, badly. The welts on his back looked to have been inflicted by a cudgel.

"This commando didn't fall down. He's been tortured," Granera shot back at Jersey. "I won't treat him here in this jail. Bring him up to the hospital."

After Rocha gained his strength in the hospital, he made his way into Tegucigalpa with two other commandos whom Jersey had tortured. All three told Sandino that Jersey had accused them of being Sandinista infiltrators.[37]

Little had changed, it seemed, in the shadows of the rebel army, and at the top, Fley found the same power struggles. Only days after his arrival, Fley read a Resistance communiqué announcing that Mack, Franklyn, and the general staff had stripped Bermúdez of his title as "commanding general." Bermúdez, finally, was out.

The final blow to Bermúdez had come when Colonel Gómez, Bermúdez's "air force chief," had sold several Resistance aircraft and some navigational equipment, and pocketed the money. Gómez couldn't have carried out the transaction without Bermúdez's connivance, and Sánchez, Mack, and Bermúdez's other enemies used the incident to engineer Bermúdez's ouster.[38]

Late one evening, Bermúdez, looking haggard, arrived at the human-rights office to visit Fley. He seemed at loose ends, but said he wanted to hear Fley's analysis of the Nicaraguan election campaign, so Bermúdez, his aide Bodán, Sandino, and Fley sat down in Sandino's second-story office. Fley reviewed his whirlwind travels through ten of Nicaragua's fourteen provinces.

"You may find this hard to believe, but these elections are going to be clean," Fley said. "And the opposition will win. The Sandinistas just don't have any strength left."

"What do people think of the Resistance?" Bermúdez asked.

"Well, *Comandante*"—Fley slipped unconsciously into his old speech patterns—"it's too bad that the Resistance didn't participate formally in the elections. People sympathize with the commandos, but many people think that we're now just fighting for power. They think we just want to install ourselves in place of the Sandinistas. They remember how the Sandinistas kicked out Somoza and then grabbed power themselves. People fear that we're trying to do the same thing."

Bermúdez listened but seemed distracted. Eventually he turned to Bodán and Sandino.

"Will you permit us a few minutes alone?" he said. Bermúdez led Fley downstairs to a kitchen, where he pulled out the general staff's decree purging him as commanding general.

"Look what they're trying to do to me," Bermúdez said. "It's against all the Resistance statutes. Only the commanders' council can remove me, and the commanders still support me. The troops are upset."

Fley stared at Bermúdez. He suddenly seemed small and very old. Was this the "supreme commander" whose orders he'd obeyed for much of a decade?

Bermúdez started to rail against Aristides Sánchez, whose behind-the-scenes machinations he blamed for his destitution. He called Sánchez a "back-stabbing dog" and a "Judas."

"*Comandante,* you've always picked the wrong friends," Fley said finally. "What you're doing now makes no sense, this squabbling over an organization that's going to disappear. What does it matter who commands the Resistance now? The opposition is going to win the elections, and the people of Nicaragua aren't going to stand for any more war. They're tired of suffering. If you want my opinion, the general staff has done you a good turn by kicking you out. Stop fighting this sterile battle, *Comandante.* Go back to Miami."

It was, for Fley, a liberating moment. When he returned to Nicaragua the week before the February 25 balloting, he felt more than ever that he was going home.

Though curious, Fley didn't attend the Sandinistas' final campaign rally four days before the vote. He was concerned that with spirits running high, Sandinista zealots might identify him as a former contra and lynch him. Instead, he watched on television as some 200,000 Nicaraguans trudged into the Carlos Fonseca Plaza for a costly fireworks display and a clumsy effort by Daniel Ortega to portray himself as a rock star rather than a revolutionary. It was the largest public rally anyone could remember, but Fley figured that many of the "Sandinistas" wearing ORTEGA FOR PRESIDENT T-shirts would end up voting for the opposition.[39]

On election day, Fley stood in line for three hours to vote at a Managua polling place, then visited a friend to await the results. The first unofficial returns were broadcast about 8 P.M. and showed the Sandinistas leading in Jalapa, a town in the far north that had suffered repeated contra attacks during the war. By midnight, however, the opposition had built a healthy lead, and throughout the night as Fley listened to the radio, the Sandinistas never regained their advantage. At 6:30 the next morning, Fley watched Daniel Ortega on television, blinking back tears, deliver a nationally broadcast concession speech. During a decade of war, Fley had come to loathe the mustachioed Sandinista President, but he found his own exultation over the opposition victory tempered by the dignity of Ortega's words.

"We entered these elections convinced that this battle would determine once and for all the end of the war and a time of peace for the Nicaraguan people," Ortega said. "The government will respect and submit to the popular mandate that arose from the vote.

"I believe that in this moment, the principal contribution we Sandinistas can make to the Nicaraguan people is the guarantee of a pure and clean electoral process, which warms our consciences.

"The election will test the will of Sandinista revolutionaries, who never have been wedded to power. . . . We were born poor and will be satisfied to die poor."[40]

In the days after the elections, Fley thought about Nicaragua and its longing for peace, about himself and the war he'd fought.

He'd learned a great deal about the Americans and their lofty rhetoric. These "allies" had used the blood of thousands of peasants to further their own interests and, in the end, had been prepared to dump the rebel army. In the days after the elections, Fley read newspaper reports that U.S. politicians from both parties were rushing to claim credit for the anti-Sandinista triumph. "This was no victory for the Americans. This was a Nicaraguan triumph," he told a reporter.

Fley had lost much: his farm, his home, his youth, even his brother. Sometimes, faced with the wartime abuses committed by his own rebel comrades-in-arms, he'd wondered why he was fighting. Now he was broke and, he had to admit, exhausted. His homeland was wasted by fighting. Had the struggle, finally, been worthwhile?

Shortly after his return to Nicaragua, Fley had spoken angrily to a group of reporters—"The war has brought nothing positive, only blood and death"—but over the weeks, talking to peasants on the campaign trail, watching Nicaragua move toward its first free elections, he regained his perspective. Fley knew that Nicaraguans had won a victory. When the Sandinistas accepted election defeat and agreed to pass on the burden of governing to their opponents—something unprecedented in Nicaraguan history—Fley knew that Nicaragua had grown as a nation.

"I knew I'd have to pay a price for liberty," Fley said, "and I did. But so did thousands of other Nicaraguans."

Epilogue

1990 and 1991

Events moved swiftly after the election. In just four tumultuous months, the contras opened negotiations with the government-elect, marched out of their Honduran bases into Nicaragua, signed an armistice with the Sandinista army, and, in June, surrendered their weapons.

Within days, the army's ten thousand fighters scattered throughout Nicaragua and dropped out of the news. In Washington and in much of the rest of the world, the contras were forgotten. Immersed in a new reporting assignment, I largely forgot about the contras, too. I was in my office in Brazil ten months later when I read the cable out of northern Nicaragua:

AGUASMARIAS, Nicaragua—A small band of demobilized contras, resentful over their plight in the first year of peace, have picked up assault rifles and resumed their lives as roving guerrillas in the rugged mountains of northern Nicaragua.

The guerrillas, baptized the "re-contra" by local peasants, number 150 to 200 in several contingents. . . . Although they are few and their return to arms is recent, the rebels have become a powerful symbol of widespread discontent among former members of the U.S.-sponsored Nicaraguan Resistance.[1]

Ten days later, I read another surprising story, this time an interview from the hills of northern Nicaragua with one of the re-contras: "Comandante Dimas." The bearded figure staring from the newspaper photograph, flanked by two aides with AK-47s, was the same Dimas who, with his older brother Tigrillo, had led one of the first contra bands in 1981.[2]

I was stunned. After a decade of fighting, why would anyone want to go back to war? Full of questions, I flew back to Managua one year after Violeta Chamorro's inauguration.

I found Franklyn, the contra army's last commander, at the Interior Ministry of all places—the heart of Sandinista police power during the war. Asking around, I learned that Franklyn had a staff of seventeen, a thirty-thousand-dollar four-wheel-drive Toyota Land Cruiser, and a new title: "Director of Inter-institutional Coordination." His top assistant was . . . Commander Mack.

Franklyn had decorated his air-conditioned office in an unmarked two-story building a block from Interior Ministry headquarters with one framed photo—of himself. We reminisced for a time about the early days. His war had begun in the blood and flames of the same 1981 ambush of a Sandinista jeep outside El Cuá that had brought Luis Fley into the contras. "We planned that attack on my farm!" Franklyn recalled.

Now that he was working for the postwar government, Franklyn was pleased to report that General Humberto Ortega and other Sandinista officials were treating him with respect, even cordiality. Franklyn's job, he said, was to fly around Nicaragua in an army helicopter talking to peasants in order to "identify their needs so that the government can solve them."

What about the re-contras? I asked. That made him mad. These were not contras, he said, just bandits and thugs unwilling to work for a living.

Years earlier, at the dawn of the war, Sandinista officials had spoken in precisely these terms about Franklyn, Tigrillo, Dimas Tigrillo, Luis Fley, and the others who laid the El Cuá ambush. These were not true guerrillas with legitimate grievances, the Sandinistas said—just bandits and thugs.

I arranged to see Rubén, the contra's general staff officer who became the rebels' top negotiator. He was now deputy minister of repatriation, the top-ranking contra in the Chamorro government. When he swept up to the lobby entrance of the Intercontinental Hotel in a new Land Cruiser with smoked-glass windows—just like Franklyn's—aides jumped out to open doors and a public-relations spokesman cleared the way.

Over a coffee shop breakfast of tortillas and eggs, I asked: Why are some former contras going back to war? Rubén conceded that a few ex-rebels were taking up arms again, mostly for self-defense. But fueling their frustrations, he said, was poverty. He began to sound like one of those early, earnest Sandinistas, eager to yank Nicaragua out of under-development.

"Our peasants need health centers, they need schools, they need financing, they need fair prices for their crops, they need roads," Rubén said. "The problem is that the government can't provide these things now. It's broke."

Events had come full circle. Nicaraguan peasants had fought for a decade in a war that destroyed scores of health centers, schools, farms, grain storage facilities, and road-building machines. Not surprisingly, their circumstances now seemed more desperate than ever.

I reviewed the events of the fifteen months that followed the 1990 elections. Violeta Chamorro's victory utterly bewildered the contra general staff; having sought military satisfaction with such fervor for so long, they were unprepared for political satisfaction. But in the days after the elections, they were suddenly under immense pressure. The U.S. aid that had sustained them for nine years was to run out at the end of April. The Hondurans no longer wanted them in their border camps, and the Bush Administration—fearful that the contras might somehow jettison Washington's windfall political victory—no longer wanted them at all.

After the elections, the contras faced an ambiguous political transition. They still had the leverage of their arms, but because they had refused to participate in the voting, they had no formal role to play in postwar Nicaragua. Their blunder became obvious after elections in Colombia, where on March 8, 1990, the M-19 guerrillas agreed to disarm and to participate in elections—and just two months later placed third in a national vote that entitled the party to several cabinet posts.

The Resistance, certainly no less popular in Nicaragua, could have done as well; Luis Fley had urged the general staff to field candidates. Now their anti-election intransigence complicated the transition from war to politics. And Franklyn, Mack, Rubén, Aristides Sánchez, and the other top contras showed no better judgment once peace negotiations got under way. Instead of concentrating on their longtime political goals, they began scheming about government jobs. Suddenly they saw Nicaragua as a pie, and they wanted their piece of it.

In their first talks with Chamorro's transition team, Rubén and Aristides Sánchez cut a deal they thought would buy some time. After March 23 talks at Tegucigalpa's Toncontín Airport, they signed a pact committing the rebels *based in Honduras* to turn their weapons over to

United Nations peacekeeping troops by April 20, five days before Chamorro's April 25 inauguration. But even as Rubén was signing the Toncontín pact, the main contra force—some ten thousand contras and another ten thousand peasant relatives—was streaming south out of the Honduras camps into Nicaragua. As a result, when UN troops moved to collect the rebel army's rifles at Yamales a month later on April 18, only a small rear guard of mostly disabled contras was left. The UN impounded only 365 arms.

But the following day in Managua, April 19, Rubén signed two new agreements, the first committing the rebels now inside Nicaragua to gather in seven demilitarized "safety zones," the second ordering the rebels to turn in their weapons after Chamorro's inauguration. These accords brought the contras one psychological victory: They held on to their arms until Daniel Ortega relinquished the presidency. That made them feel like winners.[3]

So, when Chamorro was sworn into office in a riotous ceremony in Managua's main baseball stadium on April 25, UN peacekeeping forces oversaw the physical separation of nearly ten thousand contras from the seventy-thousand-strong government army, still led by Sandinista officers. On inauguration day, the contra general staff—Franklyn, Rubén, Mack, Sánchez, and other top officers—were lying around in hammocks at a farm in a security enclave eighty-five miles north of Managua. At one point, Franklyn got up to make an anti-Sandinista speech for the benefit of visiting reporters, then invited his men to surrender their arms. Everyone broke out in laughter. "Nobody gives up his gun!" shouted one rebel. Everybody cheered.[4] But this was bluster. In two more rounds of negotiations over the next month at Managua's Olof Palme Convention Center, Franklyn, Rubén, Mack, and other rebel negotiators pledged to Chamorro aides that they would conclude their demobilization by June 10.[5]

Finally, large numbers of contras began to hand over their rifles. Nearly five hundred surrendered weaponry on May 30 alone, and over the next ten days, six thousand others followed. In a June 9 ceremony in a grass-covered square in El Almendro, a village 120 miles southeast of Managua, President Chamorro presided over the mass disarmament of two thousand troops and half a dozen top commanders—including Mack. UN troops, using blowtorches, cut up the weaponry on the spot.

Franklyn, who addressed the troops and townspeople wearing a baseball hat that read 44 MAGNUM: GOD'S FAVORITE CALIBER, held on to his weapon for three more weeks. Then, in a war's end ceremony led by President Chamorro in the town of San Pedro de Lóvago on June 27, Franklyn and a handful of other commanders turned over their weapons.[6]

Among the arms the contras surrendered for destruction were more than one hundred Redeye missiles; at that, U.S. officials heaved a sigh of relief. Concerned that the sophisticated missiles might find their way into the Central American arms trade, the Bush Administration had sent a U.S. military officer to El Almendro to negotiate with Franklyn for the Redeyes. Although the missiles had been donated to the Resistance as part of the 1987 $100 million assistance, Franklyn demanded some form of U.S. payment for their return. Eventually Franklyn accepted a trade—pickup trucks for missiles—and on June 26 and 27, contra *missileros* surrendered the Redeyes. The new trucks didn't arrive in Nicaragua until months later, but many ex-fighters learned about the trade right away, and it fueled a mounting furor about the deals their leaders were cutting.[7]

Three weeks after the demobilization, the former general staff and nearly one hundred other ex-commanders packed into the tiny El Almendro schoolhouse. They intended to found an organization to represent them henceforth inside Nicaragua: the Civic Association of the Nicaraguan Resistance. But a second agenda focused on Mack and Franklyn. Hearing in advance of trouble, Mack didn't attend, and that was just as well. Soon into the meeting, several of his own intelligence aides, men who had been with him at La Lodosa and at the CIM, stood to denounce him of thievery, cruelty to commandos, and other old abuses familiar to everyone. And Rodolfo "Invisible" Ampie—who had preceded Mack as intelligence chief and had returned from a two-year sojourn in Miami to become Rubén's closest aide—leveled new accusations.

At the climax of the contra-Sandinista peace negotiations in late May, Sandinista military intelligence chief Ricardo Wheelock had invited Mack, Invisible, and several other contra commanders to a meeting with General Ortega in the Sandinista army headquarters in the El Chipote installation behind the Intercontinental Hotel in downtown Managua, Invisible said. General Ortega wanted to discuss details of the peace agreement, but the conversation wandered once the longtime enemies sat down together in the Sandinista bunker.

"*Mi general*, we need vehicles to get around in. Can you help us?" Mack had asked Ortega, Invisible told the contras at El Almendro. Mack had adopted an annoying, ingratiating tone, Invisible said.

"We were supposed to be talking about demilitarization," Invisible said, "and Mack was pleading for vehicles, asking for little favors. And when we stood up to leave, he said, 'General, would you permit me a moment in private?'—and the two of them went off into another room together. That troubled me."

The day after the El Chipote encounter, Wheelock visited Mack at Managua's Las Mercedes Hotel, where the contra general staff was lodged during the peace talks, Invisible said. There, Wheelock met with Mack, opened an attaché case, and delivered a brick-sized stack of hundred-dollar bills. Another contra commander spoke up at the El Almendro meeting to back Invisible's accusations. He said he'd seen Mack accept the money from Wheelock—he guessed as much as fifty thousand dollars changed hands—and said he believed Mack had shared the money with Franklyn. A day or two later, aides to Wheelock drove five new Toyota Land Cruisers to the Las Mercedes Hotel and delivered them to Mack and Franklyn. Several contras said they had seen the trucks.

Franklyn listened to the charges, then rose to defend himself in a rambling speech. He conceded that he'd received money—he said five thousand dollars—from Wheelock, but he insisted that he had used the money for negotiating expenses and had distributed four of the Land Cruisers, one each, to the other members of the general staff. That embarrassed Rubén, who also took one of the trucks, but he was controlling the meeting. Franklyn's explanations didn't go down well.

The El Almendro assembly voted to expel Mack from the organization. Franklyn was told he could stay on in the Civic Association—as secretary. Rubén would be its president. Furious, Franklyn drove back to Managua and quit.[8] Soon thereafter, he and Mack began their new work with the Interior Ministry.

For their part, Rubén and Invisible moved into the posh, computer-equipped Managua offices of the Civic Association, which gave them control over a six-digit budget, two dozen patronage jobs, and the fleet of pickup trucks Washington had traded for the Redeyes. Soon, Rubén had also received from the Chamorro government an ostentatious, lakeside mansion in the southern Nicaraguan city of Rivas.[9]

By the fall, the dust had settled enough from this turbulent transition for many former fighters to see how the war had ended. After fighting for a decade and negotiating for months, many of the contras' longtime political goals were unachieved. Chamorro had abolished the draft and outlined a plan to slash the size of the military, but Sandinistas were still dominating Nicaragua's army, police, and Supreme Court as well as the country's trade unions and peasant organizations. In the contras' own negotiations with the government, they had leveraged little more than promises: that Nicaragua's security forces would pass from Sandinista control, that the government would ensure the safety of former contras in the countryside, that rebel widows and disabled would receive pensions, that the government would turn over to former contras vast tracts of land.

The contras' negotiators cashed out with government jobs, new trucks, and luxury properties. In contrast, the war's end for most contra fighters was bleak; every contra who turned over his weapon became eligible for a change of clothing, a few farm tools, a fifty-dollar U.S.-financed start-up grant, and a few months' rations of rice and beans. That was it.

During the Managua talks in May, Franklyn had bargained away several rebel political demands in exchange for a government commitment to donate unused land near El Almendro for colonization by ex-contras. He made grandiloquent predictions for the colonies, saying that contra troops-cum-farm laborers would turn them into a string of lush plantations, orchards, and even tourist centers. "We're going to build a great city," he said in one interview.

Within two months of the rebel disarmament, however, the colonization plans degenerated into fiasco. Nearly seven thousand rebels gathered at El Almendro seeking lands, but only about two hundred ever got title. Before the end of the summer, the rest had scattered to other parts of Nicaragua to live with relatives.[10]

The Chamorro government had difficulty keeping other promises, too, like the pension for contra widows. Nicaragua was virtually bankrupt, inflation was still out of control, and despite generous speeches in Washington, U.S. financial aid was disappointing. President Bush requested a $300 million reconstruction package, and a reluctant Congress eventually approved the aid. But with the fervor gone from Washington's relations with Nicaragua, the funds were a long time coming. By early 1991, less than a third of the aid had gotten to Nicaragua.

"What kind of image do the Americans want here?" an official in Chamorro's government asked a U.S. reporter. "Why was it easier for them to give the contras hundreds of millions of dollars for their war than to help a democratic government make peace?"[11]

The ex-contras' frustrations boiled over in the fall of 1990. In a dozen remote communities, bands of former rebels tried to take over cooperative farms defended by pro-Sandinista militants. Armed clashes ensued, leaving several dozen dead and scores wounded. The violence peaked in November, when ex-rebels allied with local peasants blocked the country's main east-west highway for eighteen days. Chamorro eventually ordered army troops to clear the roads. In Managua, police raided a private office that Aristides Sánchez had established, reporting the seizure of numerous rifles, grenades, and other weaponry; they accused Sánchez of masterminding the violent protests. After four days in jail, Sánchez was put on a plane to Miami and his second exile.[12]

About the time of Sánchez's expulsion, Bermúdez flew to Managua for his first visit since the end of the war. He seemed to associates who met with him to be somewhat at loose ends. At the U.S. embassy, he met with David Lindwall, who had been transferred from Tegucigalpa to Miami. Bermúdez told Lindwall that he was kicking around a couple of business ideas; he wanted to export floor tiles to Miami, and was also thinking of setting up an industrial security firm that could employ former contras.

At the same time, Bermúdez hoped to recover two modest homes and a three-acre plot outside Managua that the Sandinistas had confiscated from him. One afternoon, he drove out and talked to Cristobal Navarro, the peasant who in 1982 had been given Bermúdez's acreage as part of a land reform.

"He said these properties were his," Navarro said later. "But I answered that the revolution had given them to me, with documents. He said that was the bad thing about the revolution, that it had distributed lands and left a lot of problems. . . . The conversation was friendly."

In early December, Bermúdez drove north from Managua to the town of La Trinidad, where he had a poignant encounter with several dozen former contras. They all told Bermúdez hard-luck stories: no work, no prospects. "The general staff sold us out cheap," one ex-fighter said. Several contras asked Bermúdez to take their complaints to President Chamorro, but he said that since Rubén and Franklyn had signed the final peace treaty, he had no legal standing. There wasn't much he could do.

Bermúdez flew home to Miami for Christmas, then returned to Managua in mid-January to pursue his property claims. This time, he moved into a sister's nearly empty home in the Bello Horizonte neighborhood, where he lived alone, cooking for himself and washing his own clothes.

On the night of February 16, a phone invitation from a mystery caller lured Bermúdez to the Intercontinental Hotel to meet someone who never showed up. As Bermúdez returned to his Toyota station wagon in the hotel parking lot, a gunman wielding a silenced weapon killed him with one shot through the head. It was a professional hit.

Many Nicaraguans instantly martyrized Bermúdez, reacting to his murder with an outpouring of grief accorded only to popular heroes. Thousands filed past his open coffin in a public wake and mobbed the airport as his remains were loaded aboard a plane for his final flight to Miami, where his wife chose to bury him. Many of the Americans who engineered the contra war attended Bermúdez's funeral at Miami's St. Catherine of Siena Church, including Oliver North, James Adkins, and John Mallett.[13]

Bermúdez's killing symbolized the end of the contra era, but at the same time, by undermining Nicaragua's fragile peace framework, opened new possibilities for violence and instability. Shootings, ambushes, knifings, and other bloodshed marked the first year of contra disarmament; Organization of American States treaty verification officers received reports of thirty-five murdered ex-contras during the year. Four contras disappeared.[14] Many of the killings were committed by former Sandinista State Security officers, most of whom, after Chamorro abolished the hated agency, had simply donned National Police uniforms to continue their vendettas across rural Nicaragua.

Bermúdez's murder convinced many that no former rebel was safe, and it was in this context that several bands of ex-contras began to rearm in the spring of 1991. Francisco "Dimas Tigrillo" Baldivia was one of several former commanders who took up arms. Throughout the war, Dimas had preferred camp life in the remote jungle to the rigors of combat, and some now said that he and the other "re-contras" simply preferred life in the jungle to the rigors of farming. And some of the newly armed ex-contras were, as Franklyn said, simply bandits; after a decade of war, rural Nicaragua was alive with highwaymen. But there were scores of others with serious political frustrations.

Unlike a decade earlier, these rebels would get no foreign aid. The world had changed, and now neither Moscow nor Washington had any interest in financing a Nicaraguan war. Some said the re-contras would just fade away, but I didn't think so. New violence was brewing. To me it looked as though low-level warfare could become endemic. The emergence of the re-contras had served to underline just how little the contra war had accomplished. After a decade of fighting, Nicaragua suffered from all the maladies that had plagued it a decade earlier: elite rule, police corruption and abuse, land hunger, illiteracy, contagion. In the U.S. view, the war that made Washington feel good had come to a storybook conclusion. But in Nicaragua, it was proving harder to move on; the contra war would remain the nation's frame of reference for years to come.

During my May 1991 trip back to Managua, I went to visit Luis Fley. Throughout 1990, he had worked for the OAS, dishing out rice and beans to ex-contras from a warehouse in central Nicaragua. After the Bermúdez killing, President Chamorro had appointed Fley to sit on a commission monitoring the police investigation, and he had moved back to Managua. I found him living in a two-room wood-frame house under a grove of eucalyptus trees on the outskirts of Managua. He looked healthy but broke. He was pleased to have his family back with him, but his sons, reared in Miami on Nintendo and fast food, weren't getting along in the squalor of Managua. But as far as I could see, Fley was one of the few contra leaders who hadn't sold out.

Fley said he sympathized with the plight of the former rebels who were re-arming in the north; everybody felt unsafe after Bermúdez's murder. But the time for war had passed, he said. "Nothing justifies more fighting."

Fley seemed determined to put dogma and rancor behind him. One night in Matagalpa, he sipped sweet coffee and talked politics with his two Sandinista brothers. He tried to explain his choices. He'd never been a mercenary; he'd always fought for ideals. When he'd seen brutality in the rebel force, he had tried to set it right. And when he'd seen the movement's usefulness erode, he came home. It was a brotherly talk, and for the first time Luis believed Jorge and Francisco had begun to see why he had fought his war. "Life under the revolution had become impossible for me," Luis said.

"Undoubtedly, we Sandinistas committed errors, and I recognize them in a spirit of self-criticism," Fley's brother Jorge, the Sandinista army lieutenant, conceded in earnest. Listening, Fley found himself in rare agreement.

"In this war, nobody deserved to die," Jorge said. "Not Enrique, and not anyone else. There's been too much sadness, too many wounds, and they're not going to heal overnight. I guess we'll just have to live with the scars."

"Ideologically, we still don't get along," Fley said later. "But we're brothers. And we're trying to find reconciliation. First, our family. And maybe, someday, the entire Nicaraguan people."

List
of Characters

Abrams, Elliott. Assistant Secretary of State for Inter-American Affairs, 1985–1989.

Adkins, James. The CIA agent and veteran of CIA operations in Laos during the 1960s who was the Agency's base chief in Honduras from 1985 to 1987, succeeding Ray Doty. Oversaw CIA preparations for the contras' 1987 $100 million offensive.

Aguilar, Enrique; "Panchito." The young delegate of the Nicaraguan Association for Human Rights (ANPDH), the contra human-rights organization, in the Quilalí Regional Command.

Aguilar, Roberto; "Robespierre." Contra paramedic in the Quilalí Regional Command who pronounced murder victim Isaac González dead in November 1988.

"Alex" or "Captain Alex." CIA military trainer who worked for the contra war's first Honduras base chief, Ray Doty, from 1981 through 1984.

"Alí." See Herrera Hernández, Antonio.

Alvarez Martínez, Gustavo. The hard-line rightist Honduran general who, as top commander of the Honduran Armed Forces from 1982 to 1984, worked with Washington to establish the contras' logistical rear guard in Honduras. Assassinated, apparently by leftist Honduran guerrillas, in Tegucigalpa in 1989.

Amador, Roberto. Former National Guard Air Force major recruited into the FDN air force in 1983 and shot down by Sandinista troops over Nicaragua weeks later.

Ampie, Rodolfo Ernesto; "Invisible." Former lieutenant in the National Guard elite force known as the EEBI who became a CIA favorite after top contra commander Enrique Bermúdez appointed him intelligence chief in 1984.

Andrade Espinoza, Carlos. Alleged Sandinista spymaster said to have established residence in the Honduran town of Catacamas, adjacent to the contras' Aguacate base, to manage infiltration operations.

Arcos, Cresencio; "*Cris.*" U.S. embassy spokesman in Tegucigalpa, 1981–1985; Deputy Director, The Nicaraguan Humanitarian Assistance Office (NHAO), 1986–1987; Deputy Coordinator, State Department Office of Public Diplomacy, 1987–1988; Coordinator for Public Diplomacy on Central America, The White House, 1988–1989; Deputy Assistant Secretary of State for Inter-American Affairs, 1989; U.S. Ambassador to Honduras, 1990– .

Arias, Leonte; "*Atila.*" Former National Guard lieutenant and contra commander who sparked a human-rights scandal by ordering the execution of Sandinista prisoners in Cuapa in 1985.

"*Atila.*" See Arias, Leonte.

Azcona, José. President of Honduras, 1986–1990.

Baldivia, Encarnación; "*Tigrillo.*" Anti-Sandinista peasant rebel whose gang Jhonson joined in 1981. Became major recruiter for the contras. Deported by the CIA from Honduras to Miami in 1988.

Baldivia, Francisco; "*Dimas Tigrillo.*" Encarnación Baldivia's younger brother, one of the first contras in 1981 and after the contra army's disarmament a decade later, one of the ex-contras who—angered by the terms of the war's settlement—took up arms anew in 1991.

Baltodano, Marta Patricia. Nicaraguan lawyer hired by the State Department to administer a $3 million contra human-rights program, 1986–1990.

Barreda, Tomás. A Nicaraguan peasant whom Tigrillo and Mike Lima accused of being a Sandinista spy and murdered during their first CIA-financed incursion in 1982.

"*Beast, The.*" See López, Jr., Armando.

Bendaña, Iván. A young FDN officer who, many contras charge, was murdered by an FDN death squad in 1982 because he had criticized the rebel leadership.

Bermúdez, Elsa. Enrique Bermúdez's Dominican-born wife.

Bermúdez, Enrique; "*Three-Eighty.*" The former National Guard colonel recruited by the CIA to command the contra army throughout the war. Deposed from his commander's post by contra field commanders working at U.S. behest in February 1990. Assassinated in Managua a year later in February 1991.

"*Black Dimas.*" See Navarro, Marcos.

Blake Hurtado, Isaac Samuel; "*Israelita.*" Contra counterintelligence interrogator who committed a November 1988 murder in the Quilalí Regional Command camp in Yamales, Honduras, that provoked a human-rights scandal. Contras misspelled Blake's last name as "Blecker."

Blandón, Marlon; "*Gorrión.*" Former National Guard lieutenant who as Mack's executive officer witnessed the 1983 strangling of three contra officers.

Bodán, Harry. Former Deputy Foreign Minister under Anastasio Somoza Debayle who was Bermúdez's chief Nicaraguan political adviser from 1987 to 1990.

Bolt, Alan. Pro-Sandinista researcher who denounced abuses by Sandinista revolutionary authorities and troops against pro-contra peasants. Longtime friend of Jhonson's family.

Boyd, Maj. Gen. Charles E. "Chuck." The U.S. Air Force's western hemisphere chief who in 1979 put Enrique Bermúdez in contact with CIA recruiters.

Bravo Centeno, José Benito; "Mack." The former National Guard sergeant who was the contra army's chief trainer through most of the war and the rebels' top intelligence officer from 1988 to 1990.

Briggs, Everett "Ted." U.S. Ambassador to Honduras from 1986 through 1989. President Bush's National Security adviser for Latin America from June through December 1990.

Brown, Timothy. The political officer in the U.S. embassy in Tegucigalpa who coordinated embassy contacts with the Nicaraguan Resistance, 1987–1990.

"Bull, The." See Torres, Donald.

Busby, Morris. State Department's special ambassador for Central America in 1987 and 1988. Told Resistance leaders in Miami after Congress rejected contra aid in February 1988 that further U.S. military assistance was unlikely.

Cabezas, Omar. Sandinista guerrilla whose forces Jhonson encountered in the hills of Jinotega province in Nicaragua during the 1978 war against Anastasio Somoza Debayle. After 1979, he served in high-ranking posts in the Sandinista Interior Ministry and community movement.

Calderón, Walter; "Toño." Former National Guard lieutenant and contra field commander purged from the Nicaraguan Resistance after challenging Enrique Bermúdez in 1988.

Calero, Adolfo. Notre Dame–educated manager of Managua's Coca-Cola bottling plant. The CIA recruited him to move into exile in 1982 and head the FDN's first directorate. Served as a political director of successive contra organizations until mid-1989.

Calero, Mario. Adolfo Calero's younger brother. As the purchaser for the contra army from 1984 through 1986, he was criticized for acquiring shoddy supplies and for profiteering.

Castillo, Noel; "Trickster." Former National Guard lieutenant who was Mike Lima's counterintelligence deputy, 1988–1989.

Centeno Chavarría, Rogelio; "Pantera-Romeo." Rebel helicopter mechanic at Aguacate Air Base accused in 1987 of being a Sandinista spy and tortured by contra interrogators.

"Cerrano." See Morán Gutiérrez, Luis Ariel.

César, Alfredo. Former head of Nicaragua's Central Bank under the Sandinista government, served on the Nicaraguan Resistance directorate from 1987 to 1989, then returned to Nicaragua to campaign for Violeta Barrios de Chamorro. Elected President of the Nicaraguan Congress 1990.

Chamorro, Edgar. The Harvard-educated public-relations executive the CIA recruited as FDN spokesman in 1982. Purged in 1984 for acknowledging publicly that contra forces were committing abuses.

Chamorro Barrios, Pedro Joaquín. The son of Nicaragua's martyred newspaper publisher, Pedro Joaquín Chamorro Cardenal, and Violeta Barrios, who was elected Nicaraguan President in February 1990. Served on the Nicaraguan Resistance directorate, 1987–1988.

Chandler, Rep. Rod. A Washington State Republican who participated in a March 1989 congressional meeting with Enrique Bermúdez to pressure for a complete investigation of the reported abuses in the Quilalí Regional Command camp.

Charneco, Humberto; "Bert." U.S. Air Force colonel on loan to the State Department to oversee the U.S.-financed contra human-rights program from 1987 through 1990.

Chidester, Richard. Political officer in the U.S. embassy in Tegucigalpa who served as a liaison with the contras, 1986–1988.

"Chino." See González, Eugene.

"Chino Eighty-Five." See García, Carlos.

"Chino, El." See Lau, Ricardo.

"Clark, Col. Bill." CIA agent in charge of the Agency's contra sabotage-training base at Lepaterique, Honduras, 1982–1984.

Clark, Gerald; "Jerry." Army colonel on loan to the CIA during 1986–1987 to serve as operations chief for the contras' $100 million offensive.

Clarridge, Dewey. CIA officer who, as chief of the Latin American division of the CIA's operations directorate, oversaw the contra army's establishment.

"Coral." See Gadea, Freddy.

Correa, Juan Ramón. Sandinista organizer killed in a June 1981 contra ambush that was Jhonson's first armed attack against the Sandinista revolution.

Cruz, Arturo. Former Sandinista Ambassador to Washington, recruited by National Security aide Oliver North in 1985 to serve on the contra directorate. Resigned in 1987.

Cruz, Britolde; "X-Seven." Former National Guard enlisted man and top trainer at the contra training base known as the CIM. Strangled contra field commander "Krill" to death in 1983.

Cruz, Carmenza; "Mirna." Teenage commando who was detained, sexually abused, and tortured in the Quilalí Regional Command camp at the contras' Yamales base in November 1988.

"Cuco." See Sánchez, Enrique.

"Davis, Steve." CIA agent who helped recruit a new FDN directorate in Miami in December 1982.

"Deer, The." See Duarte, Harlie.

Delgado, Julio César. Exiled Nicaraguan lawyer who was the State Department–funded prosecutor under Jhonson on the contra legal staff.

Dellamico, Mario. Cuban-born representative in Honduras of the Miami-based arms dealership R M Equipment Inc., which tried to create an "arms supermarket" in Honduras in 1987.

"Denis." See Meza, Pastor.

Díaz, Berta. Young female commando gang-raped in 1986 in the contra unit commanded by Marcos Navarro, the ex–National Guardsman who became the contra army's final operations chief.

"Dimas Tigrillo." See Baldivia, Francisco.

"Doc." The young American paramedic who administered the contras' CIA-designed medical system in 1983 and 1984.

Doty, Ray. The retired U.S. Army master sergeant and veteran of the U.S.-financed war in Laos who, as the CIA's base chief in Tegucigalpa, administered the contra army from 1982 to 1985.

"Douglas." See Zelaya, Rudy.

Duarte, Harlie; "The Deer." Former National Guard second lieutenant who became Enrique Bermúdez's top personnel officer in 1984.

"Ecker, Tom." CIA agent who taught cryptography at the Agency's Lepaterique sabotage-training base outside Tegucigalpa, 1982–1984.

"Efrén." See Rodríguez, Rolando.

"Engineer, The." The Texas-born CIA agent who oversaw construction of the contras' main Honduran base in the Las Vegas salient in 1983.

Espinales, José; "Zero-Three." Former National Guard police sergeant who, as Mack's deputy at the contras' La Lodosa camp from 1982 to 1984, executed numerous prisoners.

Estrada, Victorino. Nicaraguan farmer on whose lands Jhonson often bivouacked his troops during 1984–1986.

Feldman, Tony. The CIA agent who as chief of the Agency's Central American Task Force was in charge of recruiting new FDN political leaders in Miami in December 1982. Later rose to head the Latin American Division of the Agency's Operations Directorate.

Fernández, Joseph. The CIA agent who as "Tomás Castillo" helped recruit the FDN directorate in 1982. CIA station chief in Costa Rica, 1984–1987. Twice indicted in the Iran-contra affair. A federal judge dismissed felony charges of lying against Fernández in November 1989 after the Justice Department barred the release of classified documents Fernández sought for his defense.

"Fernando." See Hernández, Diógenes.

"Fernando." See Midence, Eddy.

Ferrey, Azucena. Christian Democrat activist who left Nicaragua to serve on the Nicaraguan Resistance directorate 1987–1988. Returned to Nicaragua to win a seat in the national assembly in the February 1990 elections.

Fiers, Alan. The CIA's Central American Task Force chief from October 1984 through February 1988. Aside from CIA Director William Casey, the top Agency official directing the contra war during the period. In July 1991, pleaded guilty to lying to Congress as part of cover-up of Iran-contra scandal.

Fisk, Dan. A young Republican political appointee to the State Department, who worked closely with Adolfo Calero and other contra political leaders but later grew disillusioned with the corruption he saw in the Resistance bureaucracy.

Fley, Enrique. A younger brother of Luis Fley, "Jhonson." A Sandinista army lieutenant, he was ambushed and killed by contra forces in January 1988.

Fley, Francisco. A younger brother of Luis Fley, "Jhonson." He became a Sandinista army lieutenant and Jhonson took him captive during the 1987 $100 million offensive.

Fley, Jorge. A younger brother of Luis Fley, "Jhonson," and a Sandinista army lieutenant.

Fley, Luis; "Jhonson." Contra fighter and field commander from 1982 through 1988. Contra army's top legal investigator during 1988 and 1989.

Fley, Magda de. Luis Fley's wife.

"Franklyn." See Galeano, Israel.

Frixione, Donaldo. The Nicaraguan colonel who briefly commanded the air force in the days after the fall of Anastasio Somoza Debayle. Recruited as a contra pilot by the CIA during the 1987 offensive. Died in a February 1988 crash.

Gadea, Freddy; "Coral." Former Sandinista. Contra commander who formed the Quilalí Regional Command before he was purged in 1988 for opposing Bermúdez.

"Galaxias." One of Jhonson's dozen or so junior investigators in the murder case in the Quilalí Regional Command camp.

Galeano, Israel; "Franklyn." Contra field commander who in mid-1989 became the contra army's chief of staff and with U.S. backing in February 1990 succeeded Enrique Bermúdez as the army's top commander. Joined the Sandinista-run Interior Ministry at war's end.

"Gangman." See Rivera, Erwin Antonio.

García, Carlos; "Chino Eighty-Five." Rebel counterintelligence interrogator and close friend of Enrique Bermúdez and Aristides Sánchez, accused of torturing prisoners but acquitted by Resistance tribunal in 1989.

Gasteazoro, Guillermo; "Pecos Bill." Former National Guard lieutenant who worked with the CIA at the contras' Las Vegas base as an interpreter and radio scanner, 1984–1987.

"George." See Mallett, John.

Gómez, Juan "Juanillo." The former National Guard colonel and personal flyer for Anastasio Somoza Debayle who was appointed by Enrique Bermúdez as the FDN's air force commander and became Bermúdez's personal flyer.

González, Eugene; "Chino." A foot soldier in the Quilalí Regional Command who sent notes to Jhonson about a November 1988 murder in the camp.

González, Isaac; "Managua." Young commando murdered in the Quilalí Regional Command camp in Yamales, Honduras, in November 1988.

González, Pedro Joaquín. The Sandinista commander in the northern Nicaraguan town of Quilalí who grew disaffected and led the first anti-Sandinista uprising in July 1980.

"Gorrión." See Blandón, Marlon.

"Gorrión." See Siles, José.

Guillén, Carlos; "Gustavo." The son of a National Guard lieutenant, headed the contra special forces 1982–1984. Replaced Jhonson as chief contra legal investigator in 1990.

"Gustavo." See Guillén, Carlos.

Hernández, Diógenes; "Fernando." Top contra field commander and former evangelical preacher who led a dissident rebellion against Enrique Bermúdez in 1988.

Herrera Hernández, Antonio; "Alí." The young intelligence officer in the Quilalí Regional Command who provided key evidence in Jhonson's 1988 murder investigation.

Herrera, Julio César; "Krill." Former National Guardsman. Contra officer who was executed by Mack's men on higher orders in 1983. Strangled to death at the same time were two other contra officers, "Cara de Malo" and "Habakuk."

Herrera, Nicolás. The Sandinista political chief in El Cuá when Fley returned in early 1990.

Icaza, Carlos. Exiled Nicaraguan lawyer who ran a largely ineffective FDN legal office in 1985 and 1986.

"Invisible." See Ampie, Rodolfo Ernesto.

"Israelita." See Blake Hurtado, Isaac Samuel.

"Jersey." See Laríos, Francisco.

"Jhonson." See Fley, Luis.

"Joel." See Zepeda, José.

"John, Major." CIA agent in command at the Agency base on Honduras's Swan Island, which was used from 1986 to 1988 to launch weapons drops to the contras.

Johnson, Don. U.S. Green Beret colonel on loan to the CIA during 1987–1989. During the contras' $100 million offensive, Johnson was the top CIA agent at Aguacate Air Base in Honduras.

"Joshua." See Mercado Matús, Frank.

Kagan, Robert. Young Yale-educated State Department aide to Elliott Abrams who worked on the contra human-rights reform effort, 1986–1988.

"Killer Rat." See Wohl, Frank.

"Krill." See Herrera, Julio César.

Lacayo, Donald. Adolfo Calero's principal lawyer at the Coca-Cola plant in Managua before 1982. Legal adviser to Enrique Bermúdez, 1987–1988. Sided against Bermúdez in a 1988 dissident rebellion and was deported from Honduras to Miami in 1988.

Laríos, Francisco; "Jersey." Former National Guard soldier appointed by Mack as contra counterintelligence chief in 1989.

Lau, Ricardo; "El Chino." The ex–National Guard colonel from Anastasio Somoza Debayle's feared secret police who, serving as Enrique Bermúdez's CIA-financed intelligence chief from 1981 through 1984, carried out death squad executions for the Honduran military.

"Leo." See Morales, Mariano.

"Licenciado." See Sánchez, Victor.

"Lima, Mike." See Moreno Payán, Luis.

Lindwall, David E. Political officer at the U.S. embassy in Tegucigalpa who was a U.S. liaison with the contras from 1988 to 1990.

"Little Zelaya." See Zelaya, Juan José.

López, Armando; "The Policeman." Contra commander, former National Guard police lieutenant, and close associate of Enrique Bermúdez accused by other contras of murdering dozens of rebel commandos. GAO auditors in 1988 caught him diverting U.S.-financed meat deliveries destined for the contras' main hospital.

López, Jr., Armando; "The Beast." Son of Armando "The Policeman" López, one of Ricardo Lau's counterintelligence agents. Said by many contras to have executed numerous suspected infiltrators.

López, Enrique. Sandinista army lieutenant seized by Jhonson in 1987 along with Jhonson's brother Francisco Fley, during a Sandinista effort to convince Jhonson to defect.

López Contreras, Carlos. Honduran Foreign Minister, 1986–1990.

McCoy, Col. James L. Defense attaché at the U.S. embassy in Managua during Anastasio Somoza Debayle's final years. Partner in the Miami-based arms dealership R M Equipment Inc., which tried to create an "arms supermarket" in Honduras in 1987.

McCracken, Patrick. The former Marine and Vietnam veteran who, as an auditor from the U.S. Congress's General Accounting Office, carried out inspections in Honduras during 1988 that uncovered widespread torture in Resistance detention centers.

"Mack." See Bravo Centeno, José Benito.

Maldonado, Luis; "Vidal." One of the young commandos tortured during the 1988 counterintelligence roundup in the Quilalí Regional Command camp.

Mallett, John W.; "George." CIA agent who worked with the contras in Honduras from 1983 to 1986, then returned to the Agency's Central American Task Force at Langley.

"Managua." See González, Isaac.

Martin, Ronald. Partner in the Miami-based arms dealership R M Equipment Inc., which tried to create an "arms supermarket" in Honduras in 1987.

Martínez, Roberto; "Nolan." The young former student in command of the Quilalí Regional Command in 1988 and 1989.

Matamoros, Bosco. The contras' CIA-backed spokesman in Washington. Ernesto Palazio was the contra Washington spokesman whom the State Department backed.

Matamoros, Ernesto; "Dr. Tomás." The former National Guard physician appointed by Enrique Bermúdez to head the FDN's fledgling medical corps. Half-brother of contra spokesman Bosco Matamoros.

Meara, William. Assistant to U.S. Ambassador to Honduras Everett Briggs. Worked frequently with the contras during 1988 and 1989.

Medal Rodríguez, Roger; "Rambo." A twenty-four-year-old commando in the Quilalí Regional Command recruited by counterintelligence operative Isaac Samuel Blake, "Israelita," as an interrogator in 1988.

Mercado Matús, Frank; "Joshua." Deputy investigator on Jhonson's legal staff during 1988 and 1989.

Meza, Pastor; "Denis." The son of a wealthy Nicaraguan landowner. The contra army's top personnel officer, 1988–1990.

Midence, Eddy; "Fernando." The contra artillery commander who was president of the 1989 tribunal Jhonson organized to try the case of a murder committed in the Quilalí Regional Command camp in November 1988.

"Mirna." See Cruz, Carmenza.

"Moisés." See Mondragón Martínez, Efrén.

Molina, Adrian. Jhonson's Sandinista boss at the revolutionary coffee-marketing agency in the Nicaraguan town of El Cuá, 1980–1981.

Mondragón Martínez, Efrén; "Moisés." Former National Guard sergeant who became one of Col. Ricardo Lau's hitmen. Deserted from the contra army in 1985 and returned to Nicaragua. Murdered in Nicaragua by Sandinista State Security agents in 1988.

Montealegre, Orlando; "Oscar Montes." Paymaster for a succession of contra organizations. Deported from Honduras to Miami in 1988.

"Montes, Oscar." See Montealegre, Orlando.

Morales, Mariano; "Leo." The former National Guard sergeant whom Enrique Bermúdez appointed head of the rebel military police from 1985 to 1987. Accused of torture and rape.

Morán Gutiérrez, Luis Ariel; "Cerrano." Young commando accused of being a Sandinista infiltrator and detained and tortured in November 1988. Was ordered to help bury murder victim Isaac González at the Quilalí Regional Command camp.

Moreno Aguilar, Tirzo; "Rigoberto." Former Nicaraguan cattle merchant who became a top contra officer. Deported from Honduras to Miami in 1988 after challenging Enrique Bermúdez's control over the contra army in a dissident rebellion.

Moreno Payán, Luis; "Mike Lima." Ex–National Guard lieutenant. Contra field commander injured twice in 1984. Became the rebel counterintelligence chief in 1988.

Murillo Castillo, Jacqueline. Enrique Bermúdez's secretary at the Strategic Command, his headquarters. Accused of being a spy, detained and tortured in 1987.

Navarro, Marcos; "Black Dimas." Former private in Anastasio Somoza Debayle's elite force, known as the EEBI. During much of the contra war, headed the José Dolores Estrada Regional Command, one of the rebel army's most brutal and corrupt units. In 1989, became the Resistance's last operations chief.

"Nolan." See Martínez, Roberto.

Noriega, Roger. U.S. Agency for International Development (AID) official in charge of supervising U.S. financing for Jhonson's human-rights program in 1988 and 1989.

North, Oliver. Former U.S. Marine lieutenant colonel who as a National Security Council aide secretly advised and aided the contra army during a U.S. military aid cutoff from 1984 to 1986. Convicted in May 1989 on three felony counts in the Iran-contra affair. The convictions were later overturned.

Ortega, Daniel. A leading Sandinista guerrilla in the 1979 revolution. Headed Sandinista governments, 1979–1984. President of Nicaragua, 1985–1990. Brother of Humberto Ortega.

Ortega, Ernesto; "*Sherman.*" Former sergeant in Anastasio Somoza Debayle's elite force, the EEBI, who served as Enrique Bermúdez's personal secretary.

Ortega, Guillermo. Video cameraman from the contra army's Tegucigalpa public-relations office convicted of torture in a 1988 contra tribunal. Fled to Miami.

Ortega, Humberto. Sandinista Defense Minister, 1979–1990. Sandinista army general. Brother of Daniel Ortega.

Ortega, Rina. Younger sister of Enrique Bermúdez's secretary. Was Bermúdez's lover in 1984 and 1985.

Ortez, María Eugenia. Enrique Bermúdez's lover from 1986 to 1990.

Ortez Rivera, Magdalena; "*Sandra.*" The second of three teenage sisters tortured in the Quilalí Regional Command camp in November 1988.

Ortez Rivera, Otilia. The eldest of three teenage sisters tortured in the Quilalí Regional Command camp in November 1988.

Ortez Rivera, Rosa. The youngest of three teenage sisters tortured in the Quilalí Regional Command camp in November 1988.

Ortiz Centeno, Pedro; "*Suicide.*" Ex–National Guard sergeant. Contra commander who was executed by other contras in 1983. Contra leaders have never clarified how, where, or by whom Suicide was executed.

Osorio, Chilo. A peasant patriarch in northern Nicaragua. Tigrillo's younger brother Dimas ordered the murder of Osorio, along with three of his sons, at Wina, Nicaragua, in late 1982 in order to take his daughters as concubines.

Palazio, Ernesto. The contra spokesman in Washington who was backed by the State Department, 1986–1989. Bosco Matamoros was the contra spokesman backed by the CIA. Palazio became Nicaragua's Ambassador to Washington after Violeta Chamorro's 1990 presidential election victory.

"*Panchito.*" See Aguilar, Enrique.

"*Pantera-Romeo.*" See Centeno Chavarría, Rogelio.

Parker, Dana. Vietnam veteran and Huntsville, Alabama, police officer who visited contra camps in Honduras and was killed while participating in a 1984 contra air attack on the Sandinista base at Santa Clara, Nicaragua.

"*Pecos Bill.*" See Gasteazoro, Guillermo.

Peña Rodríguez, Ramón; "*Z-Two.*" Former National Guard police corporal who was Mack's longtime intelligence deputy, at the La Lodosa camp from 1982 to 1984 and on the contra general staff from 1988 to 1989.

Pineda, Denis; "*Benny.*" Former National Guard second lieutenant who was appointed by Enrique Bermúdez as his operations aide in 1984.

"*Policeman, The.*" See López, Armando.

Powell, James. A former U.S. Army helicopter pilot from Memphis, Tennessee, who joined the contras. Killed in a 1984 contra helicopter attack on the Sandinista base at Santa Clara, Nicaragua.

Pozo, Marco. Nicaraguan contra pilot killed with Americans James Powell and Dana Parker in a 1984 contra helicopter attack on the Sandinista base at Santa Clara, Nicaragua.

"*Quiché.*" See Rivas, Juan Ramón.

"*Rambo.*" See Medal Rodríguez, Roger.

Regalado, Gen. Humberto. Top commander of the Honduran military, 1985–1990.

Reich, Otto. The State Department official who, as Coordinator for Public Diplomacy, in 1985 led the U.S. attack on a series of photos taken by American student Frank Wohl of contras executing a prisoner.

"Renato." See Ruiz Castellón, Francisco.

"Ricardo, Major." A Colombian-born CIA agent based in Honduras throughout the war who reported on rebel activities to the Agency's base and station chiefs.

"Rigoberto." See Moreno Aguilar, Tirzo.

Rivas, Gerardo. A Nicaraguan peasant whom Tigrillo and Mike Lima accused of being a Sandinista agent and murdered during their first CIA-backed incursion into Nicaragua in 1982.

Rivas, Juan Ramón; "Quiché." Former National Guard sergeant. Longtime contra field commander, chief of staff from 1988 through March 1989. Confronted with ten-year-old drug trafficking allegations and forced to resign his post by CIA agents, allowing Enrique Bermúdez to return to his post as the contras' commanding general.

Riveiro, Osvaldo. Argentine colonel, attached to Argentine Army Intelligence Battalion 601, who headed a contingent of Argentine undercover agents who worked with the contras from 1980 through 1983.

Rivera, Erwin Antonio; "Gangman." The seventeen-year-old peasant commando who, after brutal interrogation by counterintelligence interrogators in November 1988, agreed to cooperate with his tormentors and became a torturer himself.

Robelo, Alfonso. Nicaraguan businessman and politician, member of the first Sandinista revolutionary junta, 1979–1980. Jhonson supported him in 1981 after he broke with the Sandinistas. Member of the contras' CIA-recruited political directorate, 1985–1987.

"Roberto." The CIA agent who was the Agency's liaison officer with Mack, the rebel intelligence chief, 1988–1990.

"Robespierre." See Aguilar, Roberto.

Rocha, Bernardo. Former peasant and longtime rebel fighter detained and tortured by contra counterintelligence agents from November 1989 through January 1990.

Rodríguez, Rolando; "Efrén." Contra commander and member of the 1989 tribunal that tried the case of a murder committed in November 1988 in the Quilalí Regional Command camp in Yamales, Honduras. Informed Mack that the tribunal had caught him in perjury.

"Rubén." See Sobalvarro, Oscar.

"Rubén, Dr." See Rugama, Francisco.

Rugama, Francisco; "Dr. Rubén." Exiled Nicaraguan physician who, during his service in the contra medical corps from 1983 to 1985, witnessed numerous murders.

Ruiz Castellón, Francisco; "Renato." Former National Guard lieutenant who headed the contras' San Jacinto Regional Command during much of the war.

Top contra finance officer, 1989–1990. Assassinated in Tegucigalpa in June 1991.
Sacasa, Marta. The contra army's spokeswoman in Miami, 1983–1988.
Sánchez, Aristides. The wealthy, exiled Nicaraguan landowner who worked closely with the CIA as a behind-the-scenes associate of Enrique Bermúdez, the contra commander. Turned on Bermúdez in 1989, helping to engineer Bermúdez's final 1990 purge.
Sánchez, Enrique; "Cuco." Aristides Sánchez's older brother and Adolfo Calero's brother-in-law. A former deputy to the Nicaraguan Congress from Somoza's Liberal Party. Coordinated the contra army's Internal Front, the unit attempting to establish a spy network inside Nicaragua, until his 1988 break with Bermúdez and deportation to Miami.
Sánchez, Victor; "Licenciado." Aristides Sánchez's younger brother. Rebel officer, 1982–1988. Watched CIA agents direct Bermúdez's activities at Aguacate Air Base in December 1987 during a major rebel attack. Quit the Resistance after backing the 1988 anti-Bermúdez dissident rebellion.
Sandino, Alfonso. Nicaraguan lawyer who, as a human-rights aide to Marta Patricia Baltodano, interviewed dozens of contra prisoners in 1988 and 1989.
Sandino, Roger. The ex–National Guard lieutenant who blew up a Nicaraguan bridge in the first CIA-directed sabotage, in March 1982. Recruited Jhonson into the FDN.
"Sandra." See Ortez Rivera, Magdalena.
"Sean, Major." Former U.S. Green Beret who was a CIA trainer at the Agency's Lepaterique sabotage-training base outside Tegucigalpa, 1982–1984.
Secord, Richard. Former U.S. Air Force major general who helped Oliver North purchase arms for the contras when U.S. military aid was barred by Congress from 1984 to 1986. Pleaded guilty in November 1989 to one felony count in the Iran-contra affair.
"Sherman." See Ortega, Ernesto.
Shields, Vincent. The CIA station chief in Tegucigalpa from 1984 through mid-1987. In the late 1960s, during the CIA's war in Laos, Shields served as the deputy chief at Long Tieng, the main base for the Agency's army of forty thousand Laotian peasants.
Siles, José; "Gorrión." One of the young commandos tortured during a 1988 counterintelligence roundup in the Quilalí Regional Command camp.
Singlaub, John. Retired U.S. Army general who raised money and brokered at least one weapons purchase for the contras in 1985, when official U.S. military aid was illegal.
"Six-Seven." See Tijerino, César.
Skelton, Rep. Ike. A conservative Missouri Democrat and contra supporter who led the March 1989 efforts to pressure Enrique Bermúdez for a complete investigation of reported abuses in the Quilalí Regional Command camp.
Sobalvarro, Oscar; "Rubén." Member of the rebel general staff, 1988–1990. Signed an agreement demobilizing the contra army in March 1990.
Somoza Debayle, Anastasio "Tacho." The last of the Somoza family dictators. Son of Anastasio Somoza García. Ruled Nicaragua from 1967 through July 1979.

Somoza García, Anastasio. The first commander of the Nicaraguan National Guard. Founder of the Somoza dynasty and dictator of Nicaragua from 1936 to 1956.

Somoza Portocarrero, Anastasio "Tachito." Somoza Debayle's Harvard-educated son. In 1979, became the commander of the National Guard's most elite unit, known as the EEBI.

Somoza, Julio. Anastasio Somoza Debayle's second son, the child raised in the dictator's residence by National Guardsman José Benito Bravo, "Mack."

Stenholm, Rep. Charles W. A Texas Democrat who participated in a March 1989 Capitol Hill meeting aimed at pressuring Enrique Bermúdez for a complete investigation of reported abuses in the Quilalí Regional Command camp.

"Steve, Captain." Vietnam veteran and CIA agent based in the contra base at Yamales, Honduras, in 1986 and early 1987.

Suazo Córdova, Roberto. President of Honduras, 1982–1986.

"Suicide." See Ortiz Centeno, Pedro.

"Tanga." Former National Guard soldier who commanded the contra military police force in 1988 and 1989.

"Ted, Mr." A CIA agent and longtime veteran of Agency paramilitary operations in Laos and other Asian countries who worked with the contras in Honduras during the mid-1980s.

"Terry." CIA paramilitary agent in Laos, 1963 to 1965. CIA station chief in Honduras, 1987 to 1989. Chief, Latin American Division of CIA's Operations Directorate 1989–? As an active-duty intelligence agent who has not been previously identified in print, it is illegal to publish his full name.

"Thomas, Major." CIA trainer at the Agency's Lepaterique sabotage-training base outside Tegucigalpa, 1982–1984. Later in the war, he was based at the Yamales Strategic Command camp, often debriefing returning rebel officers about their field experiences.

"Three-Eighty." See Bermúdez, Enrique.

"Tigrillo." See Baldivia, Encarnación.

Tijerino, César; "Six-Seven." Former interrogator from Anastasio Somoza Debayle's secret police agency, the Office of National Security, who became a contra interrogator. Accused by the State Department of torture in 1989.

"Tim." A CIA agent based at Langley in 1989 who worked with the contras and who, like many State Department officials, turned critical of the corruption among the Resistance politicians whom the Agency had recruited to represent the rebels.

"Tomás, Dr." See Matamoros, Ernesto.

"Toño." See Calderón, Walter.

Torres, Donald; "The Bull." Former National Guard major appointed by Enrique Bermúdez to be the contra army's counterintelligence chief, 1984–1988. Accused by the State Department of torture in 1989.

"Trickster." See Castillo, Noel.

Ubeda, Yorlin María. Young woman repeatedly raped in the contras' counterintelligence interrogation center between 1986 and 1988.

"Vidal." See Maldonado, Luis.

Villagra, Hugo; "Visage." Former captain in Anastasio Somoza Debayle's elite force, known as the EEBI. Recruited by the CIA to replace Enrique Bermúdez as the FDN's theater commander in 1983, then forced from the movement when the American plot to oust Bermúdez failed.

"Villegas, Santiago." An Argentine Army intelligence agent who trained contra fighters in Honduras, 1981–1983.

"Visage." See Villagra, Hugo.

"West, Major." The first CIA agent to command the contra air base at Honduras' Aguacate Air Base when it opened in 1983.

"Wilfredo." See Zeledón, Santos.

Winters, Donald. The CIA station chief in Tegucigalpa from 1982 to 1984 who worked with base chief Ray Doty to establish the contra army in Honduras.

Wohl, Frank; "Killer Rat." The Northwestern University student who sold *Newsweek* magazine photos of contras slashing the throat of a prisoner, which the American took during a 1985 visit to Mack's base camp.

"X-Seven." See Cruz, Britolde.

Zelaya, Juan José; "Little Zelaya." The former personal secretary to Gen. Samuel Genie, Anastasio Somoza Debayle's intelligence chief, whom Enrique Bermúdez made his intelligence aide in 1984.

Zelaya, Rudy; "Douglas." Contra field commander who traveled with Jhonson to Washington in April 1985. By 1990 he was the contras' top logistics officer.

Zeledón, Santos; "Wilfredo." Jhonson's executive officer during the $100 million offensive. Served on the 1989 tribunal Jhonson organized to try the case of a murder committed in the Quilalí Regional Command camp in Yamales, Honduras, in November 1988.

Zepeda, José; "Joel." The former National Guard sergeant who was Mike Lima's counterintelligence deputy in the contras' Yamales base camps, 1988–1989. Accused of torture by the State Department in 1989.

"Zero-Three." See Espinales, José.

"Z-Two." See Peña Rodríguez, Ramón.

A Note on Sources

Although I covered the Nicaraguan war intermittently from 1983 through 1988 for the *Miami Herald*, I learned most of the history I recount in this book while conducting research during a 1989–1990 leave of absence, working under the auspices of an Alicia Patterson Foundation fellowship. During my research, I conducted about 250 separate interviews. I talked to about sixty-five different contra rebels, about twenty present and former U.S. officials who worked with the rebel army, and about twenty Nicaraguan and Honduran government officials. Most of those interviews I taped and transcribed.

Several rebel commanders who administered offices that maintained written records bearing on the contra army's history allowed me to read, take notes from, and in some cases copy those files. These included the public-relations office, the counterintelligence section, the legal adviser's office, and the Asociación Nicaragüense Pro-Derechos Humanos (ANPDH), the Nicaraguan Association for Human Rights. Those interviews and original records provided my basic source materials.

I have portrayed dialogue and other personal encounters only when I have been able to draw detailed firsthand accounts from interviews or written records.

During 1989 and 1990, I taped about forty interviews with Luis Fley, some one hundred hours of conversation. Unless otherwise noted, I have drawn my accounts of passages in which Jhonson figures as a character from interviews with him.

Central to my account of the Quilalí case was the voluminous file Jhonson and his staff collected during the nine-month investigation, tribunal, and appeal. I photocopied the file—127 documents—including Jhonson's memos, radiotelegraph messages, typed depositions taken from rebels involved in the Quilalí abuses, transcripts of testimony by witnesses before the tribunal, and other documents.

Notes

1: The Pit

1. Jhonson later stored the anonymous notes in the Quilalí tribunal documents.

2. This and subsequent discussions of the rebel army's intelligence and counterintelligence sections were drawn from interviews with Jhonson; Luis "Mike Lima" Moreno, the counterintelligence chief from February 1988 through July 1989; Noel "Trickster" Castillo Burgos, Mike Lima's counterintelligence deputy; and several other rebel counterintelligence agents. During a series of February 1989 visits to the safe house serving as the rebel army's counterintelligence headquarters, I took notes from numerous counterintelligence files. Mike Lima described the two CIA agents working in direct liaison with his section in several interviews. U.S. officials confirmed that the CIA had established special liaison relationships with the rebel army's intelligence and counterintelligence sections.

3. Loosely modeled on U.S. ground forces, the Resistance army was led by a "general commander": Bermúdez. Below Bermúdez was the chief of staff, Juan "Quiché" Rivas, and his five staff aides. Staff officers, numbered one through five, held responsibility, respectively, for S1 personnel, S2 intelligence, S3 operations, S4 logistics, and S5 psychological operations.

4. My description of the Yamales Valley and the general staff camp was drawn from notes I made during several visits.

5. I called Meara long distance at his new diplomatic posting on October 25, 1989. I outlined this and other incidents in which various sources had described his participation and asked to hear his version of the events. He declined to comment.

6. Acting on Charneco's tip, Jhonson days later obtained the release of the teenage commando detained by contra counterintelligence agents. I interviewed several U.S. officials familiar with Bert Charneco's November 1988 visit to Honduras.

7. The funding for the Resistance legal office had run out on September 30, 1988, at the end of the 1987 U.S. Government fiscal year. Jhonson's office received no additional U.S. funding until mid-February 1989, when the U.S. Agency for International Development (AID) funded his office to sponsor human-rights training. Jhonson and much of his staff pursued their probe of the Quilalí case essentially without remuneration.

8. I drew my description of Jhonson's office from personal visits during 1989.

9. Several U.S. officials described the financial austerity to which Jhonson had to accommodate himself late in 1988.

10. In the course of the investigation and trial of Isaac Blake for abuses in the Quilalí camp, Jhonson and other contras routinely mispronounced and misspelled Blake's name, referring to him as "Isaac Blecker."

11. In most military organizations, the intelligence staff collects information on the enemy, and a special counterintelligence section of the larger intelligence staff works to protect against enemy espionage. In the Resistance army, Colonel Bermúdez had established a counterintelligence section in February 1988 that was equal in power to the intelligence section. But from the beginning of the war, the functions of the two staffs had been hopelessly blurred as well, with intelligence agents spending much of their time tracing suspected spies within their own ranks. The CIA assigned liaison officers to work closely with both sections.

12. My characterization of Mike Lima's safe house draws on several visits during February 1989.

13. I interviewed Pastor "Denis" Meza about his background and work in February 1989.

14. Jhonson detailed his conversations with Commanders Rubén and Denis in several interviews.

15. Jhonson described the counterintelligence interrogation center at Yamales in an interview on October 26, 1989.

16. Jhonson described Joel, as well as the December 9, 1988, visit he and Denis made to Joel's interrogation center, in an interview on October 26, 1989.

17. The note signed by Jhonson and Denis was later stored along with other documents in the Quilalí case file.

18. Jhonson recounted his conversation with Bermúdez in several interviews. Jhonson's message to Joshua was in the Quilalí documents.

19. Jhonson described his discovery of the file on Blake in his office and detailed his December 13, 1988, visit to the Yamales camps in several 1989 interviews.

20. Freddy "Coral" Gadea, who recruited Alí into the rebel army and was his commander during several years of war, detailed Alí's family background and rebel career in an October 18, 1989, interview in Miami.

21. Alí's December 13, 1988, statement to Joshua—eight typed legal pages, single-spaced—was filed with the Quilalí case documents.

22. Jhonson detailed Joshua's visit to the Quilalí camp, as well as the hard times Joshua faced pursuing his investigation in the camps. The threat against Enrique "Panchito" Aguilar was documented in Aguilar's December 12, 1988, statement to Joshua, filed in the Quilalí case documents.

23. I drew details of the November 30, 1988, prison inspection by GAO and Price Waterhouse auditors from interviews with participants and from a five-page December 2, 1988, draft letter from Price Waterhouse to Coinage Gothard, AID's Regional Inspector General for Audit at the U.S. embassy in Tegucigalpa.

24. Rebel counterintelligence chief Mike Lima, Jhonson, and several U.S. officials said that Blake's interrogations in the Quilalí camp came amid a much larger hunt through the rebel camps for "infiltrators."

25. Jhonson, in a November 1988 interview in Tegucigalpa, discussed the mounting introspection among young rebel commanders about the origins of the rebel army.

2: Insurgent Roots

1. At its numerical peak in early 1987, the rebel army had some eighteen thousand combatants, according to U.S. officials, including a former CIA officer monitoring the contra army's personnel lists at the time. But during the course of the conflict, thousands more were rebels at one time or another before deserting, dying, falling prisoner, or leaving the army in some other way.

2. For my account of Luis Fley's youth, I drew on July 1989 interviews with Luis Fley; his wife, Magda; his father, Federico, eighty-four; his mother, Teodora, sixty-eight; his sister Mercedes; his brothers Jorge, Francisco, and José Spencer; and his sister-in-law Sonia. Richard Boudreaux of the *Los Angeles Times* also generously loaned me transcripts of his own interviews with Luis Fley and family members.

3. The Escuela de Entrenamiento Basico de Infantería (EEBI), the Basic Infantry Training School, was commanded by Somoza Debayle's son, Anastasio Somoza Portocarrero, known as "Tachito." Though designed for training, the EEBI became the Guard's most elite infantry combat battalion. The Armor Battalion, the other Guard unit with a modicum of discipline and fighting resources, was commanded by José Somoza Rodríguez, Somoza García's illegitimate son. I discussed both units with former Guardsmen, including Mike Lima and Walter "Toño" Calderón. For more details on the Somoza family and the Guard in Nicaraguan life, see Bernard Diederich's *Somoza and the Legacy of U.S. Involvement in Central America* (New York: Dutton, 1981); Richard Millett's *The Guardians of the Dynasty* (Maryknoll, N.Y.: Orbis, 1977); David Nolan's *FSLN: The Ideology of the Sandinistas and the Nicaraguan Revolution* (Coral Gables, Fla.: University of Miami, 1984); and Shirley Christian's *Nicaragua, Revolution in the Family* (New York: Random House, 1985).

4. Cabezas, later a senior official in Nicaragua's Interior Ministry, drew

worldwide fame for his memoirs recounting these guerrilla experiences: *Fire from the Mountain* (New York: Crown, 1985).

5. For an inside look at the details of the Sandinistas' early organizing techniques in northern Nicaragua, see the folder of essays written by Sandinista Front officials in May and June 1983 and dedicated to Daniel Teller, a Sandinista Front official ambushed by the contras in early May 1983. They are available for public review at Managua's Instituto para el Estudio del Sandinismo.

6. The literacy worker was Georgino Andrade. Details of his death filled the May 23, 1980, issue of *Barricada*, the Sandinista party organ. Andrade appears to have been one of the very first victims of the contra war.

7. The attack came on July 23, 1980. Its organizer, Pedro Joaquín González, was entrapped, ambushed, and killed by Sandinista Interior Ministry agents near Quilalí on September 13, 1980. The State Department mythologized González as a contra hero in a January 1988 publication, *Nicaraguan Biographies*. State's account vastly exaggerates González's military rank before his defection, suggesting that he complained personally to Sandinista Defense Minister Humberto Ortega about the aristocratic composition of the army's general staff. González's widow, Eva Soila López Medina Viuda de González, now living in Danlí, Honduras, said in a March 1989 interview that González never met Ortega. State's account also misnames González's betrayer, who was Mamerto Herrera, not Mamerto Torrera. And it misdates his death, putting it in August. The July 24, 1980, *Barricada* reported the attack. The September 21, 1980, *Barricada* reported González's death. The contras' Quilalí Regional Command was named to commemorate González's uprising, and another unit was given his name.

8. Fley's boss, Adrian Molina, was among fourteen political prisoners released in the 1974 seizure by a Sandinista commando group of a number of wealthy Managuans, including Somoza's foreign minister, attending a party hosted by Chema Castillo. The prisoners were flown to Cuba.

9. The Pedernales del Cuá ambush was detailed in *Barricada* on June 16, 1981. I also drew on interviews with Luis Fley; Fley's wife, Magda; Encarnación "Tigrillo" Baldivia; Francisco "Dimas Tigrillo" Baldivia; Israel "Franklyn" Galeano; Oscar "Rubén" Sobalvarro; and several others who participated.

3: The Rise of the Ex-Guards

1. I drew the account of Bermúdez's fall 1981 visit to Maquengales from interviews with Bermúdez, Luis Fley, Encarnación "Tigrillo" Baldivia, Francisco "Dimas Tigrillo" Baldivia, Freddy "Coral" Gadea, Pastor "Denis" Meza, and others.

2. Santiago Villegas was a pseudonym. He was later identified as José Hoyas by an Argentine intelligence officer, Hector Frances, who offered an extensive analysis of Argentine involvement with the contras in a statement videotaped by Sandinista government interrogators on November 6, 1982. The other Argentine who accompanied Bermúdez to the Maquengales meeting remains unidenti-

fied. A book by former FDN Director Edgar Chamorro, *Packaging the Contras* (New York: Institute for Media Analysis, 1987), includes a transcript of the Frances videotape.

3. Bermúdez's biographic details were drawn from a January 3, 1990, interview in Miami.

4. Bermúdez, in a January 3, 1990, interview, denied that he had any contacts with the CIA before late 1981. He could not recall meeting General Boyd. Boyd and several other U.S. officials contradicted Bermúdez. They said that the CIA "put Bermúdez in touch" with the September 15 Legion in Guatemala. Some writers have argued that Bermúdez's CIA contacts began before 1979, perhaps as early as 1965, during his participation in the Dominican intervention. That may be true, though Bermúdez was a mere lieutenant in 1965. U.S. officials familiar with the history argue that Bermúdez's relationship with the CIA—if he had one—changed qualitatively in late 1979.

5. Although U.S. aid to the contras didn't begin, even covertly, until 1981, the CIA already had other funds available to begin financing the activism Bermúdez suddenly adopted in mid-1980. Even during the Carter Administration, the CIA had a political budget under the terms of its annual intelligence authorization that allowed the Agency to channel funds to the Sandinistas' opponents: anybody that fell under the umbrella "democratic opposition."

6. Lau's background in the Office of National Security and his involvement in the 1980 killing of the El Salvador archbishop is discussed extensively in Chris Dickey's book *With the Contras* (New York: Simon and Schuster, 1985).

7. Some have reported that Lau was a classmate of Bermúdez's at Somoza's Academia Militar from 1948 to 1952. But Bermúdez said in an interview that Lau entered the academy several years after Bermúdez's own class, the academy's seventh promotion, had graduated.

8. Bermúdez discussed his Buenos Aires trip in the September/October 1987 issue of the CIA-financed contra magazine *Resistencia*. For other details on the trip, see page 52 of Roy Gutman's *Banana Diplomacy* (New York: Simon and Schuster, 1988). Former National Guard Colonel Guillermo Mendieta, one of the founders of the September 15 Legion, outlined his embezzlement allegations against Bermúdez in a June 1986 interview with me. Bermúdez denied Mendieta's accusations.

9. The Reagan Administration intelligence findings during 1981 are chronicled in the National Security Archives' book *The Chronology: The Documented Day-by-Day Account of the Secret Military Assistance to Iran and the Contras* (New York: Warner Books, 1987).

10. On August 5, 1989, I drove through Tegucigalpa with Luis "Jhonson" Fley, visiting more than a dozen once-secret rebel facilities. I drew my descriptions of the Florencia South and other contra safe houses from that tour.

11. The August 1981 creation of the FDN in Guatemala City is discussed in Gutman's *Banana Diplomacy*, page 56. Bermúdez claimed to have chosen the name FDN and to have paid the bills out of his own pocket—falling behind on his credit card—but this smacks of the picturesque hyperbole at which

Bermúdez and other contra leaders became experts. Edgar Chamorro, a former FDN director, said in his 1985 testimony before the World Court at The Hague, the Netherlands, that the CIA chose the name FDN, wrote up the group's founding documents, and paid the bills. Victor Sánchez, brother of Aristides Sánchez, recalled that some Nicaraguan exiles wanted the force called Guardia Nacional.

12. Bermúdez numbered the Guard and its officer corps in his September/October 1987 interview with *Resistencia.*

13. The March 28, 1983, issue of *Barricada* includes an interview with one of Bermúdez's traveling recruiters.

14. The motivations of the ex-Guardsmen who signed on to the contra army were varied. Some young officers like Mike Lima just wanted to fight a war. Lima said that because he was single, he received no family-aid payments from his March 1982 recruitment until May 1983, when he said he began to receive the equivalent of two hundred dollars per month. Other contras suspect that the payments were higher and began earlier. Bermúdez, in his interview in the September/October 1987 issue of *Resistencia,* complained about the high salaries some officers demanded. The family-aid payments, first extended only to ex-Guard officers, broadened over the years into a full-fledged salary system that covered hundreds of contra staff and field officers. See the March 15, 1987, *Miami Herald* for an article by Sandra Dibble discussing the salary system in detail. When the CIA turned administration of the contras over to AID in April 1988, AID took over the salary payments. Roger Noriega, an AID spokesman, described the workings of the system in interviews in May 1988 and September 1989.

15. Bermúdez listed the FDN's three original border bases in a January 3, 1990, interview.

16. Tigrillo detailed his encounter with Bermúdez in a May 1988 interview. In a January 3, 1990, interview, Bermúdez said he first met Tigrillo not in Danlí, but in the nearby border village of Las Trojes.

17. I drew my account of Mike Lima's youth from eight interviews with him in 1989.

18. José Benito Bravo Centeno, "Mack," was born on March 21, 1946, in Santo Tomás, Chontales. I interviewed him in June 1986, February 1988, and May 1991. Mike Lima, Victor Sánchez, Fley, and two of Mack's officers—former Guard Sergeant Filemon Espinales and former Guard Lt. Marlon Blandón—also provided information on Mack.

19. Mike Lima, Tigrillo, Dimas Tigrillo, Israel "Franklyn" Galeano, and several other contras described the La Lodosa training.

20. Many contras met Alex, the CIA agent. Among those who provided information were Mike Lima, Walter "Toño" Calderón, Enrique "Cuco" Sánchez, and others.

21. Mike Lima detailed the weapons deliveries.

22. My account of the 1982 expedition into upper Jinotega was drawn from interviews with Mike Lima, Tigrillo, and Dimas Tigrillo. The accounts of the murders of peasants accused as State Security agents came from Mike Lima. On

July 7, 1982, Tigrillo and Mike Lima ambushed a Sandinista army patrol led by Lieutenant Fidel Tinoco, capturing Tinoco's diary. Mike Lima began using the diary himself to record the executions of suspected agents, writing down names, dates, and places.

23. Mike Lima described his interrogation by Alex and the Argentines.

24. Dimas Tigrillo recalled his views of Bermúdez in a February 1989 interview at the Yamales camps.

25. The November 4, 1982, *Barricada* featured extensive reportage on Dimas Tigrillo's Wina base, which Sandinista troops had just overrun. There were photographs of the bamboo houses, the holding cell, and the cemetery. Ironically, *Barricada* claimed that U.S. advisers had learned to build similar bases in Vietnam and had taught the contras how. Mike Lima described Dimas Tigrillo's execution of Chilo Osorio and his sons.

26. Mike Lima, Dimas Tigrillo, and Tigrillo offered accounts of their confrontation.

27. Mike Lima described the organized effort to strip the Baldivia brothers of recruits. Walter "Toño" Calderón, Victor "Licenciado" Sánchez, and other contras confirmed his account.

28. The rifles were Belgian FALs that the Honduran Army was passing on to the contras. The Reagan Administration, in turn, was replacing the Honduran military's stocks with new U.S.-made M-16s. Efrén "Moisés" Mondragón Martínez, a regional commander who defected from the contra army in March 1985, discussed the arrangement in several published interviews. See Robert McCartney's piece in the *Washington Post* on May 7, 1985. Two extensive interviews with Mondragón were translated by the Congressional Research Service of the Library of Congress, and circulated widely in Washington.

29. My description of La Quinta comes from an August 5, 1989, visit, as well as from watching archival video footage of various television interviews taped at La Quinta. Rafael Tercero at the CBS News office in Tegucigalpa helped me by arranging the video viewings.

30. Details of the contra attack on the Puerto Viejo construction site were recounted in the August 31 and September 1, 1982, issues of *Barricada*.

31. For examples of the October and November 1982 U.S. media coverage of the contra war, see the *Miami Herald* series, October 24, 1982, and the November 8, 1982, *Newsweek* cover story, "The Secret War."

32. Although the Pacific zone amounts to just 15 percent of Nicaragua's territory, it is inhabited by 2.3 million of the country's 3.7 million people, according to a government publication, *Ten Years of Revolution*, distributed to reporters in July 1989 by the Dirección de Información y Prensa de la Presidencia.

33. Federal laws punish the publication of the names of U.S. intelligence agents. In cases where the Americans who worked with the contras are believed to be still working under cover and are thus potential targets, and whose security has not already been compromised by publication of their names, I have identified them only by their public pseudonyms. Most contras knew the CIA officer

in charge of Lepaterique in 1983 just as "Colonel Bill," though several identified him as Colonel Bill Clark. A retired ranking CIA official who worked in Honduras with the contras also identified him as Bill Clark. The CIA agents who worked with the contras routinely took on military ranks with their pseudonyms in order not to be outranked in their dealings with their counterparts among the contra commanders and Honduran military officers. It is unlikely that Clark had ever reached the rank of colonel or lieutenant colonel in the U.S. military.

34. Colonel Bill's second, "Major Thomas," left Lepaterique in 1984. In 1986, he showed up at the contras' Yamales base, where he introduced himself as "Major Ramirez." One of the contras who met him at Lepaterique, Guillermo "Pecos Bill" Gasteazoro, an FDN communications officer who often worked for the CIA as an interpreter, said Major Thomas told him once that he was a Marine reconnaissance officer, originally from California. Again, it is unlikely that Major Thomas ever really reached the rank of major in the U.S. military.

4: The Project

1. The history of command-and-control in the FDN passed through at least five distinct phases. During the war's early years, 1981–1983, strategy was plotted and key decisions taken in tripartite meetings bringing Honduran and Argentine military advisers together with the FDN general staff. CIA agents sat in as observers in most of the tripartite meetings. The CIA took direct control in late 1983 when the Argentine advisers left the Project, and the Honduran Army reduced its participation after a 1984 coup deposed Gen. Gustavo Alvarez. Some strategic control reverted to Bermúdez and the contras themselves after the U.S. aid cutoff in mid-1984. The result was that the war drifted with little central direction for two years, although Oliver North tried to direct some operations by sending plans and orders to Honduras with personal couriers. In the fall of 1986, after the passage of a $100 million U.S. aid package, the CIA again took virtually complete control of the war, rebuffing Honduran military attempts to participate in the planning of rebel operations during the rebels' $100 million offensive. After the February 1988 U.S. aid cutoff, State Department officials increased their direct involvement in the management of the rebel army.

2. U.S. officials detailed the numerical strength of the Honduras CIA station in late 1982 to *Miami Herald* correspondent Juan Tamayo. See the *Miami Herald*, December 19, 1982.

3. Winters's name has appeared many times in print. For instance, see Roy Gutman's *Banana Diplomacy*, page 153 (New York: Simon and Schuster, 1988).

4. I drew my description of the CIA's successive Tegucigalpa bases from an interview with a former CIA officer who worked in several of them.

5. Ray Doty became a well-known figure in Honduras during his 1982–1985 tenure as CIA base chief. Several contras, including Hugo "Visage" Villagra and Mike Lima, described to me their dealings with Doty. I also discussed Doty's

career with a former CIA officer who worked with him. For a description of a visit to Colonel Doty's CIA base, see Bob Woodward's *Veil*, page 230 (New York: Simon and Schuster, 1987). Woodward incorrectly identified Doty as a Special Forces lieutenant colonel; a CIA officer who worked with him said he had never risen above army sergeant major.

6. I drew my thumbnail account of the CIA's war in Laos largely from a review of the *New York Times'* coverage of the conflict from 1969 through 1975. Two especially fascinating pieces were Henry Kamm's initial October 26, 1969, article first announcing that the CIA had secretly recruited an army of Laotian peasants, and Kamm's wrap-up piece six years later on July 13, 1975, at the war's close. At that time, Gen. Vang Pao, like Enrique Bermúdez, the CIA's handpicked rebel commander, had just gone into exile. Some eighteen thousand panicked Meo tribesmen had fled Thailand, and tens of thousands of others were roaming the country in panic. Christopher Robbins's book *Air America* (London: Macmillan, 1979), discusses the role of the CIA-run airline in Laos.

7. I discussed the similarities between the CIA's Nicaraguan and Laotian experiences with an American agent who worked for the CIA in both. One important difference was that in Laos, American agents fought alongside rebel troops in combat. In Honduras during much of the war, CIA agents were prohibited from going any closer than twenty miles to the Nicaraguan border—much less from engaging Sandinista troops in combat.

8. Two of the camps were in Choluteca. A third, Mack's La Lodosa, was in southern El Paraíso province. Pino Uno, near Arenales, was in Honduras's "recovered territory" in eastern El Paraíso province. And farther east in the recovered territory was the Maquengales camp, which later became known as Las Vegas. I draw the account of camp development from interviews with Bermúdez and other contras.

9. At least one other FDN border camp took on importance, not for its convenience in supplying the FDN troops, but for supplying the FDN *with* troops. Tigrillo brought thousands of "recruits" out of Nicaragua in 1983, crossing the Coco River into Honduras at Banco Grande, a riverine clearing at the northeast tip of Nicaragua's Jinotega province. It was several days' march from Banco Grande southwest to Las Vegas. The CIA decided it would be most convenient to equip and train the recruits right at Banco Grande. They cleared a helicopter landing strip, threw up a medical clinic, and put a Guard sergeant in command.

10. Details of the early supplies purchased by the Argentines for the contras came from interviews with several contra leaders and from an article by Juan Tamayo in the December 19, 1982, *Miami Herald.*

11. A CIA officer in charge of the supply system at the time described it in an interview. Although successive U.S. spokesmen at the Tegucigalpa embassy repeatedly insisted indignantly to reporters that no FDN supplies were passing through Palmerola Air Base, the CIA officer said that in the early years most rebel supplies were flown into Palmerola. Later the Honduran military insisted that rebel supplies pass through Palmerola or other military sites for inspection by Honduran soldiers.

12. A former CIA officer said the Agency made a single monthly payment to the Honduran Armed Forces to cover the use of the helicopters and other aircraft, as well as to compensate Honduran military pilots and mechanics for services rendered to the contras. He said three or four helicopters were flying an average of five hours daily to supply the rebels during some periods. That would put monthly helicopter rental costs to the CIA at nearly $500,000.

13. Several contras described "The Engineer" and "Mr. Ted." A former CIA officer who worked with them provided further background.

14. The Engineer's construction of Las Vegas was described by Guillermo "Pecos Bill" Gasteazoro, an FDN communications officer who often worked for the CIA as an interpreter, and by other contras as well.

15. Former FDN Director Edgar Chamorro, who worked in Honduras as a rebel spokesman during 1983 and 1984, identified the FDN's two earliest planes in an interview on August 11, 1989.

16. The U.S. Army's 46th Engineering Battalion's improvements at Aguacate were detailed by Alfonso Chardy in the July 2, 1988, *Miami Herald,* citing a classified 1984 General Accounting Office report. Also, see the July 7, 1984, *Congressional Quarterly,* page 1656. The GAO report calculated the cost of army improvements to Aguacate at $199,000 for materials alone.

17. I and several other U.S. reporters interviewed Amador in Managua in October 1983, days after he was shot down. See the *Miami Herald,* October 23, 1983. Amador was imprisoned from 1983 until March 1988, when he was released in an amnesty a week after the Sapoa cease-fire accords. He immediately returned to salaried work for the Nicaraguan Resistance in Miami.

18. The Pentagon, at CIA urging, classified the three Cessna O-2s as "surplus materials," turning them over free-of-charge to a Delaware firm for outfitting with rockets. Then the CIA delivered the planes to the FDN. See the December 9, 1983, entry in *The Chronology: The Documented Day-by-Day Account of the Secret Military Assistance to Iran and the Contras* (New York: Warner Books, 1987), edited by the staff of Washington's National Security Archives. A CIA officer who served in Honduras said the planes were to be used for close air support during contra attacks in northern Nicaragua.

19. Most of the details on the FDN medical system were drawn from interviews with Francisco "Dr. Rubén" Rugama, a Nicaraguan physician now living in Miami who worked for the FDN from 1983 to 1985.

20. "The weakest part of the whole program in the early period was the contra army's inability to collect intelligence and use it properly," a CIA officer who worked with the contras in Honduras said in a March 1990 interview.

21. I drew my portrayal of the history of the FDN intelligence system from interviews with Bermúdez; Mike Lima; another senior FDN officer who worked with Lau in his Florencia South safe house and requested anonymity; and a CIA officer who worked with the FDN in Honduras. In addition to intelligence and counterintelligence, Lau had initial responsibility for a third secret organization called "the Internal Front," whose mission was to infiltrate agents into Nicaragua to set up safe houses and recruit collaborators. Bermúdez said in an

interview on January 3, 1990, that Lau had a staff of just five paid agents: three working in Tegucigalpa, one in Choluteca, and one in Danlí. "Lau had no real intelligence capacity. We were just a gang," Bermúdez said.

22. Mike Lima, one of Lau's successors as FDN intelligence chief, identified Iván Bendaña in an interview on November 20, 1989, as one of Lau's first victims. Lima said he believed the FDN's Argentine advisers ordered Lau to kill Bendaña after Bendaña complained about the terrible food at a leadership course run by the Argentines at La Quinta. "Lau just had a group of killers, men that would kill whomever Lau considered a danger to the commander," Lima said. I first heard of Bendaña's murder in June 1986, and interviewed two of his brothers in Miami: Milciades, a onetime Guard cadet, and Pedro, a former Guard second lieutenant. They showed me the April 25, 1982, Bermúdez telegram. After learning of Iván's murder, Milciades and Pedro traveled to Honduras to investigate. There, Lau's personal secretary told them Lau had arranged the execution, Milciades said. Milciades said he believed Iván had been murdered because he had threatened to reveal crimes committed by Lau in Guatemala. In a January 1990 interview in Miami, Bermúdez said: "People have suggested that Chino Lau was executing people on my orders. That is false. Totally false . . . . We've been accused of everything: as thugs, thieves, drug addicts—everything. But nobody has ever proven anything."

23. My account of the 1981 agreement to put FDN death squads at the service of the Honduran military comes from interviews with a former senior FDN officer. He himself did not participate in the negotiations between the Argentines and the Hondurans, but learned of the agreement directly from one of the participants. The officer's position gave him access to the FDN's secret intelligence and counterintelligence files starting in 1983, and he uncovered detailed evidence of FDN executions coordinated by Argentines after Honduran targeting. FDN record keepers employed a euphemism to describe the operations: "Noxious elements were eliminated."

24. Honduran Army officers revealed in January 1985 that Lau's unit had worked closely with General Alvarez's 316 battalion. See Juan Tamayo in the *Miami Herald* on January 15, 1985. The officers especially stressed the FDN squad's involvement in the deaths of Salvadorans. General Walter López, Honduran Armed Forces Commander from 1984 to 1986, claimed in a March 29, 1987, interview on CBS's "60 Minutes" that the CIA had actually targeted many of the alleged arms traffickers for elimination by FDN killers. No eyewitness accounts or other hard evidence have confirmed those allegations, however. CIA targeting of FDN death squad victims would have been consistent with Reagan Administration policy; the CIA originally described the FDN's purpose to congressional oversight committees as a force designed to interdict arms.

25. The account of the murder of the two Hondurans was told in the August 1986 *Progressive* magazine.

26. Juan Tamayo reported that eighty-two Salvadorans disappeared in Honduras during the period. See the *Miami Herald*, January 15, 1985.

27. Several contras described the use of the ovens in the Choluteca gold mine

to burn bodies and, some said, to murder live victims. One was a former senior FDN officer who worked with Lau, who requested anonymity. Another was Efrén "Moisés" Mondragón, a regional commander who defected from the contra army in March 1985.

28. Edgar Chamorro, a former political director of the FDN, said that the CIA channeled funds to Lau and his staff of agents through Bermúdez during the period that Chamorro was working in Honduras, from early 1983 through mid-1984. Chamorro said Lau's counterintelligence unit was a line item on the monthly FDN budget, funds which were provided by the CIA. Chamorro described the unit's function: "to look for subversives and eliminate threats." I interviewed Chamorro on February 17, 1987, about the payments to Lau.

29. The CIA's training of Honduran interrogators and the Agency's contacts with the 316 battalion were discussed in *Human Rights in Honduras*, a publication of the human-rights monitor Americas Watch (New York, May 1987).

. 30. Numerous contras had dealings with "Ricardo." All have described him as a CIA investigator and reporter.

31. For Doty's boasts about the CIA's spying on the rebels, see Woodward's *Veil*, page 231.

32. The commanders were: army, former Guard Colonel Enrique Bermúdez; air force, former Guard Colonel Juan Gómez; "navy," former Guard Colonel Isidro Sandino; medical corps, former Guard Colonel Ernesto Matamoros; intelligence, former Guard Colonel Ricardo Lau.

33. Somoza's *jueces de mesta* were armed sheriffs who arrested drunks, murderers, and bootleggers, and kept an eye cocked for subversives in thousands of Nicaraguan hamlets.

34. My account of Aristides Sánchez's background comes from interviews with Aristides and with his two brothers, both of whom also worked with the FDN. Enrique Sánchez, Aristides's older brother, went to work on the Project in late 1981 in Honduras, at first helping the CIA build angry Miskito Indians into a rebel army, and later forging the FDN's U.S.-financed "Internal Front" network inside Nicaragua. Victor Sánchez, Aristides's younger brother, joined the FDN as a fighter in September 1982.

35. For insight into the diversity of views within the CIA on this division of labor between combat and politics, see Woodward's depiction of the 1983 argument between CIA Director Casey and Dewey Clarridge, then the head of the CIA's Central American Task Force, in *Veil*, page 260.

36. The two others were Mariano Mendoza and Francisco Cardenal.

37. Details of the December 1982 CIA recruiting drive in Miami were drawn from several interviews with Edgar Chamorro and from "Confessions of a Contra," an article by Chamorro and journalist Jeff Morley, published in the *New Republic*, August 5, 1985.

38. Joe Fernández's name became public when he was indicted in Washington in April 1989 on charges of lying to Iran-contra investigators about his activities as the CIA station chief in Costa Rica from 1984 to 1986, after leaving Honduras. A federal judge dismissed the case in November 1989 after Attorney

General Dick Thornburgh blocked Fernández from using certain classified information in his defense. Several career details were drawn from Fernández's profile in the State Department's Biographic Register. Other information came from an article by Knight Ridder's Washington legal reporter Aaron Epstein, published in the *Miami Herald* on November 25, 1989.

39. I drew the biographic information on Calero from a 1985 State Department handout and from numerous published interviews. Chamorro said in a 1988 interview that Calero had long worked for the CIA in Nicaragua. Several U.S. officials identified Tony Feldman to me as the CIA agent who brought Calero into exile.

40. Calero remained sensitive for years to any suggestion that he was not an independent patriot but rather that the CIA had recruited him to work as a rebel politician. "That's the goddamnedest lie in the world," he fumed at a reporter who asked him in March 1985 if he had been recruited by the CIA. Calero claimed that after going into exile, he had gone to visit Bermúdez to answer the question "Who are these Guardias who are running this?" He conceded he had met some American officials working with the FDN. "None of the Americans I have associated with was older than me, or had more education," he said, denying again that he had been recruited by the CIA. "That's ridiculous," he said. "I was not interviewed. I did not receive payments."

41. Details of the FDN parallels with the CIA's 1961 Project were arrived at after reading *The Bay of Pigs* by Haynes Johnson (New York: Norton, 1964), an account based on interviews with 2506 Brigade veterans.

42. The details on John Mallett's career were drawn from the State Department's Biographic Register and from interviews with several present and former U.S. officials who worked with him. My description of him comes from a photo of Mallett published on page 144 of *La Contra*, a book on the contra war written by former FDN negotiator Jaime Morales Carazo (Mexico: Planeta, 1989). Mallett was identified as a CIA agent in a 1983 German publication, *CIA in Mittelamerika*, by G. Neuberger. He was first identified as the "George" working with the contras on pages 11 and 50 of Chamorro's *Packaging the Contras*.

43. Walter "Toño" Calderón, an FDN officer who occasionally visited Sánchez at FDN safe houses in Tegucigalpa, quoted Sánchez on his dealings with the CIA.

44. The bogus lumber company was Maderero del Norte. Juan Tamayo identified it in the *Miami Herald* on December 19, 1982. Chamorro described Fernández's inspection of the FDN safe houses in a February 1987 interview.

5: Dirty War

1. Mike Lima described, among other details, how he named his Diriangén regional command, used horses for mobility, and visited his parents at the head of his troops in interviews in Tegucigalpa March 5, 6, and 7, 1989.

2. Several contra commanders recalled Mike Lima's early abuses in separate interviews. I interviewed Walter "Toño" Calderón in Miami on May 16, 1989;

Freddy "Coral" Gadea also in Miami on October 18, 1989; and Luis Fley in Tegucigalpa on June 20, 1989.

3. Mike Lima's "I killed a lot . . ." quote came from a Tegucigalpa interview on March 10, 1989.

4. I drew details of Mike Lima's attack on Pantasma from interviews with Lima and his aide Benjamín Salazar, "El Politico," on March 7, 1989, as well as a half dozen other rebels who served under Lima in the attack. *Barricada* reported the Pantasma attack in detail on October 21, 1983. The Pantasma damage and casualty figures came from Julia Preston's October 21, 1983, article in the *Boston Globe.* Mike Lima said that eighty people had been killed. The government said forty-seven. Lima claimed that his two execution victims were an army lieutenant and a State Security officer. Preston, in her *Globe* article, quoted townspeople as saying that the victims were "peasants suspected as Sandinista sympathizers."

5. In an interview published in the January 30, 1985, issue of the Honduran daily *El Tiempo*, Honduran schoolteacher Juan José Espinal alleged that former EEBI Private Marcos "Black Dimas" Navarro had kidnapped him in Choluteca, along with a Honduran student, Hipólito Rodríguez. Espinal, who escaped, claimed to have seen Navarro execute Rodríguez with a pistol. Espinal also accused Black Dimas of sending contra troops into Nicaragua to rustle cattle for resale in Honduras. Those charges have been repeated many times in the years since. Black Dimas was, at the end of the war, the Resistance's operations chief.

6. José Efrén Mondragón Martínez, a contra counterintelligence officer who defected from the FDN in March 1985, listed the clandestine graveyards in interviews March 30, 1985, and May 30, 1985, that were later translated by the U.S. Congressional Research Service and circulated in Congress.

7. Details on Mack's style of command at La Lodosa were drawn from interviews with Lieutenant Marlon Blandón Osorio, Mack's executive officer, in interviews on June 21, 1986, and May 19, 1989, and with Dr. Francisco Rugama, a physician who was based at La Lodosa during the period. Blandón Osorio and several other rebels offered details on Mack's aides, Zero-Three, Z-Two, and X-Seven. Former FDN spokesman Edgar Chamorro, in an interview on July 13, 1989, in Managua, described how Mack's killings at La Lodosa became common knowledge within the rebel movement.

8. Suicide, posthumously, became one of the most famous insurgent field commanders after *Washington Post* correspondent Chris Dickey chronicled his rebel career in his book *With the Contras* (New York: Simon and Schuster, 1985).

9. In an October 1983 interview with the author in Tegucigalpa, FDN Director Adolfo Calero said that Suicide's most serious crime had been embezzlement.

10. In a January 1990 interview in Miami, Bermúdez insisted that a tribunal of FDN officers had court-martialed Suicide and his staff officers. But Bermúdez couldn't recall the names of the tribunal's supposed members, where the tribunal had met, or what crimes they had attributed to Suicide and his officers. Pressed for details, Bermúdez said, "I don't have any further information to give you on that case."

11. Dickey, in *With the Contras,* page 247, describes Krill's arrest days after a failed attack on the northern Nicaraguan town of El Jícaro during the last week of August 1983. *Barricada,* on August 25 and 26, 1983, reported on the Jícaro attack. Krill and Suicide's other staff officers were held only days, or at most a couple of weeks, at La Quinta, according to several rebels who guarded them.

12. I drew details of the multiple execution at Alauca from Blandón Osorio, Mack's executive officer, in two interviews three years apart: June 21, 1986, and May 19, 1989. Blandón's version of the executions did not change in any detail between the two interviews.

13. Jhonson told the story of his attempt to enlist American help to stop the killings at La Lodosa in an interview on June 20, 1989.

14. Clarridge's briefing to Congress was reported by Alfonso Chardy in the October 20, 1983, *Miami Herald.* Dickey refers to the briefing on page 257 of *With the Contras.*

15. Bermúdez's involvement with rebel commandos was described by several FDN officers working closely with him at the time. The complaints about embezzlement of salaries and food money were detailed by several rebels, including former National Guard Lt. Marlon Blandón and former Guard Lieutenant Javier Gómez in interviews on June 21, 1986. The *New York Times* of the same date, June 21, 1986, detailed the same charges.

16. Mike Lima and other contra commanders understood clearly that the FDN couldn't defeat the Sandinistas in set-piece engagements. "I knew how to fight the Sandinistas," Mike Lima said in a March 1989 interview, "and I knew that we could win one or two battles, but not a whole war. They had better armament than we had. We could hurt them economically. But we couldn't defeat them."

17. Some sixty FDN fighters were killed in the CIA-ordered offensive in December 1983—about as many as had died in the previous eleven months. See Juan Tamayo's excellent account of the fighting and the FDN reorganization in the March 11, 1984, *Miami Herald.*

18. I assembled the account of the CIA-backed conspiracy to remove the general staff from interviews with several rebels who participated, including Walter "Toño" Calderón, Marlón "Gorrión" Blandón, Javier "Wili" Gómez, Hugo "Visage" Villagra, Francisco "Dr. Rubén" Rugama, and Luis "Mike Lima" Moreno. I obtained a copy of the January 10, 1984, letter signed by forty-two commanders and sent to Adolfo Calero asking for Bermúdez's replacement. I also discussed the CIA's goals in the rebellion with a CIA officer serving in Honduras during this period.

6: The Cutoff

1. The attempts on the Paso Caballos bridge by Fley's unit were only three of many mounted by the CIA. Nicaraguan Interior Ministry official Lenin Cerna announced one of the early aborted attempts in a press conference reported in the February 19, 1982, *Barricada.* The CIA's own sabotage squads of "unilaterally

controlled Latin assets," called UCLAs, using diving gear, failed in at least one attempt reported by David Blanco, the top Interior Ministry official in the Corinto region, in a press conference reported in the September 17, 1983, *Barricada.* Commander Cerna, looking back across ten years of revolution in a July 19, 1989, *Barricada* interview, cited the disruption of CIA attempts to destroy Paso Caballos as one of his State Security Directorate's greatest accomplishments.

2. Articles detailing attacks by combat units directly controlled by the CIA are included in the October 12, 1984, *New York Times,* the October 12, 1984, *Washington Post,* the December 20, 1984, *Miami Herald,* and the April 18, 1984, and March 6, 1985, issues of the *Wall Street Journal.*

3. For a convenient summary of the complicated history of the legislation on U.S. assistance to the contras, see *Contra Aid: A Brief Chronology and Table Showing U.S. Assistance to the Anti-Sandinista Guerrillas, Fiscal Years 1982–1988,* by Robert E. Sanchez of the Library of Congress, Congressional Research Service, March 10, 1988.

4. Because of Victorino Estrada's collaboration with the contras, the Sandinista army confiscated his hacienda in 1986, turning it into a state farm. Then Jhonson's men burned it.

5. The May 3 and 4, 1983, issues of *Barricada* feature articles detailing the Sandinista Front's efforts in the El Cuá area to suppress rebel supporters. The articles focus especially on the targeting and suppression of the La Perla cooperative as an alleged counterrevolutionary organization.

6. The figures on the Popular Anti-Somocista Tribunals come from "Human Rights in Nicaragua, 1985–1986" (New York: Americas Watch, March 1986). For a good summary of rights abuses by both sides throughout the contra war, see "Nicaragua, A Human Rights Chronology, July 1979 to July 1989" (New York: Americas Watch, July 1989). An article I wrote in the May 3, 1987, *Miami Herald,* headlined "Sandinistas Accused of Jail Abuses," was another discussion of the treatment of detainees inside the Sandinista detention centers.

7. See my article in the April 15, 1984, *Miami Herald* for details of the January–March 1984 Pantasma investigation and trial. A parallel scandal erupted during the same period after Sandinista Front officials supervised similarly brutal suppression of peasants around Yalí. Sandinista officials told me that the Agrarian Reform Ministry had investigated the incidents and written a report, "The Case of Yalí," which was never published publicly.

8. See the September 15, 1983, *Miami Herald* for a summary of the draft law. It required men aged eighteen to twenty-five to register for a two-year stint in the army, and men aged twenty-six to forty to register for service in army reserve battalions. Conscription began in January 1984.

9. Besides Jhonson, other former civilians who rose to significant command positions during the period included Oscar "Rubén" Sobalvarro, Pastor "Denis" Meza, Rudy "Douglas" Zelaya, Tirzo "Rigoberto" Moreno, Israel "Franklyn" Galeano, Diógenes "Fernando" Hernández, and Freddy "Coral" Gadea. Pastor "Indio" Palacios became an influential task force commander. Some former National Guardsmen served under these men. And the top commander of the

Jorge Salazar operational group, who coordinated operations by Rigoberto, Franklyn, and Fernando, was a former Guard sergeant, Juan "Quiché" Rivas. It cannot be said that the units commanded by these men committed no abuses. But an examination of the investigative files of the Nicaraguan Association for Human Rights and many interviews showed that these men forged qualitatively different relations with Nicaragua's peasants than did the ex-Guardsmen, most of whom quit fighting during the period. Three of Tigrillo's officers also became regional commanders during the period. They were José "Tiro al Blanco" Galeano, Abelardo "Iván" Zelaya, and Francisco "Dimas Tigrillo" Baldivia, Tigrillo's brother. Paradoxically, however, though these men enjoyed firm roots among the peasantry, they continued to commit such systematic abuses—rapes and murders—that their records are virtually indistinguishable from those of the ex-Guardsmen.

10. Dickey, in *With the Contras*, dates Winters's departure to about June 1984, and suggests that Winters was in disgrace for failing to foresee the coup against General Alvarez. See page 262.

11. Vincent Shields's involvement in the CIA's war in Laos was mentioned in Christopher Robbins's book *Air America* (London: Macmillan, 1979). I discussed Shields's work as Tegucigalpa station chief with a former CIA officer who worked for him in Honduras.

12. For a quick summary of the Saudi payments to Calero's FDN account, see the July 1984 entry in *The Chronology*, National Security Archive.

13. The Iran-contra affair has been studied widely in other books. I discuss the U.S. scandal only where necessary to understand the course of Jhonson's rebel war.

14. Edgar Chamorro, working closely with Bermúdez at the time, was quoted widely on Bermúdez's continuing ties to Lau: "He [Lau] was still the last person to speak to Bermúdez at night and the first person to talk to him in the morning," Chamorro said. "Absolutely absurd," Bermúdez called Chamorro's claims in a January 1990 interview.

15. Several U.S. officials said as late as 1989 that they believed Lau was still receiving an FDN stipend, financed by the CIA. But they had no proof.

16. A senior FDN officer who worked with Lau's office and lived in Bermúdez's safe house for a time said Bermúdez arranged a U.S. visa for Armando López, Jr., who moved to Los Angeles.

17. Among the rebels who detailed Bermúdez's philandering were Walter "Toño" Calderón, Luis "Mike Lima" Moreno, Victor "Licenciado" Sánchez, Guillermo "Pecos Bill" Gasteazoro, as well as a senior FDN officer who lived at the Strategic Command during the period but declined to be identified. Bermúdez's affair with Rina Ortega was so well known in Honduras that a reporter for the Sandinista organ *Barricada* learned of it during a March 1986 reporting trip to Honduras and published details in the April 3, 1986, *Barricada.*

18. My account of the Santa Clara incident was drawn from interviews with Mike Lima, Guillermo Gasteazoro, Carlos Guillén, and another senior FDN officer who asked for anonymity.

19. The causes of the accident remain in dispute. Mike Lima blamed the accident on the CIA, whose logistical officers he claimed gave him four Soviet-made 82-mm. mortar tubes, and, days later, boxed Chinese-made ammunition for an 82-mm. recoilless rifle. The much more powerful recoilless rifle ammunition blew apart the thin steel of the mortar tubes, he said. Walter "Toño" Calderón, a friend of Lima's at the time, said that Lima captured the Soviet-made mortar tubes in his takeover of Pantasma, then asked the CIA for 82-mm. ammunition. The CIA's logistical men believed the request was for 82-mm. recoilless rifle shells. Furthermore, Calderón said Mike Lima altered the artillery shells with a knife to make them fit the mortar tube. In any event, the accident left Mike Lima angry at the CIA. "I lost my arm and four of my men died because of those sons of bitches in the CIA. We Latins think of ourselves as fools, and I was a young kid. I believed you Americans are the maximum: intelligent, capable people. So when they sent me the wrong ammunition, I didn't doubt them."

20. There undoubtedly were enemy spies in the camp, because the Sandinistas boasted later about their successes at infiltrating rebel ranks. But other rebel officers said Mike Lima—and other ex-Guardsmen—routinely labeled disorder, indiscipline, and insubordination as the work of enemy infiltrators.

21. An interesting inside look at the operations of Mike Lima's intelligence section at the time and Bermúdez's close involvement with it came in the November 20, 1985, issue of *El Tiempo*, the Tegucigalpa daily. María Mercedes Rivas Obregón, a pretty twenty-three-year-old Nicaraguan teacher held prisoner at Las Vegas starting in November 1984, escaped in 1985 and told her story to Honduran reporters. She said that after being seized by Tigrillo's men inside Nicaragua, she was raped, then forced to carry cargo with a contra column to Banco Grande, an FDN base on the Coco River, and then west to Las Vegas. There, she said she was "investigated" by Bermúdez, Z-Two, and Mike Lima. She was not raped there, but she claimed to have learned of the rapes of several other prisoners during her imprisonment at Las Vegas. Bermúdez asked her if she wanted to join the FDN and become his secretary, she said. She demurred. Instead she was made a cook, she said.

22. In a Miami interview in November 1989, Mike Lima recalled of his intelligence work: "I discovered the first network of infiltrators, and if we didn't capture all of them, at least we made them afraid to act with impunity . . . Bermúdez didn't realize that we weren't playing with just kids—there were people out there that were shooting and that were killing. So what I did, I did because I needed to protect my own life . . . I was in intelligence only a couple of months, because in a certain way, it didn't appeal to me. It was going to dirty me after so much glory in the field. Intelligence work gets you dirty, because you're a son of a bitch whether you do it well or badly."

23. Reagan made his "Founding Fathers" speech before the Conservative Political Action Conference on March 1, 1985. See the *New York Times*, March 2, 1985.

24. The corollary of the Reagan Administration's policy of dismissing reli-

able reports of contra atrocities as unfounded was to consistently exaggerate reports of Sandinista abuses. Americas Watch, the New York–based rights monitor, complained in a 1986 report: "The United States has detracted from its credibility in speaking out about human-rights abuses anywhere by exaggerating abuses in Nicaragua, most recently by disseminating accusations that the Nicaraguan government has murdered thousands of its political opponents according to a centrally directed plan. These charges are unsubstantiated and almost certainly false. It does a disservice to the human-rights cause to disseminate war propaganda and pass it off as human-rights information." From *Human Rights in Nicaragua, 1985–1986.*

25. Veldhuyzen, who after graduation took a job in Washington and was in 1989 attending law school at George Mason University, heard North make his comments about Wohl in a briefing for the Washington-based American Security Council early in 1986.

26. "Their focus was not on who did the killing, but on who let the photographer into the camps," a U.S. official involved at the time said of the CIA investigation of the Wohl affair. "They were really pissed off about who let this guy in. But they weren't going to lift a finger in terms of pinpointing the guys with the knives."

27. Wohl stuck by his version during many retellings, always maintaining that the rebel execution had taken place near the comarca of Balsama, near San Juan del Río Coco in Nicaragua's Madriz province. I know of no reason why Wohl would have lied about the location of the murder. Jhonson, however, was certain that the killing occurred in Honduras.

28. Two of Wohl's classmates at Northwestern University, Tom Holt and Albert Veldhuyzen, enumerated Wohl's bonanza photo earnings, which they said he invested in a mutual fund. After graduation, Wohl sold real estate in Miami Beach until May 4, 1987, when he died at twenty-four in a motorcycle crash in Key West. Wohl's obituary appeared in the May 5, 1987, *Miami Herald.* His photos sparked extensive media coverage after they appeared in the April 29, 1985, *Newsweek,* which hit the newsstands on April 22. The *Washington Times* led the charge of conservatives portraying the photos as Sandinista fakes. See the April 24, April 25, April 29, May 6, and June 5, 1985, issues. Also see the April 25, 1985, Associated Press dispatch, and articles in the *Chicago Tribune* on April 24 and April 26, 1985.

29. A 1986 Sandinista government publication distributed to foreign journalists, *El Revés de La Contrarevolución—The Defeat of the Counterrevolution,* said that 250,000 Nicaraguans were under arms: 60,000 in the Sandinista army, and 190,000 in the militias and reserves. Diplomats said the army figure was low.

30. "If I hadn't lost my arm, maybe I might have won a few more victories," Mike Lima said in 1989. "But probably they would have killed me, I knew it. The Sandinistas are brave, they're good soldiers, they're well trained. The Simon Bolívar, the German Pomares—those are great battalions."

31. See my articles from December 30, 1985, and June 15, 1986, in the *Miami Herald* for a longer discussion of the Sandinista buildup.

32. Tigrillo detailed his experiences in a May 1988 interview in Miami. His brother Dimas described his encounter with Tigrillo at Aguacate in a February 1989 interview.

33. A U.S. State Department officer who worked with the rebels described to me in a September 1989 interview the ordeal "Sergeant" suffered through.

34. Oliver North closely monitored the 1985 Sandinista artillery barrage of Las Vegas and sent lots of advice down to Bermúdez with his courier, Robert Owen, about how to protect, and finally move, the camps. See North's memos to Robert McFarlane on February 6, 1985, and April 11, 1985, published with McFarlane's testimony to the Select Committees on the Iran-Contra Investigation. I also drew on interviews with Mike Lima and other contras who participated in the move. See the March 26, 1985, issue of Tegucigalpa's *La Tribuna* for an article on the Sandinista shelling of La Lodosa.

35. I drew the figures on land titling from the 1986 Sandinista government publication *El Revés de La Contrarevolución—The Defeat of the Counterrevolution.*

36. The Nicaraguan government did not maintain official figures on the numbers of people its agents arrested, but investigators from Americas Watch, the New York human-rights monitor, concluded that arrests had surged in 1986 by analyzing the number of persons charged before the Popular Anti-Somocista Tribunals, the emergency courts set up to try contra collaborators. Tribunal prosecutors received cases for prosecution as follows: 513 cases in 1983, the year the tribunals were established; 302 in 1984; 301 in 1985, and 976 between January and August 1986. Many other people were arrested and released after investigation by State Security. The figures, by extrapolation, suggest that arrests quintupled in 1986. Americas Watch published its findings in *Human Rights in Nicaragua, 1986* (New York: Americas Watch, February 1987).

37. See the *Miami Herald* from March 17, 1985, for details of the resettlement. The June 4, 1985, *New York Times* numbered the internally displaced at 180,000. The government publication *El Revés de La Contrarevolución—The Defeat of the Counterrevolution* numbered the government settlements at 145 in 1986.

38. Alan Bolt, a dissident Sandinista activist, recalled the conversation with his cousin, a Sandinista army officer, during a July 1989 interview at his home outside Matagalpa, Nicaragua. The controversial study was "Dos Pasos Atrás y Dos y Medio Adelante—Two Steps Back and Two and a Half Forward," published in 1986 by the Agrarian Reform Ministry.

39. See the *Report of the Congressional Committees Investigating the Iran-Contra Affair*, page 60, for details of Bermúdez and Calero's Miami meeting with North in July 1985.

40. Mike Lima quoted Bermúdez demanding a "spectacular attack."

41. For the account of the Trinidad attack, I drew on the *Miami Herald*,

August 2, 1985, and on interviews with several commanders involved in the strike.

42. For a concise statement of the government's view about how it defeated the contras in 1985, see the October 15, 1985, *Barricada* account of Sandinista army chief of staff Gen. Joaquín Cuadras's exposition on the subject.

43. For an extensive analysis of the politics surrounding Congress's $27 million "humanitarian" aid appropriation in June 1985, see John Felton's articles in the *Congressional Quarterly* on June 15, 1985, as well as his nineteen-page analysis starting on page 61 of *Congressional Quarterly*'s 1985 Almanac.

44. Mondragón Martínez's statements were widely disseminated. See the *Washington Post*, May 7, 1985. Two lengthy interviews with Mondragón, conducted in March and May 1985, were translated into English by the Library of Congress's Congressional Research Service and circulated widely in Congress. Mondragón was the highest-ranking field commander to defect from the contra movement. His charges about contra abuses have been amply corroborated by numerous other rebels over the years since. The Sandinistas rewarded Mondragón for the propaganda he gave them with an atrocity of their own. Two years after Mondragón's 1985 amnesty and return to Nicaragua, he told reporters that Sandinista authorities had constantly harassed him since his return and complained that his life was in danger. He was jailed twice by local State Security officials. A year later, Mondragón turned up beaten, stabbed, and shot in the square of his hometown, the northern village of Somotillo, where a local Sandinista militia commander kicked his body in a public warning to villagers. There were no witnesses to the murder, but his mother said he was last seen leaving his home in the custody of State Security agents. Richard Boudreaux's investigative reporting documented Mondragón's story in the June 11, 1987, and the April 7, 1988, issues of the *Los Angeles Times*.

45. Arturo Cruz, Jr., described Alan Fiers's background on page 213 of *Memoirs of a Counter-Revolutionary* (New York: Doubleday, 1989). Cruz referred to Fiers by his pseudonym, "Cliff."

46. Doyle McManus disclosed the seven-thousand-dollar monthly stipend North channeled to Cruz from January through October 1986 in the February 20, 1987, *Los Angeles Times*.

47. Icaza described the Código de Procedimientos in an interview with the Tegucigalpa daily, *El Tiempo*, published on August 23, 1985.

48. I drew my account of the history of the FDN prisons from interviews with Marta Patricia Baltodano and Alfonso Sandino, both lawyers with the State Department–funded Nicaraguan Association for Human Rights; Guillermo "Pecos Bill" Gasteazoro, the ex-Guard lieutenant who worked with Leo at both Las Vegas and Yamales; Walter "Toño" Calderón, the FDN regional commander who was good friends with Leo; and Mike Lima, who helped Leo set up the Military Police.

49. A Honduran woman, Ildefonsa Funez de Maldonado, forty-four, provided macabre testimony in December 1987 of the violent atmosphere that reigned at

Yamales during the period when contras had their Strategic Command there. She drove in a taxi to the Danlí, Honduras, offices of the Honduran daily *La Tribuna*, carrying the skeletons of her husband and seventeen-year-old son. She said both had been murdered at Yamales on November 8, 1986, one shot, the other bayoneted. She said that since their deaths she had sought to recover their bodies for Christian burial. The article suggested that contras committed the murders, but she made no direct accusations. *La Tribuna* published her story on December 10, 1987. Another violent incident during the same period demonstrated the extreme sensitivity of the FDN's leaders to internal criticism while Calero and Bermúdez were under fire in Washington. Leonardo Zeledón Rodríguez, a former sergeant from Somoza's EEBI, was a personal aide to Bermúdez early in the war. But he resigned from the FDN in 1982, then worked for three years as an adviser to the CIA-backed Miskito Indian army also based in Honduras. In September 1985, Zeledón Rodríguez showed up in the Honduran newspapers, complaining that FDN counterintelligence chief Donald Torres was plotting to kill him because he had criticized FDN corruption. He pleaded for the protection of the Honduran government. His comments appeared in the Honduran daily *El Tiempo* on September 25, 1985. Five months later, in January 1986, FDN counterintelligence agents seized Zeledón as he emerged from a Tegucigalpa restaurant, beating and kicking him senseless. The assault left Zeledón paralyzed from the waist down. Zeledón told the story of his attack in a hospital bed interview published in *El Tiempo* on April 26, 1986. Four days after the attack was reported, the UNO-FDN bought a paid advertisement to describe Zeledón's accusations as "Soviet propaganda." The contra advertisement appeared in *El Tiempo* on April 29, 1986. Jhonson, who met Zeledón Rodríguez when he first came to Honduras in 1982, said it was well known in the FDN that Donald Torres and his men from FDN counterintelligence had carried out the assault that paralyzed Zeledón. Jhonson said Bermúdez paid for some of Zeledón's medical costs and bought him a wheelchair after the 1986 attack to quiet his public criticisms.

50. John Felton's article in the June 28, 1986, *Congressional Quarterly* analyzed the $100 million contra aid vote.

7: The $100 Million Offensive

1. The formal name of the Honduras-based rebel army changed several times during the war. From 1981 through mid-1985 it was the Nicaraguan Democratic Force, FDN. Then, with Alfonso Robelo and Arturo Cruz joining Calero in the political front United Nicaraguan Opposition, the army became known as UNO-FDN. In mid-1987, its formal name became the Army of the Northern Front of the Nicaraguan Resistance—though most of Bermúdez's ex-Guardsmen continued to think of themselves as the FDN. I refer to the army as "the Resistance" for events after early 1987.

2. Salvador Stadthagen, deputy director of the Nicaraguan Resistance's Wash-

ington office, told a reporter from the *Ft. Walton Beach Playground Daily News* in Ft. Walton Beach, Florida, in September 1987 that seventy contra leaders had trained at a base in the Florida panhandle in late 1986. Eglin Air Force Base is adjacent to Ft. Walton Beach. I showed a wire-service pickup of the *Playground Daily News* story reprinted in the September 3, 1987, *Miami Herald* to a retired CIA officer who was working with the rebels at the time of their U.S. training, and he confirmed that the rebels were trained at Eglin Air Force Base.

3. I drew my discussion of contrasting U.S. strategies from interviews with U.S. officials in September 1989. For an account of the CIA's view then of what U.S. strategy should be, see my article in the January 22, 1987, *Miami Herald*, based on a strategy document distributed to the press by Bosco Matamoros. Matamoros, the rebel spokesman in Washington, liked to call himself a nationalist. Often, however, as in this case, he was a mouthpiece for CIA views.

4. My account of the U.S. training comes from interviews with the following contras: Jhonson, Jacinto "Campéon" López, Freddy "Coral" Gadea, and José Angel "Chakal" Talavera. Also see the January 9, 1987, *New York Times*. Two U.S. officials involved in the training, one a military officer and the other a civilian, also detailed the instruction and its objectives.

5. Many contras met and dealt with James Adkins, known as "Colonel Jaime." The *Washington Post*, on December 18, 1987, reported his dismissal by CIA Director William H. Webster, publishing his name, misspelled as "Atkins." I reconstructed his career from the *Post* and other newspaper articles, from information given me by the contras and by using the State Department's Biographic Register. Adkins's work in Guyana was detailed in the June 1980 issue of *Covert Action Information Bulletin*, though the magazine incorrectly identified him as deputy chief of station; he was station chief in Georgetown. I also discussed Adkins's career with a former CIA officer.

6. The loosening of the CIA restrictions was little-noted at the time. John Felton mentioned them in his nineteen-page analysis of contra aid starting on page 61 of *Congressional Quarterly*'s 1985 Almanac. I discussed the impact of the changes with a former CIA official.

7. I discussed the defects of the rebels' previous communications security and intelligence gathering, as well as the improvements brought by the U.S. aid in 1986, with three U.S. officials who worked with the rebels at the time.

8. The February 26, 1987, *Washington Post* published a long article detailing Martin and McCoy's contra arms transactions. Oliver North testified about the CIA's suspicions about the group's arms supermarket during the Iran-contra hearings. See the *Report of the Congressional Committees Investigating the Iran-Contra Affair*, page 50. I discussed the CIA's frictions with the Honduran Army over the arms supermarket with a U.S. official who watched the relations fray from a posting in Tegucigalpa during the period.

9. Colonel Gerald Clark was well known to reporters because of his prominent role in the U.S. military exercises in Honduras during the decade. He died in an automobile crash in Panama on February 26, 1989. The Reuters news agen-

cy moved an obituary on February 27, 1989. I called his wife at her home in suburban Virginia to request an interview about Clark's career, but respected her plea to be left alone when she expressed pain about discussing his memory.

10. Ironically, it wasn't the Honduran military that sent Adkins home. The CIA itself turned Adkins out of his job in May 1987, accusing him during the Iran-contra scandal of being a rogue officer. Higher-ups accused Adkins of using CIA helicopters to fly contra wounded from border bases to the Aguacate hospital and other tasks when such assistance was technically illegal. The May 29, 1987, *Los Angeles Times* first reported on Adkins's suspension, without naming him. "The agent told investigators that he acted not on orders from his CIA superiors or from White House aide Oliver L. North . . . but out of humanitarian concern for the contras," the *Times* story said. "Leave in an empty helicopter when a guy's leg has been blown off and his life's blood is draining out? Not me, mister!" Adkins told associates angrily. Adkins never denied helping the contras when such aid was technically illegal, but he said he was scapegoated by CIA superiors who needed to satisfy congressional calls for an Agency housecleaning. The *Washington Post,* on December 18, 1987, reported his dismissal by CIA Director William H. Webster, misspelling his name as "Atkins."

11. I interviewed several rebels about the evolution of the FDN air force and the two successive mercenary forces U.S. officials recruited to supersede it. Most knowledgeable was Gustavo "Waiky" Quezada, a rebel pilot based at Aguacate who flew frequently to Swan, whom I interviewed in Miami on May 21, 1989.

12. Description of Aguacate in 1987 comes from Victor "Licenciado" Sánchez, based there throughout the year as Bermúdez's operations officer; Diógenes "Fernando" Hernández, also based there as personnel officer; Donald Lacayo, who traveled to Aguacate as the rebels' legal adviser, and others.

13. I drew details of the CIA operation on Swan Island from interviews with Noel "Trickster" Castillo Burgos, an FDN officer based on the island in 1987, and Victor "Licenciado" Sánchez, who traveled to the island. Alejandro Sánchez Herrera, a cargo kicker based on Swan and captured by the Sandinistas in January 1988, provided extensive details during a Managua press conference after his capture. See the UPI report of the press conference, published in Tegucigalpa's *El Tiempo* on January 26, 1988. Francisco "Lester" Sánchez Picado, also based on the island during 1987 and later captured by the Sandinistas, also described the CIA operation on the island. For Sánchez's statements, see the March 18, 1988, *Barricada.*

14. Walter "Toño" Calderón, Victor "Licenciado" Sánchez, and other contras described the U.S. pressure on Bermúdez to move to San Andrés de Bocay.

15. The May 23, 1987, *New York Times* detailed the Sandinistas' operation against San Andrés.

16. I interviewed numerous contras and Americans about Don Johnson in 1988 and early 1989, then met him in Tegucigalpa in August 1989. I requested an interview with Johnson in March 1990, but he declined.

17. The downing of the helicopter by Jhonson's unit came on June 12, 1987. It was mentioned in an Associated Press dispatch, datelined Managua, June 19,

1987. Technical details on the Redeye missile are from page 194 of Tom Gervasi's *Arsenal of Democracy* (New York: Grove Press, 1977).

18. Bermúdez numbered the 1987 airdrops at 470 in a January 1990 interview in Miami.

19. Scores of newspaper accounts documented the dramatic economic deterioration. See the *Miami Herald* for April 13, 1987, and February 18, 1988, for two examples.

20. Along with Ortega, the signers were Presidents Oscar Arias of Costa Rica, José Azcona of Honduras, Vinicio Cerezo of Guatemala, and José Napoleon Duarte of El Salvador.

21. Marjorie Miller described Bermúdez's fury over the Guatemala Peace Agreement in the September 6, 1987, *Los Angeles Times*.

22. The destruction of the rebel aircraft at Aguacate before an impending visit by the International Commission on Verification and Follow-up was reported in the January 6, 1988, edition of the Tegucigalpa daily *La Tribuna*. Victor "Licenciado" Sánchez, stationed at Aguacate at the time, provided further details on the incident.

23. Richard Boudreaux first wrote of the encounter between Jhonson and his brother in the January 2, 1988, *Los Angeles Times*. I drew on that story, on interviews with Jhonson, and on several July 1989 interviews in Matagalpa with Jhonson's parents and various siblings.

24. The December 12, 1987, Miami banquet was reported in the December 13, 1987, *Miami Herald*.

25. I reconstructed details of Enrique Fley's January 5, 1988, ambush and Jhonson's phone call to his mother from interviews with Jhonson and July 1989 interviews with his mother, Teodora, his sister Mercedes, and his brother Jorge.

26. "We didn't use the word 'interrogators,' " the former CIA officer recalled. " 'Debriefers,' we said. It was another one of those horse-shit things with Congress. They don't like the word 'interrogator.' "

27. Rodolfo "Invisible" Ampie, the Resistance intelligence chief, told Agustin Lacayo on May 1, 1987, of Bermúdez and Calero's eagerness for information about the counterintelligence investigation. Lacayo, a staff member of the Asociación Nicaragüense Pro-Derechos Humanos (ANPDH), the State Department–funded monitor established to improve the rebels' human-rights image, recorded Invisible's comments in an internal ANPDH memo. "Dr. Calero and 380 [Bermúdez] had told him [Invisible] that they wanted him to keep them closely informed about the investigation," Lacayo wrote. I obtained a copy of the memo.

28. I have drawn my account of the 1987 spy roundup from a copy I obtained of the rebel counterintelligence file on the case. According to the fifty-page file, called "Analysis of the Wilson Case," José Wilson Jackson's real name in the Sandinista army was José Luis Martínez Montoya. Also according to the file, Carlos Andrade Espinoza's real name in the Sandinista army was Lieutenant Roberto Enrique Espinoza. I also interviewed Mike Lima about the case.

29. The identities of the interrogators emerged in dozens of interviews by

Alfonso Sandino and other ANPDH officers with Resistance prisoners after their release in December 1988.

30. Centeno Chavarría made his statements in a January 17, 1989, interview with the ANPDH's Sandino at Honduras's Las Vegas refugee camp. I obtained a transcript.

31. Alfonso Sandino cited the examples of Mike Lima's involvement in the brutality.

32. I interviewed Guillermo "Pecos Bill" Gasteazoro about the interrogations in Miami in June 1989.

33. The September 12, 1986, plane crash was reported in the Tegucigalpa daily *El Heraldo* on September 15 and 17, 1986.

34. Details of the May 1987 DC-6 crash at Aguacate were drawn from Resistance counterintelligence files, as well as from Gustavo "Waiky" Quezada, a rebel pilot, whom I interviewed in Miami on May 21, 1989.

35. The American officials expressed their views in the only extensive article written about the alleged infiltration ring at the time. It appeared in the May 9, 1987, *Los Angeles Times.*

36. For an example of Sandinista Interior Ministry boasts about having infiltrated the contra army, see the interview with State Security chief Lenin Cerna published in the July 19, 1989, *Barricada.*

37. "I realized that many of those accusations were just based on ignorance, even on personal jealousies," Bermúdez said of the investigation in a January 6, 1990, interview.

38. Alfonso Sandino, a lawyer for the Nicaraguan Association for Human Rights (ANPDH) who dealt with rebel prisoners, made his remarks in several August 1989 interviews in Tegucigalpa.

39. I took notes from Colonel Gómez's memo while reviewing files at the rebels' counterintelligence safe house in Tegucigalpa in March 1989.

40. I arrived at the figure of 110 prisoners by adding the 80 or 81 prisoners released on September 18, 1987, and the 30 prisoners Bermúdez acknowledged to a reporter that his forces were still holding at Aguacate a week after the release. See the September 24, 1987, ACAN-EFE cable reprinted in Tegucigalpa's *El Heraldo* on September 25, 1987, for Bermúdez's remarks. Marjorie Miller reported in the June 27, 1987, *Los Angeles Times* that the contras were holding a total of 105 prisoners at that time. See Julia Preston's article in the *Washington Post* on September 19, 1987, for an account of the Costa Rica prisoner release.

41. During August 1989 interviews in Tegucigalpa, Alfonso Sandino described how Bermúdez and Mike Lima interviewed the prisoners to divide them into two groups.

42. Jhonson described the 1988 transfer of the blindfolded prisoners from Yamales to San Andrés de Bocay.

43. I interviewed Baltodano about her youth and early career in Miami on January 3, 1990.

44. Baltodano's quote comes from an interview conducted by Julia Preston in Costa Rica on February 24, 1987.

45. I drew the biographical information on Arcos from several interviews, and from page 808 of the 1989 Federal Staff Directory (Mt. Vernon, Va.: Congressional Staff Directories Ltd.).

46. Officials at Americas Watch, the New York–based human-rights monitor, described the ANPDH's funding as the second-largest in the world.

47. I drew the biographical and career information on Briggs from page 830 of the 1989 Federal Staff Directory, and from several interviews with people who worked for him at the Panama and Tegucigalpa embassies.

48. Several U.S. officials posted in Tegucigalpa and at the State Department described Briggs's relation with Baltodano, the CIA, and the Bermúdez clique.

49. John Lantigua's *Washington Post* article on the Cuapa attack appeared on August 8, 1985. The ANPDH published public reports on its activities in July 1987, January 1988, June 1988, and March 1989. The ANPDH's July 1987 report quoted the October 21, 1986, letter from Ian Martin, Secretary General of Amnesty International, to George Shultz.

50. I drew my account of Baltodano's Cuapa investigation from the extensive ANPDH file on the Cuapa case, successive Americas Watch reports documenting the case, especially *Human Rights in Nicaragua, 1985–1986*, and from interviews with Baltodano.

51. Baltodano recalled the obstacles thrown up by Bermúdez and Sánchez, and discussed their likely reasons, in an interview on January 3, 1990.

52. Several contras and U.S. officials discussed Chidester's visit with Bermúdez.

53. I drew the account of the Tegucigalpa meeting between Arcos, Chidester, Bermúdez, Calero, Baltodano, Mallett, and others from interviews with several participants.

54. Biographical details on Lacayo were drawn from a January 23, 1990, interview with him in Miami.

55. The account of the angry 1987 confrontation between Baltodano and Bermúdez, Sánchez, Mike Lima, and others at Aguacate was drawn from interviews with several participants in the meeting.

56. I drew the account of Baltodano's investigation of the Berta Díaz case from a January 3, 1990, interview with Baltodano and from reviewing the ANPDH file on the case, which included a transcript of the 1987 interview conducted in the Yamales Military Police stockade.

57. I obtained a transcript of an interview Baltodano conducted with Yorlin María Ubeda in Danlí in 1987. I also interviewed Baltodano about the case. A six-part series published in *Barricada* in August 1989, based on interviews with Ubeda after she returned to Nicaragua, contains some interesting details, as well as some sensational allegations that appear to be disinformation, including the claim in the August 16, 1989, issue that Bermúdez raped Ubeda himself.

58. The June 1988 ANPDH report, page 21, summarizes the Jacqueline Murillo Castillo case. I interviewed Baltodano and Lacayo, and reviewed the file Lacayo assembled on the case at his legal adviser's office in Tegucigalpa. In a January 6, 1990, interview in Miami, Bermúdez conceded that Murillo had

worked at his Strategic Command, but denied that she was his secretary. She was "just a girl who took notes," he said. He conceded that his counterintelligence "did not handle that investigation well," but asserted that he had tried to correct the problem by ordering his interrogators to "be careful with the persons during your investigations." Bermúdez denied that he had asked Lacayo to suspend the investigation into Murillo's torture. He asserted that Lacayo was trying to slander him because of their dispute during the April 1988 dissident rebellion. "Do you believe that I, as the commanding general, am going to be interested in a girl that has no importance?" Bermúdez asked.

59. The Lawyers Committee for Human Rights, a New York–based rights agency whose attorneys monitored Marta Patricia Baltodano's performance, concluded in late 1987: "While the Lawyers Committee has no reason to doubt the dedication and good intentions of Dr. Baltodano and her staff, the ANPDH's efforts have yet to be directly translated into any discernible improvement in the human-rights record of the contras. . . . A major impediment to any improvement . . . is the recalcitrant attitude of the military command to any outside effort to monitor their performance." From page 37 of *Human Rights in Nicaragua: 1987* (New York: Lawyers Committee for Human Rights, November 1987).

60. I discussed the planning and coordination of the attack on the mining complex with a former CIA official based in Honduras during 1987 as well as with several other U.S. officials. I also interviewed Fernando, Rigoberto, and Mack, three of the rebel regional commanders who participated in the attack. They provided many details of the fighting on the ground itself. The August 1988 *Soldier of Fortune* featured an extensive first-person article by Steve Salisbury, a young American who fought with the rebels during the attack. The piece offers many insights into the positive and negative aspects of the rebel force. An Associated Press dispatch from Managua on December 21, 1987, cited the $23 million gold production figure, as well as many other details of the December 20 attack.

61. Sánchez described the scene at Aguacate during the December 1987 attack on the mining complex in several 1989 interviews.

62. Several journalists generously discussed with me their flight to the border for the encounter with Bermúdez during the fighting at the mining complex. For a nice example of the dispatches that moved from the Bermúdez interviews, see Wilson Ring's pieces in the December 23, 1987, *Chicago Tribune* and the *Washington Post*.

63. Victor Sánchez and Mike Lima described the CIA's insistence on the airdrops that led up to the January 23, 1988, crash. See the January 25, 1988, *Miami Herald* for June Erlick's report from Nicaragua on the crash. Carlos Harrison in the January 26, 1988, *Miami Herald* reported Frixione's biographic information, as well as the CIA's call to the Frixione household.

64. The February 4, 1988, *Miami Herald* reported on the defeat of the contra aid package, quoting Representative Coelho. John Felton's article in the February 6, 1988, *Congressional Quarterly* offers a good analysis of the vote. The Senate voted to approve the contra aid package on February 4, 1988. Senate approval

was of course moot in the wake of the House defeat, but two Democratic senators, Bill Bradley of New Jersey and Alan Dixon of Illinois, made good speeches that explain the politics of the administration's defeat. "I blame Ronald Reagan," Bradley said. "There is a difference between speeches that rail at Communists and a policy that effectively counters them. Speeches are easy; policy takes effort and care." See the *Congressional Record*, February 4, 1988.

8: Back in the Camps

1. The July 18, 1987, *Washington Post*, in a story credited to the *Los Angeles Times*, reported that Fiers "may lose his job." The December 18, 1987, *Washington Post* reported CIA Director William Webster's announcement that Fiers had been reprimanded. The *Post*, on February 27, 1988, reported Fiers' resignation from the CIA.

2. I drew my account of the March 8, 1988, Miami meeting from interviews with U.S. officials who participated and from contra negotiator Jaime Morales Carazo's book *La Contra*, page 342.

3. Bermúdez, in a January 3, 1990, interview, confirmed the "No somos Chinos" quote attributed to him by various U.S. officials.

4. Noel "Trickster" Castillo, a contra officer stationed on Swan Island during the $100 million offensive, described the standoff between "John," Swan Island's CIA commander, and the Honduran Army officer over the leftover Redeye missiles.

5. The March 17, 1988, *Washington Post* cited the figure of three thousand metric tons dropped into Swan.

6. Julia Preston, in the March 18, 1988, *Washington Post*, wrote a good account of the fight for San Andrés. The March 17 *Post* reported extensively on Reagan's deployment of U.S. troops to Honduras.

7. U.S. officials, in several September 1989 interviews, offered a more concrete explanation for why Calero signed the Sapoá agreement. They said the CIA, more conscious than anyone else of the mounting vulnerability of rebel forces after the U.S. aid cutoff, urged Calero to sign a cease-fire as soon as possible. "I think his orders were to sign an agreement," said one State Department official.

8. A May 24, 1987, article by Marjorie Miller in the *Los Angeles Times* discussed the ironies in Azucena Ferrey's move into exile. Nicaragua's Christian Democrats, affiliated with the Christian Democratic movement worldwide yet divided into several small parties, call themselves "Social Christians."

9. The original Resistance directorate, unveiled in May 1987, included Adolfo Calero, Alfredo César, Aristides Sánchez, Pedro Chamorro, Azucena Ferrey, and Alfonso Robelo, representing his own centrist party, the MDN. Robelo's resignation nine months later was announced in the February 6, 1988, *Washington Post*. Another seat on the Resistance directorate was to be reserved for an Indian leader, but the army of Indian rebels fell apart before the CIA could recruit a rep-

resentative. The May 17, 1987, *Washington Post* has an early article on the emergence of the Resistance.

10. Several U.S. officials described the evolution of the secret CIA-funded *tendencia* payments. I found the payments quantified at $180,000 per year, or $15,000-per-month-per-director, in a secret 1989 State Department document. I confirmed the figure with State Department officials.

11. I drew the account of the post-Sapoá meeting in Tegucigalpa from interviews with Fernando, Toño, Jhonson, and Mike Lima.

12. Chris Marquis's story in the March 26, 1988, *Miami Herald* described the post-Sapoá confrontations at the Viscount Hotel.

13. Toño detailed his Guard career in interviews in January and May 1989. Marta Patricia Baltodano saw Toño weight-lifting in Tegucigalpa.

14. Diógenes "Fernando" Hernández described the 1983 murders by Armando "The Policeman" López and César "Six-Seven" Tijerino during a June 12, 1989, interview in Miami. The murders by López and Tijerino were widely discussed in the contra army. Dr. Francisco Rugama, "Dr. Rubén," a Nicaraguan physician now living in Miami who worked for the FDN from 1983 to 1985, was traveling with López and Tijerino at the time and witnessed several of the murders. He described his experiences with López in Miami interviews on April 9 and May 17, 1989.

15. Several rebels described the anger in rebel ranks occasioned by Bermúdez's retreat into his new safe house with María Eugenia Ortez during the confusing early weeks of 1988. Among them were Jhonson, Walter "Toño" Calderón, Freddy "Coral" Gadea, Encarnación "Tigrillo" Baldivia, and Enrique and Victor Sánchez.

16. Tigrillo and Rigoberto, who attended the meeting at the Danlí clinic, described it in a May 8, 1988, interview.

17. The new general staff, elected at the San Andrés meeting that was held February 29 through March 2, 1988, was the following: Chief of Staff, Juan "Quiché" Rivas; Personnel, Pastor "Denis" Meza; Intelligence, José Benito "Mack" Bravo Centeno; Operations, Walter "Toño" Calderón; Logistics, Rudy "Douglas" Zelaya; Civic Affairs, Tirzo "Rigoberto" Moreno; Counterintelligence, Luis "Mike Lima" Moreno. After the dissident rebellion, Bermúdez replaced Toño with Israel "Franklyn" Galeano as operations chief and Rigoberto with Oscar "Rubén" Sobalvarro as civic action chief. I drew my account of the San Andrés meeting from interviews with Toño, Tigrillo, Mike Lima, and Jhonson, and from Jaime Morales's book *La Contra.*

18. I drew the biographical and career information on "Terry" from interviews with present and former U.S. officials and from the State Department Biographic Register. U.S. officials identified Terry's full name to me, but in early 1989, "Terry" became director of the Latin American Division in the Operations Directorate at Langley. Since he is an active-duty intelligence agent, it is illegal to publish his full name.

19. The account of the dissidents' Tegucigalpa meeting with Terry came from interviews with several of the Nicaraguans and Americans who participated.

20. I reported the deportations of Toño, Rigoberto, Tigrillo, Enrique Sánchez, Donald Lacayo, Orlando Montealegre, and two other dissidents to Miami on May 6, 1988, in the May 7, 1988, *Miami Herald*. The story of Fernando's deportation was drawn from interviews with Fernando and Chamorro.

21. The June 10 and 11, 1988, issues of the *Miami Herald* chronicle the final breakdown of the cease-fire talks.

22. The new contra humanitarian aid voted in late March 1988 came in a larger $47.9 million package that also included about $17 million in medical care for Nicaraguan children and about $10 million to finance operations of a Verification Commission established by the Sapoá cease-fire agreement.

23. Officials at the Tegucigalpa embassy described the April 1988 transition from CIA to AID during several interviews in August 1989.

24. Several U.S. officials discussed with me the CIA's continuing secret political payments to the rebel army, and Doyle McManus mentioned them briefly in the January 28, 1989, *Los Angeles Times*. The CIA's continuing secret financial support for Resistance intelligence and counterintelligence operations have never been discussed publicly. Jhonson, Mike Lima, and other Resistance officers described them to me.

25. These and other details of AID's assumption of the formerly covert program were drawn from a September 21, 1989, interview with Roger Noriega, an AID spokesman.

26. For details of the 1988 resettlement of Yamales, see the April 21 and 22, 1988, issues of the *Washington Post*. The August 12, 1988, *Post* reported that 80 percent of the contra force had crossed back into Honduras.

27. See the April 28, 1988, *Washington Post* for an example of many similar reports during the period from rebel field commanders confident of their abilities to prosper inside Nicaragua.

28. See the August 12, 1988, *Washington Post* for an account of the desperate condition of the civilians marching into Honduras.

29. U.S. officials posted at the embassies in Tegucigalpa and Managua, in September 1988 interviews, described Bermúdez's self-serving reasons for ordering the mass withdrawal of rebel fighters and their supporters.

30. The June 1989 GAO Report to Congress, *Central America, Humanitarian Assistance to the Nicaraguan Democratic Resistance*, revealed on page 16 the $2,750 monthly salary Bermúdez was drawing from the Family Assistance Program. That salary was the highest in the Resistance army, but not necessarily Bermúdez's only U.S.-financed salary. CIA salary payments to Bermúdez have never been revealed.

31. U.S. officials, in September 1989 and April 1990 interviews, discussed the CIA's secret *tendencia* funds and the extravagant expenditures they spawned.

32. The *Semi-Annual Report from the Legal Adviser and the Military Prosecutor* published in January 1988 contains budget figures and descriptions of the workings of the legal adviser's office.

33. Baltodano described her deepening disillusionment during a February 1989 interview.

34. The biographical details and description of Timothy Brown were drawn from the State Department's Biographic Register, as well as from a March 1990 interview which he insisted remain off the record.

35. Jhonson, Baltodano, and several U.S. officials described Jhonson's routine reporting calls to the State Department. The distrust between the State Department and Briggs's Tegucigalpa embassy were well known throughout both bureaucracies.

36. Resistance tribunals heard thirty cases during the last half of 1987. Seven dealt with true human-rights abuse cases, while twenty-three were for camp crimes ranging from murder and rape to minor disciplinary infractions. See the *Semi-Annual Report from the Legal Adviser and the Military Prosecutor.*

37. The Resistance obstruction of Baltodano's attempts to visit contra prisons during 1987 and 1988, as well as the Tegucigalpa embassy's diffidence to Baltodano's complaints, were discussed by Baltodano in several interviews, as well as by half a dozen U.S. officials during interviews in September 1989.

38. See the June 1988 ANPDH Report, page 33, for Baltodano's account of her May 24, 1988, visit to the San Andrés prison with Jhonson. Baltodano and Jhonson also discussed the visit in interviews.

39. The number of prisoners reported executed at Cuapa has varied. The original August 8, 1985, *Washington Post* article by John Lantigua reported eleven prisoners executed. Later, Marta Patricia Baltodano concluded from interviews that ten prisoners had been executed. See her January 1988 ANPDH report, page 7.

40. A December 17, 1987, legal adviser's memo written by Lacayo detailing the proceedings of his December 16 meeting in Washington with Robert Kagan, Humberto Charneco, and several other State Department officials about the Cuapa case indicates that the Americans were handing down detailed "recommendations" to the Resistance in this, and presumably other, human-rights deliberations.

41. Atila served his three-month sentence in the Yamales lockup. Upon his release, he traveled to Miami, where he had relatives. There, outraged State Department officials discovered that during 1989, Atila was still receiving family-assistance payments from AID. Bermúdez was in charge of drawing up the FAP list. I drew my account of the Cuapa tribunals from reading the ANPDH's records of the case and from interviews with Baltodano, Jhonson, and several other rebels.

42. In several interviews during 1989 and 1990, Baltodano described how she gradually accumulated the evidence for her counterintelligence case. The Resistance counterintelligence interrogators against whom Baltodano presented charges in the fall of 1988 included Carlos "Chino Eighty-Five" Garcia, José "Joel" Zepeda, César "Six-Seven" Tijerino, Donald "The Bull" Torres, Ramón "Z-Two" Peña Rodríguez, and another interrogator with the pseudonym "Pepe." Mike Lima's name was added to the case months later, after prisoners released in December 1988 complained of tortures that he had committed.

43. Preston's article, headlined "Peasants Say Sandinistas Kill Suspected Contra Supporters; Atrocities Laid to Lax Discipline in Army," appeared on

September 9, 1988. Jemera Rone, an attorney for Americas Watch, the New York–based rights monitor, had been drawing similar conclusions during the same period. Throughout the war, Americas Watch displayed healthy skepticism toward reports of Sandinista abuses, but successive Americas Watch reports starting in 1987 discussed the abuses Jhonson was complaining about: "From 1987 through the early part of 1989, Nicaraguan military and security forces engaged in a pattern of killings of contra supporters and contra collaborators in remote communities of northern Nicaragua. . . . Americas Watch documented 74 murders, 14 disappearances, and two severe beatings; in addition, we obtained some evidence about another 20 possible killings and one disappearance." From the November 1989 Americas Watch report *The Killings in Northern Nicaragua*.

44. Marta Patricia Baltodano, Jhonson, and Mike Lima described the CIA funding for the intelligence and counterintelligence sections. Mike Lima said his monthly cash budget was small: 7,000 lempiras, just $3,500. Two U.S. officials interviewed in September 1989 confirmed that the CIA continued to fund the sections after the March 1, 1988, military-aid cutoff. Roberto, Mack's CIA liaison, was a well-known figure in the Resistance. Mike Lima described his two CIA liaisons and their work.

45. I drew my discussion of the 1988 staff and other changes in the intelligence and counterintelligence sections from interviews with Mike Lima, Noel "Trickster" Castillo, Jhonson, and others.

46. Mike Lima described his developing worries about infiltration during the disorderly resettlement of the Yamales Valley in an April 1989 interview in Miami.

47. The experiences of Gema Velásquez, sixteen, one of the young women detained during the successive anti-infiltration sweeps of 1988, demonstrate how Mack's intelligence and Mike Lima's counterintelligence sections worked together during the 1988 sweeps. Originally detained in Yamales in mid-1988, Velásquez was taken to Mack's intelligence section at the Strategic Command, where Mack's deputy, Ramón "Z-Two" Peña, accused her of being an infiltrator. Z-Two then turned her to Mike Lima's deputy, José "Joel" Zepeda, who took Velásquez to the counterintelligence center for interrogation. There, bound and blindfolded, she was beaten, kicked, and smothered with a rain poncho tied around her head. Eventually, Velásquez was among the ninety-two prisoners interviewed at Yamales by the GAO auditing team in December 1988. In July 1989, a researcher for the human-rights monitor Americas Watch interviewed Velásquez in Managua and detailed her experiences in the November 1989 Americas Watch report *The Killings in Northern Nicaragua*.

48. On whose authorization Blake began detaining commandos in November 1988 remained a mystery throughout the Resistance's own Quilalí tribunal. But on March 23, 1990, Blake clarified that and other questions about his career in an interview with the author at the Managua offices of the Permanent Human Rights Commission, whose director, Lino Hernández, helped me locate Blake in Managua eleven months after Blake's deportation from Honduras. He walked

into the human-rights offices smiling and serene. He said he was earning a modest living as a car salesman. He was not born in Bluefields, on Nicaragua's Atlantic coast, as various contra witnesses during the Quilalí tribunal believed. He was the son of an electrician living in Managua. Chain-smoking Windsor cigarettes throughout the encounter, Blake described his contra career and his involvement in the Quilalí case. He described his return to the Yamales camps in late summer 1988 from Nicaragua, bearing suspicions about Sandinista infiltrators in the Quilalí Regional Command. He recounted the meeting at the Yamales general staff camp with Mike Lima and Mack that led to his transfer to the Quilalí Regional Command for work as a counterintelligence agent.

49. The Tegucigalpa embassy, in a classified December 13, 1988, cable to the State Department, reported that Bermúdez had informed the embassy on December 9 of Isaac González's death, and that Bermúdez was calling for a complete investigation. The cable called the murder "an isolated act."

50. Accurate statistics on the Resistance's prison population in late 1988 don't exist, because record-keeping was sloppy and many detentions were never recorded. The Honduran Army, to whom the Resistance was reporting some of its detentions, had a list of 280 prisoners in December, according to ANPDH official Alfonso Sandino. But Sandino said in an August 1989 interview that 280 was well above the number of detainees the Resistance was by then holding because the Resistance released many prisoners without notifying the Hondurans. The problem was aggravated because Marta Patricia Baltodano, a meticulous statistician, was blocked from prison visits after mid-October. One U.S. official said he believed that the number of commandos detained during the period may have approached five hundred.

51. Noel "Trickster" Castillo, after leaving the Resistance in November 1989, described how the counterintelligence section had routinely briefed Bermúdez during the period of mass detentions in the fall of 1988.

52. Bermúdez's rejection of ANPDH prison visit requests between October 16 and December 9 were noted in the ANPDH's March 1989 report, page 8. The report said the Resistance general staff had refused the requests; Baltodano's deputy, Alfonso Sandino, said Bermúdez made the decision personally.

9: The Quilalí Tribunal

1. John McPhaul, in the July 30, 1988, *Miami Herald*, reported on the Inter-American Court's decision. A year later, the Court ordered the Honduran government to indemnify the families of two victims disappeared by a Honduran death squad with payments totaling $695,000. See McPhaul's story on the indemnity ruling in the August 2, 1989, *Miami Herald*.

2. López Contreras's October 4, 1988, General Assembly speech was reported in the October 5 *Washington Post*. U.S. officials described López Contreras's late 1988 letter to Shultz during Washington interviews in September 1989.

3. The biographical details on Virgilio Galvez were provided by the Honduran Foreign Ministry. Details of the encounter between Jhonson, Galvez, and

Brown came from interviews with Jhonson and Alfonso Sandino, who learned details of the incident from friends in the Honduran Foreign Ministry. Galvez declined to be interviewed. The Honduran Foreign Ministry communiqué on the Resistance prisoner release appeared in the December 21, 1988, issue of the Tegucigalpa daily *La Tribuna.*

4. In several interviews in Tegucigalpa during August 1989, Alfonso Sandino described the ANPDH's debriefing of prisoners before their December 1988 release. Sandino and Jhonson both described the meeting with Bermúdez and Brown.

5. The December 30, 1988, issue of the Tegucigalpa daily *El Heraldo* reported on the repatriation of forty-four prisoners and the resettlement of the rest at Teupasenti.

6. Jhonson's memo calling for a tribunal was included in the Quilalí tribunal documents.

7. Sandino and Marta Patricia Baltodano described the January 17, 1989, ANPDH interviews with Blake.

8. Mike Lima's description of the CIA's repeated attempts to explore Blake's relationship to counterintelligence came in an April 1989 interview in Miami.

9. My interview about Blake's deportation with Charles Barclay, then the spokesman for the U.S. embassy in Tegucigalpa, was conducted by phone on May 4, 1989. After my Managua interview with Blake on March 23, 1990, I was not convinced of the veracity of his claim that an "American adviser" drove him with Honduran authorities to Las Manos for his deportation. Blake made a similar, though not identical claim, in the *Barricada* interview written by Jilma Rodríguez, the *Barricada* stringer in Ocotal, which appeared on February 12, 1988, two days after his deportation. I interviewed Rodríguez by phone from Managua in March 1990. She said she often interviewed detainees held by Ocotal State Security officials, much the way U.S. reporters cover the police beat. Her article on Blake is a mix of fact and fantasy, a result, I believe, of Blake's silver tongue rather than deliberate distortion by Rodríguez. She misspelled Blake's name as "Blayker."

MIRACULOUS RETURN FROM HONDURAS!
ATLANTIC COAST MAN TELLS OF TORTURE BY CONTRAS!

OCOTAL — After being cruelly tortured by the contras, the Honduran Guardia, and U.S. advisers, citizen Isaac Samuel Blayker crossed into his homeland last week at Las Manos.

The repatriated Atlantic Coast man, 34, of strong complexion and agile with words, told Barricada how he was kidnapped, forced to be a contra, and of his attempts to escape as he was held prisoner during four years . . . Col. O'Connor of the Honduran Guardia personally came to the place where he was held prisoner and took him to Ojos de Agua, where he was held four days.

"They beat me until I lost consciousness," he recalled. He was held in a dungeon without water or food, then sent to the 316 battalion. He said he was kicked and slugged in the face and stomach. When he fell, he was brought up for more. "Those were days of agony," he recalled.

Blayker was interrogated by U.S. military advisers.

"They asked me how long I'd been a Sandinista," Blayker said. "I told them I wasn't a military man. I had to say that—otherwise, I'd have been dead."

The U.S. military advisers told Blayker that the Honduran government would send him back to Nicaragua.

"They blindfolded and handcuffed me and kicked me into a truck. I believed it was the end. I was thinking of my family," Blayker said. . . .

"Uniformed Hondurans working with the contras arrive at all hours at the refugee camps to take people away for interrogation. Some return, some don't," he said. Blayker said he had witnessed the death of a young refugee.

"Through a hole in the plastic tent that served as a prison in the contra camp, I saw Col. O'Connor arrive with a security officer, looking for a young prisoner. They pulled him out, completely covered in blood, hitting him in the head with their rifle butts. O'Connor took out his pistol and shot him four times," Blayker said.

Blayker said he was glad to be home, and enthusiastic about the life waiting for him.

10. I interviewed Briggs in September 1989 at the National Security Council, where he was President Bush's top Latin American security adviser for a few months in 1989 after he left the Tegucigalpa embassy in June.

11. Several U.S. officials, requesting anonymity, described the differences between the Tegucigalpa embassy and the State Department over the Quilalí abuses. I also obtained temporary access to several classified embassy cables discussing the Quilalí case. Briggs, in a September 1989 interview in Washington, insisted that his embassy always reported contra abuses that came to his mission's attention to Washington in a timely fashion.

12. I reviewed Charneco's career with several State Department officials.

13. I drew the account of Charneco's dinner with Bermúdez from interviews with Resistance and U.S. officials familiar with the encounter.

14. Commander Denis's memo to Jhonson was filed in the Quilalí trial documents.

15. I put together my account of the women's tribunal testimonies from the Quilalí tribunal transcripts and the statements the witnesses gave to Joshua during Jhonson's initial investigation. For reasons of clarity in the narrative, I have not recounted the women's testimony in chronological order.

16. I pieced together my account of the tribunal's first sessions from the transcripts of the proceedings and from interviews with Jhonson and other Resistance officials.

17. I put together my account of Bermúdez's encounter with the three congressmen from interviews with congressional staffers who arranged and attended

the meeting and with Resistance officials familiar with the meeting, including Ernesto Palazio, the Resistance's Washington spokesman, who attended.

18. Jhonson's message to the general staff was contained in the Quilalí tribunal documents.

19. Mike Lima read the messages between Joel and Trickster into the Quilalí tribunal transcript.

20. Alí's memo to Mack was contained in the Quilalí tribunal documents. Many other documents contradict the memo on one detail: Alí gives the impression that González died the same day he was seized. Actually, he was seized one day and died at midnight the next.

21. I put together my account of Bermúdez's meeting with the ex-Guardsmen in interviews with Jhonson, Trickster, and others.

22. Alí referred to the threats by Mack's men in a March 29, 1989, memo to the members of the Quilalí tribunal, requesting protection for his family.

23. Deputy Assistant Secretary of State Cresencio Arcos and two other U.S. officials informed the Resistance directorate of the suspensions in a meeting in Miami on March 24, 1989, according to U.S. officials interviewed in September 1989 and March 1990. A memo outlining the meeting was in Jhonson's Quilalí case file.

24. I compiled the account of the encounters between Arcos and Briggs over the Quilalí case after interviews with Arcos, Briggs, and other U.S. officials who worked for both men.

25. The general staff's letter that Denis read aloud was later contained in Jhonson's Quilalí case file.

26. The account of Arcos's meeting with the Resistance commanders at Yamales comes from interviews with Arcos, Jhonson, and several other U.S. officials.

10: Final Verdicts

1. See the March 25, 1989, *Washington Post* for coverage of the Bush Administration's announcement of the bipartisan accord.

2. I drew details of the Tesoro Beach accord and the Calero quote from the February 15 and 16, 1989, editions of the *Washington Post.*

3. The March 18, 1989, *New York Times* reported on the release of the 1,894 imprisoned former Guardsmen.

4. Pedro Sevcec reported on Ferrey's return to Managua in Miami's *El Nuevo Herald* on May 26, 1989. Sevcec also reported César's return to Managua in the June 11 and 12, 1989, editions of *El Nuevo Herald.* Julia Preston, in the May 15, 1989, *Washington Post,* reported on the atmosphere in Managua with dozens of former contras returning to campaign.

5. Several U.S. officials described the secret CIA *tendencia* payments. A 1989 State Department document quantified them at $180,000 per year, a figure I confirmed with State Department officials. The figures on U.S. subsidies

to the political directorate and to the Miami Resistance office were also reported in the June 8, 1989, *Los Angeles Times* and the June 25, 1989, *El Nuevo Herald.*

6. Details of Dan Fisk's career were drawn from September 1989 interviews in Washington with several State Department officials.

7. I drew my account of the State Department meeting from several September 1989 interviews with U.S. officials and rebel leaders who participated. Sánchez repeated his vow to "support the armed struggle to the end" in an interview with Pedro Sevcec, reported in *El Nuevo Herald* on June 25, 1989. Doyle McManus, in the June 8, 1989, *Los Angeles Times,* also reported on the dispute between Bush Administration officials and the contra leaders.

8. State Department officials later questioned the numerical accuracy of their own casualty estimate. A February 1990 State Department study estimated on the basis of figures provided by the Nicaraguan Resistance army's personnel staff, headed by Commander Denis, that only some 5,300 contra combatants were either killed or wounded from 1981 through 1989. But Department officials conceded that lapses in rebel record-keeping had probably resulted in that extremely low estimate. In contrast, the Sandinista government's Ministry of the Presidency, presumably exaggerating contra casualties, reported 16,781 contra dead and 3,940 wounded from 1981 through 1987.

9. The September 2, 1989, *Washington Post* told Bosco Matamoros's side of this dispute. Palazio told me his side of the story in a Washington interview on September 26, 1989.

10. In interviews in September 1989, State Department officials described Calero's threats to expose CIA agents.

11. Mike Lima described the CIA firing of Quiché in a Miami interview in November 1989. I confirmed the details with U.S. officials.

12. Several U.S. officials, in separate interviews, traced Sánchez's 1989 campaign to destroy Bermúdez.

13. Two U.S. officials recounted Bermúdez's comments to Arcos.

14. Several U.S. officials in separate interviews described the U.S.-ordered sanctions against Mack. See Wilson Ring's April 18, 1989, article in the *Washington Post* about the brief controversy that followed when rebel leaders allowed Mack to work at Yamales despite the U.S. order barring him from the camps.

15. I discussed the new information about Mack's long career of violence with several U.S. officials in September 1989.

16. The appellate tribunal's July 1989 verdict—part of the Quilalí trial documents—listed the appellate judges. I researched their political backgrounds in interviews with Bodán and other Resistance officials.

17. Bermúdez's influence on the appellate tribunal was strong because Bodán, one of the magistrates, was Bermúdez's paid personal adviser. But two U.S. officials who followed the Quilalí case told me that Aristides Sánchez was the man most responsible for Mack's exoneration.

18. Among other spurious arguments, the appellate panel claimed that no evidence emerged during the Quilalí trial to suggest that when Commanders

Franklyn and Mack visited the Quilalí camp on November 1, 1988, they learned that Blake was torturing prisoners. But the appellate panel had to ignore plenty of testimony in the trial record to make this argument. For instance, Roberto "Robespierre" Aguilar testified: "Commanders Mack and Franklyn visited the Quilalí base and visited the place where the prisoners were held, and they saw the prisoners and they could see the signs of the tortures."

19. Jhonson detailed the July 28, 1989, Alameda Hotel meeting in a Tegucigalpa interview the following morning.

20. Jhonson filed a copy of the congressmen's letter to the directorate with his Quilalí trial documents.

21. Richard Boudreaux reported on the Tela accord in the August 8, 1989, *Los Angeles Times.*

22. A memo that circulated in the State Department in July 1989 reported Sánchez's attempt to sidetrack Jhonson.

23. The April 14, 1989, *Washington Post* reported on the passage by both houses of Congress of the $49.8 million contra aid package on April 13.

24. Pastor "Denis" Meza, the Resistance personnel officer on the general staff, told Jhonson in late 1989 that more than seven hundred fighters deserted from the rebel army between March 1988 and fall 1989.

25. Jhonson, Alfonso Sandino, and several other Resistance officials recounted the moves by which Mack extended his powers in the fall of 1989.

26. Pedro Sevcec, in the June 8, 1989, *El Nuevo Herald*, reported on the formation of the UNO anti-Sandinista coalition. Richard Boudreaux, in the August 5, 1989, *Los Angeles Times*, noted the importance of the electoral reform package to which the Sandinistas agreed on the eve of the Tela summit. Mary Speck, in the September 3, 1989, *Miami Herald*, reported on Violeta Chamorro's nomination as the UNO's presidential candidate.

27. Efrén "Moisés" Mondragón, a former regional commander, accused Marcos "Black Dimas" Navarro of participation in the contra death squads in published interviews after he defected from the contra army in March 1985. Honduran student Juan José Espinal aired kidnapping and murder charges against Dimas in the January 30, 1985, issue of the Honduran daily *El Tiempo.*

28. Investigative reporting by Richard Boudreaux in the November 7, 1989, *Los Angeles Times* pointed to contra responsibility for the Claymore mine explosion that killed the nine Sandinista soldiers on October 21. Boudreaux's *Los Angeles Times* piece on October 28, 1989 described Ortega's cancellation of the nineteen-month truce.

29. Jhonson gave me a copy of his letter to Franklyn.

30. Jhonson gave me a copy of Franklyn's radio message.

31. I reconstructed the phone conversation from interviews with both Jhonson and his secretary.

32. Among other press accounts of Jhonson's return to Managua, the Associated Press's Doralisa Pilarte filed a January 8, 1990, dispatch from Managua.

33. I reconstructed the details of Jhonson's trip to El Cuá in interviews with Jhonson and Marta Patricia Baltodano—who went along, too—and by watching

the Dutch documentary, produced by Marijke Vreeburg of Interkerkelijke Omroep Nederland.

34. The crowd estimate for the February 11, 1990, rally in Matagalpa came from Richard Boudreaux of the *Los Angeles Times*, who reported on it.

35. Lee Hockstader, in the February 26, 1990, *Washington Post*, enumerated the election observers.

36. After hearing Jhonson's account, I confirmed the Choluteca violence in interviews with Alfonso Sandino and with the same frightened contra who had talked to Jhonson.

37. I pieced together the account of the new violence in the Yamales counter-intelligence center in interviews with Sandino and by reading the interview conducted by ANPDH human-rights activists with Bernardo Rocha after his release on January 27, 1990.

38. Both U.S. and Resistance officials confirmed Gómez's sale of the Resistance aircraft. Gómez sold the Beechcraft Baron that had served for Bermúdez's personal use, the motors from a rebel DC-7 transport, and several pieces of expensive navigational gear. The total proceeds were probably well above $100,000.

39. Julia Preston described Ortega's effort to appear as a rock star in her article "The Defeat of the Sandinistas" in the April 12, 1990, issue of the *New York Review of Books*.

40. The Associated Press ran a transcript of Ortega's concession speech on its February 26, 1990, news wire. The February 27, 1990, *Los Angeles Times* reprinted it.

Epilogue

1. Edward Cody wrote the story in the April 9, 1991, *Washington Post.*

2. Shirley Christian's interview with Dimas Tigrillo and Raoul Shade's photo appeared in the April 22, 1991, *New York Times.*

3. Richard Boudreaux's March 24, 1990, article in the *Los Angeles Times* was an excellent account of the Toncontín negotiations and accord. Boudreaux also reported in the April 20, 1990, *Los Angeles Times* on the war's definitive armistice, signed April 19, 1990, in Managua, and on the results of the symbolic April 18 contra demobilization in Honduras.

4. Douglas Mine's April 25, 1990, Associated Press dispatch from El Destino, Nicaragua, provides a good picture of the contra leadership during Chamorro's inauguration.

5. Boudreaux's May 31, 1990, *Los Angeles Times* piece discusses the third and fourth rounds of rebel-government talks.

6. Doralisa Pilarte's June 9, 1990, Associated Press dispatch and Boudreaux's June 19, 1990, *Los Angeles Times* piece, both datelined from El Almendro, provide good accounts of the first major contra demobilization. Boudreaux described Franklyn's hat; Pilarte noted that Mack was among the commanders

who gave up arms. Filadelfo Aleman filed for the Associated Press on Franklyn's June 28, 1990, demobilization at San Pedro de Lóvago.

7. Franklyn told me about the June 1990 negotiations with the U.S. Military attaché in Managua at El Almendro for the Redeyes during an interview in May 1991. How many trucks were traded for how many missiles remains undisclosed. One contra version of the deal was that Franklyn demanded seventeen trucks, intending to donate one truck to each of the Resistance's seventeen missilemen. A U.S. diplomat in Managua who confirmed the outlines of the trucks-for-missiles deal, however, denied that trucks were given to individual contras. Instead, they were donated to the Civic Association of Former Resistance Fighters. The Associated Press reported the surrender of the Redeyes in a June 27, 1990, dispatch from San Pedro de Lóvago.

8. I pieced together my account of the July 18–19 El Almendro meeting and the accusations discussed there from May 1991 interviews in Managua with Rubén, Invisible, Franklyn, Mack, and Luis Fley.

9. The contra fighters who took government jobs in the first year of the Chamorro Administration included Franklyn and Mack at the Interior Ministry; Rubén, who became deputy minister of repatriation in January 1991; and Boanerges "Pepe" Matús, who had been an adviser to the general staff and became deputy minister of agrarian reform. See Pilarte's January 10, 1991, Associated Press dispatch from Managua. Rubén's fleet of pickup trucks became an increasing point of irritation with former contras in 1991, particularly because he gave one truck to his wife and two to his brother, who wrecked the first. A U.S. diplomat said that the pickup trucks traded for the Redeye missiles were donated by the U.S. government to the Civic Association; that put them under Rubén's control. Bermúdez said in January 1991 that the U.S. government had also donated $360,000 to the Association to help the contras get started in postwar politics, and that Rubén had used the money to buy more trucks and to pay himself a two-thousand-dollar-per-month salary. But a U.S. diplomat denied in an interview that the U.S. government donated any cash to the Association.

10. Boudreaux filed good detailed reports on Commander Franklyn's colonization scheme. See the May 6, 1990, and August 31, 1990, *Los Angeles Times.*

11. In the *Washington Post,* Al Kamen on October 16, 1990, and Lee Hockstader on December 13, 1990, detailed how quickly Washington's fervor over Nicaragua faded after the Sandinistas turned over power. Hockstader reported the figures on the delayed U.S. reconstruction aid. The "What kind of image?" quote comes from a Boudreaux piece in the *Los Angeles Times* on May 19, 1990.

12. Doralisa Pilarte filed more than a dozen Associated Press dispatches on violent clashes between ex-contras and pro-Sandinista peasants during fall 1990. A good early dispatch was on September 25, 1990. Another useful roundup came on November 15. On November 20, Pilarte reported in detail on Sánchez's arrest and second exile.

13. I drew my account of Bermúdez's return to Nicaragua and his murder from interviews with those who met with him in Managua, and from the San-

dinista Police's two-hundred-page investigative file on the assassination. Photos of crowds mobbing the airport as Bermúdez's remains were flown to Miami appeared in the February 19, 1991, *La Prensa.* Luis Fley attended Bermúdez's funeral in Miami and described it to me.

14. The OAS figures come from an April 8 report from the OAS's International Commission of Support and Verification. Bermúdez was not included in the figures, because OAS said that nobody filed a complaint.

Index